A HISTORY

OF

TEDSTONE DELAMERE

in north-east Herefordshire

Jennifer Weale

Bromyard & District Local History Society
5 Sherford Street, Bromyard. HR7 4DL

ISBN 0-9546212-3-9

All rights reserved. No part of this publication
may be reproduced, stored in a retrieval system,
or transmitted, in any form or by any means,
electronic, mechanical, photocopying, recording
or otherwise, without the prior permission,
in writing, of the publisher

Set in Times New Roman Monotype and printed in Great Britain by
Orphans Press, Leominster, Herefordshire

Cover illustrations

Front:
Arthur Griffiths, John Roper & John Griffiths at Bromyard Market. *Kathleen Harris*
Tedstone Court in 1908;
Bellville children on their donkeys. *Jane Hawksley;*
Mr. & Mrs. James Grubb at Woodend. *Evelyn Whistance*
Inside front cover: Map 1. Roads, Relief & Drainage. *Geoff Gwatkin*

Back:
Watercolour of Tedstone Delamere Church, 1850, by Walker. Pilley Collection. *Hereford City Library*
Inside back cover: Map of the Tedstone Court Estate 1908. *Gail Bellville*

Other publications of the Bromyard & District Local History Society

*Bromyard A Local History (1970)
*Bromyard Parish Registers by E. D. Pearson (1974)
*Bromyard: The Day Before Yesterday. A book of photographs (1979)
Whitbourne: A Bishop's Manor by P. Williams (1979)
*Little Cowarne: A Herefordshire Village by J. Hopkinson (1983)
*Herefordshire Under Arms by C. Hopkinson (1985)
Bromyard: Minster, Manor And Town by P. Williams (1987)
*A Pocketful of Hops. Hop Growing in the Bromyard Area (1988)
Bromyard: Round And About by D. Waller (1991)
Two Churches: Two Communities. St Peters Bromyard and St James's Stanford Bishop by E. D. Pearson (1993)
*A History of Bredenbury and its Landed Estate by Jennifer Weale (1997)
Avenbury and the ruined church of St Mary by P. Williams (2000)
Where Have All the Courts Gone? A monograph by J. Hopkinson (2003)
The Churches of the Bromyard Rural Deanery An Informal Guide by D. M. Annett
Bromyard's Victorian Heritage A book of photographs (2005)
The Three Stanfords A History of Stanford Bishop, Stanford Falcon and Stanford Regis by P. Williams (2007)
A Pocketful of Hops. A New Edition (2007)
An analysis of the historic fabric of fifty buildings in the central area of Bromyard, Herefordshire
by Duncan James (2009)

* OUT OF PRINT

Acknowledgments

It gives me great pleasure to thank all the people who have assisted with this book. Sadly it is impossible to name each one. I especially thank all the people of Tedstone Delamere who have welcomed me into their homes, so generously allowing me to inspect their properties. Many have provided photographs, documents and reminiscences. I thank the Publications Committee of the Bromyard and District Local History Society for all their helpful encouragement.

Audrey Lowery, Beryl Hunt and the late Barry Phillips all helped with research in the very early days of this project. Research has been carried out in the Bromyard Local History Centre and I thank the History Society for use of their records and photographs. Much of the research has been carried out in the Herefordshire Record Office and I am very grateful to Elizabeth Semper O'Keefe, Rhys Griffiths and their staff for much help and for permission to reproduce documents. I particularly thank Sue Hubbard, former manager of the Record Office, who has painstakingly translated nearly all the Tedstone Delamere court rolls which were in Latin. She has also read and helpfully commented on my Chapter III which is based on the court rolls and wills. Polly Rubery has transcribed the more difficult wills. I thank Anne and Chris Evans of the Dial House, Whitbourne who have made the Whitbourne Estate records so readily available and provided maps and photographs to copy. Rosemary Keep has generously allowed me to use her dissertation 'Survey on Tedstone Delamere and Tedstone Wafre', made when an archaeology undergraduate.

Sue Haffenden and Jane Hawksley have read some of the chapters and their local knowledge has been most helpful. Sue has provided a delightful chapter about the Bellvilles at Tedstone Court. There is always an anxiety to reproduce reminiscences and photograph-captions correctly, any errors remaining are my responsiblility and mine alone. Members of the Bromyard Local History Society: Allan Wyatt, Jean Hopkinson, and Phyllis Williams have spent much time carefully reading the text and making many useful suggestions and corrections. Hugh Langrishe has carefully read and corrected the proofs. I thank them all. I am most grateful to Joe Hillaby who has written the foreword; Joe has been tutor and adviser to the Society since its inception. It was Joe who advised me to give due prominence to the description of Tedstone's important Saxon church.

I am indebted to Bruce Coplestone-Crow for generously supplying information on the early descent of the manor and also to John Freeman who has suggested meanings for some of the place-names. I thank Hereford City Library who have provided the watercolour and sketches of the church, and also English Heritage for photographs and plans from the RCHME. Geoff Gwatkin has drawn wonderfully clear maps which enable the buildings, fields and other features to be shown in the right context. I thank archaeologists, Neil Rimmington for his aerial photograph of the possible prehistoric enclosure round the church, and Tim Hoverd for his drawings of the prehistoric flint scrapers and axe-head that were found by Francis Clarke. I thank Francis Lowden for loan of the hunt scrap-books. I am very grateful to the many Tedstone and other local people who have lent photographs without which this book would be so much the poorer; where possible, there names appear with the captions. Brian Pepper, Neville Page-Jones and Brenda Allen have all helped to copy photographs.

Finally, I thank the staff at Orphans Press, (Gary Nozedar, Amy Oakley, and especially Neil Chapman) for their patience and expertise in arranging this book.

Jennifer Weale
October 2013

Preface

The Bromyard & District Local History Society was founded in 1966. Jennifer Weale became a member in 1967. Its first volume, Bromyard: A Local History, was published in 1970; 1,500 copies were printed. Sadly it was soon out of print. Jennifer's contribution was a discussion of 'Some Aspects of Victorian Bromyard from the 1851 Census'. This was based on a detailed analysis of the enumerator's returns. From these she was able to build up a clear picture of the census occupations of its citizens, the economy of the town, household size, age structure and the birth places of its 292 heads of households: 111 were born in Bromyard; 136 within Herefordshire and Worcestershire; and only 45 from beyond. 2% of the population were visitors. Here, as in Jennifer's other studies, the problem of poverty was discussed. It would be very interesting to have a comparable study of Bromyard at the last census.

In 1987 Phyllis Williams published Bromyard: Minster, Manor and Town, looking at the town in the broader context of the ecclesiastical estate and the lands held by military service. The Society published more general volumes of which the most popular was A Pocketful of Hops (1988). This sought to provide 'some record of the excitement of hop-picking before memories fade and pass into folk lore'. Many of the photographs which play such an important part in the book were drawn from the Society's own collection.

Even earlier, members of the Society had embarked on detailed studies of individual parishes of the Bromyard parochia, a district which has a unity that goes back more than a thousand years. The first, by Phyllis Williams, was Whitbourne: A Bishop's Manor, published in 1979. A review by Philip Rahtz in West Midlands Archaeology 23 (1980) described it as 'perhaps the nearest we can get to "total history"', with a range extending 'beyond the documents to the topographic and archaeological evidence – the geology, communications and especially buildings and farms described and illustrated in loving detail'. Whitbourne thus established a tradition cherished by other Society members in later parish volumes. In 1984 Jean Hopkinson published Little Cowarne, a village were plague and population crises virtually rendered it a deserted village; in 1428 there were fewer than 10 villagers. Although it became a chapelry of Ullingswick, it survived. In 1871 there were 213 people living in 43 houses.

In 1997, the Society published Jennifer's History of Bredenbury and its Landed Estate. Here she traced the history, not only of a parish, but of an estate: 'Boarded Burg to Modern Village'. Bredenbury village and estate were transformed after 1865 when Edmund Higginson, a bachelor who had purchased the estate for £17,000, gave it to his nephew, William Henry Barneby, as a wedding present. Jennifer's description of the latter's transformation of Bredenbury is assisted by a wealth of remarkable photographs, including the nine 'staff at the laundrey', a gardener, a gamekeeper, the carpenters in their shop, grooms and stable lads. The village is represented by the WI percussion band in 1920; the large cast of 'Bluebeard', the parish play in 1936; the Mother's Union in 1937; the 2nd Bredenbury Guides camping at Porthcawl, and at home in full uniform, in the 1920s; the children of the village school in 1913, 1931-2, 1938 and c1946; and the wonderfully attired Bredenbury Home Guard in 1944. Such photographs portray the tone of village life in the 20th century. Nevertheless, Jennifer characteristically devotes an interesting chapter to 'The Poor Law of 1834 and Care by the Gentry'.

The Society's most recent project was the publication, with support from the National Lottery, of An Analysis of the historic fabric of fifty buildings in the central area of Bromyard, Herefordshire (2011). The report was prepared for the Society by Duncan James who records his very special thanks to Jennifer for 'arranging the very many visits ... made throughout the town'. As he explains, 'without her (support) the project would not have been brought to a satisfactory conclusion.

With A History of Tedstone Delamere Jennifer has returned to the tradition of full-volume parochial studies. Tedstone Delamere is the only parish within the Bromyard parochia with firm architectural evidence of Saxon foundation. From a wide range of documentary and other sources, Jennifer provides a remarkable description of the development of the parish from this pre-Conquest period until the end of the last century.

Joe Hillaby, Hollybush
July 2013

Contents

			Page
Acknowledgements			iii
Preface			v
Introduction	Early Beginnings		1
Chapter I	The Church of St James. Part I. From Earliest Days to the Beginning of the 19th Century		9
Chapter II	The Manor and Lordship – from the Domesday Survey to the end of the 17th century		31
Chapter III	Our Tedstone Forbears, who they were and how they lived and farmed during the 15th – 17th Centuries		43
Chapter IV	The Eighteenth Century Manor and Tenants		77
Chapter V	Farms and Smallholdings West of the Sapey Brook - before 1841		87
Chapter VI	Farms and Smallholdings East of the Sapey Brook - before 1841		114
Chapter VII	The Wight Family and their 19th Century Tedstone Court Estate		137
Chapter VIII	The Church of St James. Part II. The Nineteenth Century Rebuilding of the Rectory, Restoration of the Church and Stories about some of the Parsons		145
Chapter IX	The Estate to the East of the Sapey Brook and its Owners – after 1841		162
Chapter X	The Farms and Smallholdings – after 1840		173
Chapter XI	The Cottages		210
Chapter XII	Schooling in the Parish		234
Chapter XIII	The Bellville Family at Tedstone Court 1908 – 1996		241
Chapter XIV	The Changing Centuries		252
Appendix A	Lords of the Manor of Tedstone Delamere		256
Appendix B	Taxes of Henry VIII		259
Appendix C	Probate and Administrative Acts		261
Appendix D	Patrons and Incumbents		262
Appendix E	A Lewne made by the overseers of the Poore of the parish of Tedstone Delamere for collecting Money for the poore at 2d in the Pound to be collected monthly as oft as needful in the year 1739		264

Errata

p56 Militia Assessments
    Delete horizontal line at base of 1st column
    The figure for Will: Wynne should read '4 10 0'
    Add 'Tho: Lewis 1 0 0'

			Page
Table	1	Composition in lieu of Tithes proposed to be paid annually to the Rev. Mr. Tomkyns 1792	28
Table	2	Tedstone Delamere Wills and Inventories 1556 - 1696	73
Table	3	Inventory Values	74
Table	4	Eighteenth Century Wills and Inventories 1700 – 1782	82
Table	5	Land Tax Assessments 1790	84
Table	6	Farms and Smallholdings in Western Tedstone Delamere 1841 – 1901	174
Table	7	Farms and Smallholdings in Eastern Tedstone Delamere 1841 – 1901	193
Table	8	Occupants of Cottages in Western Tedstone Delamere 1841 – 1901	217
Table	9	Occupants of Cottages in Eastern Tedstone Delamere 1841 – 1901	224
Table	10	Population in Tedstone Delamere from the Censuses	253
Map	1	Roads, Relief and Drainage	inside front cover
Map	2	Tedstone Delamere and Surrounding Parishes	5
Map	3	Earthworks near the Church	7
Map	4	Tedstone Delamere Field Names 1841	46
Map	5	Hedge House Farm - from the Saltmarshe Estate Survey 1841-42	95
Map	6	Plan of the Woodham Hall Estate 1787	121
Map	7	Plan of the Tedstone Delamere Estate of James Moore 1848	122
Map	8	Tedstone Delamere Landowners 1841	164
Map	9	Tedstone Delamere Tenants 1841	175
Map	10	Cottages in Western Tedstone Delamere	216
Map	11	Cottages in Eastern Tedstone Delamere	225
Map	12	Tedstone Court Estate in 1908/09	inside back cover
Index			274

INTRODUCTION

Early Beginnings

Tedstone Delamere lies in what must be one of the most beautiful parts of the country. It is a medium sized parish covering some 1677 acres and is situated in the far north-east uplands of Herefordshire bordering the county of Worcester. The parish is on some of the highest land of the Bromyard plateau, thus commanding exceptional views, part of a landscape of gentle hills and valleys. Old red sandstone has been broken down through the ages into the typical reddish coarse loamy soil seen in Herefordshire and is particularly good for the production of corn, grassland (especially for sheep), orchards, and in former years the growing of hops was widespread. Although providing good farmland, the geology and soil does not produce the lush pasture found in the Frome Valley and central Herefordshire. A limestone band appearing in the Sapey Valley just north of the parish runs southwards more or less parallel with the brook until it leaves the parish; there is another limestone band to the east. This limestone is the source of the springs in the centre and east of the parish and seepage from it is the reason for the thick belt of trees that have grown along the sides of the Sapey Brook and also along the Whitbourne Brook on the south-eastern boundary. It has provided building material together with lime for improving the land and preserving buildings. The deep valley of the Sapey Brook separates the parish in two from north to south; this has been an important division between estates, and a physical barrier that can make travelling between the two halves of the parish difficult.[1]

Pre-history and a recent exciting discovery
Worked flints and arrowheads from the Neolithic and Bronze Ages have been picked up nearby: Deborah Waller made an impressive collection, mostly from around Keephill, just north of Bromyard, and eagle-eyed Ivan Turner has a huge number he found at Netherwood in Thornbury. And here in Tedstone Delamere, Francis Clark has picked up a number of worked flints, scrapers and a stone axe-head from the fields close to Ireland Cottage where he lives. Recently, aerial photography has shown up a very interesting large bank feature curving round on the south side of the church. What could it be? Archaeologist Neil Rimmington says: 'my gut instinct is that it is a prehistoric monument judging from its scale and form and probably of Bronze Age date judging from its position in the landscape'. It would need archaeology to test his strong suspicion and this would need funding. At the moment this remains just a dream for the future. If it is an ancient enclosure, it may be significant that the churchyard would probably have been at least partially within its boundary and when the Saxon church was built, the enclosure's bank and ditches would have been much more prominent. An interesting question springs to mind:

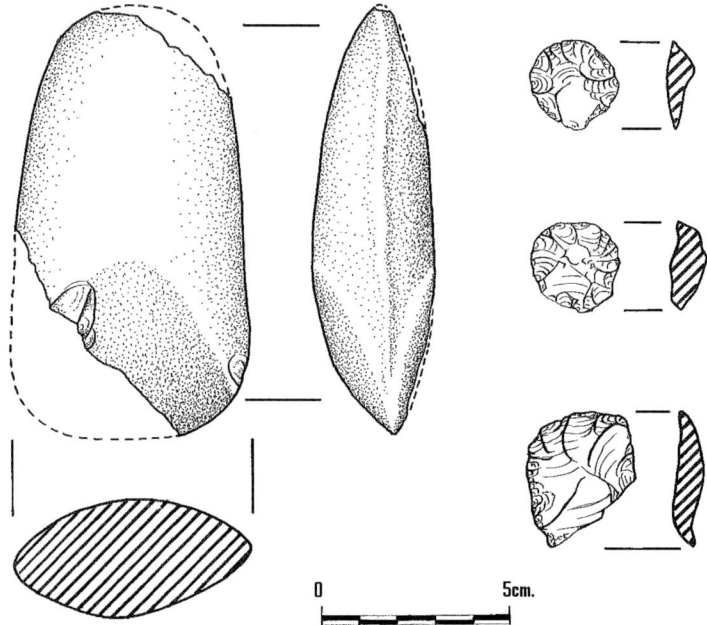

Polished stone axe from the Neolithic period probably made of volcanic tuff from south-west Wales

Thumb scrapers made of flint from the south Welsh coast and the larger example possibly from Norfolk. Late Neolithic or early Bronze Age.

Pre-historic artefacts found by Francis Clark near Ireland Cottage where he lives. *Tim Hoverd*

was the church built on its present site in some way because of the ancient enclosure? Because of the importance of this early church, it is discussed in some detail at the beginning of Chapter I.

The earliest inhabitants were hunter-gatherers; these were followed in time by nomadic peoples with herds of domesticated animals. In roughly around 5000 BC, people learnt to grow crops and it was at this stage that they developed permanent settlements. Eventually men learnt how to exploit metal, firstly bronze and then iron. It was during the so-called Iron Age, from 500 BC, that this part of the country became dominated by hill forts, some of them massive structures like the British Camp at Malvern that could be seen for miles around. The rural population at this point in time is thought to have achieved a height that was not reached again until the 19th century and surely the land at Tedstone Delamere must have been farmed to feed the people from nearby Thornbury Camp and perhaps those from around the equally large hill fort at Whitbourne[2], both occupying about 25 acres. The tribe in this part of the country was called the *Dobunni;* they were good farmers, had a rich artistic culture and traded widely with the Continent. The Roman Conquest of Britain took place from 43 AD and quite early on at Tedstone Wafre on the High

INTRODUCTION

Photograph showing a large bank feature curving round on the south side of the church. Could this be Bronze Age?
Neil Rimmington, Hereford Archaeology

Lane, they established a marching fort. Another was established at Upper Sapey. Romano-British pottery has been found in the area and a kiln was busy firing pottery at Batchley in Grendon Bishop. The Romans left nearly 400 years later but before this time, raiding Germanic tribes were beginning to make sorties from the Continent. Angles, Saxons and Jutes crossed the sea and came up the rivers to settle in ever increasing numbers. They were a pagan people whereas the Romans in the latter stages of their occupation were Christians.

The Anglo-Saxon kingdom between the Severn and the Wye
Herefordshire became part of the land of the Western *Hecani*, the name probably being derived from its inhabitants, the *Hwicce*. It was later to become the kingdom of the *Magonsaete* who occupied the land between the Severn and the Wye. These farming peoples seem to have absorbed the indigenous Celtic population and cultivation of the land would have continued much as before but what did change were the place-names. The Anglo-Saxons gave us our language.

Plegelgate Hundred
In late Anglo-Saxon times, the hundreds, approximately 100 hides*, were the principal sub-divisions of the shire. Plegelgate Hundred lay within a radius of about

---
* A hide in this part of the world is thought to have been approximately 120 acres

4 miles from Bromyard, and Tedstone Delamere was on the eastern boundary of this Saxon local government administrative unit. *Plegelgate* probably means either 'the gap of a man called Plega' or 'the gap where the deer play'.[3] As a member of the hundred, Tedstone Delamere would have had to send a delegate to the hundred moots every 4 weeks.[4] These courts are thought to have taken place at Flaggoners Green on the western outskirts of Bromyard, the unusual name of 'Flaggoners' appearing to be a corruption of *Plegelgate*.[5] The system of minster churches was developed to serve these territories and the minster church of Bromyard is at the heart of the hundred of Plegelgate. This and the beginnings of Christianity in the area will be discussed further in Chapter I relating to the parish church.

Origins of the place-name
The name 'Tedstone' means *Teod's thorn-tree*. Teod is a personal name and the thorn tree was perhaps an important boundary marker. Estates had Anglo-Saxon names by 1066; often a parish name referred to a manorial lord, for instance Edwyn Ralph and Edvin Loach were named after one Gedda, an Anglo-Saxon who settled on what was *fen* or marshy land then later when the estate was divided, one Norman landowner was called Ralph and the other de Loges. In the same way, Wafre and la Mare were the names of the Norman families who held two parts of this now divided Tedstone estate some time after the Conquest.[6] In Anglo-Saxon times, Tedstone Wafre and Tedstone Delamere had been one estate but sometime before or around the time of the Domesday Survey in 1086, this large estate had become three: they are all three recorded in the Domesday Survey: as *Tedesthorne* listed among the Bishop of Hereford's lands, as *Chetestor* listed amongst Gilbert fitz Thorold's lands and as *Tetistorp* listed among the lands of Roger de Lacy.[7] 'Teod's thorn-tree' was a name which French speakers found difficult and these earliest forms of the name show a good deal of corruption. The first two which were to become Tedstone Delamere are discussed in detail in Chapter II but the tenurial history of the third manor which became Tedstone Wafre is mentioned briefly here: its Norman lord was Roger de Lacy who came to England with the Conqueror and was the chief recipient of lands in Herefordshire. His lands were confiscated for his part in the rebellion of 1095 and Tedstone Wafre was given to Bernard de Neufmarche. It seems probable that Bernard gave lands which included Tedstone Wafre to Hugh *cognomine Guafre* (Wafre) soon after 1095, in return for military service. The manor remained with the Wafre family until 1275 when a Wafre daughter married into the important Mortimer family.[8]

Parish boundaries
On the west, the parish of Tedstone Delamere is separated from Tedstone Wafre by the B4203 main road from Bromyard, a road that has long been considered to be an ancient ridgeway.[9] At High Lane, the boundary turns eastwards and shortly joins the Worcestershire county boundary. This northern boundary of Tedstone Delamere shares the county boundary together with the Lower Sapey parish boundary until, at its most easterly point, it adjoins the parish of Whitbourne and follows the Whitbourne Brook southwards to Horners Mill. It then takes a westerly direction

INTRODUCTION

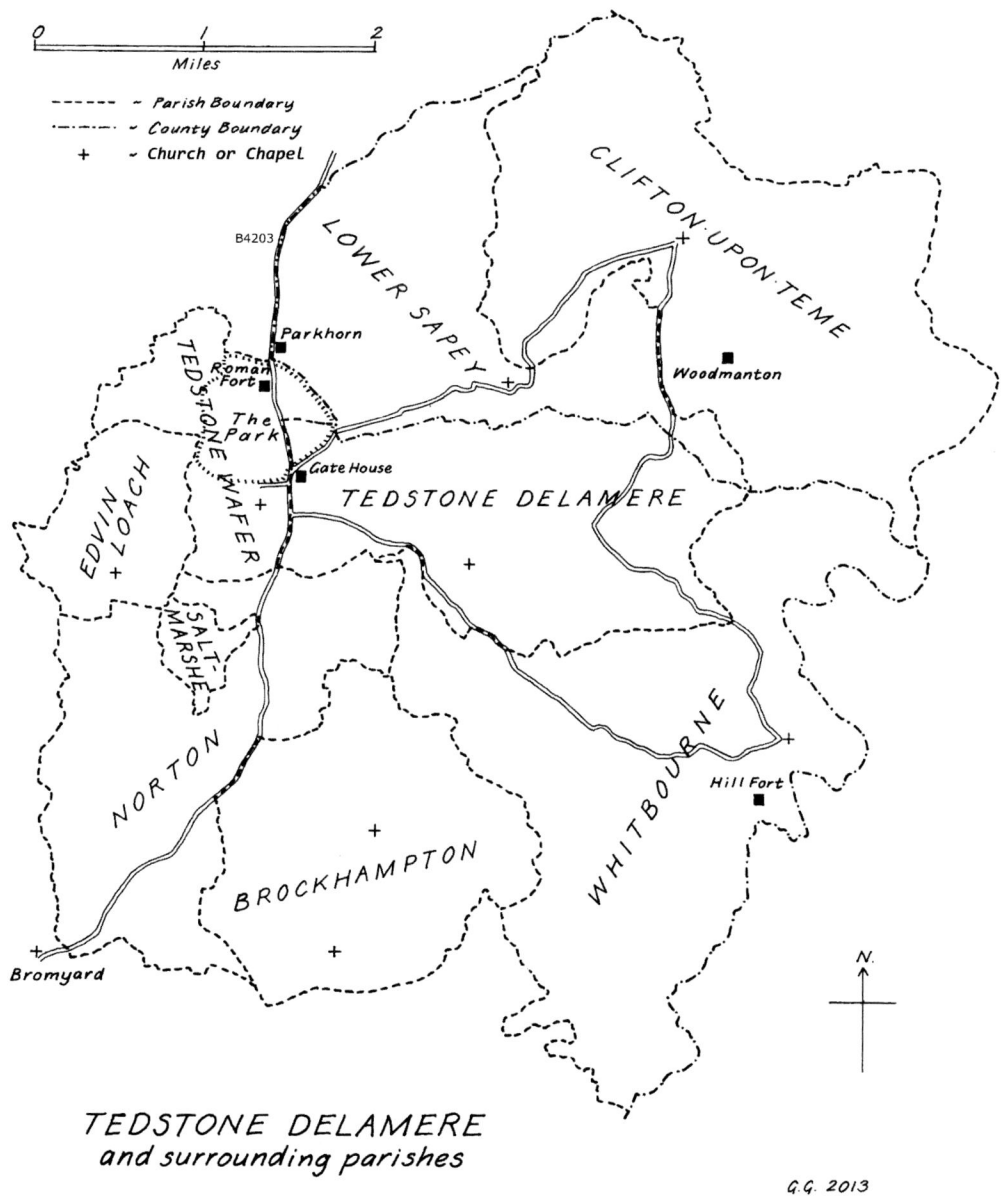

Map 2. Note the medieval deer park of the Mortimers to the north-west of the map.

along a small tributary of the Whitbourne Brook, crosses the Sapey Brook, and continues westwards until it meets the Whitbourne/Tedstone road which it follows upwards for a short distance, then crosses the road below Brick Cottages, skirts along Hole Coppice and above Vinschurch, until it leaves Whitbourne for the final stretch westwards, bordering Norton township, until it meets the B4203 road and Tedstone Wafre. Parish boundaries are ancient: in the 12th century, the Church had utilised the secular boundaries of the Anglo-Saxon estates, that had been in existence for many years previously, as parish boundaries and this is explained in more detail in Chapter I.

Settlement areas
It is probable that there was a small area of settlement around the church although the visible earthworks appear to relate only to two or three house platforms. This is now described officially as a 'deserted medieval village or DMV' but the survey that was carried out, see Map 3, only shows two or three house platforms which could possibly relate to a former parsonage with associated buildings or one farmstead; archaeology may discover more signs of occupation in this area. The small circular feature may have been a dovecote. Apart from the ancient enclosure by the church, the remaining earthworks in the field (not mapped) appear to show lines of former hedgerows cleared to create the Victorian parkland. But what is clear is that dispersed settlement of scattered farmsteads seems to have been the norm in Tedstone Delamere from an early date. The court rolls, some of which have survived from the mid 1400s, make no mention of any habitation round the church, so it is possible that this settlement, if there ever was any, became deserted at the time of the Black Death, some 80 years earlier. Population density in Herefordshire as a whole has been low at all periods, particularly in the eastern part and large villages are not common.[10] Tedstone Court occupies a defensive position on top of a hill and was probably moated. In 1440, three tenants held land at Tipton and there is known to have been more than one household at Winley in the 16th century and these may be the sites of further hamlets.[11] And for the eastern side of the parish, Rosemary Keep suggests that the late clearance of woodland here as demonstrated by place-names and the survival of wild service trees and small-leaved limes as hedgerow trees means that this side of the parish may have been settled later than the western side. These tree species were found near Woodend and Woodhall, along the Whitbourne Brook on the far eastern parish boundary, in the Ladywood area and at Winley.[12] There could well, at one time, have been a hamlet in the Woodend/Woodhall vicinity, an area where there were several houses in the 18th century. Woodend had extensive fish ponds and may possibly represent the demesne farm of the ancient eastern manor.

Settlement areas have changed through the centuries: in the 18th century, farms and smallholdings were amalgamated by the landlord to create larger units, some small former farmhouses became labourers' cottages for a while, then becoming unoccupied as the result of the agricultural depression and movement to the towns in the 19th century. These events are traced in the chapters relating to the farms and cottages. In the 17th, 18th and 19th centuries, there was considerable cottage

INTRODUCTION

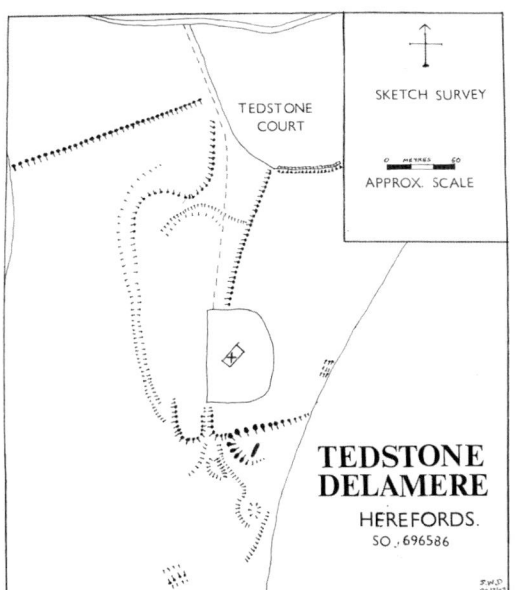

Map 3. Sketch survey showing two possible house platforms below the church. Landscaping to enlarge a pond has largely removed these features.   *HRO*

settlement along the Sapey Brook, most of it having originated as squatters on the manor's wastes. Modern settlement has largely replaced that lost but this has taken place where there are good roads and modern amenities.

What is special about Tedstone Delamere records?

Some classes of records ought to be of equal usefulness for all parishes but vary, either because of the form in which they were made, or because of illegibility due to damp and decay and many records have been lost. One of the reasons for selecting Tedstone Delamere for study, as opposed to other parishes in the Bromyard area, was because, apart from the manors of the bishops of Hereford in the area, namely Bromyard, Whitbourne, Stanford Bishop, Bishops Frome and Grendon Bishop, it seems to be unique in that a substantial number of its manorial records have survived. Only about 4% of manors have surviving records before 1500.[13] The manor of Tedstone Delamere has manorial records dating from the late 14th century and so is rather special. These are now in the Hereford Record Office. There is always a downside and the surviving church records apparently contain no overseers' books, no rate books and the churchwardens' accounts only date from 1855-95 and parish registers from 1698, but other records relating to the church partly compensate for this omission and we are particularly fortunate that old title deeds have survived for nearly every property, mostly either in the Hereford Record Office or amongst Whitbourne Estate papers kept at the Dial House, Whitbourne.

How this book is arranged

It begins with the first of two chapters on the church: Chapter I 'The Church of St James' tells of the development of Christianity in the area and the continuing story of the Saxon church, one of only five Saxon churches in Herefordshire; it covers the patrons of the living and the incumbents, explaining the difficulties associated with supporting the clergy and maintaining the church and parsonage before the Tithe Commutation Act of 1836. Chapter II, 'The Manor and the Lordship', begins with the Domesday Survey. It goes on to trace the descent of the manor from Anglo-Saxon times until the end of the 17th century. Chapter III is based mainly on the manorial records, wills and inventories and is about the people, who they were and how they lived and farmed during the 15th to 17th centuries. Chapter IV traces the manor and its tenants through the 18th century and tells how the wealthy industrialist lord of the manor, Robert Moore, invested in more land and finally how the second of his bachelor sons, James, divided this now much larger estate by bequeathing it to two cousins. The three chapters on the history of the farms are arranged geographically as west and east of the Sapey Brook and chronologically before and after 1840/41, the dates of the tithe map and apportionment. Chapter VII is about the Wight family and their Victorian estate in the west of the parish. A chapter about the church in the 19th and 20th centuries follows; this includes the rebuilding of the rectory and major restoration of the church together with stories about some of the parsons. Chapter IX traces the eastern estate and its owners from 1840. Another chapter maps the many 19th century cottages and gives a detailed account of their history suggesting reasons for the disappearance of many of them. A brief piece on schooling is followed by a chapter by Susan Haffendon née Bellville and tells of the Bellville family's time at the Court in the 20th century. A short final chapter summarises some of the changes that have taken place through the ages, the population changes in the 19th and 20th centuries, and discusses the situation in the parish today.

Aerial photo showing clearly the circular medieval deer park of the Mortimers that is shown on Map 2. See also pages 94 and 95.

© *Getmapping Plc*

CHAPTER I

The Church of St James

Part I
From Earliest Days to the Beginning of the 19th Century

The little church in Tedstone Delamere is situated on the side of a hill and just below the manor house. It is approached by a footpath across parkland and is in a beautiful position with stunning views; if visited in the spring, one finds the churchyard has been lovingly planted with daffodils and is a picture to behold; a beautiful and tranquil place. As one enters the building, one gains the impression of an attractive but entirely Victorian church but on closer inspection there are clues that this is largely a very much earlier building. The church was much restored in 1856 and the chancel is Victorian.

Christianity was introduced to Britain by the Romans but we don't know to what extent it had spread to the indigenous Celtic population by the time of their departure. The so- called Dark Ages were to follow with the invasion of the country by hordes of pagan peoples. The re-Christianisation of England began in the 6th century and came from two directions: firstly, by Celtic missionaries from Ireland; locally a missionary from Lindisfarne converted the Anglo-Saxon kingdom of the Magonsaeten which is thought to cover the same area as that of the Hereford Diocese today. First wooden and then stone crosses served as a focus for worship and at Acton Beauchamp, now used as a lintel over a doorway into the tower, is a very finely carved cross shaft of the 9th century. And secondly, from the south-east came St Augustine and his monks arriving on the Kent coast from Rome in 597 and they brought a church based Christianity. The two factions met somewhere in the Welsh Marches and at first failed to agree but in 664 at the Synod of Whitby, matters were finally settled in favour of the Roman system of St Augustine and this system included the *Minster Church*.

Part of the *parochia* of Bromyard Minster.
The Anglo-Saxon minster churches were the first stage in the development of our parish system. The converted kings of the separate English kingdoms founded 'minsters'; these were large churches, usually with attendant buildings that housed the priests serving the surrounding district or *parochia*. The see of Hereford was in existence by the end of the 7th century and we know from an Anglo-Saxon charter that a minster church had been established at Bromyard by 840[1] but very probably

this took place in the first part of the 8th century and soon after the establishment of the diocese. Bromyard Minster became the centre for missionary activity in the north-east of the county before the area was divided into parishes; a small group of priests would have gone out from Bromyard, sent by their bishop to convert the remaining heathens in the district and to serve the spiritual needs of the community there, the minster's 'district' covering a similar area to that of Bromyard Deanery today. Tedstone Delamere is on the far eastern perimeter of this ancient *parochia* of Bromyard's minster and borders Worcestershire. Tithes, which were a tenth of the produce of the land were collected from this extended parish to maintain the priests at Bromyard and people were expected to attend the mother church there for special occasions.

Only just over a mile from Tedstone's northern boundary lay another minster church; that of Clifton-on-Teme, probably on the same foundations as Clifton's present 14th century church dedicated to the Saxon saint, St Kenelm. The parishes of Edvin Loach, Lower Sapey and Kyre Wyard looked to Clifton rather than Bromyard as their minster church; it is sometimes forgotten that until a date as late as 1919, all these parishes, including Clifton, had been in the diocese of Hereford.[2] Edvin Loach, alone of the above, remained in the diocese of Hereford.

The next stage in the development of our parochial system was the building of small estate churches by local lords of the manor to serve their own and their tenants' needs; many of the earlier churches were of wood and have not survived. They would at first have been used by the visiting priests from the minster for the celebration of mass, for preaching and the baptism of converts; they were a closer and more convenient place for Christian burial than Bromyard and might also have been a place of sanctuary in those uncertain times.

The Saxon church on an ancient site
Situated on a hill with magnificent views east to the Malvern Hills and beyond, the Georgian manor house is built on or close to the site of an earlier house; it lies just above the important church which is one of only five Anglo-Saxon churches in Herefordshire. The church is sited on an unusual sloping site that necessitated cutting into the hillside. The recent discovery, mentioned in the Introduction, of a probable prehistoric enclosure of possible Bronze Age date partially surrounding the churchyard, suggests that the site of the church may well have been chosen in some way because of this ancient enclosure. When the church was built, some 1000 years ago, the banks and ditches of this small enclosure would have been much more prominent than they are today. We do not know whether its purpose was defensive or perhaps sacred but it is not unusual for churches to be built within ancient enclosures; a famous example is at Knowlton in Dorset where the church is within an Iron Age hill-fort.[3] Nearer to hand is the church at Hanbury in Worcestershire, also within an Iron Age hill-fort.[4] A strategy advised by Bede was to deliberately take over old sites thus avoiding rival religions being practised nearby. He records an instruction in a letter from Pope Gregory to Abbot Melitus, asking him to tell

The church before the 19th century restoration. *Hereford City Library*

St. Augustine: 'that the idol temples of that race [the English] should not be not destroyed, but only the idols in them'.[5]

What can the fabric of the church building tell us? The nave walls are built of local sandstone, rubble and some tufa. Tufa was often used in dressings, being an extremely durable stone of calcium carbonate resembling petrified sponge. Both Saxon and Norman builders used it for external facing on churches and because of its lightness it was used for vaulting, as in Bredon Church in Worcestershire; the herringbone masonry at Edvin Loach is of tufa. The nearest good source is thought to be at Shelsley Walsh, about five miles away, but it is also found in the Sapey Brook so it was a very local source of building stone.

Writing in 1965, H. M. and J. Taylor, in describing the church say that:

> the aisle-less nave is Saxo-Norman in character,... the triangular-headed blocked doorway in the middle of the north wall [only visible from the outside] is of distinctly Anglo-Saxon type, even though the hood-moulding over its head has now been cut back flush with the walls. The south doorway which now serves as the entrance to the church is of pointed form, but it is still possible externally to see traces of the original, triangular-headed shape, and it is therefore clear that the church had two of these doorways, placed opposite each other, in the centre [or just east of central] of its side walls.[6]

North doorway. This photo shows the pointed 14th-century arch of a doorway that is now blocked. Above it, the triangular strip-label in tufa, cut back flush with the wall, is Anglo-Saxon.

The west end of the church showing the Anglo-Saxon quoins of tufa with corbels projecting above.

H. M. Taylor's later book comes down firmly in favour of the nave of the church being Anglo-Saxon[7] and the new edition of *The Buildings of England, Herefordshire* by A. Brookes and N. Pevsner, states categorically, leaving no room for doubt, that the church is of Saxon origin:

> The nave W quoins, flush with the W wall must be Anglo Saxon. Of blocks of travertine or tufa, with corbels projecting above; the third block from the ground, SW, shows signs of a cut back. Above the blocked N doorway (and faintly above the S), outlines in tufa of former gables. The S doorway's inner surround is also of tufa, ... [8]

It is suggested that these were doorways to side-chapels or porticos. The Saxon church at Bradford-on-Avon contains famous examples of these.[9]

Taylor thinks that the two simple, round-headed, single-splayed windows high up in its side walls, towards the west, are also Saxon.[10]

The Saxon quoins - detail.

One of the two round-headed single-splayed windows which H. M. Taylor considers to be Anglo-Saxon.

The mysterious skeleton at Lower Sapey

Just across the county boundary, and little more than a mile away as the crow flies, lies the unassuming little church of Lower Sapey. This building is thought to date from the late 11th century and a priest was recorded here in the Domesday Survey. It had been thought that the church had always been a chapel of ease; this would mean that there would have been no burials. So it was surprising when, in 1994, an extraordinary discovery was made there: one evening after a period of heavy rain, Mr. and Mrs. Prosser were returning home to Church House when something was picked up in the car headlights in the steep bank bordering the churchyard. On archaeological investigation in 1997 and subsequent radio carbon analysis, it was found to be part of a human skeleton dating from the early 9th century.[11] The skeleton was complete except for the foot and some leg bones which had been washed away. The burial was in a Christian east-west alignment and the arms had originally been crossed.[12] Clearly, Lower Sapey had been a very early place of Christian worship where burials took place.

In 781, King Offa of Mercia had granted some land to Worcester Monastery in exchange for land at Sapey, but Sapey must have been returned to the church of Worcester, as Bishop Brihteah was able to give it 'to a certain man who had married his sister' ...[13]. At the Conquest, one of the two manors of Tedstone Delamere was held by the church of Hereford (see page 32). If one could assume, as suggested on pages 32-33, but this is pure guess work, that the church of Hereford's manor was on the west side of the Sapey Brook and was the one in which our church is built, one could argue that the Bishop of Hereford, not wishing to be outdone by the church at Worcester, might have been the person who built the little church at Tedstone; perhaps his tenants had been attracted by services to Lower Sapey. It does raise the possibility that there might conceivably be burials of almost the same period in the churchyard at Tedstone Delamere.

The Norman Conquest led to renewed efforts to build on a grand scale and churches were built, rebuilt and added to in stone. With the proliferation of these small churches, there was a certain resistance from the priests at the minsters who were concerned about the loss of their tithes and other revenues which would now be needed to support the new parish priests. We know the extent of the minster's *parochia* at Bromyard, for after the Reformation the Crown attempted to prove that Bromyard was a collegiate church and should therefore become the property of the Crown. However it was successfully argued that it was instead a portionary church and that every Whit Monday the priests of the fifteen 'inferior' churches attended the church at Bromyard, 'confessing the same to be the mother church'. Indeed, if they did not attend, they were fined 6s. 8d.[14] Some of these 'inferior' churches are identified in a terrier of 1589 which records that ancient dues were paid by their priests to the vicar of Bromyard every Easter and these are listed as follows: Stoke Lacy 6d., Tedstone Delamere 2s. 6d., Upper Sapey 6d., Collington 6d., Edwyn Ralph 6d., Stoke Bliss 3s. 4d., Wolferlow 2s., and out of the lands of the Hide in Stanford Bishop, 4d.[15] Stoke Bliss and Tedstone Delamere appeared to pay much more than the others. It seems to have been during the 12th century that parish boundaries became fixed. These boundaries usually mirrored the ancient estate boundaries of the Anglo-Saxon manorial lords, or their Norman successors, who had built the churches. Once money was needed to pay priests, it became imperative to fix the area from which each estate church got its funds and so the boundaries of these Saxon estates were taken for those of the new parishes; that is why parishes today vary so enormously in extent. Their size was not organised systematically by a higher authority.

What would the church have looked like?
Roy Strong in his excellent book: *A Little History of the English Country Church,* discusses the omnipresence of images in the medieval church. Pope Gregory the Great who had sent Augustine to England in 597 laid down reasons for their use: 'for a picture is introduced into the church so that those who are ignorant of letters may at least read by looking at the walls what they cannot read in books', and so churches became increasingly elaborate. Roy Strong continues:

> In order to comprehend the importance of images we need to understand the medieval mindset. Today we take reading, writing and visual stimulation for granted. We encounter more images in a day than a medieval villager would have seen in a lifetime. Yet virtually the only images he or she ever saw were displayed in the parish church: the statue of the Virgin over the porch, the interior depicting stories from the Bible, the Last Judgement or Doom, and images of the Virgin and the saints. There would also be the sculpted figures of the Saints and those of saints attached to various altars. As stained glass became more common from the twelfth century, the windows too were a phantasmagoria of images. The impact of this visual world on the many worshippers who were unable to read or write must have been overwhelming: spelled out before their eyes was the whole story of Creation and Salvation – and their own place within it.

Roy Strong is describing larger churches than this one and there may not have been much if any stained glass, which was very expensive, but there would certainly have been colourful wall paintings at Tedstone Delamere. These would have been whitewashed over during the violent disruption following the Reformation. Anyone wishing to see surviving medieval wall paintings should visit nearby Martley church where there are some fine examples. There would have been no heating or lighting in our medieval church apart from candles and there would probably have been an earthen floor, perhaps covered with straw and no pews. One stood or knelt to hear matins or the Mass. Church going for our medieval forebears was a rigorous experience.

The simple font dates from the 12th -13th century[16] and was presumably ejected during the 19th century restoration but has been brought back in and now stands side by side with the grander Victorian one.

The simple carved oak screen is *c*15th – 16th century. The wrought-iron hour-glass stand from the *c*17 century pulpit is now rather incongruously banished to the porch. The congregation of those days would have enjoyed hour-long sermons. This pulpit, pictured, is now moved to nearby Upper Sapey church.

The two mid-13th century coffin lids, now out in the churchyard, may have belonged to members of the La Mare family after whom the parish is named, see more details on pages 34-35.

Churchyard Cross
The square plinth is modern. The RCHME considered that the square base is possibly medieval in origin, but the upper part has been cut back and the date 1629 cut on the east face. The shaft and existing head are modern. The original-medieval cross head has been reset to the side of the entrance gate to the churchyard. It is sadly eroded but the RCHME photos show more detail than can be seen today:

> It has a shouldered, pedimental top and in each of the two sides is a sunk panel with trefoiled head. The E panel has the Virgin and Child carved in low relief; in the W panel is a Crucifix. 14th C.[17]

The nave and carved oak screen of c15th - 16th century.   *Howard Painter*

The Black Death

It is impossible when writing a parish history to completely ignore one or two cataclysmic national events that we know would have affected Tedstone Delamere although there are no records to prove it. The Black Death in 1349 was a hugely momentous and devastating occurrence, beyond anything we can imagine today when between a third and a half of the inhabitants of the country died in one year. We can't do more than mention it in passing because there are almost no local records. We don't know how badly Tedstone Delamere was affected but the people of nearby Collington petitioned the bishop to merge their two parishes for 'so

Wrought-iron hour-glass stand which would have been beside the pulpit.

great and grievous hath been the late pestilence and plague and so diminished the number of men …' that they had difficulty maintaining one church and its priest, let alone two.[18] The clergy are known to have suffered badly, particularly if they were conscientious and ministered to the sick. There was quite a rapid turnover of Tedstone Delamere clergy at that time: in the diocese of Hereford in 1349, the vacancies to benefices created by the deaths of incumbents had risen from one in January to 19 in July when there were also five resignations.[19] John de la More (Mare?) was instituted on the death of the previous incumbent in 1349.[20] Only a year later, a new man, Llewellen de Blakebache, acolyte, was instituted.[21] Llewellen perhaps took fright, and who can blame him, and resigned in 1351 when Thomas de Hylycombe of Odycombe (what a name!) was instituted.[22]

The patronage
The lords of the manors had the right to present priests to the living which was only appropriate considering they had built churches on their estates and had endowed the livings with glebe land for the priests' support. The patronage or advowson of a church was a valuable asset which could be sold or bequeathed. Until around 1700, the patrons of the church had all been lords of the manor, apart from Sir William de Caple who presented in 1289 and Richard de Bagyndon in 1349 (for reasons as yet unknown but it may have been during the minority of firstly, one of the de Plesseys and secondly, one of the Wyshams). In about 1700, the financial difficulties of Robert Mason, lord of the manor, (see page 77) caused him to sell the advowson to the rector, George Hay. Hay's widow and daughter successively presented clergy to the living, and then the patronage changed hands several times before being purchased in 1811 by Brasenose College, Oxford. It was very clearly an attractive country living with which the college could reward people who perhaps needed a quiet time for academic study. For a complete list of the patrons and rectors, see Appendix D.

Some of the early parsons
There was plenty of variation in the priests' backgrounds, origins and learning. Some were simple men and very little different from the peasants; as well as fulfilling the office of priest, they had to be farmers, in the early days cultivating their glebe land which was in strips in the common fields and probably stocking their pasture with the tithed lambs and calves. At that time, ordination appeared not to be a prerequisite of being presented as rector; sometimes acolytes were instituted: in 1318, Eustace de Chandos, rector of Tedstone Delamere, acolyte, was granted a year's dispensation for absence for the purposes of study. There is a note that 'he is allowed to put out his benefice *ad firnam* for the same time' presumably meaning that he could lease it.[23] In 1367 there was another dispensation for absence given to 'Hugh Haukeleye, rector, for study at Oxford or some other university, provided he proceeds to sub-deacon's orders and assumes the tonsure and dress of suitable width – length'.[24] He was ordained sub-deacon the following June. (Hugh de Hawkesley, surely the same family if not the same man, held the manor of Edvin Loach in 1346.)[25]

The parsons' revenues

Until quite recently, each benefice was supported by tithes, lands and offerings, the most important of these sources being **tithes**. Originally claimed by the minsters, tithes were a tenth of the produce of land in the parish and at first were paid in kind, hence the need for a tithe barn. They were required for the support of the clergy from Anglo-Saxon times and can briefly be divided into great tithes and lesser tithes. 'Great tithes' were owed upon corn, hay and wood. All other tithes, which included milling and fishing, were known as small tithes. Tithes were a heavy tax on the parishioners and were frequently a source of bad blood between a rector and his flock, were hard to collect and generally came to be considered a hindrance to the improvement of agriculture and there was much litigation. The means of assessing tithes in a parish depended on long usage and we are fortunate that the following agreement concerning 'small tithes' for this parish is to be found amongst papers in the Herefordshire Record Office:[26]

An Agreement between the present Ministers and Parishioners of Tedstone Delamere concerning the manner of paying certain tithes which is as followeth:
Impr: That the pay for the fall of a calve four pence for all that are yearly, under ten, and if they amount to that number, that then a calve be paid in kind.
It: For the fall of a Colt Sixpence.
It: For every Cow kept on the lands one penny.
It: For the fall of every Lamb under ten one penny and at that number one in kind.
It: For every Fleece of Wool under ten one penny and at that number one in kind
It: For every Hogshead of Cyder made at their own Houses four pence And for every tenth Bushel of apples sold Sixpence
It: That the tithe of Hourding Winter fruit be paid in kind

Bradshaw

The above was copied from the Book kept for parish Accounts from 1616 to 1767 this 12th day of April 1791. And is Contained or Wrote upon the 1st leaf in the sd Book.

John Bury
Church Warden

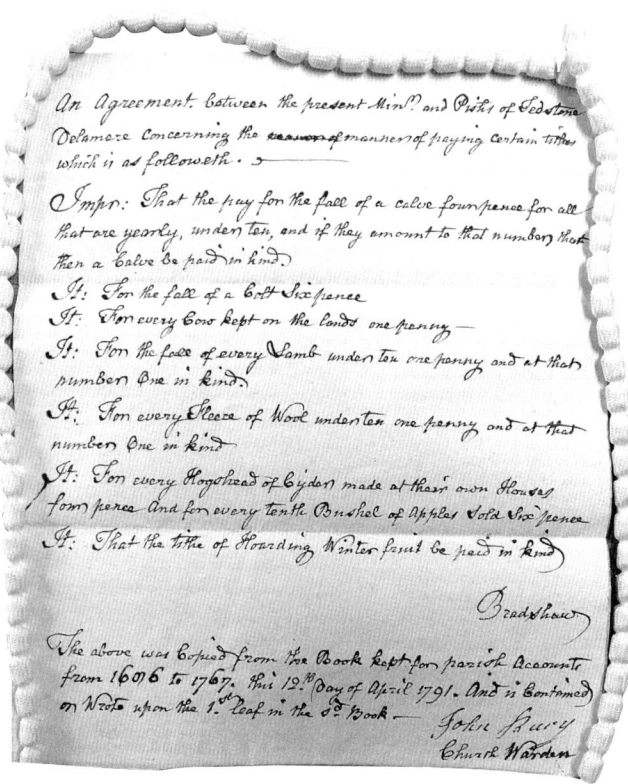

A later copy of an early 17th-century tithe agreement. *HRO*

J. H. Bettey wrote that a tithe notebook kept by the vicar of Minety (Wilts) during the late 17th and early 18th centuries (now in the Wiltshire Record Office):

> ... shows the watchful eye he kept on his parishioners' livestock, records the sales and purchases they made, whether the cows calved in the parish or the sheep were shorn there, and the attempts which the parishioners made to hoodwink him by moving livestock into neighbouring parishes, overwintering stock and selling them in the spring, or by attempting to conceal the true number of lambs, calves or pigs which they had bred.[27]

The second source of the priest's income comprised **offerings from the congregation** including those given at major feast days and at weddings and funerals and the priest would have put some pressure on his flock to see that weddings and funerals took place in their own parish *ie* Tedstone Delamere. The third source of income was from **glebe land**; as explained, the builders of the churches had usually endowed the benefice with land which originally the priest farmed himself. This was once scattered about the parish in the common fields and meadows and the priest would have cultivated his strips alongside his peasant parishioners. A typical customary tenant's holding in this part of the country was a virgate of land which averaged about 40 acres, varying according to the quality of the land. A holding of one virgate in this parish would have been one of the larger farms. Tedstone Delamere's glebe land amounted to 45 acres which was fairly similar to that of most nearby parishes: Whitbourne with 35 acres, Collington with 46 acres, Avenbury with 62 acres, Little Cowarne with 52 acres, but poor Bredenbury only had 5 acres in its early days.

Glebe terrier

The parson and churchwardens were probably moved to take action to make a terrier of the glebe land in the fear of an impending visit from the archdeacon. Archdeacons were to:

> Take account in writing of all the vestments and books and they shall require them to be presented before them every year ....[28]

The terriers were likely to have been needed at the same time. The following Tedstone Delamere terrier is undated but is known to be before 1598, (George Wysham who is mentioned in the terrier died in the previous year). The handwriting appears late 16th century. Many of the local parishes have terriers dating from about 1600. There is an 18th century copy which is much easier to read but with the possibility of copying inaccuracies:[29]

> **Glebe Terrier**
> Extracted from the Registry of the Consistory Court of the Diocese of Hereford
> The Presentment of the Churchwardens and sworn men of the parish of Tedstone Delamere as followeth:
> George Wissomme Gent is reputed and taken patron of our Parsonage of Tedstone. The quantity of lands and houses belonging to the same: Imprimis a Hall, a parlour with chambers over the same, a kitchen, a barn with other houses. The parsonage closes and meadow ground belonging to the same by estimation twelve acres or thereabouts, the one side adjoining upon the parsonage house and the highway. Eleven acres of arable land lying in **Held Field** leading on the one side by

the highway and butting on the south side on the land of George Wisshame Gent. One parcel of old leys lying in **Binde Field** shooting along by Whitinges ground containing by estimation two acres or thereabouts one other parcel of land called the *You* one shooting upon the Corteway, one acre lying in the same field of arable land shooting down by Worcester way, one parcel of old leys at *Pixwells well* by estimation one acre and a half. Two parcels lying in **Smallstye** shooting by the pathway containing by estimation two acres, one other acre of old land lying in the same field by a parcel of ground of the Widow Lane called *Hollowbache*, one parcel of land lying in **Westfield** by estimation two acres or thereabouts lying next to the land of George Wyssomme Gent on the north side & other parcel of land lying on the over end of *Rotherpolle* Shooting to the same highway by estimation three acres or thereabouts, one parcel of land lying in **Manley Field** shooting on *Burrall Meadow* by estimation one acre, one other acre of old leyes lying in the same field called the *Harpe acre* lying within John Capper's new land. One other parcel of ley ground shooting down of the land of John Capper by estimation two acres and one other acre of old land lying in **Churchfield** ley … of Thomas Fidowe on the north side, one other parcel of meadow and old land lying in **Hamstoll** by estimation two acres or thereabouts within the ley of **Manley Field**, two ridges lying by the same in the same field of **Hamstolls** shooting up by the Widow Lane's hedge, one other acre of Woodland lying in **Dunleys** Ley butting upon Dee's land. The whole land belonging to the said parsonage containing by estimation forty five acres or thereabouts besides the Churchyard. The houses above mentioned are for the most part down and utterly defaced and for the most part carried away.

Willm Capper, Edward Elt - Churchwardens

Roger Conny, Augustine Horner, John Stallard, Richus Perkins, Thomas Baker, John Perre, Willm Howell, John Capper Senr, John Sherree, Roger Hunt, Willm Baker, John Whitledge, John Millward

The signatures above were all made with a mark because nobody could write their name. Field names in bold are suspected common fields; other field names are in italics. The probable whereabouts of most of the common fields are suggested on Map 4, page 46. The terrier begins by naming the patron, George Wysham, and then goes on to describe the parsonage house: a hall (not at this time ceiled), a parlour with chambers over the same, a kitchen, a barn with other houses, this description being much the same as that of a typical farmhouse of that time; it then goes on to list the land in 20 small pieces scattered throughout the parish. All 15 parishioners and churchwardens signed their names at the bottom of the Terrier with a mark so it is unlikely that the parish had a school. One can conclude that by this date, some consolidation of the land had already begun. Two ridges are recorded in Hamstolls, one of the open fields, but the remaining land is in numerous small 'parcels', not strips, many in what were formerly the open fields showing that the first small steps towards consolidation of the glebe-land by agreement was taking place; this was not complete until 1793. From the description of the parsonage and its buildings, one has to conclude that they were too dilapidated for the rector to have been living there!

The Reformation
The Reformation was another cataclysmic event for which we have no records, and like the plague, its effects ebbed and flowed; the severity of the changes varied with the religious beliefs of the monarchs. The break with Rome came about, as everyone knows, when Henry VIII wanted to divorce his wife to marry Ann Boleyn.

It eventually resulted, amongst many other things, in devastation of the parish churches, the chief loss visually in a little church like Tedstone Delamere probably being colour. Painted stone and woodwork, wall paintings, crosses, candlesticks as well as vestments and needlework for the altar, the smell of incense together with the old services, all went. Many of the church's treasures would have been donated by local families. People's faith must have been very sorely tested. The troubles reached their peak during the Commonwealth period; it is said that Cromwell's soldiers used Thornbury church for target practice, cannon balls being found lodged in the masonry.

An Episcopal Visitation 1600-1601
The Bishop kept a very close eye on the morals of the inhabitants and the fabric of the church. After the above Visitation, the following were presented:

> William Turford clerk curate excommunicated ad gratiam for solemnising a clandestine marriage on 9 June 1601
> William Turford for refusing to deliver the register book to William Howells the churchwarden being requested thereunto
> William Howells and Henry Pytte, churchwardens – they lack a service book and the Homilies and Paraphrases of Erasmus,* a sufficient pulpit and cloth, and a covering of silk for the communion table but they have a good linen cloth for the same
> Francis Wisham for not frequenting church
> Margaret Lane illicitly impregnated
> Roger Hunte not cohabiting with his wife
> The churchwardens – the church is out of repair as to its walls and buttresses, two main slits, one in the steeple and the other in the church wall, churchyard gate wants repair, church needs tiling
> Blanche Thomas accuse by William Capper that she said to the curate that you lie and could lie all manner of lies [this is just as it is written]
> The curate for not publishing the names of those he baptised in the church
> Churchwardens for not collecting 12d from the parishioners because they themselves were absent from the service
> Churchwardens and other parishioners for not taking communion since Easter notwithstanding that the minister warned them to provide bread and wine for Whitsuntide last and they did not.
> Francis Wisham not paying 6s 8d to the church of Tedstone nor 10 bushells of corn given by his father (as it is said) in his last will and testament for the use of the poor.[30]

Oh dear! What problems! William Turford, the curate, appears in other records: he witnessed wills of parishioners and George Wysham, lord of the manor, felt sufficiently highly of him to leave him £3 in his will, quite a large sum for that time.[31] One would like to know more about the clandestine marriage that Turford solemnised! We shall read about the rather casual lord of the manor, Francis Wysham, in Chapter II, page 40 Poor Margaret Lane; we hope she didn't have to appear in church dressed in a white sheet; she was probably one of the Lanes from Tipton; even then, these things happened in the best of families. Roger Hunt held one of the holdings at Woodend. The churchwardens do seem to have been

---

* In 1547, Edward VI had ordered that Cranmer's 'Book of Homilies' and 'Paraphrases by Erasmus' be placed 'in some convenient place' for reading in parish churches. This was to ensure that all parishes had access to Protestant ideas

A HISTORY OF TEDSTONE DELAMERE

particularly laid back although the state of the church with two main slits in the steeple and church wall can't have happened overnight; we know that plans to repair were underway in 1596 when Ellenor Stallard left money towards the 'Reparacions' of the church, see page 61. Enormous buttresses are portrayed in a later water colour of the church on page 11.

Parish registers and burials in woollen

It was in 1538 that Thomas Cromwell ordered that all weddings, christenings and burials be entered in a book after Sunday service in the presence of a churchwarden. The earliest surviving register for Tedstone Delamere dates from 1689 and the burial of the rector, Thomas Dolman, is recorded on the first page: 'Thomas Dolman AM Rector was buryd with Affid. Feb 13th.' Burials in woollen are sometimes recorded in parish registers; an act of 1678 provided that:

```
No. 20.

                                          of the Parish of
                    maketh Oath, that the Body of
late of the Parish of
which was buried at
was not wrapt in, or put into any Suit, Sheet or Coffin,
lined, faced, or covered with any Materials but what was
made of Sheep's Wool only, according to the Direction of an
Act of Parliament, Intitled An Act for burying in Woollen.
DATED the                    Day of
in the Year of our Lord 17
witness                                  Sworn before me
```

Form for burial in wool. *Manuscripts and Special Collections, The University of Nottingham, Galway Collection, Ga 2D 2953*

> No corpse of any person (except those who shall die of the plague), shall be buried in any shirt, shift, sheet or shroud or anything whatsoever made or mingled with flax, hemp, silk, ... or in any stuff or thing other than what is made of sheep's wool only .... [32]

The act provided that within eight days of the funeral, an affidavit was to be made that the law had been complied with and these, abbreviated to 'Affid.', are meticulously recorded in the Tedstone Delamere register. Penalties of £5 were imposed if somebody was not buried in woollen; the very rich might regard it as a tax worth paying but almost everybody in Tedstone Delamere was buried in woollen including the rector, Thomas Dolman. The object of course was to assist the wool trade. The act was not repealed until 1814 but for a number of years before had been only partially observed and entries of affidavits ceased to be made.

Parsons and parsonage during the 17th and 18th centuries

For a complete list of rectors and incumbents, see Appendix D. As related, the church was going through very difficult times in the mid 17th century. *A Puritan's Survey* of *c*1642[33] lists the clergy in the county, gives the value of their livings together with a usually derogatory and probably bigoted description of each incumbent:

> Tedstone Delamere. Worth per annum 60li [£60], supplied by Mr. Parry a very negligent preacher, Mr. Creswell Patron in right of his wife.

£60 for the living can be compared with £15 for Tedstone Wafre, £50 for Upper Sapey, £40 for Thornbury and £100 for Whitbourne. To obtain an idea of how the priest's incomes compared with others in the parish during the 17th century, the Militia Assessments of 1663, which are based on the value of estates (see page 56), show that the largest assessment was that of the lord of the manor, Robert Mason at £27. There were only three people in the parish with estates assessed at £12, the second largest sum, and one of these was poor Mr. Parry, 'our very negligent preacher'. In 1664, Parry was paying tax on 3 hearths, and assuming this to be at the, hopefully rebuilt, rectory, it was one of the bigger houses in the parish. The only larger ones were the Court with 5 hearths and Tipton with 4. The substantial inventory of Parry's belongings is given on p... where it is noted that the poor of Tedstone Delamere were bequeathed £10, a large sum, and for the church there was money for a communion table and a 'fair carpet'. Thomas Dolman, rector 1679 – 1689, whose burial in woollen we have just read about, was also rector and patron of Broom where he presumably employed a curate. His was an educated family; in his will he left his books to his brother 'excepting some English authors which my wife shall choose' and a legacy to the poor of £5 to be divided equally between Tedstone and Broom.

George Hay, who, as we shall read in Chapter IV, bought the advowson from the lord of the manor, Robert Mason, was clearly another educated man, leaving a 'study of books' to his son John in 1727. There was provision in his will for his wife to have first pick of up to twelve books for herself and her daughters. He asked to be buried in the chancel of the church. George Hay owned the Line House and farmed part of it himself. He may actually have lived there; what is clear, though, from the answers to the questions at the Bishop's Visitation (see page 24), was that he lived within the parish but we are not told whether he lived in the rectory. His inventory names the rooms in his house as a hall, what must have been quite a large parlour as it had twelve chairs and two tables, a little room over the pantry, a chamber over the kitchen, a hall chamber, a best chamber, a garret, and a pantry. This sounds rather larger than the parsonage and buildings recorded in the above late 16th century terrier which were described as *'for the most part down and utterly defaced and for the most part carried away'* and may have been the earlier wing attached to the rebuilt Victorian rectory, that stands today. Some of the other items listed in Hay's inventory such as two looking glasses, a clock and a 'silver wier drawer' show that the rector's possessions were a cut above the average farmer of the time. Farming items included corn and lent grain (spring corn) in the barn, corn upon the ground, four cows and two year-old calves, hay and straw, carts, wagon and tack of the team (harness), implements of husbandry, four horses and one colt, five store pigs and the usual 'lumbar & things unseen'.

Rector John Landon, who was possibly followed by his son, came next. John senior was presented to the living by Ann Hay in 1749. The Landons also owned the Line House, having bought it from the Hays. The rector buried both his wife and son on the same day in 1750, perhaps after childbirth. There is a rather nice stone wall tablet to Rev. John Landon dated 1777, now hidden away in the vestry and sadly flaking. It is by John Broad of Knightsford Bridge.

Churchwardens

Churchwardens were firstly ecclesiastical officers, but following the decline in the powers of the manor, from the late-16th century until the mid-19th century, they carried out various secular functions in addition, such as care of the poor, maintenance of the highway and appointment of the constable. Unfortunately for us, no overseers' account books have survived and the only churchwardens' accounts date from 1842. The *archdeacon's visitation* took place every year to inspect the church and parish and make sure everything was in order. In 1736 the church was presented as being out of order and Benjamin Bough, churchwarden, had to appear before a court to certify when the repairs had been carried out. The *episcopal visitations* took place less regularly; the resulting list of misdemeanours, after an earlier visitation, having already been reproduced on page 21; there was one in 1716 when a printed questionnaire had to be filled in. The numerous questions covered all aspects of the church and parish: those concerning the condition of the building including roof, windows, floor, furnishings, books and also the churchyard were all answered satisfactorily. They answered that the parsonage house was in good and

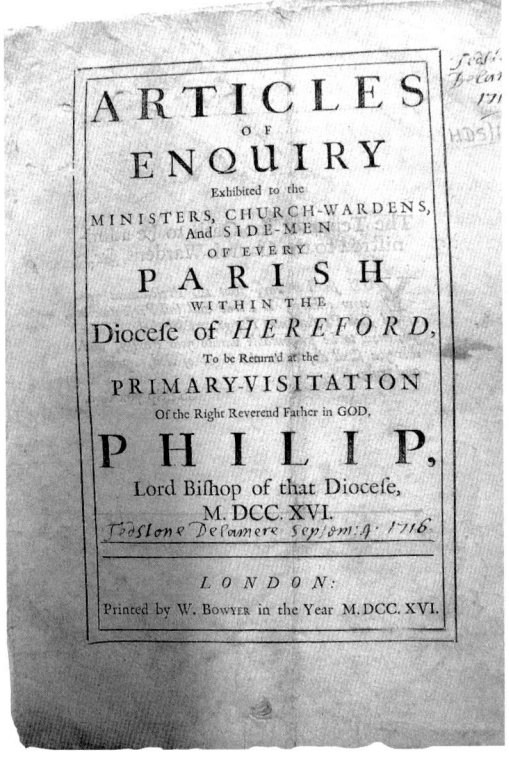
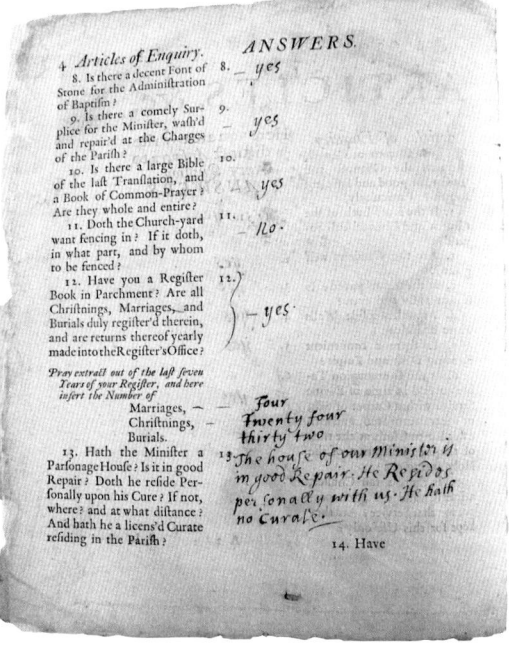

An episcopal visitation in 1716.

HRO

sufficient repair and that the minister lived personally in it and had no curate. They satisfactorily answered questions about the conduct and frequency of services, they had no chapel, the Minister catechised the children during winter and Lent time, the Sacrament was administered four times a year at Easter, Whitsuntide, Michaelmas and Christmas. In answer to a question 'Doth every person that keepeth a school in your parish come to Church himself, and cause his scholars also to come to Divine Service', they answered in the affirmative but it is possible that this answer referred to Sunday school; to another question they answered that there was no charity school in their parish. To a question about people following worldly employment on Sundays, they replied that they did not know of any; they had no dissenters and no public penances had been performed in the church. The document was completed by presenting John Barnes (of Winley) as churchwarden for the ensuing year; it was signed by the rector, George Hay and the then churchwarden, Aaron Cook (of the present Woodhall).

Glebe exchange
For much of the 18th century, the patronage was in the hands of the clergy and members of their families and this may have given the parsons added influence and interest in the outcome of attempts to consolidate the glebe land. What was probably the final step in creating a glebe farm within a ring fence and convenient to the rectory took place in 1793 with two exchanges of land between the Rev. Packington George Tomkyns, the rector, and Robert Moore, the lord of the manor. Mr. Tomkyns was a very wealthy man who lived at the nearby mansion of Buckenhill in Norton; his great-great-grandfather, Dr. John Tomkyns, had inherited Buckenhill in the mid-17th century and later generations had enlarged and rebuilt the house and extended the estate. So this parson clearly would have had an eye for business and was determined to get the glebe land and tithes on a proper footing. Mr. Moore was a go-ahead lord of the manor who was busily consolidating his own lands and would have been sympathetic to the rector. A total of about 12 acres of glebe land was exchanged for an equal amount of Mr. Moore's land in two separate exchanges. The plans help to pinpoint the whereabouts of the common fields of Smallsty and Hamstolls.[34] The field called Hampstead on the tithe map is probably part of the latter common field and is shown in Map 4, page 46 The exact position of Smallsty is unknown but it is probably north of the Whitbourne road near Hill Cross.

Location of Rectory
One of the glebe exchange plans proves that in 1793 the Rectory was near to or on the site of the later Victorian Rectory. The description in the 16th century terrier: 'The parsonage closes and meadow ground belonging to the same by estimation twelve acres or thereabouts, *the one side adjoining upon the parsonage house and the highway*' could indicate that it might have been on the same site at that time. Duncumb, writing in 1812 makes this odd comment: 'The situation of the church and parsonage-house on the declivity of a hill, is highly interesting'; he could not have been looking at the same parsonage house as the one described in the terrier and glebe exchange. What building Duncumb was looking at remains a mystery but

could this be connected with the earthworks of two house platforms just below the church shown on the plan in the Introduction?

Glebe Farm
The Rectory, formerly occupied by tenant William Tombs, was in 1791 re-let together with the glebe land and the tithes to John and William Smith, husbandmen of Pencombe for £200 per annum. It seems that the farm buildings were in a poor way for the lease included the provision that some buildings be repaired by the tenant but 'Mr. Tomkyns to provide the straw ready watered and also lugs, twigs and buckles for such of the buildings as shall be thatched'. £14 was allowed for erecting a barn, the Smiths themselves spending £30 on its building. The tenants did not have to pay any rent for the first year of the term, presumably because of doing the repairs. There was also provision for use of the fireplace in the kitchen and one room in the house by a servant; it is not clear what the servant's duties were.[35]

A late 18th century tithe agreement
The Tithe Commutation Act of 1836 made provision for conversion of tithes to a money rent but in many cases this Act merely completed the process that had begun many years before. Rising land values, increased agricultural production and higher prices for agricultural produce all helped to raise the value of tithes during the 18th century. Compositions of cash payments in lieu of tithes were very common at this time, making life much easier for the rector, but before 1836 such compositions could be upset upon every change of incumbency resulting in endless arguments; we are fortunate to have such records for Tedstone Delamere and these show how negotiations were fraught with problems.[36] The parishioners were not at all happy with the arrangement made that leased the tithes to the Smiths. The cash being claimed had greatly increased and to get their money, the rector and the Smiths had to take legal action. The parishioners asked the brother of John Chreese of Winley, who was a Worcester attorney, to act for them. A test case had been made against only one of the parishioners, Mr. Bedintun of Brierley (a now disappeared farm near the Thrift). One wonders why he was selected and whether it was because he, unlike the majority of the farmers at this time, was unable to read or write and therefore perhaps easier game.

The lord of the manor, Robert Moore, took a leading role helping the parishioners in their proceedings and many of the papers appear to be in his hand. A number of questions to ask their attorney were listed: had Lord Foley (owner of Hedge House), Mr. Jones (owner of Tipton), Mr. Lane of Norton, Mr. Norman and other landowners & their tenants been consulted about the defence and should they not bear a proportion of the expenses? Why was the action being brought against Bedintun only? Is the present lease to Smith a good or bad lease? They made it particularly clear they didn't like the lease of the tithes to Smith:

> For if Mr Smith is continued as Lessee to Mr Tomkyns of the Glebe and Tithes (or any part thereof) there will be no end of disputes.

Questions to be asked Mr Chreese Attorney Relative to the Defence to be made Respect.d the Tythes at Tedstone, Tomkyn & Smith ag.st Bedintun Oct.r 20th 1792.

Has Lord Foley or his agents been consulted ab.t this Defence and if they have not, Whether or not It is not proper to do it. And whether or not his Lordships Tenants are agreeable to join to try the Merits of the Tythes And what Tythes the Parson is intitled to. &

Likewise Mr Jones and his Ten.t Three Mr Lane of Norton Mr Norman and other Land owners within the p.ish —

What Reason can be assigned for bringing the present action ag.st Bedintun only — Why was it not bro.t ag.st Lord Foley's Tenants Mr Jones's Tenant Mr Norman or other Land owners Tenants —

Quere If proceedings sho.d not be stayed till they have all been Consulted Respect.d the Business And to see if they will bear a proportional Share of the expences And if they can be got to do it For all to sign It shall be done And a proper Undertakeing to be hewed ab.t —

The Action is Certainly partial by being Bro.t ag.st Bedingtun And had Mr Jones and Mr Price as Laymen any Right to Purchase & Sell the Living And is the present Lease to Smith a good or bad Lease There is Certainly a Terrier of the Glebe Tythes as well as the Glebe But if a Composition is agreed upon that Matter is out of the Question — Or otherwise must be seen after —

Mr Huck, Mr Chreese Mr Lane Benj.n Pitt Sen.r Mr Norman & such others as your Bro.r may think right may be good Evidences Respect.d the Terrier and the Tythes —

Questions to be asked Mr Chreese, Attorney, Relative to the Defence to be made Respect[ing] the tithes at Tedstone. Tomkyn and Smith v. Bedintun. Oct 20th 1792.   *HRO*

It does seem to have been a foolish decision of the rector to have made mere husbandmen responsible for collecting tithes from farmers at a time when he had massively raised the charges. Finally on 13th November 1792, after endless meetings trying to get all the parishioners to agree to the increase, and with papers flying to and fro, a composition was produced and agreed upon; a sum of £155 13s. 0d. was to be paid to Mr. Tomkyns. The previous incumbent, Mr. Cox, had received only £105 10. 0d. so Tomkyns had achieved a significant increase, probably justified if there hadn't been a rise for some time.

TABLE 1
A Composition in lieu of Tithes at Tedstone proposed to be paid Annually to the Reverend Mr Tomkyns

1792 Nov 13th

	£	s	d		£	s	d
John Portman	0	3	0	Brought in	31	2	6
James Gittins	0	11	6	Thomas Corbett	0	14	0
Francis Eaton	0	5	0	Richard White	17	17	0
Thomas Jones	0	14	0	Thomas Knill	15	7	6
John Price, Woodend	18	0	0	John Lawrence	12	0	0
William Griffith	1	2	0	John Cheese	13	7	6
Benjamin Pitt Junr	0	10	6	Joseph Barnbrooke	10	10	0
Robert Moore, Blakeways	1	1	0	Edward Haynes	4	4	0
Benjamin Pitt Senr	1	0	0	Giles Berrow	1	17	6
Phillip Griffith	0	5	0	William Lokyer	10	10	0
Martha Brazier	0	5	0	John Bury	11	10	0
John Mortiboys	0	15	6	John Bedintun	15	0	0
Benjamin Birch	3	3	0	Thomas Grubb	11	0	0
Joseph Caswell Senr	0	10	0	Robert Moore, coppices	1	1	0
John Acton	0	5	0	Mrs Shangold	0	2	0
Richard Portman	0	6	0				
John Callow	0	6	0				
Joseph Caswell Junr	0	4	0				
William Beard	0	8	0				
John Davis	0	7	0				
Edward Price	1	1	0				
	31	**2**	**6**		**155**	**13**	**0**

I consent and agree to accept and take the composition of tithes above expressed for and in lieu of the tithes due to become due to me from the parish of Tedstone Delamere to be paid to me Annually Viz from each person and their representatives, the respective sums, placed opposite their respective names. Witness my hand the 13th day of November 1792

Witness to the Sighning hereof by the Reverend Mr Tomkyns

Signed R G Tomkyns

We each of us Consent and agree to pay the respective sums placed opposite our respective names to the Rev Mr Tomkyns for and in lieu of the tithes due or to become due to him from the parish of Tedstone Delamere to be paid to him Annually

THE CHURCH OF ST JAMES

Witness our hands this thirteenth day of November Seventeen hundred & Ninety Two
John Chreese   the mark of John Bedintun   Benj. Birch   Joseph Barnbrooke,
Thomas Grubb   John Bury   William Lokyier   the mark of Thomas Jones
Thomas Corbett   the mark of Thomas Eaton   Richard White

Witness to the Signing by the above names parishioners

It was decided the Smiths should receive £50 compensation for giving up the lease which was to be raised as follows:

Rev. Mr. Tomkyns	£21	0	0
Mr. Moore	10	10	0
Mr. Chreese	5	0	0
The parish in proportion to the value of their estates	19	0	0

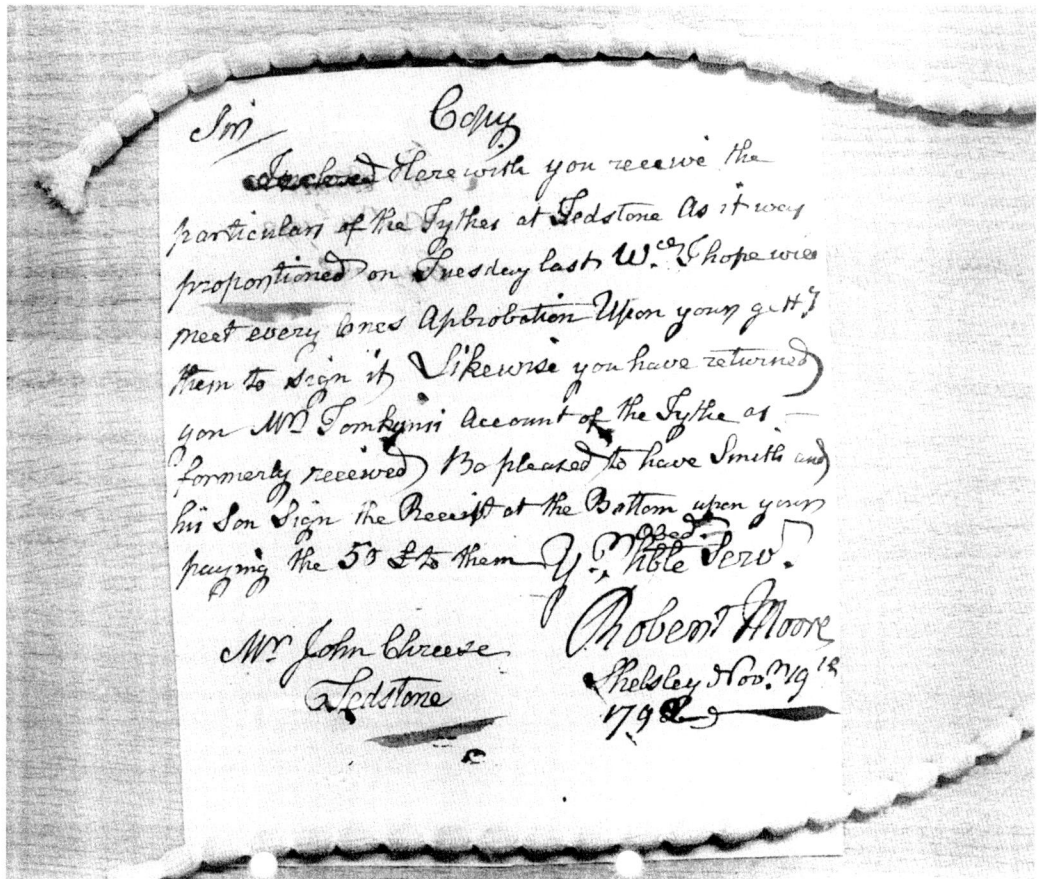

Letter to John Chreese [of Winley] from Robert Moore [lord of manor] regarding tithe apportionment 1792.

HRO

Two clergymen, the Rev. Mr. Glasse of Pencombe and the Rev. Mr. Jennings of Whitbourne acted as arbiters to decide the cash the Smiths should receive in lieu of the tithes that were not collected during the two years of dispute. At the bottom of this document is a brief note by Robert Moore (lord of the manor) that the tithes were admitted. He adds an additional note 'I had only to settle with them for three bags of apples and half a hogshead of cider'! One can sense his relief! It is possible that these difficulties went on with every change of incumbent, a somewhat lowering thought!

Tithe Commutation Act of 1836
This Act must have been received with relief all round and no longer were decisions made at parish level. The Act provided for a fluctuating money payment known as a corn rent charge adjusted each year on the basis of the seven year average price of wheat, barley and oats. Tithe maps and apportionments were drawn up for each parish. The parson was provided with a regular and reliable stipend. The Tedstone Delamere map is dated 1841 and together with its apportionment is an enormous boon to local historians. It provides the first large scale map of the whole parish showing all the farms, cottages and fields. The apportionment gives details of the owner, occupier, acreage, crops and field names of every field in the parish.

Glebe Farm
The tithe survey tells us that in 1840, 34 acres of glebe land were let to James Bevan which included one acre of the churchyard which was grass. It seems as if Bevan was expected to allow stock to graze the churchyard. There was no farmhouse. Another five acres were let to James Palmer. There had been 45 acres in the 1585 glebe terrier so a fairly similar figure and probably the missing six acres were rectory garden, orchard and so forth.

For the continuing story of the church, read Chapter VIII.

CHAPTER II

The Manor and Lordship - from the Domesday Survey to the End of the 17th Century

at Gloucester at midwinter ... the King had deep speech with his counsellors ... and sent men all over England to each shire ... to find out ... what or how much each landholder held ... in land and livestock, and what it was worth ...
The returns were brought to him.

The Saxon Chronicle 1085

The Domesday Survey
We must now take a leap back in time to the Norman Conquest in 1066. After the Conquest, the ordinary people would have noticed little change to their daily lives. It was the top strata of society only that changed, most of the lands of the Anglo-Saxon nobility being granted to King William's followers; the Normans made very little change to the system which they took over and life continued in the villages and countryside much as before. The survey made in 1086 was most detailed and thorough; William needed to know what land he had and the names of the people who held it. The term *'manor'* is a Norman word they used to describe an Anglo-Saxon estate. It is a word which, to the average person today, means simply a large country house but the Normans meant much more than just the lord's hall or house which in this part of the country usually goes by the name of 'court'; to them it was also an administrative unit or system of economy by which the land supporting that house and its owner was managed.

The following is a translation of the *two* Domesday entries for Tedstone Delamere for, as discussed in the Introduction, there were almost certainly two Anglo-Saxon manors,[1] these estates being, most probably, on either side of the Sapey Brook which is a natural division between the two:

1. The first manor is listed amongst the lands of Gilbert, son of Thorold:

> In PLEGELGATE Hundred
> Gilbert also holds **Chetestor** [Tedstone]. Ernwy and Godwin held it as two manors; they could go where they would. 2 hides which pay tax.
> In lordship 3 ploughs;
> 7 villagers with 7 ploughs; 1 further plough would be possible in lordship.
> 6 slaves; a mill at 4 1/2s.
> Value before 1066, 50s; later 45s; now 70s.

Gilbert was the new owner and Ernwy and Godwin were the Anglo-Saxons who were dispossessed. These two had been free to choose their own overlords and sell or bequeath their land ('they could go where they would') and they had worked it as two manors. Ernwy was one of King Harold's thanes and held other land in Herefordshire including some at Thornbury. Godwin's other holdings included land in the very large manor of Leominster owned by Queen Edith.

It has been suggested that a **'hide'** or taxable area, in this part of the country, averaged about 120 acres of arable land and was the amount of land that could be cultivated by a team of eight oxen in a year and could support one free family, but there was variation. The lord's demesne or home farm at Chetestor ('in lordship') had three plough teams and seven villagers or peasants had a further seven plough teams. We know that this home farm was not fully exploited because it is recorded in the survey that another plough team 'would be possible' there. The manor had gone up in value from 50s to 70s since the Conquest, probably because more land had been brought into cultivation.

2. The second manor is listed amongst the lands of the Church of Hereford:

> These hides paid tax with Bishop Walter before 1066: in *Tedesthorne* [Tedstone] 2 1/2 hides, in Sawbury [now in Bredenbury] 1/2 hide, in Yarsop 3 virgates of land, and in Noakes [now in Bredenbury] 1 hide and 1 virgate.

Bishop Walter was the Saxon Bishop of Hereford. The record of this second manor is much less useful than the first one for although two and a half hides, no other information is given. *Chetestor* and *Tedesthorne* are both derived from OE 'Teod's thorn-tree'. As explained in the Introduction, it was a name which French speakers found difficult and this is probably the reason why there was a good deal of corruption leading to many spellings of the name and indeed it is likely that *Tetistorp* (Tedstone Wafre) has the same derivation.[2] 'Delamere' comes from the name 'La Mare', the family who held the manor later.

Hides and ploughs and associated problems

The area of a hide seems to have varied, most likely according to land conditions but if the readers have carried out a simple sum, they will have realised that two hides or 240 acres in the first manor and two and a half hides or 300 acres in the second manor is a small proportion of the 1840 parish of 1677 acres. It must surely only refer to the arable land with perhaps the meadow land. Was the rest of the parish pasture, useful woodland, or just waste? And the *10 working ploughs and another possible one* provide us with an additional dilemma for there are too many plough teams here to have been working land only assessed at two hides in the first manor of Chetestor so surely they must also have worked the land at Tedesthorne.[3]

Another unknown is which manor was which; but the fact that the bishop had the second one does incline one to believe that this manor was perhaps the one on the west side which contains the church but it is no more than a suggestion. Gilbert fitz Thorold, the Norman lord who held the first manor, Chetestor, very quickly appears to have acquired the second manor, Tedesthorne, and thereafter the two manors continued under one lordship. Another reason for suggesting that the bishop's manor was on the west side is that Hedge House, or part of it, a farm that borders the main Bromyard to Stourport road and for which there is no record amongst the Tedstone Delamere manorial records, was recorded in the court rolls of the bishop of Hereford's manor of Bromyard (see page 97). For some reason, lost in the mists of time, Hedge House land, or part of it, seems to have been retained for the Bishop when the rest of his Tedstone manor passed to Gilbert fitz Thorold. It is possible that the Saxon Bishop Walter was the church builder. If *Chetestor* is the eastern manor, then the mill mentioned in the survey might be on the site of Horners Mill on the Whitbourne Brook, see Map 1, (inside front cover). On the other hand, if it was the western manor then the mill might have been on the Sapey Brook at Whitehall where fieldnames indicate the presence of a former mill there. This one became the manorial mill of the later combined manor.

A period of prosperity
The two hundred years following the Conquest were a time of relative prosperity and the population expanded. With more mouths to feed, more land was pressed into service and archaeologists know this because signs of ancient cultivation have been found in the very last places that one would choose today to grow crops; it is very possible that the now wooded areas and steep land by the Sapey Brook were at that time under cultivation. During this period market towns grew up at Bromyard and also at Clifton-on-Teme. Bromyard was a long way from Tedstone Delamere, especially from its eastern side so a market at Clifton would have been very handy whilst it lasted. By a charter of 1270, Roger Mortimer was granted a weekly market at his manor of Clifton to take place on Thursdays and also a four-day fair there 'unless that market or fair be to the harm of the neighbouring markets'.[4]

Norman lords
But back in time to the Domesday Survey, the only person who actually *owned* land was the king. Most of it he let to between 50 and 80 tenants-in-chief: dukes, earls, and barons. These men who were busy attending the king or building their castles, usually sublet most of their land to local lesser lords: knights, esquires and gentlemen who were not lords in the sense that they had a title but merely lords over their manorial tenants. In addition, the church was endowed by the king with vast tracts of land going to bishops, abbots and other churchmen. The lords of Tedstone Delamere have taken some tracking down and a summary is given here but as full a list as possible is given in Appendix A.

Tenants-in-chief:
Gilbert, son of Thorold, the new Norman lord who had supplanted Ernwy and Godwin at Tedstone, was an important follower of William fitzOsbern, earl of Hereford, who was the man who brought about the conquest and settlement of

Herefordshire; at one point Gilbert had been Sheriff of Herefordshire. His lands, which were in several counties, were valued annually at nearly £100 which makes him one of the more minor Domesday tenants-in-chief. But times were uncertain and in 1095, he joined an unsuccessful rebellion against William Rufus and all his lands were confiscated. But we know that before this happened, both of the two above manors, Chetestor and Tedesthorne, were in his hands. The king then shared out Gilbert's barony amongst those who had supported him in the rebellion and Tedstone Delamere (both parts) was given to **Bernard de Neufmarche,** baron of Brecon.

Neufmarche's daughter, Sybil, married **Miles of Gloucester**; on Neufmarche's death in 1125, Miles inherited his father-in-law's lands, which included Tedstone Delamere. He was made earl of Hereford in 1141 and died in a hunting accident a couple of years later. After he inherited the Neufmarche lands but before the death of Henry I in 1135, Miles of Gloucester sub-let several manors which included both parts of Tedstone Delamere to his cousin, **William de la Mare**.

The sub-tenants:
William de la Mare was to hold Tedstone Delamere together with lands in North Cerney, Gloucestershire, by the service of one knight. (The service of one knight was generally that the man concerned would maintain himself as a knight and would be in his lord's army or in his castle or accompany him on a journey for forty days yearly at his own cost. If he was required any longer, then his lord would pay him at the going daily rate).

Mid 13th-century coffin lids in Tedstone Delamere churchyard. They may have belonged to members of the La Mare family after whom the parish is named. *Reproduced by permission of English Heritage*

The La Mare family after whom Tedstone was named

The La Mares had become fairly widespread by the end of the 12th century, holding land in Herefordshire and neighbouring counties. They remained as lords of Tedstone for about 150 years. They may well have come from an area of Normandy near Sainte-Pierre-du-Chatel, by the Seine estuary between Honfleur and Pont-Audemer. For the descent of the manor through generations of this family, read Appendix A. It is not known whether the La Mares actually lived in Tedstone as they held land in many other places but as the parish is actually named after them, it would be nice to think, that the two very worn 13th century coffin lids, now banished outside to the churchyard, belong to La Mares:

Coffin Lids

The coffin lids, refered to in Chapter I as possibly belonging to members of the La Mare family after whom the parish is named, are three yards south of the porch. Now sadly eroded, they would once have been inside the church. They date from the mid-13th century. In 1931 they were described by the RCHME when a little less worn than they are now:

> (1) Tapering lid, now in two pieces, with moulded edge. The top ... retains traces of a human head and foliage, carved in low relief, and of a cross shaft. (2) Tapering lid, larger than (1) and broken into five pieces. The edge is moulded. The top is worn but retains considerable traces of elaborate carving in low relief. The top has a male head within a large trefoil, and infillings of interlacing foliage. Beneath is a large cross-head, built up out of a complicated arrangement of 'stiff-leaved foliage. The bottom of the shaft is terminated with the same type of foliage.
>
> Both lids are an unusual, very yellow limestone, not seen elsewhere in this part of the county.[5]

Further sub-tenancy under the de la Mares

A further sub-tenancy, held under the de la Mares, seems to have been created by the end of the 12th century. This was probably the messuage and lands called Catley (the Gatehouse) that Humphrey Dore had in 1501 (see page 98), held as of the manor of Tedstone Delamere for ¼ knight's fee.[6] He also had a messuage called Lyndehouse (Line House). At the end of the 12th century, this sub-tenancy was probably held by *Eliam filius Willelmi* who appeared in 1200 as Thomas de la Mare's essoiner* in the case of Jordan de Mara.[7]

Land that belonged to Malvern Priory

Somebody must, at some time, have given some land in Tedstone Delamere to the Priory of Great Malvern. A man called *Elye*, in whose demesne lands the Priory had 2/3 tithes in 1271 is probably this *Eliam filius Willelmi* recorded in the paragraph above as holding the sub-tenancy of Gatley.[8] Could this land be that called *Dean Meadow* and *Dean Orchard* on the tithe map, near Hedge House marked on Map 4, page 46. It is suggested that Elye may have been related to the de la Mares. In 1291 the Priory's rents in Tedstone Delamere were worth 13s. annually to them.[9] Duncumb alludes to a pension of ten shillings payable to the priory.[10] After the dissolution of

---
* Someone who appears with an excuse for the non-appearance of a person at court

the Monasteries in 1543, Henry VIII granted the rents in Tedstone Delamere and Bilfield [Hatfield] to Richard Callowhill and his heirs.[11] The Callowhills feature in the court rolls and taxation lists at this time, recorded in Chapter III, and were obviously people of some importance in the parish and at one time held Woodmanton in Clifton-on-Teme.

In 1296, Joan de la Mare, to whom the manor passed, married John de Plessey and was succeeded by their son **Robert de Plessey** who died c1301. In 1294 Philip Burnel held Hanley Child & Hanley William in Worcestershire of Hugh de Plessey 'by attending him armed with a light horse upon Robert de Plessey's charges in the wars in Wales'. In 1335/6 both the above places were held of the lord of Tedstone 'by finding two well armed footmen in defence of the castle at Hereford for forty days at the charges of Edward de Plessey'. Peter de Plessey was lord of Tedstone in 1316.[12] Peter's sister, Hawise, inherited and she married John of Wysham.

The Wyshams - lords of Tedstone Delamere for 300 years

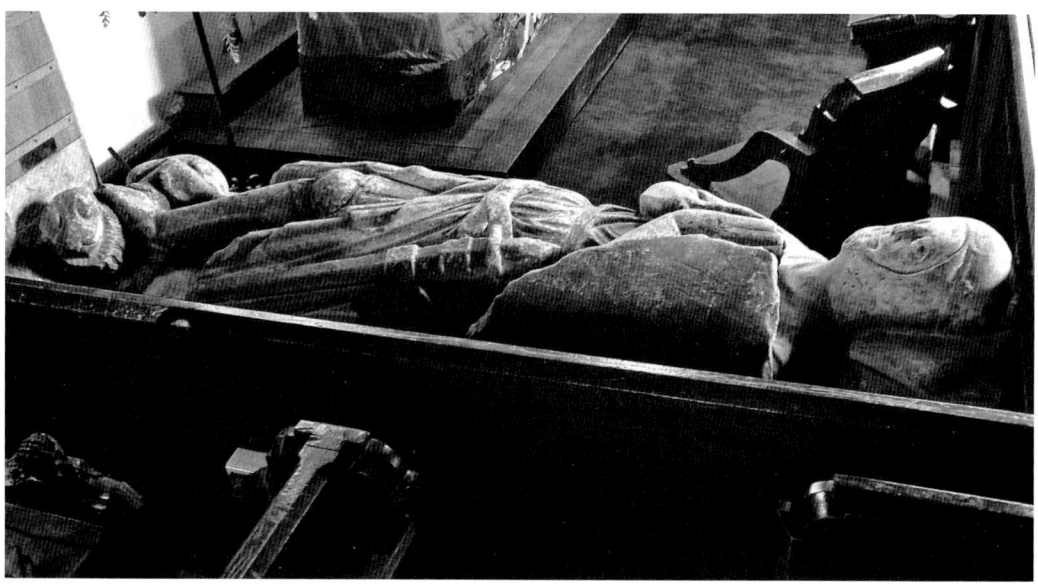

Ralph de Wysham of Woodmanton. His monument is in the south aisle of Clifton-on-Teme church.

The Wyshams were already established at nearby Woodmanton (see map page 5) in Clifton-on-Teme, and Tedstone Delamere would have been a useful extension to the Woodmanton estate; at one time the Wyshams held the manor of Clifton. Ralph de Wysham of Woodmanton is supposed to have erected an aisle in Clifton Church, he died in 1332 and had been Steward of the King's Household and Justice of North Wales. His cross-legged effigy with a lion at his feet is in the south aisle, the east end of which was formerly the chantry chapel of the Wyshams.[13] The lion, which looks a bit like a dog, may have given rise to a legend that Sir Ralph's ghost is sometimes

The medieval chapel at Woodmanton.
Duncan James

seen along the road from Woodmanton to Clifton where he is supposed to have died underneath a yew tree, his dog refusing to leave him.[14] In 1328 there was 'a grant, of special grace, to John of Wysham and his heirs, of free warren, meaning the right to hunt beasts and fowls in all their demesne lands in Tedsterne de la Mare'.[15] And of course today, hunting and shooting are still of prime importance in Tedstone Delamere! In 1333, a licence was granted to John de Wysham to crenellate (or fortify with battlements) his 'manor of Wodemanton' and some of the existing remains of the old house appear to be of that date. At the inner north-west angle of the moat, which was partly filled in when the house was rebuilt, is what appears to be the foundation of a circular stone tower, probably part of John de Wysham's fortifications. It seems that Woodmanton was occupied by another family soon after John's death.[16] However, the line continued as lords of Tedstone Delamere and successive generations of Tedstone Delamere people would only have known Wyshams as lords of their manor for nearly three centuries.

How the manors worked
A manor would be managed for the lord by his steward. The manorial courts, which met at intervals, dealt with administrative matters connected with the land and its occupants within the manor, all very necessary when the land was farmed communally. The manor would have its demesne land or home farm together with a bailiff, bailiff's house and associated buildings. The six slaves in the Domesday Survey above would have worked full time on the lord's demesne land. The seven villagers or senior serfs were granted land which they would cultivate to feed their families but in return for this they had to work regular hours on the lord's demesne together with extra hours at busy times such as haymaking and harvest. The lord supplied them with cattle, especially oxen with which they ploughed their own land but only after first ploughing the lord's. On the serf's death, the land and cattle were initially taken back and re-allocated. The land issued was based on the *virgate* or yardland, a variable amount dependent on the quality of the land; it could be anything from 15 to 60 acres; Phyllis Williams, in her history of the neighbouring parish of Whitbourne, states that in that parish, in 1285, the acre used appeared to be the old Herefordshire acre which was two thirds of the statute acre and like the virgate, it varied according to the quality of the land. The virgate or yardland was 60 Herefordshire acres or 40 statute acres, and she quotes the scribe who wrote in Swithin Butterfield's survey of the manor of Whitbourne in 1577:

> Further the said jury do say that by the custom of the country, 60 acres of land is a yardland, 30 acres is a half yardland, and 15 acres is a nooke of land[17]

It seems fair to assume that in neighbouring Tedstone Delamere, the virgate would have been 40 statute acres but few holdings were of this size, most were of a *noke or nooke,* and using the Whitbourne calculation, this would have been usually about 10 statute acres. A manor would have had its own separate field system in which the villagers and their lord had their share of the strips; these fields were cultivated communally but the produce of the strips was the villagers' own. The villagers were compelled to have their corn ground at the lord's mill, another profitable enterprise for the lord. Both Tedstone Delamere manors would have had at least three large common fields with the usual rotation of two years of crops and one of fallow. Crops grown were wheat, oats and rye for bread, barley for beer and beans for cattle, a whole field being given over to growing one crop. Land would have been allocated for hay, permanent pastures and rough pastures. We don't know their size, but in Bredenbury in 1282, some land had been the subject of a grant by the bishop and it was noted that it included three very large fields of 54 acres, 52 acres and 51 acres which were probably the three common fields of that manor.[18] However, there seem to have been more fields in Tedstone Delamere and they may have been smaller. We know from later records that the common fields in eastern Tedstone Delamere (see Map 4, page 46) were *Collins Field, Dunley Field* and possibly the *Riddings* and *Hopley*; a couple of fields on the tithe map called *Hopley Alders* and *Long Hopley* are situated close to the northern boundary (also on Map 4). In 1545, at the manorial court, six men were ordered to:

> take a view of bounds and meres in Hoppley which are in dispute between Thomas Wysham gent, lord of the manor and Richard Dee.[19]

Thomas Wysham or Richard Dee were probably accusing the other of having moved the marker (mere) stones and the six unfortunate men were to go and try to work out where the original boundary was. On the west side, the common fields were *Manley Field, Smallstye, Binde Field, Hamstoll, Held Field, Church Field* and *Westfield*. These are taken from a glebe terrier (see page 19) We know the approximate whereabouts of all except the last one; some of the names survive as field names in the tithe survey of 1840/41, again see Map 4; the Held Field was probably in the vicinity of Hill (*Held*) Cross and Smallstye seems to have been somewhere in that area but on the north side of the road.

The 14th century was a disastrous time. The country had become over populated and the strips in the fields had had to be shared out between more people; the century started with several years of drought which was followed by a period of floods so that animals drowned in the fields, crops rotted in the ground and famine followed. The population was already in a poor physical state when plague struck; the Black Death reached Herefordshire in 1349; between a third and a half of the people in England are said to have died within two years and this county is known to have been particularly badly hit. It is hard for us today to imagine what it would have been like; many households were entirely wiped out and others escaped, but often with no-one to bury the dead, no-one to till the land and with the animals dying of

A distant view looking westwards towards the church. *Rosemary Keep*

starvation in the farmsteads and fields, the times were horrendous indeed. A less labour intensive system of agriculture had to be found and grassland farming increased. Many holdings had become unoccupied and land probably returned to scrub. A slight lessening of the lord's hold over his tenants resulted, men were able to move elsewhere for better pay, peasants were able to purchase uncultivated strips and estate owners may well have found that it was more satisfactory to have a paid workforce than help given grudgingly by serfs. The demesne land began to be let to tenants and it was at this time that the class of yeoman farmers started to emerge.

The manor house

The Wyshams, who as we have read, succeeded the Plessys as lords of the manor and held Tedstone for nearly three centuries, would have had a fine house to live in at Tedstone Delamere, perhaps something along the lines of Lower Brockhampton. As discussed in the Introduction and at the beginning of Chapter I, an earlier Tedstone Court, occupying this defensive position on a hill may well have been of ancient origin; a moat is visible today in the garden of the Georgian house. It was taxed for five hearths in 1664 making it the same sort of size as Wicton in Bredenbury;[20] also by way of comparison, Tipton in Tedstone Delamere was assessed for 4 hearths at the same time (see page 57). It is likely to be this house

Tedstone Court in the 20th century.
Rosemary Keep

of the Wyshams that Richard Wight demolished to make way for the grand new house he built at Tedstone Court in 1809 and recorded in Chapter VII. In 1597, George Wysham died and his will is an interesting one. He left 6s. 8d. to the local church, 1s. to Hereford Cathedral and in lieu of money, the much more practical gift of 10 bushels of rye or muncorn (mixed corn, often rye and wheat sown together) for the parish poor. After leaving money for his daughter, Margaret Powell and his two granddaughters, he made careful provision for various servants:

> Itm I geave vnto Fraunc Walker Tenne pound and his Table vntill he shalbe conveniently placed
> Itm I give unto Anne Walker Twentie poundes
> Itm I give vnto Elienor Walker fortie markes vpon Condicon that she shall leave her stock & yf she will not leave her stock then I geave vnto her Tenn pound besides her stock
> Itm I geave vnto Fraunc Hodgekins ... Tenne poundes and his Table vntill he shalbe of the age of xv yeares
> Itm I geave vnto Richard Abevan five poundes, & his table as longe as he live ...
> Itm I geave vnto Martha Langeford vjs viijd to be paid yerelie for the space of xx yeares next ensuinge out of her mothers rent.[21]

The odd phrase 'his table' meant that his servants would be fed at the manor house. George Wysham seems to have been a caring and thoughtful man. He left his son Francis two mares and Francis was to get money from bonds he had entered with his father. The manor house was left to his wife Anne and she and his son-in-law, Anthony Hodgekins, were made executors. After George's death, the executors renounced the administration in favour of Francis, the deceased's 'natural and lawful son' and Anne went on to assign the property to Francis, with the careful provision that she should have the use of the upper chamber being over the parlour in the manor house of Tedstone Delamere and a rent of £20. Francis was to:

> Provide for her and one servant maid to attend her sufficient and compotent meat, drink, fire & lodging meete and fit for her estate and calling in the manor house of Tedstone Delamere. And if it shall happen that Ann Wysham be minded to take the same elsewhere then Francis Wysham was to pay her £10 over and above the £20 before mentioned in lieu of her diet.[22]

Francis's father must have had concerns about his son and heir as he did not make him an executor of his will. In renouncing the administration of the will in favour of Francis, George Wysham's executors trust in Francis may have been misplaced, for as we have read in Chapter I, he was presented at the time of an Episcopal Visitation for, firstly, 'not frequenting church' and secondly, for 'not paying 6s. 8d. to the church of Tedstone nor 10 bushells of corn given by his father ... in his last will and testament for the use of the poor'.[23]

Francis was the last of the Wyshams at Tedstone Delamere; he died fairly early in the 17th century and the manor passed to Richard Cresswell in the right of his wife Elizabeth who was Francis Wysham's widow. Their last Court Baron for which there is a record was held in 1616. Elizabeth Cresswell left £5 in her will dated 1645 for the parish poor, to be administered according to the advice of the Minister and the Overseers.[24]

The impecunious Mason family

Negotiations to purchase the manor and estate from the Wyshams were started in 1614 by William Mason, a clergyman, and were continued by Robert Mason I, but they purchased the property in bits and it wasn't until 1651 that finally the whole property with the manor and advowson was purchased from George Wysham, the grandson of Francis & Elizabeth, by Robert Mason II. The legal business with the Masons at Tedstone continued for about 100 years and must have seemed like a godsend to the lawyers, as demonstrated by the endless documents that flowed from them.[25] The family's desperation for cash is demonstrated in four letters shown in the Court of Wards on 17th November 1640 when a very young Robert Mason is being forced into a marriage he did not want.

> James Bethell, uncle to Robert, in a letter to Wm. Cooke of Worcester, another uncle.
> 'I have a match in hand for your nephew Mason. Unless you can procure him a better I pray you to come over and see the gentlewoman.'

> James Bethell to James Newton. 'You know I have no means of raising money but by the marriage portion of the ward. If you will get me a licence to marry the ward, I hope money will be had to give us content.'

> Same to the same. 'You wish to have money from me for Mason's business, but you have had large sums already. For three years I have had no allowance for the ward. The lands that I hold are Wm. Mason's, and held by me for a considerable valuation. You threaten a suit against me. I have had so many already that I know not which to put off first'.

Finally there is a pathetic letter from the poor lad to his uncle Wm. Cooke:

> 'My uncle Bythell says that if I will not marry he will cut down all the wood at Tedstone. For the maid, she is handsome enough, but I am not minded to marry, and am but a child. I pray you to come to me at Tedstone for I know not what to do'.[26]

In 1651, there was a dispute with the Wyshams over £100 which George Wysham claimed was still unpaid and he questioned Mason's title to the manor but on 20th October 1651 the business with the Wyshams was at last satisfactorily concluded.

Unfortunately there isn't a Wysham or Mason will that gives us a glimpse inside the 17th century Tedstone Court but Robert Mason's sister, Mary Marston, was living in part of the house with her husband Richard Marston who had at one time acted as steward for his brother-in-law. Her will is a long and interesting one, rather different from the more basic ones of the farmers we read about in Chapter III. Some of her belongings were at Eyton where the family had property and some were at Tedstone Court and a short extract follows:

> First I give and bequeath unto my sister-in-law Hester Mason the beds in the chamber where I lodge and all the furniture to them, one trunk with drawers, one silver sugar dish & three silver spoons two pairs of flaxen sheets and a pair of pillow beares, one dozen flaxen napkins & a flaxen table cloth, my late husbands signet ring & one plain gold ring. I give and bequeath unto Richard Mason, son of the said Hester, forty pounds of money in the house, all the

books in the study at Tedstone & the desk there, one damask tablecloth and napkins thereto belonging, one pair of flaxen or Holland sheets & one pillow beare.[27]

Bedding was always highly valued. The lengthy will continued with numerous bequests to a large number of people including 4s. each to her 'Brother Mason's servants'. Altogether 27 separate items of silver or gold were listed. It also included 'a boulster in the Rectory Chamber'. Why this room was so named is a mystery.

Part of Mary Marston's will. She was the sister-in-law of Robert Mason, lord of the manor, and was living in part of his house at Tedstone Court. *HRO*

Duncumb records an inscription on the south wall of the chancel:

> Robertus Mason, qui fuit praetorii dominus et hujus ecclesiae, fatis cessit, April 16, A.D. 1684, aetat. 63
> Et in eodem tumulo depos: reliquiae Hesterae uxoris, quae obit Sept. 28, 1709, aetat. 83[28]
>
> Robert Mason, lord of the manor and patron of the church died April 16, A.D. 1684 aged 63
> And in the same tomb lies: Hester his wife who died Sept. 28, 1709, aged 83

We don't know whether Hester was the maid, that as a youngster, Robert didn't want to marry. It is recorded that Robert and Hester left five sons and two daughters.[29] The century and also this chapter end with the Masons being in increasingly grave financial difficulties and unable to redeem their mortgages and it was becoming clear that they would be unable to continue much longer at the Court.

CHAPTER III

Our Tedstone Forbears, who they were and how they lived and farmed in the 15th - 17th Centuries

The past is a foreign country; they do things differently there ...
L. P. Hartley, *The Go-Between,* (1953)

The Records
A variety of records are available to the local historian; none were specifically designed for recording a history but were for entirely different purposes; so often the information given is of limited use but taken together with that provided by other documents, it can be illuminating. Many of the records are of church or state and were for the purposes of taxation. Some of these, especially the earlier ones, assessed the parish rather than an individual person and others provide the numbers of taxpayers in a parish but give no names. The parish taxation lists can provide us with information regarding the relative wealth or prosperity of a particular parish compared with that of its neighbours or with more distant parishes; and in a similar way taxation lists of named individuals, usually without addresses, can, if nothing else, provide us with the relative prosperity or otherwise of a person compared with other people in the parish or with people from neighbouring parishes. And indeed, to have an actual name of a *real* person who lived in the parish centuries ago, even if there is no address, is valuable; addresses were not needed because then, everybody knew where a person lived! One always hopes that another record might provide further clues and help to complete the picture and provide an address. Henry VIII's reign was a period of heavy taxation because funds were needed to pay for his expensive foreign wars. These taxes involved far more of the ordinary people than any since the poll taxes of 1377 – 81. We are particularly lucky in Herefordshire in that recently the publication by the Woolhope Club of the important book by M. A. Faraday makes this source easily available to all.[1] The tax records provide us with some useful early names and the assessments reflect the beginnings of the gradual decline of the manor as the primary unit of taxation and its replacement by the parish. These records are recorded in Appendix B. Also recorded in Appendix B are the names of those in Tedstone Delamere and Wafre who were recorded in the Herefordshire Muster Book of 1542[2] as being 'able', when war with Scotland was threatened. The Scots were thoroughly beaten at Solway Moss on 23rd November 1542 and it is probably here that the Herefordshire men fought. These Tedstone names can be compared with those who were assessed for taxes under the 1543 Subsidy Act. Another invaluable book by Faraday, *Calendar of Probate and Administration Acts 1407 – 1581*[3] has provided more very early names of people in

the parish and these are recorded in Appendix C. But the records which have been most particularly illuminating in bringing people to life during the 15th – 17th century period are the court rolls, and wills and inventories:

Tedstone Delamere court rolls[4]
The manorial records do actually provide some addresses as well as names. These records for Tedstone Delamere consist mainly of court rolls which are fascinating documents. A medieval manor was an administrative unit for managing the local countryside, usually run by the lord's steward. Courts, which probably took place at or near to Tedstone Court (hence the name), were held at intervals through the year and their records were kept in Latin. The court rolls are where the minutes of the courts were written. They are on a mixture of parchment and paper, some are in the form of a long length of parchment in a roll or as separate membranes sewn end to end; one particular roll consists of a dozen sheets of parchment and paper tied at the head. Nobody but the steward or his clerk were ever thought likely to read them so they were written in a terse and abbreviated form which they could understand, but are fiendishly difficult for local historians to read today. The surviving Tedstone Delamere court rolls can only be just a fraction of the original number and some of these are too faded, fragile or torn to decipher. Nine of the reasonably legible ones are from the 15th century, 28 are from the 16th and 11 from the 17th centuries.

The usual form of the business was to start with the lord's and sometimes the steward's name, then came the date which was usually the regnal year and a saint's day, or less frequently, the day of the month. The stewards would have had to have lived either in the parish or else close by. They seemed to be members of the gentry and one in particular, Richard Marston who was steward in 1648, was brother-in-law to Robert Mason, the lord of the manor. He and his wife actually lived in part of Tedstone Court. Sometimes the roll began with a list of *essoins* which were excuses for non-attendance, often followed by a list of *defaults* which seem to be people who hadn't bothered either to come or send their excuses. Those who defaulted were likely to be fined. A list of the *homage* normally followed: these were the more important tenants who acted as a kind of jury to decide on the many day to day local problems that arose. In the early days in a large manor, *presentments* for the homage to consider fell into two main categories: firstly, transfers of land were dealt with at a *Court Baron* or great court and secondly, the day to day problems concerning maintenance of roads, hedges, bridges etc together with tenants' misdemeanours, would have taken place at a Court Leet. In Tedstone Delamere, by the 15th century, everything took place at the Court Baron.

Things had moved on since the early days described in Chapter II. Norman lords began to intermarry with Saxons. To start with, men had been tied to the manor and could not leave; running away was severely punished. Over the years, the Saxons learnt to work the system, the cleverer serfs had managed to buy their freedom and after the Black Death there was an acute labour shortage which enabled serfs to demand payment for work done. The one time bond serfs had become manorial tenants. Services on the lord's demesne and extra ones at harvest were now commuted to cash. After a serf's death, instead of his land being taken back, it began to be passed to the eldest son or heir; former serfs had become entitled to an almost perpetual tenancy, paying a very small annual rent and a *relief* on death or transfer. In addition, rather than all the cattle, only the *heriot* or best beast was taken back, due to the lord on the death of a tenant. A *relief* was the fine or payment that a new tenant paid on entering the property. The best beast or heriot soon became commuted to a money payment although in Tedstone Delamere, a payment of the best beast, carefully selected and valued and described in the court rolls, as for example, a *red cow* or *black ox*, continued in some cases. In 1556, Edward Ingram bequeathed his best brown ox to Edward Dyll, his son-in-law, 'excepte the sayd ox be chosen to harryot and yf he be so chosen then the sayd Edward to take my gelding horse'.[5] Right into the 19th century occasional references occur to best beasts being required although by then they were very difficult to collect.

As explained, the presentations which took place at the court can be divided into two sections:

1) Land transactions: When a tenant died, his death was presented to the Court by his neighbours: the Homage. Some of the earliest entries are given below:

> 1428 The homage report the death of John Caluhull who was seized of **Wynleslond;** he gave a heriot at his death and so his widow Alice has agreed with the lord to pay 8s as heriot and William Caluhull is her guarantor
>
> 1428 Nicholas Love did homage for lands formerly held by John **Catteleye** in Tedisterne and gave to the lord's chamberlain 6s 8d, and 25s as relief for the 4th part of a knight's fee
>
> 1429 The tenants of **Catteleyns** have defaulted and a distraint is ordered against them
>
> 1429 The homage presents the death of John **Pykeshale** who held land, but they don't know how much. William Byry claims the land and he is given until the next court to prove his claim[6]

Seized means 'in ownership of'. In those early days, surnames were sometimes derived from a person's occupation, for instance, Adam the smith, or John the joiner or, as in the cases above, surnames might come *from* the place where a person lived, or alternatively a person might have given their name *to* the place in which they lived. 'Catteleyn', which became Catley or Gatley, is believed to be the present Gate House and of course 'Pykeshale' is the present Pixhill and Wynleslond is Winley's land.

> 1443 Homage present the death of Agnes Porter who held 1 messuage and 2 nokes of free land called **Sewalles** for which 1 cow worth 8s is due as a heriot. John Wyse and William Welonde are her nearest heirs in blood by inheritance through their mother. They came into court and asked to be admitted to the lands, upon which Thomas Chaleston also came and claimed to be the heir. The parties were told to produce evidence of their claims and after considering the evidence the homage agreed unanimously that John Wyse and Willam Welonde are the right heirs. Then Wyse and Welonde acknowledged the rents and services due for the land and 6s 2d is due to the lord for feudal relief [fine paid to the lord by the heir on succession][7]

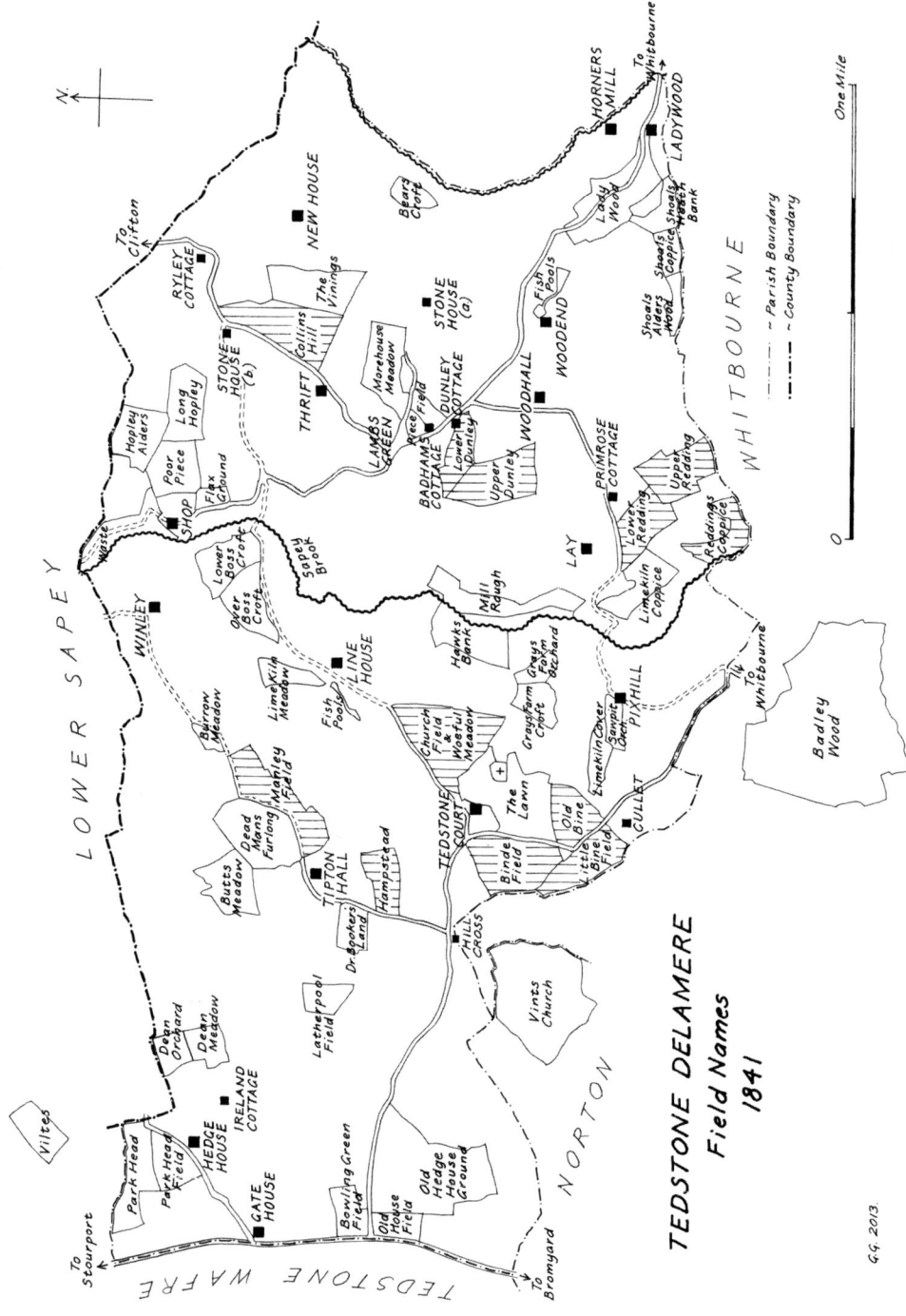

Map 4. This map shows the fields that are mentioned in the text. The hatched fields were once part of the common open fields of the manor. *HRO*

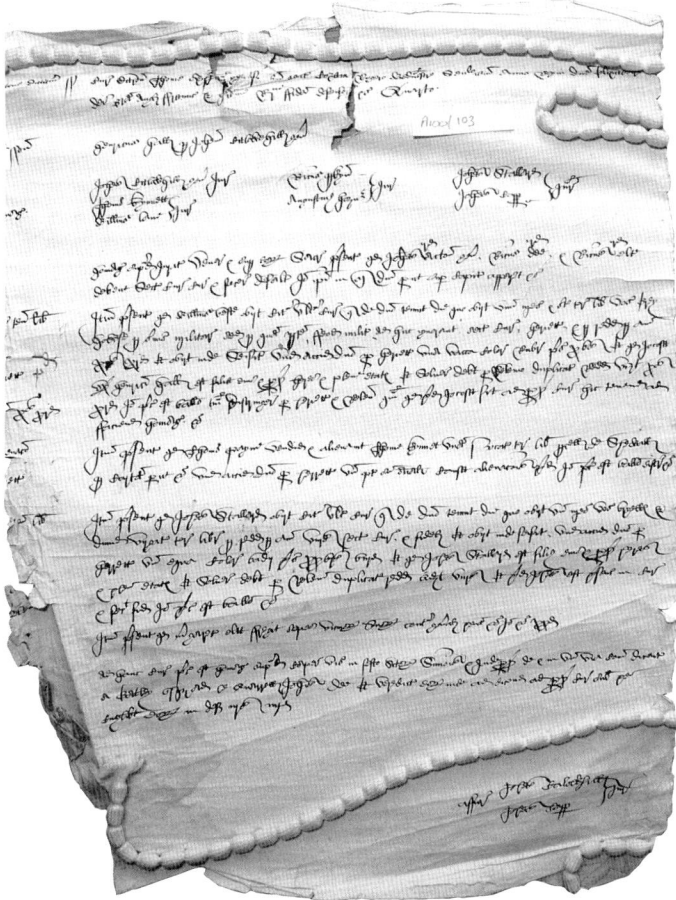

A typical court roll.   *HRO*

Sewalles is one of the lost holdings. It was on the eastern side of the parish probably south of Woodend and close to Ladywood. The above examples illustrate how land transactions were carried out during the 1400s. The vital document was the title deed and in the extract above, the parties were told to produce this evidence before the homage could decide on the rightful heirs. There is evidence that considerable care was taken over this; it was never allowed to go through on the nod as it were. It is clear from what has survived that the steward had a rough version that he worked up into the finished article. They used the rolls for reference because there were odd notes such as 'as appears in the rolls' and people would be told to produce evidence (their deeds), as in the extract above, at the following court to support a claim. To repeat, the old manorial system, when the lord took back the serf's land and livestock on his demise, had changed. The land could now be passed to a tenant's heirs or sold by him to somebody else. It was, in fact, effective ownership. The only livestock to be handed over was the best beast, called a *heriot*, often now commuted to cash after the particular beast was valued and the new tenant had to come to the next court to do fealty and be admitted. When Edward Horner (probably from the mill), died in 1558 the following entry appears in the court rolls:

> Death since the last court of Edward Horner a free tenant who held 1 messuage and 1 noke of land and there is due to the lord as heriot a red cow worth 20s. Augustine Horner is his son and nearest heir and he is of full age and a relief of 3s 1d is due to the lord. He came to the court and acknowledged tenancy by rent of 3s 1d pa and heriot when it should be due and did fealty and was admitted[8]

One must assume that there was the option here of paying cash for the heriot but what is quite clear was that if they thought this cash might not be forthcoming, the bailiff would be ordered to go and forcibly take the best beast. When John Capper, a chap who had not been particularly prompt paying his dues in the past, died in 1615 holding Winley, the bailiff had 'seized a red ox worth 46s 8d and was ordered to deliver it into the lord's store'.[9]

If an heir was a minor, great care was taken that he or she was looked after and, probably more importantly, that the land was properly farmed until he reached his majority. In 1573, after the death of Richard Elt, there came the following entry:

> Edward Elt is his son and heir. He is aged 12 and is said to be in the guardianship of Edward Whore of Bewdley. A relief of 7s 3d is due and the bailiff is ordered to take the body of the said Edward into the lord's hands, together with the said lands, to answer for the issues and profits of the said lands until the said Edward comes of age[10]

And at the next court:

> The lord granted to William Howell the body of Edward Elt aged 12, son and heir of Richard Elt deceased, together with 1 messuage and 1 noke of land called Briers Held ... To hold during Edward's minority (except for the last year of the same) for which grant William has paid 40s to the lord[11]

Taking the 'body' of the poor boy seems an odd phrase today but it was probably a caring system, although of benefit to William Howell: what often happened in such a case was that the person who was to farm the land in the meantime, *ie* William Howell, would marry the boy to his daughter, thereby getting the lands into his own family, quite a profitable thing to do! Briers Held or Brierley is a lost farm in the east of the parish near the Thrift.

When a new lord of the manor took over, everyone had to come to the court to confirm what land they held and acknowledge their tenancy to the new owner (to *attorn* and do *fealty*). One of the surviving court rolls was for this very purpose. (In medieval times a tenant did *fealty* by placing his hands between the lord's and swearing loyal service.) Those tenants who did not appear were distrained by the bailiff to appear at the next court:

Court Baron for acknowledgement of lordship and attornment of Francis Wysham gent [1599]

Essoins: Margaret Coninge widow, Francis Hall gent.

Homage: Thomas Fidoe, John Kynnett, John Capper, William Howells, Robert Arden, Roger Hunt, John Whitlegg, Henry Pitt

Defaults: Ann Welshe widow fined 2d, John Acton gent 4d, John Hopton [edge of document torn] 4d. Richard Perkins 2d, Baldwin Cowghley 2d, Ann Langford widow 2d, Ann Capper widow 2d, John ... [edge of document torn], Thomas Eckley 2d

Thomas Fidoe came into court and acknowledged his tenancy of 1 messuage and 1 virgate of free land called **Greyhouse** by knight's service viz wards, marriage, homage, 'scutage incertum' and relief and the annual rent of 10s 11d, suit of court, heriot and fealty and he attorned tenant to the lord and did fealty for the property

The remaining entries are abbreviated for reasons of space:

John Kynnett – ackn. tenancy of 1 noke of free land, part of **Shewelles**. Rent: 3s 1d pa

Richard Perkins holds tenancy of messuage & ½ virgate of free land called **Winleyhou** [edge of doc. torn] rent 5s 10d pa. He is ordered to appear at next court

Anne Walshe [Welshe] holds messuage & lands called **Ryley**. Tenant to come to next court

Margaret Coninge, widow of Richard Dee, holds messuage & 1 virgate of free land called **Whitewoods Crofte** rent 23d pa. Tenant must appear at next court

John Acton holds free lands called **Burbage**. Rent & services unknown, enquire before next court

John Hopton gent holds messuage & 2 virgates free land [**Tipton**] 2s 6d pa. Bailiff ordered to distrain for 3 years back rent

William Howells, by right of wife Joan, formerly wife of Richard Elte, holds moiety of messuage, 1 virgate & 1 noke of free land [**Woodend**] for term of Joan's life, reversion to Robert Arden & heirs, rent 3s 6d pa. Did fealty

Robert Arden ackn. tenancy of moiety of above messuage & lands, rent 3s 6d

Ann Capper wid. holds for term of her life, remainder to son William C, messuage & ½ virgate called **Pixall** 4s pa. Must appear at next court

Francis Hall gent holds by right of wife Elizabeth, dau & co heir of Augustine Horner, free lands called **Impye & Midlefield**. Must appear at next court

Eleanor Horner, wid, John Bradford & Joan, dau & co heirs of Augustine Horner & said Francis & Elizabeth Hall sold **Peckmill** [Horner's] & lands to Thos Eckley who owes one year's rent as relief. He must appear at next court. A heriot is due from him

John Stallard holds 1 messuage & free lands called **Bryells**, rent 8s pa. Must appear at next court. Homage to enquire whether part of the premises has been sold to his brother Edward

Tenants by indenture
Roger Hunt, William Baker, Baldwin Cowgley, John W..., John Capper, Henry Pytt, Geoffrey Nicholls and John Whitlegge, tenants by indenture, attorned tenants to the lord by payment of 1d each in court and did fealty[12]

Significant holdings are omitted from the above list and one must assume that these are included among the *tenants by indenture* above; for instance, we know from other records that the Line House was held by John Capper and one of the holdings at Woodend was held by Roger Hunt. Evidence suggests that at least some of the *tenants by indenture* held property that was part of the lord's demesne land and were let by him for a fixed period or 'for lives'.

Important family names which persisted over a period were the Callowhills at Winley for at least 72 years, from 1428 – 1510; followed there by the Perkins, for at least 82 years, from 1534 – 1616. Another important family were the Cappers at Pixhill, active from 1510 – 1710. The land transactions recorded in the court rolls which can be related to today's farms are mostly included in Chapters V and VI about the farms.

By today's standards, the recorded holdings were mostly very small. The largest was Tipton with two virgates; next came the Line House with one and a half virgates; Woodend, Grey House and that important lost holding of Whitewoods Crofte were all one virgate. Winley; and Brierley, that lost farm near the Thrift; were each half a virgate. The remaining holdings were of one or two nokes or were of unspecified amounts of land. Virgates and nokes were variable according to the quality of the land but a virgate in Tedstone Delamere was probably about 40 statute acres and a noke about 10 acres.

Tipton Hall

Holdings west of the Sapey Brook, with dates when first recorded in the surviving rolls, are the Gate House 1429, Tipton 1440, Winley 1428, the Line House 1615, Pixhill 1510, the Grey House 1451; and also on the west side although of course not recorded in the rolls, was Tedstone Court itself. Apart from the ruined Grey House, these farms all exist today. Hedge House was never part of the manor of Tedstone Delamere, see Chapter V.

Holdings certainly or probably east of the Sapey Brook, with dates when first recorded in the surviving rolls, are Whitwoods Croft 1534, Brierley 1428, Sewalles 1443, Morehouse 1451/52 (Morehouse Meadow is on the tithe map, south of the Thrift, see Map 4, page 46), Mesers 1615 (became Mazers), Ryley 1599, Burbage 1599, Impye and Middlefield 1599, Peckmill (Horner's) 1532, Woodend 1518 (more than one holding), Woodhall 1648, Pitts land 1689, Homs/Hams 1689. A local person today will hardly recognise any of these names on the east side! So what has happened? Only Peck Mill (Horner's) together with Woodhall, Woodend, and Ryley which is no longer a farm, survive today. Two of the lost properties were sizeable farms: firstly Whitwoods Croft was a farm of one virgate held by John Dee in 1534. In 1599, Margaret Coninge, widow of Richard Dee, held the farm which in 1657 featured in title deeds of the Thrift Farm, as part of the marriage settlement of Richard Hill and Elizabeth Hay.[13] Secondly, a farm of half a virgate that disappeared was Brierley. It was merged with the Thrift at the end of the 18th century. A family by the name of Stallard lived at Brierley for around a hundred years from the mid-16th century. The remainder, all now disappeared, were smaller properties.

The reason for this extraordinary state of affairs is that the western side survived the predations and sweeping changes made by acquisitive lords of the manor much better than the eastern side (this becomes clear in Chapters V and VI). On the west side, the Grey House and Pixhill were purchased by Robert Moore (the lord) at the end of the 18th century. He immediately merged the two farms and the farmhouse at Pixhill was the one that was retained, the other farmhouse quickly fell into disrepair and has now disappeared. The Gate House, Tipton, Winley and the Line House, although not continuing in owner occupation, were acquired by different individual landlords and somehow managed to retain their separate identity. On the east side however, the Moore family purchased almost all the land there during the 18th century and made huge changes, merging holdings to create larger more viable farms.

2) Maintenance of roads, hedges, ditches, bridges etc and reports and complaints by the tenants against each other: as well as dealing with transactions of land, manorial courts coped with day to day administrative matters connected with the land and its occupants within the manor. What seems like compulsory snooping by one's neighbours was absolutely essential when the land was farmed communally. Tenants must have spent a great deal of time walking about between their homes and their land, much of which was scattered all over the parish in the common fields and, just as it is today, looking over other people's hedges was of great interest to farmers. One of the most frequent entries in the court rolls concerned the maintenance of the many roads and trackways crossing the parish and the trimming back of hedges and overhanging trees and cleaning out ditches.

> 1532 The road between le Hurstway and Wall Grene is badly out of repair by default of Richard Baker, Richard Irelond, and John Dee. To repair by Pentecost, pain 20p each[14]

The *pain* was the fine that would have to be paid if the job was not done by a certain date, in this case, Pentecost. There are a number of lost names which one tries to place, sometimes without success; Wallegrene and the Hurstway are such names. The personal name 'Irelond' is remembered today by Ireland Cottage, near Hedge House.

> 1532 A church road from the Barcrofts Glatt to le stable is out of repair, Thomas Wysham gent, Thomas Capper, John Elte and Thomas Elt to repair by St John Baptist, pain 20d each. And Thomas Wysham's pain for default will be forfeited to Teddesterne church[15]

The above entry is particularly interesting because it appears to illustrate true democracy; Thomas Wysham was lord of the manor. He couldn't have his fine being paid to himself and so it was to be paid to the church instead. Barcroft/Bearcroft was a holding east of the Clifton to Whitbourne road and south of New House. The Elts farmed a noke of land at Woodend.

All tenants had the right to graze a fixed number of cattle or sheep on the pastures and wastes at certain prescribed times of year, depending on the amount of land they held. In the early 15th century, the population was expanding again after the devastation caused by plague and it is probable that more land was ploughed up at this time for corn. At times of year when the grass got short, tenants were tempted to allow their animals to stray and in 1428, various tenants were presented to the court for trespass:

> 1428 The tenants present William Calluhulle for trespass with his draught animals in the wood (fined 2d)
> John Byrche for 2 bullocks in the wood (fined 1d)
> John Deykyns, John Wylyams and Roger Wylyams, trespass on the common [or common fields] with pigs and draught animals, each fined 2d[16]

And a later entry:

> 1581 Edward Perkins [of Winley] trespassed in the lord's pasture so he was fined. John Capper [Pixhill] trespassed in the lord's pasture several times with his beasts as aforesaid. He confessed in court in front of the homage and was fined.
> It was ordered that no tenant within the manor should maintain or support any subtenant keeping beasts or cattle on the common belonging to the demesne under pain of 6s 8d for the tenant and 20d for the subtenant as ordered previously in the court rolls. No tenant is to keep more than 30 sheep in le Commons for one virgate of land and so for each same amount of land on pain of 3s 4d[17]

On occasions, a tiresome tenant could cause a lot of trouble and at the manorial court in 1496, Humphrey Dore was presented for various misdemeanours:

> Humfrey Dore fined 4d for digging a ditch in Court Meadow contrary to the wishes of the lord and to the harm of his neighbours
> Humfrey Dore has pastured his beasts on Perycroft and other of the lord's pastures
> Humfrey Dore is enclosing the lord's waste lying between ye Held Cros [Hill Cross] and Owdlow and the head of Vynchurch. Ordered not to enclose any more on pain of 3s 4d[18]

Humphrey was a very considerable landowner. He had served Henry VII as purveyor of the king's buttery and had a house at Westminster. His brother, William, held Burton (Burton Court in Lower Sapey)[19] and Humphrey was to inherit this from his brother two years later. His mother was a Mortimer, a member of the powerful family of Mortimers who held Tedstone Wafre. When he died in 1501, he was in possession of considerable property including land in Norton, Saltmarshe, Edvin Loach and also Catley or Gatley (the Gate House) together with the Line House in Tedstone Delamere. So perhaps all this was why he thought he could cock a snook at poor John Wysham, lord of Tedstone Delamere.[20] The urge to enclose land, legitimately or otherwise, had begun: two years later, in spite of fines and warnings, Humphrey was at it again and was obviously a thorn in the flesh of Wysham and his tenants:

> Humfrey Dore has enclosed more common land at Vynchurch Hed and is fined 3s 4d as set at last court
> Humfrey Dore has enclosed the common church way to the harm of all the parishioners[21]

Humphrey was not the only person who tried to enclose what didn't belong to him, probably hoping that nobody would notice. A number of others seem to have made a similar push to enclose or encroach on land that wasn't theirs:

> 1588 John Capper [Pixhill] has enclosed part of an empty piece of land adjoining the end of the wood called Badley Woode and the road leading to Heldecrosse [Hill Cross] and has kept it enclosed for the last 15 years or thereabouts to the damage of the lord. He is ordered to open it up before Michaelmas and to let it lie open as it used to be on pain of 10s[22]

> 1589 John Capper hasn't opened up the piece of vacant land that he recently enclosed adjoining Badley Woode and kept it open as he was ordered to do, so he has incurred a fine of 10s. He is ordered to open it before the Invention of the Holy Cross [Holy Cross Day, 14 September] on pain of 20s[23]

We don't know what the outcome was, whether he paid the fine or got away with it. One suspects that at this date, the power of the manor wasn't quite what it had once been. Another way to get more land was to move a boundary. In 1529, William Brown was presented for 'removing and ploughing out part of a boundary' between his land and church land and was to put it back by Christmas; John Dodying had committed a similar crime. In 1545, another rather different boundary problem occurred, as recorded in Chapter II: it was ordered that six members of the homage 'take a view of *bounds and meres* in Hoppley'[24] in dispute between the lord and Richard Dee. This is an unusual entry: it is suggested that as Hoppley was on the northern boundary of the parish bordering Lower Sapey, perhaps the *bounds and meres* marked the parish and county boundary.[25] Richard Dee held the lost farm of Whitwoods Croft which one suspects was in the north of the parish as it is mentioned in deeds of the Thrift (see page 116) so it is possible that his land was partly in Lower Sapey.

The court rolls include a number of references regarding encroachments onto the wastes. It is clear that the common's wastes were scattered in several places over the parish. There was waste between Hill Cross and Vynchurch, at Whitehall, at Tidbatch, and the next two entries refer to waste at Riley and also at Shewells on the southern parish boundary:

> 1603. 4d fine on William Ingram because he made encroachment on the waste at Ryley.
> 4d fine on John Whitlegge because he made an encroachment on the waste at Shewells land and enclosed a parcel there and made a garden from it[26]

He later claimed he had permission to do this. And just to show that nothing changes, Bringsty commoners today occasionally fall foul of the manorial court in the same way. They might begin by mowing the grass outside their property, then after a year or two they will plant one or two ornamental trees there, and after another year or two they might surreptitiously make a small flower bed, hoping that nobody will notice!

Woodland
The lord had the important right to all growing timber in his woods and demesne land, and originally also on copyhold land, because it could be purported that the ground on which the timber grew was his. Over the years, this right became increasingly difficult to prove but the records do show that the lord claimed the woodland, including the underwood, from tenants who held their land *by indenture* (see following page). Much of the court's time was taken up with disputes and misdemeanours relating to woodland and the following are just a few examples: in 1428 the wood bailiff presented William Callowhill for trespass with his beasts twice in the wood (fined 4d.) and Isobel Bruton for trespass in the wood (fined 1d.). The total court fees that day amounted to 33s. 5d. so the courts were a good source of income for the lord. In 1429 'the wood bailiff presents for attachments* from the woods 4s 5d as appears in his accounts'.[27] Also in 1429, Thomas Whyting was fined 2d. for cutting down an oak tree and Richard Grey was fined for having 11 pigs in the 'lord's park'; this is the only reference found relating to a possible deer park in Tedstone Delamere held by the Wyshams. In 1558 there was a general injunction that no-one should cut down trees in the lord's wood, break down any hedge, carry off timber, plough or dig up the roads or the lord's waste in the period till the next court under pain of 6s. 8d. In 1578, Hugh Price was fined 20d. for keeping pigs contrary to the ordinance of the court. An injunction followed that no tenant was to take acorns in the lord's waste to feed their pigs or to damage the oaks there on pain of 20s. In 1581 'Henry Pitt took and carted away, for his own house and fences, timber belonging to the lord from a pasture called le Viltes, therefore he is fined';[28] the Viltes was in the north-west of the parish on what is now Hedge House land. In 1589, Richard Owen, who was Edward Elte's sub-tenant, cut down and carried away a sally tree from the lord's wood and was fined 6s. 8d. In 1606, 'George Whitinge, William Adams and Walter Dallabere were each fined 12d because they dug in the lord's waste and made pits there called sawpits';[29] pit saws began to be used in preference to trestle saws in the mid-16th century. In 1630 an injunction ordered the tenants to ring their pigs and keep them ringed on pain of 6s 8d. The above are just a few of many examples that the court dealt with associated with woodland which has always been a very valuable asset.

Another important right that the lord of the manor enjoyed was to all wild creatures which walked, flew or swam. Hunting and shooting of deer, pigeons and partridges were particularly important as were pigeons in the dovecote. *Pigeon House Meadow* is recorded in Tedstone Court deeds (see page 78). In 1329, John Wysham had a grant of free warren in his demesne land at Tedstone Delamere. Farmed rabbits were a very important source of meat in medieval times.[30] Eventually of course they escaped

---
* *Attachments* here probably mean the value of goods confiscated as evidence of wrongdoing

and the rest is history. There is a small field called Burrow Meadow on the tithe map which lies beside the road from Tipton to Winley, see Map 4, page 46. The reference to the lord's park above probably means that venison was farmed by the lord and must have involved substantial ditches and fencing. The lord's fish were important too: one can feel real sympathy for William West, John Hamons[?], George Bennett, Richard Fudger and Richard Simons who in 1606 were each fined 2s. for fishing in the Sapey Brook and some of them had dug in the lord's waste to make a pond to raise the water in the brook. There are said to have been trout in the Sapey Brook until the 1960s when pollution from milking parlour chemicals cleared the stream of its rainbow trout.[31]

There are several unusual entries that don't fall into any particular category. One of these relates to bakers: in 1558 there is a reference that 'Richard Ireland and Thomas Fawkener are common bakers and are in mercy'.[32] This entry is likely to mean that the two men had been breaking the assize laws. You weren't allowed to sell bread without a licence from the lord of the manor. This was to make sure that the weight was correct. Another unusual entry in the same year was a concern about somebody becoming a charge on the parish: 'John Callowhill must not allow a certain William Hostler to wander around and live in idleness or else must exclude him from the lordship on pain of 6s. 8d'. A parish or manor was responsible for its own poor and if it was feared that someone from another parish showed signs that they might need help in the future, they were hustled out pretty smartly. Care of the poor was always a concern; from the early 16th century this responsibility had begun to be taken over from the manorial courts by the vestry, but for a time the responsibility was shared in varying degrees by the two bodies.

In 1529, it was reported that the roof and walls of Richard Ireland's were in a bad state and he was ordered to repair them before the Nativity of the Virgin Mary on pain of 20s. At the same court, he was told to scour a ditch from his [house?] to Wallgrene by All Saints on pain of 3s. 4d. It seems as if Richard was not a good tenant for again in 1551, there is the following reference to him: 'Richard Ireland holds certain lands by Indenture and has allowed them to become derelict. And a building of two parts [bays?] has fallen into disrepair and Richard has cut down some oak trees from the lord's wood and so he is amerced'.[33] The land *held by indenture* possibly means that it was what had been part of the demesne land which now the lord was letting out, probably on shortish leases, and this is maybe why there was a special concern about the state of the buildings.

After these various problems and misdemeanours had been presented at the courts, some members of the homage were usually compulsorily despatched to make sure the matter had been put right or the problems had been sorted out:

> 1610 The homage are ordered to take a view at All Saints to find the way for William Greenwiche clerk [the rector] to come and go with his carts from the rectory to his lands at Dunleys Hey and similarly to find the way for Thomas Cony to go to his lands called Burbage

Acre. And also to see whether George Lane or Joan Lane widow [from Tipton] have made an encroachment on the lord's land called Deane Croft. And to bring their verdicts to the next court under a pain of 3s 4d each[34]

For reasons of space, these extracts from the surviving rolls are restricted to just a small sample but they are enough to illustrate how day-to-day local government worked at this time, bringing it down to a human level. It also tells us that the advantages of enclosure were understood by farmers of the time and indeed was well under way even though their efforts were not always legal!

Militia Assessments of 1663
Charles II's advisers had learnt from experience that the restoration settlement depended on its military arrangements. They also knew that a standing army could be a dangerous thing. What was needed was a force of adequately trained men, capable of rapid mobilisation and officered by loyal men with a stake in the society they were defending. The purpose was to put down plots and risings. In Herefordshire, their main task appears to have been harrying the poor papists. The king appointed lords lieutenant and deputy lieutenants. Property owners were charged with providing soldiers, arms and supplies and the amount charged was based on the value of their estates. People were used to paying church and poor rates so the concept of a yearly value was familiar to them.[35]

Tedston Delamer	£	s	d		£	s	d
*Mr James Parry, Rect.	12	0	0	*Rich: Stallard	4	10	0
William Acton Esq	12	0	0	Anne Pitts land	3	0	0
*Robert Mason gent	27	0	0	Rich: Hacklett [*Hackluitt*]	1	10	0
Mr Salloways land	5	0	0	Simon Collins	1	0	0
*John Batman gen	2	10	0	*Antho: Lea jun		15	0
	(13v)						
*Geo: Lane	12	0	0	Tho: Ingland		7	6
*John Barnes	4	10	0	John Whiteing		7	6
*John Cooke	6	0	0	Henry Norgrove		10	0
*John Hill	2	10	0	Katherine Cony		15	0
John Capper	4	10	0				
Anne Lewis wid	2	10	0	Charge	127	0	0
*Rich: Hill	6	10	0		[*124*	*15*	*0*]
*James Batman	5	0	0				
Eliz: Howlders land	4	10	0				
Will: Wynne	4	0	0				

*Also listed as paying Hearth Tax

There is an error in the calculation and the figure in square brackets is the correct one.
The raters, John Hill, John Barnes and John Mathewes would have been chosen from the more substantial farmers and probably estimated the incomes of their own class fairly accurately but their estimate of the income of the gentry would have been less accurate for it is unlikely they would have had access to the farm or rent accounts of

their betters, so the figure of £27 for Robert Mason, the lord of the manor, may well be an under assessment and a bit of a guess! With each succeeding century we know a little more from other records, so that we are now able to say that Robert Mason, gent (in the above list) was lord of the manor from the Court, William Acton Esq. was probably the same gentleman who sold Burton Court, Lower Sapey to the Foleys in the mid-17th century;[36] he held the Gate House and almost certainly Hedge House. Mr. Salloway's land was probably Riley. James Batman (or Bateman) was from Woodam (or Woodham), near the present Woodhall. George Lane was from Tipton, John Barnes held Winley and John Capper held Pixhill. John Cooke was probably from the present Woodhall; John & Richard Hill, father and son, held Whitewoods Croft, Howan, Showley Heath and the Thrift; the first three are 'lost' farms, Whitewoods Croft being one virgate in 1534. Anthony Lea may have held Lea Lay. William Wynne probably held Homs and Richard Stallard held Brierley.

Hearth Tax

In 1662 Parliament tried to raise an annual tax to augment the income of the Restoration monarchy. It was an extremely unpopular tax; every householder who owned property worth £1 or more (in terms of annual rent) and was not otherwise exempt on the grounds of poverty was liable to an annual payment of 2s. per annum for every fireplace or stove in his house. It was collected twice yearly and a return had to be made by the village constable and delivered to the justices at quarter sessions, a copy being sent to the Exchequer. This of course involved intrusion into the house and was much disliked and there was a good deal of evasion. The tax was abandoned in 1689.

Hearth Tax 1664[37]

*James Parry [Rectory]	3	William Mayo	1
*Robert Mason gent [Court]	5	George Ley	1
*George Lane [Tipton]	4	William Finch	1
*John Barnes [Line House ?]	1	*Richard Stallard [Brierley]	2
Richard Corbett	2	Philip Hamans	1
Richard Barnes [Winley ?]	2	William Gunny	1
+Edmo: Capper [Pixhill?]	1	+Thomas Lewis	1
John Turner	1	William Hill	1
*John Cooke [Woodhall]	1	*Antho: Lea [Lea Lay?]	1
+John Mathews	3	John Floyd [Woodend?]	3
*John Hill [Whitwoods Croft]	4	William Southhall	1
*Richard Hill [Thrift?]	1	Thomas Colley	1
*James Batman [Woodam]	1		

The columns of figures denote numbers of hearths.
* also mentioned in Militia Assessments and so are owner/occupiers
+ a *John* Capper and an *Anne* Lewis wid were listed in Militia Assessments and John Mathews is mentioned there as one of the Raters.

The charged houses total 25. This tax can be compared with the Militia Assessments only a year earlier when there are also 25 names but three of these are for land. It will be seen that 10 names appear in both lists indicating that these people were owner-occupiers. The remaining 15 names in the Hearth Tax assessment would have been tenants. Sometimes, people with more than one hearth stopped up a chimney to avoid some tax and in 1666, Richard Barnes and John and Richard Hill had each stopped up a hearth. Robert Mason, lord of the manor, was listed amongst the owner-occupiers.

In 1664, as well as the charged properties listed above, it was also noted in that year that 15 properties were exempt for reasons of poverty giving a total of 40 houses in the parish at that time. To get a figure for the population, it is usual to multiply the number of houses by five so giving a total of 200 people. In 1671, the total number of houses was 30, a reduction of one quarter in seven years and to date, there is no accounting for this fall. The figure for charged houses at this time remained almost the same at 24 so the shortfall was in the houses that were exempt because of poverty.

Hearth Tax Assessments[38]

Lady Day 1664			Michaelmas 1671		
Charged Hearths	Charged Houses	Total Houses	Charged Hearths	Charged Houses	Total Houses
49	25	40	44	24	30

This phenomenon did not occur in neighbouring parishes. The number of houses can be compared with the 1841 census when there was an increase to 42 inhabited houses. We have next to no information about the parish poor except that they were always with us. The poor law records have not survived. Some people, if they could afford it, left money for the poor in their wills.

The Compton Census 1676[39]

Only five years after the 1671 Hearth Tax Assessment, we have the Compton Census: this return was made to find out how many people worshipped in the parish church and were of an age to receive communion, *ie* all those over the age of 16. It also gave figures for the number of papists and nonconformists in the parish. The figures below include those for some neighbouring parishes to enable comparisons to be made; the instructions to the incumbents as to how to fill in the forms were ambiguous and were interpreted differently in different areas. The figure given for Tedstone Wafre is thought to be its total population:[40]

	Conformists	Papists	Nonconformists
Tedstone Delamere	95	2	2
Thornbury	113		
Whitbourne	300		
Tedstone Wafre	73		
Edwyn Ralph	88	3	
Bromyard	938	4	31

It is usually estimated that the number of people below the age of 16 in the mid-17th century was one third of the population which would mean that the total population of Tedstone Delamere at this time was approximately 132 persons, that is if the incumbent had interpreted his instructions correctly. This is rather less than the figure of 150 estimated from the Hearth Tax returns in 1671. In 1801, the census gives a parish population total of 245, a very considerable increase since the 17th century if we are to believe the range of possible Compton figures: *ie* total population of 99 – 132 and the figures derived from the Hearth Tax. The 1841 census gives a parish total of 207 persons living in 42 houses. So whichever way you look at it, there appears to have been a substantial increase in population between the second half of the 17th century and 1801, and also, to a lesser extent, 1841. It would be interesting to know who the two papists were in the above table. Papists had a very difficult time during this period. The nonconformists were George and Mary Primrose, Rev. George Primrose M.A. was removed from his living at Hereford and he later lived at Tedstone Delamere and was licensed here as a Presbyterian preacher in 1672. He died in 1695 and he and his wife are buried in the chancel of the parish church, a prestigious position which shows that he must surely have had had the approval of the rector and the lord of the manor. It is possible that Primrose Cottage and Primrose Hill in the east of the parish were named after George Primrose.

'Feather beds and sheep' - wills and inventories[41]

These are really enlightening records which can tell us a great deal about families, their homes, their possessions and their farming. They give us a glimpse inside the homes and farmsteads of our forebears. Probate administration was a responsibility of the ecclesiastical courts from 1529 until 1858 when it was taken over by the civil authorities. Until 1858, an inventory and valuation of a deceased person's goods and chattels had to be made if the value exceeded £5 but unfortunately those for the Hereford Diocese for the period before 1662 have been lost. This valuation included a person's clothing and cash in the house, household goods, tools of the trade, livestock, harvested and growing crops, fodder, provisions, and money owing to the deceased. The valuation did not include houses or land. Sometimes, rooms in the house are mentioned and these can be of particular interest if the house is standing today. The ecclesiastical courts charged a probate fee according to the value of the estate. The money owing to the deceased might be unpaid bills or loans made and this seemed to be an essential part of the rural economy; people such as widows would often lend money as an investment. The inventories and valuations were normally made by the deceased's neighbours or sometimes their relatives and at least one of them had to be able to write; they were called the 'appraisers' and they probably tried to make the valuations as low as possible to help the family. Inventories are usually to be found with the wills although many are missing. If somebody died intestate, and a great many did, the next of kin had to make application to a probate court for letters of administration and these are stored with the inventories. The wills, inventories and letters of administration for this diocese are now kept at the Herefordshire Record Office. If a person died during the Interregnum in the mid-17th century, or if somebody had property in more than one county, usually just the rich people, wills were proved by the Prerogative Court of Canterbury and these are stored at the National Archives and can be found on line.

The Tedstone Delamere wills and inventories, apart from a selected few, are far too numerous to reproduce here (a few are either too fragile to handle or faded to decipher) but those from the 16th and 17th centuries are listed below, those from the 18th century are listed in Chapter IV and copies of these documents with transcripts will be placed in the Bromyard Local History Centre. A few of the more interesting ones together sometimes with other information about the families are reproduced or discussed here and others have been scattered fairly liberally through Chapters V and VI relating to the farms wherever they can be reasonably attributed to a particular property.

Wills usually started with a similar phrase to that below:

> In the name of God Amen, I Richard Perkins [of Winley] late of Tedstone Delamere in the county of Herefs yeoman the 26th daie of Aperil in the yeare of the Raigne of our soveraigne lord James by the grace of God Kinge of England, Scotland, Ffrance, and Ireland, defender of the faith that is to say of England, France & Ireland etc the eight of England & of Scotland the XLIIIth [year] 1610, beinge sicke in bodie & pfect in mind thankes be to god for the same do make my last will and testament in manner & form following vizt I bequeath my soule to the almighty god my maker & redeemer by whom I hope to be saved and my bodie to the earth from whence it cometh.

Variations of the above, particularly the last two lines, can be extended over a whole page. Interestingly, the content of the last two lines is entirely dispensed with in two wills of the clergy. Most wills seem to have been made a short time before death and a great many begin, as above, with the phrase 'being sick in body and perfect in memory thanks be to God'.

The Callowhills
The will of John Callowhill of Worcester, clothier, who died in 1573 is most intriguing.[42] The Callowhills had been in Tedstone Delamere for over 100 years, holding three messuages and land including Winley although by the date of John's death above, the Perkyn or Perkins family were at Winley. John had inherited property from his father in 1545. He left money to each of his five sons together with various household items which included 'one great pott which was brought from Tedstone to Worcester … the second pott wch was brought from Tedstone with my great paier of Andirons wch were brought from Tedstone … my cuborde standing in the hall with the great candlsticke wch I brought from Tedstone'. Other bequests included a great charger, his clothes such as his best gowns, his best doublets and jerkins and the usual household linen. 'Item. I will that Alice my wife shall bringe up my two sones Anthonye and Francis at schole until they be placed wth some master or until they cann write and reade. Item I give to everie of my fouer prentices [apprentices] 6s 4d apece. Item my will is that if my said wife shall refuse and doe not bringe up my children orderlie as aforesaid, that all my corne and graine growinge at Tedstone be reasonablie prised And that my wife shall paie unto them the value thereof towards their bringing up beside my other bequests.' He gave his brother Richard a doublet, a jerkin, a black coat and 'my must myll at Tedston'. He gave to

his brothers Richard and Charles: 'three score trees in Ladie Woode [in south of parish] which trees I had of Mr Wisham by covernant between him and me which trees shalbe equallie devided between my said brethren'.

The Stallards of Brierley
The Stallards had farmed Brierley (a lost farm of a half virgate near the Thrift) since at the latest 1558 when John succeeded on the death of his father, another John. John Stallard died in 1595 and clearly he had not been too certain about how his son Edward would turn out: he left him his cottage or house in Neldsley (another lost place) and two acres in the Riddinge (on southern parish boundary) and to pay 12d. rent pa for the house Briells [Brierley] where John was living 'yf the saide Edward will so be contente to enioye them & take them as a gifte From me his Father & if the saide Edward Stallward doe or cawse to be donne ani trowbles by law any vexation or anye huttes [hurts] against my wife or against my soonne John for any matter or cawse that then he the sayde Edward shall haue no part or portion of This my gifte ...'. Everything else was left to John after the death of his wife Ellinor. The delightful spelling is part of the charm in reading these documents. John's widow, Ellenor, died a year later in 1596, leaving 12d. towards the 'Reparacions' of the church. Repairs and restoration of the parish church is a problem that is forever with us which today's parishioners know all about, having just themselves completed a major restoration. Ellenor went on to leave a best feather bed, a second best feather bed and a flock bed to her three daughters, along with tablecloths, brass & pewter items, bullocks (colours specified, black, brown, spotted etc). Beds seem to be highly valued and often came first amongst bequests, and indeed one's own comfortable bed is one of the most important things in life! Her son Edward was to have some growing corn and a white sow with black spots. Everything else was left to her son John who was made her executor. James Stallard, probably the grandson of John & Ellenor, died in 1661, having made a lengthy will listing numerous household contents including the smallholding called Burbage (now gone, south of New House). His son, Richard, was assessed for two hearths (probably for Brierley) in 1664.

The Coninges of Whitwoods Croft
The Coninges were a prosperous family who farmed Whitwoods Croft. This was a sizable farm of one virgate, probably in the north-east of the parish that disappeared in the 18th and early 19th century reorganisations, see Chapter VI, page 116 Thomas Coninge left 3s. 4d. to the poor, his son Miles was to have a house and four acres in Tedstone Delamere, sons Anthony and Thomas were each left a house and land in Avenbury. Thomas was also left two leases of Whonall which may have been what is now represented by Primrose Cottage, and half of the family home (Whitwoods Croft).

It is worth reproducing most of Thomas's widow Ann's will, 1627, as it is full of interesting household items:

> First I geve unto my sonn Miles Coning a blanckett, one canvase, a peyr of hempen sheets, on pillow, five slipes of yearne [certain measures of yarn] & an half, a coffer vnder the windo a pipin [small earthenware pot] of butter, a pewter dishe a malt sive & hures [coarse cloth made from horse hair used for spreading the grain in the malt kiln], a mattocke & an axe, a brazen candellsticke, a dozen of trenchers, the second ketell, two barrels, a payle, halfe the wooll a peyr of sheets & half the hempe Item I geve to Mary his wife a smocke & a smocke peticote Item I geve to Anthonne Coning a blanckett, a bushel, a pewter dishe a brooch [spit], a dripping pann a paynted cloth & too bags, the third kettell, a wheele [spinning wheel], a lincke [upright drop for pot hooks] & pothooks a flaxen sheete & a peyr of sheets. Item I geve to Ann the daughter of Richard Coninge a Holland pillow beere [pillow case] Item I geve to Thomas Coning five slips of yearne & a half a coffer att the beds feete, a flascett, a salting tubb, a great skeele a … skeele, a pewter dishe a pott of brasse, an Iron wedge, a pickle a brasse candlesticke a hatchel a half hogge [half hogshead barrel] a bucking Cowle [washing tub] on brewery stoynd [stand for a barrel] a lethern bottell five shelfs half the wooll a flaxen sheete a peyr of s[hee]ts, three table napkins an andiron, a strake [piece of iron to tyre a cart wheel], nayls & other Iron & half the hempe. Item I geve to my daughter Jane a coffer att the beds [sy..e] a pewter dishe a brasse pan a frieing pan a gridiron a possnett the best peticotte & wast cott & the best of my weareing apparel Itm I geve to Ann Brucking a bede bolster a pewter dishe a brass pan the best ketell, a table cloth & a blew towel Item I geve to Ann Aiden the second peticote, a pewter dishe, a smocke & a waistcoat Item I geve to Zacy Aeden a peyr of sheets And make Thomas my sonn the sole executor of this my last will & testament.

This will helps us to picture life in a busy 17th century farmhouse and the many activities that went on within it. People had their own wool which they spun and weaving was carried out on some farms and also by professional weavers within the parish. Hemp was grown and used for coarser sheets; flax was still being grown and processed on the farm to produce the best linen sheets. A much coarser cloth was made from horse hair. Almost all clothes were home produced. Tanning leather was also carried out within the parish. Ann's son, the farmer, lived in the other half of the house, and that is why there were no dairying and brewing items mentioned in her will.

The Cappers of Pixhill

Another important Tedstone farming family were the Cappers. Richard Capper bought Pixhill in 1510. The will of Anne Capper who died in 1605 can't help but make the reader smile:

> Item I bequeath vnto Edmond Perkins my sonne in Lawe the some of fower pownd three shilling & fower penne of currant English money vpon condicon, that the said Edmond Perkins shall see me honestly broughte home which fower pownd three shilling & fower pennc debt my sonne William Capper doe owe vnto me the said anne Capper for catteles which the said William Capper had to Bargaine of me the said Anne Item I bequeath vnto the said Edmond Perkins the somme of fower pownd six shilling and eighte Penc of Currant Englishe money, which the said William Capper doe owe vnto me … for the rent of Pixall due vnto me for divers yeres Last past Item I bequeath vnto Anne, Susane, Roger, Katherine, and Elizabeth Perkins, the somme of fower pownd to be equally devided between them. Which fower pownd my sonne John Capper doe owe vnto me … foe one yocke of oxen which John Capper did sell for me diverese yere past. Item I bequeth vnto the fore said Anne, Susane, Roger, Katherine and Elizabeth the some of thirtie shilling my said sonne John Capper doe owe vnto me for a yocke of heyfferes which the said John Capper did bye of me the said Anne Capper for divers yeres past, and the said five shilling due for the Latter math [second growth of grass after a

hay meadow has been mown] of her medow Item I bequethe vnto John Perkins, the sonne of Edmond Perkins, one three yere olde Bullocke … which Bullocke was deliued vnto John Serre for divers yere last past …

And so the will continues! One doesn't know whether to be most sorry for Anne, her family or her poor executor! As we have read on page 53, her son, John Capper, was known for being rather a tiresome manorial tenant, enclosing land that didn't belong to him and not paying his dues. He died in 1614 holding the Line House, then a farm of one and a half virgates, so one of the largest in the parish; and Winley which he had bought from the Perkins for his daughter, Christiana, the wife of John Barnes. Another John Capper sold Pixhill to Edward Tymmings in 1712. The Cappers had held Pixhill for over 200 years and must have built the present attractive farmhouse.

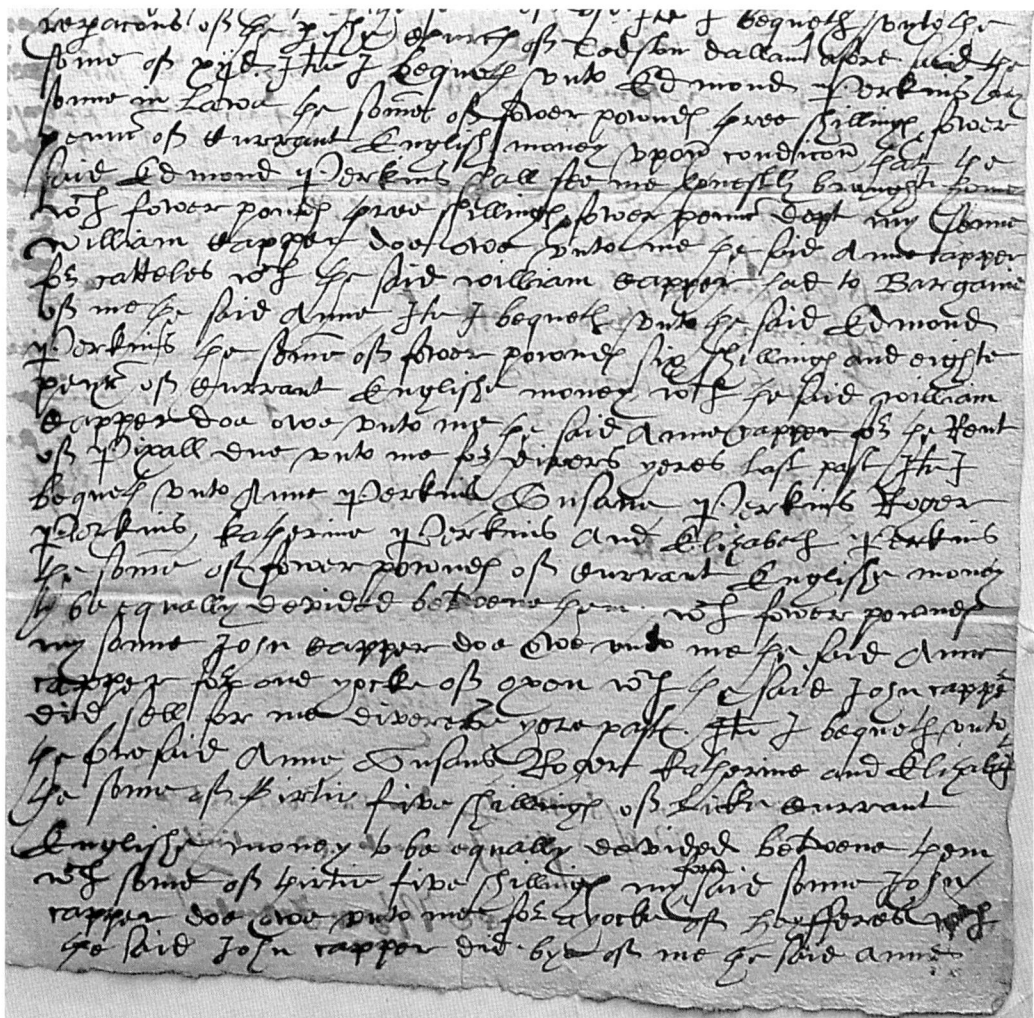

Part of the will of Anne Capper, widow.   *HRO*

Anne Gough, spinster, died in 1630. She had clearly been a fashionable lady with many clothes to bequeath. She left her black gown to Daniel Collins, the son of William Collins [of Tedney, Whitbourne] and a red petticoat; her green waistcoat was left to her goddaughter, Ann Dodson. To the 'Goodwife Saunders' she left her best 'Ruffeband and one smocke that is in my coffer and my best hat and one linen shocked apron'. She gave Anne Boswoode her best red wool petticoat, Katherine Perry her best green apron. She seems to have been related to the Ruffordes, a gentry family from Lower Sapey and she left Francis Rufforde £3 5s. that was in the hands of William Gabb and four cows in the keeping of Roger Rufforde, Francis's brother. Francis was made executor.

Examples of some inventories:
The following inventory is that of John Barnes who was probably living at either the Line House or at Winley. The Barnes family owned them both. The inventory lists the rooms of this seemingly and surprisingly rather modest establishment. Usually, if the hall has been ceiled a 'chamber over the hall' is referred to but this does not occur here so it is possible that this was still an open hall. From the description of the items, there would, as expected, have been a hearth in the hall and as there were 'pott hangings', some cooking went on there. One should realize that, in those days, rooms were multi-tasked and one frequently comes across beds in a parlour. Cooking here went on in the hall rather than the kitchen where there was no fire and which seems to have been used for mixing the dough and making beer and cheese. It appears that cooking also took place in the chamber where they must all have slept (five of them in the will). We are looking at an entirely different lifestyle to that of today; whole families slept together, there was no privacy, no bathrooms with a lock on the door, the privy outside could well have been a two or three-seater; life then was very matey! The division between living accommodation and farm was also less marked than today: hop treading holes are often found in 17th century houses proving that hops were commonly stored inside the house; malt and threshed grain were also often stored in the house as were hogsheads and barrels etc. If there was a cellar, it was often underneath the parlour, enabling the farmer to keep a close eye on his drink.

Line House.

Inventory of John Barnes, Yeoman, Tedstone Delamere, 5th April 1670

An Inventory of all and singular the goods Chattles & Cattle, late of John Barnes of Tedston Dalamere in the County of Herefford yeoman Deceased taken valued and prized the Fifth daye of Aprill 1670 in the Two & Twentieth Yeare of the Raigne of our Soveraigne Lord Charles the second by the grace of God Kinge of England etc by Edward Holder Rowland Barnes and William Barnes as followeth:

	£	s	d
Imprimis his wearing Apparell and money in his purse	3	0	0
In the Hall			
Item one long Table board with an old Frame Two Formes one shelf one Cratch[x] and Fower little Chaires one ioyned stoole one fire shovel one paire of Tonges one Andiron and Pott hangings	1	0	0
In the Kitchin			
Item one Malting Phatt one Meale trowe one Cheese Presse seaven Hogsheads nine half Hogsheads Two barrels one great skeel[∞] and other Treene Ware	4	10	0
one old ioyned Cupboard	0	5	0
In the Chamber			
Item one Ioyned tester bedstead one piece of wainscot and boardes lying in the Copp loft for the sealing thereof	2	10	0
one ioyned Chest two lowe bedsteads one Table board with another side board and one Coffer and a Cheese Cratch and Two Flasketts[#]	1	0	0
Item Two Dripping Panns Two iron spits & one paire of Cobirons	0	10	0
In the Chamber over the Kitchin			
Item one kill hair Cloath and one bagg of hopps	2	10	0
Malt and Graine in the house threshed	2	6	0
Corne in the Barne	0	12	0
Item Cider and Beere in the House	2	0	0
Item one iron Pott one brasse Pott and Two little brasse kettles	0	15	0
Item Butter and Cheese and other Provision in the House	5	0	0
Item one perry Mill	0	5	0
Item one Dung Wayne Two paire of Harrowes and the Tacklings of the Teeme			
Item plowe Timber and implements of Husbandry	2	0	0
Item Fower acres of Corne groweing upon the ground	2	0	0
Item one Grey Mare	4	0	0
Item three Cowes and Calfs	10	0	0
Item 12 Sheepe	3	13	4
Item three store swine	1	10	0
Item Debts oweing to the Testator at the time of his Decease by speciality	99	0	0
The Sume is	£148	6	4

Rowland Barnes)
Edward Holder his marke) Apprisers
William Barnes sen)

---

[x] A cratch in this context is likely to be a rack of some kind, a flight of shelves or less possibly a cradle
[∞] A skeel is a wooden bucket, pail or tub used for holding water or milk
[#] A flasket is an oblong or oval tub used for washing clothes

One is always surprised that so few stock were kept although as this was April, some livestock may well have been sold off before the winter and there was only a little corn left in the barn. We are still seeing very much a form of subsistence farming here with just a few stock, probably mostly for the family's own use. The occasional animal would be sold together with surplus dairy produce, poultry, fruit and vegetables to enable them to purchase those few things they would need and to pay the rates and taxes. The very small farmers rarely ate meat themselves, it was far too valuable.

Inventory of Richard Hill, Tedstone Delamere, buried 8th Jan 1678
A righte and true Invitarie of Richard Hill of Tedston Dallamere of all his goods and Cattell and all that he died Ceased of he was buried the eight day of Jenuarie in the yeare of our lord god one thousand six hundred sevente and eight 1678

	£	s	d
Item his wearing aprell and money in the house	1	0	0
Item one yoke of bollockes at	5	10	0
Item 4 Cowes and a Calfe	9	10	0
Item one yearling and 2 toyeareouls and 2 sheep and 4 piggs	4	0	0
Item 2 beeds and 2 beedsteds and furniture there vnto belonging	4	0	0
Item all the brasse and pewter	1	0	0
Item the hopes in the house	0	10	0
Item the Corne in the barne and Corne in the filde	3	0	0
Item the heaye and fodder in the barne	1	0	0
Item tacke of the Tieme and 2 hoghsheads and all other trumper vnthought	0	15	0
Item Richard Lawrence of Whitbourne Cooper owith [different hand]	0	14	8
The whole sume is	29	07	00

wee prisers heare vnto
haue put our hands
James Batman
The marke **J** of
John Fide
Thomas Lewes

The above is fairly typical of a small farmer who has died in harness. Often farmers near death have run down their stock and clearly have been living in retirement. Richard Hill died mid-winter so there was still food stored in the barn for the small number of stock. Sometimes the arithmetic is questionable as in the above example. Richard probably farmed at the Thrift, then just a quite small farm.

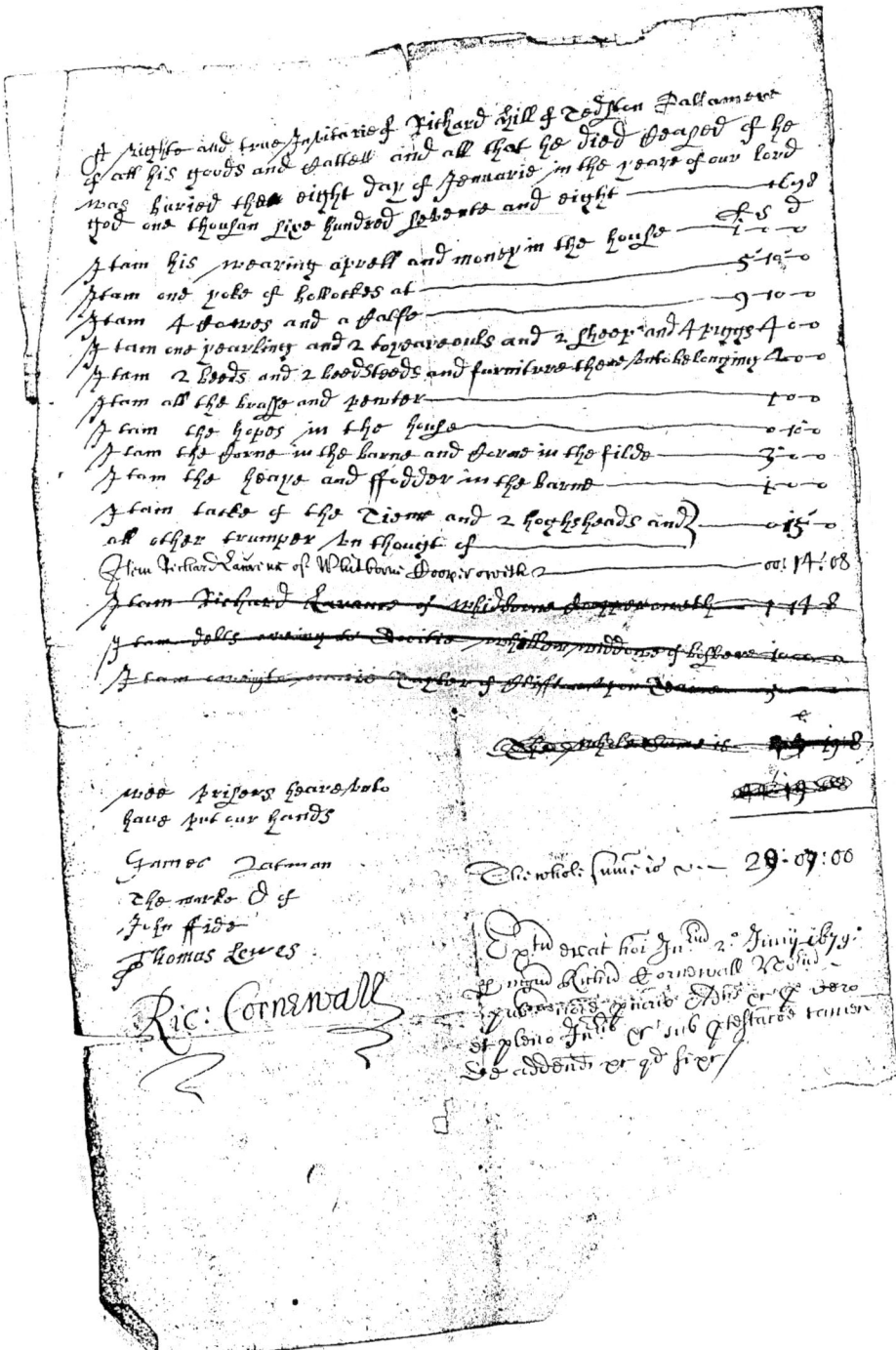

Inventory of Richard Hill. HRO

Catherine Coney, widow, died in 1665. She was assessed in the Militia Assessments for 15s. so we know she owned property (see page 56). She was clearly not farming at her death and her small inventory, which only included household items and the inevitable hogshead (everybody had their drink), is as follows:

	£	s	d
Item one bed steade	0	4	0
Item one featherbed one bowlster	0	6	0
Item one coverled one thumcloth	0	4	0
Item one paier of flaxen sheets	0	4	0
Item one paier of hempen sheets	0	3	0
Item one paier of hurden sheets	0	3	0
Item three tabell napkins & taborl cloth and all other linings	0	6	0
Item to brase pots	0	5	0
Item to brase kettels	0	6	0
Item 3 pewter dishes	0	2	0
Item 1 Cuboard	0	2	0
Item one halfe hogshead ... one skeele with all other coopiri ware	0	3	0
Item one table board & forme	0	4	0
Item to coffers & stoles	0	1	0
Item one friying pan ? and ...	0	3	0
Item all her wearing aparel	0	6	0
Item forti shillings of money wich William Joone oweth her	2	0	0

The whole sume is 4 pounds seaventine shillings 4 pence

Hear unto wee have pute our hands
Thomas Lewes   } Apprizers
Philip Hammand }

Most of the inventories were those of yeoman, husbandmen or their widows but some were for members of the clergy:

Inventory of James Parry, Clerk, 1671

	£	s	d
Imprimis his wearing Apparell & silver plate	£8	0	0
Item all his bookes	5	0	0

In the hall
Item one long table board upon a ioyned frame one old forme and a little piece of wainscott		7	8

In the kitchen
Itm Two great brasse kettles & three little brasse kettles & three brasse potts, one iron pott, two warming panes and three little posnetts	2	0	0
Item one iron jacke, two paire of Andirons & the pott hangings one fire shovell, one paire of tongues, three spits, one dripping pann, one paire of cob-irons and an old frying pan		10	0

Item nineteen pewter dishes, fower pewter plates, one pewter
Gunn, two Basons, three Chamber potts, one pewter candlestick

four small porringers and spoones and sallett dishes, a pewter Still and a tinn dripping pann	1	10	0
In the parlour Itm one table board & two ioyned formes, four old Chaires some other stooles and one paire of little Andirons		6	8
Item one ioyn'd tester bedstead with curtains and valance one feather bed and bolster and the furniture thereton belonging	2	0	0
In other lodging chambers Item two half headed bedsteads, three trundle bedsteads five feather beds, seaven feather boulsters, three paire of curtens with pillows, coverings and blankets hereunto belonging & one carpet & cushions	6	0	0
Itm Table cloaths, Sheets, Napkins & all other linens	6	6	8
Itm one chest three old trunks & one standing presse	1	0	0
In the Butterye Itm five old half hogsheads, one brewing vessel and all other treene ware	2	5	0
Itm all the hopps in the house	4	0	0
Itm corne & grain threshed in the house	3	0	0
Itm a little parcel of wooll		10	0
Itm all the provision in the house	2	0	0
Itm two kilnhaire cloaths		6	0
Itm all the corne & graine, haye & fodder in the Barn	5	0	0
Itm three cowes & one yeareling heifer	7	0	0
Itm one Mare & a young Colt	3	0	0
Itm Twelve Sheepe	1	4	0
Itm Two great swine, four little pigs & the poultry	1	0	0
Itm certain implements of husbandry		3	4
Itm the Mucke & Compost & the Wood in the yard	1	0	0
Itm all other things unnamed		10	0
Itm good debts owing to the deceased and ready money in the house	176	0	0
The sume is	236	18	4
Desperate debts owing to the deceased £5 The total sume is	£241	18	4

John Cooke
Richard Barnes   **X**   Apprisers
William Barnes

The wealthiest people in the parish, apart from the lords of the manor, were usually the clergy. This inventory of the rector, James Parry, was valued at £242. The rectory at the time, which seems to have been on the site of the Victorian rectory, was probably similar in size to the larger farm houses. James Parry was quite a wealthy man. He left no proper will but just a list of bequests to 32 individuals or bodies. The poor of Tedstone Delamere were to receive £10, a substantial sum, and for the church there was money for a communion table and a 'fair carpet'. He left a widow, Sarah. He had £176 invested, a considerable sum of money in those days ('good debts owing to the deceased' listed in the inventory above) and far more possessions than the average farmer. He had silver plate and books and 25 pewter plates and dishes. In the lodging chambers were such unheard of comforts as curtains, cushions and a carpet. At this time, the clergy themselves were farmers and 45 acres of glebe land was a good sized farm in Tedstone Delamere in those days. It was unusual to mention the 'little parcel of wool' at 10s. Surely most farmers had wool but it is not often listed in the inventories. It was also unusual to value the muck and compost and the wood in the yard.

A less common occupation was that of Richard Summers, a weaver. His possessions in 1696 were valued at £19 18s. and included 'utensils of the shop & trade' at £2. He also possessed two 'wheeles', probably spinning wheels which together with a warming pan were worth 8s.

Another inventory belonging to someone with a different occupation was the detailed one of John Cooke the Younger, tanner, who died in 1686. He was also a farmer and clearly quite a wealthy man with an inventory totalling £188 and probably farmed what is now Woodhall Farm. His household belongings were much the same as the smaller farmers only there were rather more of them and they included books, 'three little spinning wheels & a great one' and also five bushels of salt which was probably to do with the tannery but kept in the house to keep it dry. His farm stock, which was more than in the majority of inventories, included four oxen, four cows, a bull and two horses. Other items included:

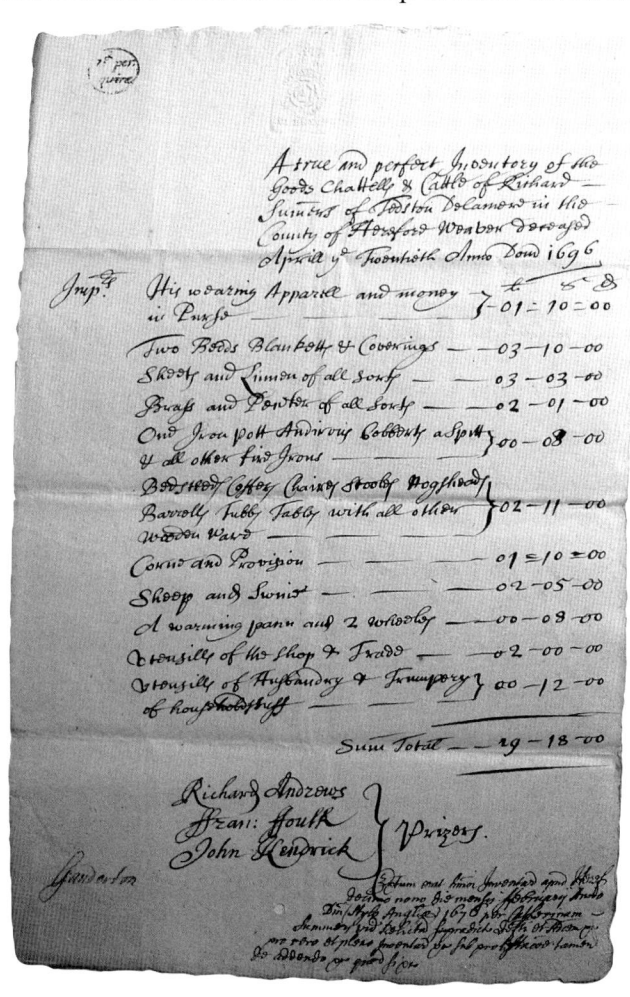

Inventory of R. Summers, weaver 1696.   HRO

	£	s	d
In the Tannage			
Bark valued at	20	00	00
The Tann phatts	18	00	00
Leather at	17	00	00
The bark mill at	01	00	00

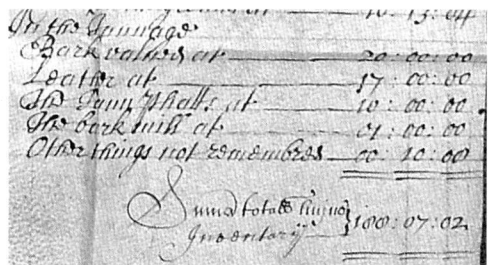

Part of inventory of John Cooke, tanner 1686. He probably lived at Woodhall. *HRO*

The oak bark was needed for the tanning process. With a tannery, it was important to have a reasonably good water supply. We don't know whether the tannery was at Woodhall but if it was somewhere else, one would perhaps have expected this to be mentioned.

Literacy

During the 16th and 17th centuries, only four out of a total of 26 people who made wills signed with their names, of whom two were gentry, one was a clergyman and one a yeoman (see Table 2, page 73). The wills of Elizabeth Cresswell, who held the manor, and George Dolman, rector, were proved by the Prerogative Court of Canterbury (PCC); they appear to be copies and so don't contain signatures. The remaining 20 people signed with a mark or not at all. Wills were usually made a very short time before death so it is possible that one or two might have been too ill but as we have read in Chapter I, at the end of the 16th century, all of the 15 churchwardens and parishioners signed the glebe terrier with their marks so clearly there had been no school in the parish. This is in marked contrast to the situation found in Edvin Loach where only 12.5% who signed the probate records in various capacities were *unable* to write their names: Allan Wyatt, in the manuscript for his forthcoming book on Edvin Loach, attributes this to the probability of a school in which children were taught by the rector. At this time the only people to teach children would have been the clergy.

It is noted in the following table that the five people who left bequests to the church died in the 16th century. Augustine Horner's bequest was to Whitbourne Church which he had probably attended. One asks oneself whether there was any significance in there being no bequests to the church after 1600. Were people poorer or less religious? Perhaps church rates were greater in the later period and people felt they had paid enough or was it something to do with the disillusion felt after the continuing troubles following the break with Rome and the 'chucking out' of so many church treasures given by local benefactors?

There were six bequests to the poor, four of them as cash and two in kind as bushels of corn but these were scattered through both centuries.

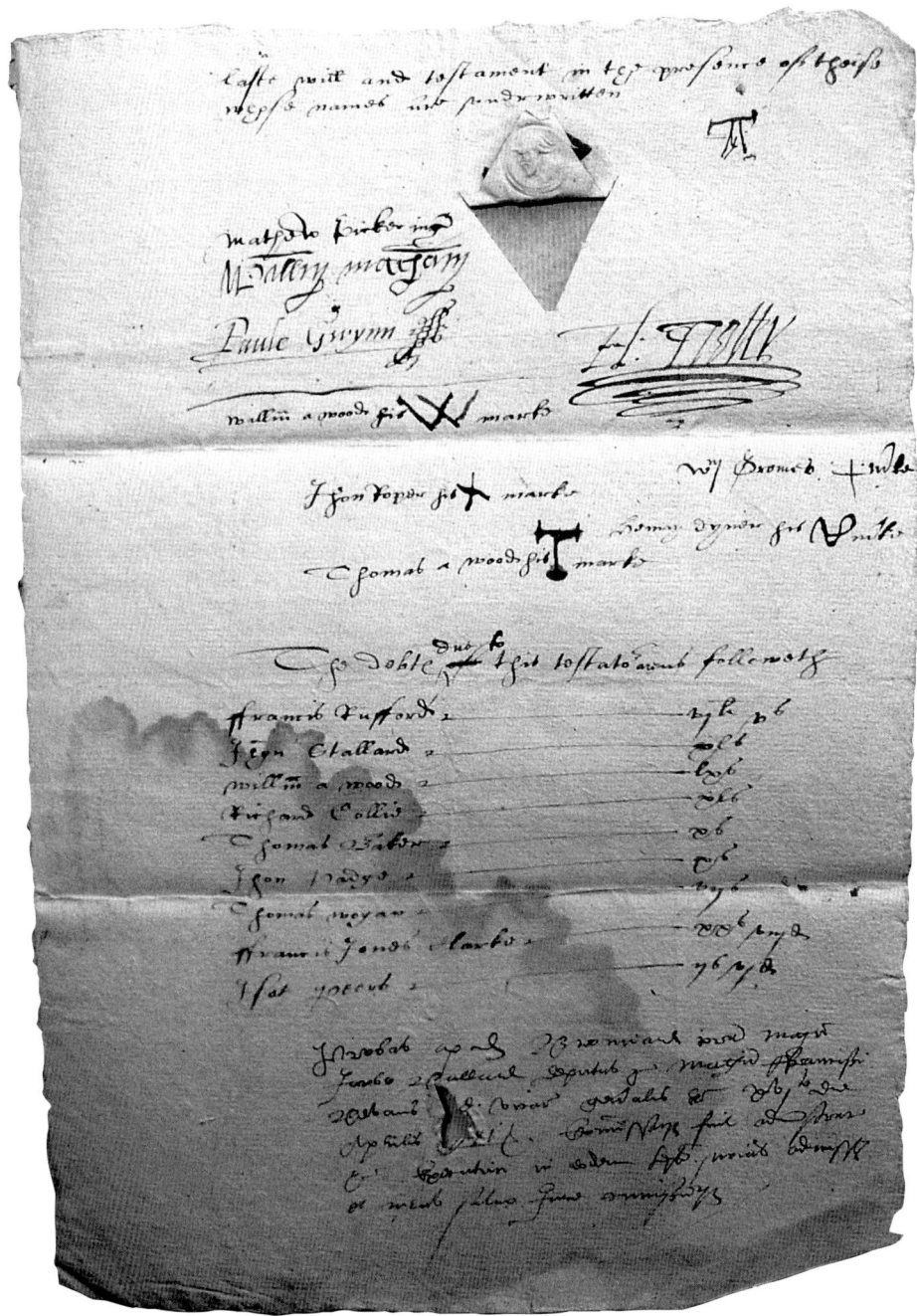

An interesting array of marks used by the illiterate witnesses to Augustine Horner's will in 1591. A list of Augustine's debtors follow. Augustine lived at Horner's Mill. His signature is the rather distinctive A (right hand top corner).

HRO

TABLE 2
TEDSTONE DELAMERE WILLS & INVENTORIES

Date	Name S = signature	Doc Will / Invent.	Status or Occ.	left Church	Poor	Value	House L = likely
1556	Edward Ingram	W	husbandman	6d.			
1558	John Peyrs	W		2s.			
1591	Augustine Horner	W	yeoman	3s. 4d.	2 bushels corn		Horners Mill
1592	Roger Conynge	W	yeoman			£97	Whitwoods Croft
1595	John Stallward	W					Neldsley ?
1596	Ellenor Stalard	W	widow	12d.			Brierley
1597	George Wysham S [1]	W	gent	6s. 8d.	10 bushels rye		Tedstone Court
1610	Richard Perkins	W	yeoman				Winley
1613	William Turford S	W	clerk (curate)				
1617	John Whitledge	W				£27	
1620	Thomas Coninge	W	yeoman	3s. 4d.			Whitwoods Croft
1630	Anne Gough	W	spinster				
1633	George Lane[2]	W & I	yeoman			£78	Gatley (Gatehouse)
1645	Elizabeth Cresswell[3]	W. PCC	widow		£5		
1660	Anne Stallard	W	widow				Brierley
1661	James Stallard S[4]	W	yeoman				Brierley
1665	Henry Norgrave	W & I	yeoman			£4	
1670	John Prattenton[5]	W	yeoman				
1665	Catherine Coney	I					
1670	John Barnes	W & I	yeoman			£148	Line Hse. or Winley
1671	James Parry	W & I	rector			£242	Rectory - L
1672	Richard Marston[6]	W & I	gent			£25	lodged at Court
1673	Mary Marston S	W	widow		£5		lodged at Court
1677	John Cooke senr [7]	W & I	yeoman			£49	Woodhall - L
1678	Richard Hill	I				£29	Thrift - L
1682	Richard Hackluit	W & I	yeoman			£52	
1686	J. Cooke the Younger[8]	I	tanner			£188	Woodhall - L
1689	Thomas Dolman[9]	W. PCC	rector		£2.10s		
1695	George Primrose S[10]	W	clerk				
1696	Richard Summers	I	weaver			£20	

[1] Wysham was lord of the manor. The church may never have got this bequest (see page 21)
[2] Formerly of Tipton
[3] Widow of Francis Wysham, lord of the manor. PCC will
[4] Also bequeathed Burbage. PCC will
[5] Security by land of £400 from James Newman of Chaddesley Corbett. PCC will
[6] Former steward of the manor, brother-in-law to Robert Mason, lord of the manor
[7] John Cooke senr. Managed a childish signature as a witness but did not sign his will
[8] Grandson of above
[9] PCC will. Also rector of Broom. Wealthy
[10] Nonconformist minister

The Tedstone Delamere inventories are listed below and the format for analysis here is similar to that used by Phyllis Williams in her books: *Avenbury and the ruined church of St Mary* and *The Three Stanfords, A History of Stanford Bishop, Stanford Falcon and Stanford Regis*, thus enabling a comparison to be made with these other parishes but it mainly enables comparisons to be made between the various Tedstone Delamere inventories. The inventories from the 18th century are included in the next chapter

TABLE 3
INVENTORY VALUES

A	Total value of inventory to nearest £
B	Value of farm livestock
C	Value of crops growing and harvested, including corn, grain, pulses and hay
D	Value of farm implements
E	Value of household goods including furniture, kitchen, provisions, hops, cider, flax, hemp etc
F	Money owing to or owed by deceased
G	Number of oxen
H	Number of cows
I	Number of other cattle
J	Number of sheep
K	Number of horses
L	Number of pigs or if mentioned
M	Number of rooms mentioned in house

Inventories Name of deceased	date of inventory	A £	B £	C £	D £	E £	F £	G No	H No	I No	J No	K No	L No	M No
1. George Lane, Gatehouse	1633	78	38	13	2	15	0	4	6	13	32	2	5	0
2. Catherine Coney	1665	5	0	0	0	3	2	0	0	0	0	0	0	0
3. Henry Norgrave	1665	4	0	0	0	4	0	0	0	0	0	0	0	0
4. John Barnes, Line Hse	1670	148	19	5	2	13	99	0	3	3	12	1	3	5
5. James Parry, clerk, Rectory	1671	242	13	9	0	31	5	0	3	1	12	2	6	6
6. Richard Marston gent. [steward]	1672	25	3	0	0	23	0	0	0	0	0	1	0	0
7. Richard Hill	1678	29	19	4	1	5	1	2	4	4	2	4	0	0
8. John Cooke the Elder, yeoman	1678	49	1	0	3	34	9	0	0	0	0	0	0	7
9. Richard Hackluit, yeoman	1682	52	0	0	0	3	40	0	0	0	0	0	0	0
10. John Cooke, tanner	1686	188	58	21	3	73	0	4	4	3	all	2	12	7
11. Richard Summers, weaver	1696	20	2	2	2	14	0	0	0	0	?		?	0

Richard Marston, gent. was brother-in-law to Robert Mason, lord of the manor, with whom he was living. His valuation was made by two of his brothers-in-law, so they were likely to have tried to keep it as low as possible. The inventory included a close stool; it seemed it was only the gentry who had such comforts!
Richard Hackluit must be retired. His household goods included 1 stall of bees.
John Cooke, tanner. His sheep are not numbered but described as 'all the sheep'.

It is difficult to ascertain from these documents how prosperous the community was at this time. One would expect that the 17th century farmers in Avenbury and Stanford Bishop in the more fertile Frome Valley would be more prosperous than those in Tedstone Delamere and so it has proved, but even in these parishes one is amazed at the very small numbers of stock kept and wonders how people ever made enough to live on, let alone build the wonderful timber-framed houses which anyone trying to farm on the same acreages today could only dream of doing. The Civil War must surely have had an impact in this area. Cromwell's soldiers engaged in target practice at Thornbury church, cannon balls having been found lodged in the masonry. The Scottish army is said to have marched along the B4203, living off the land and causing considerable damage. The Hearth Tax records tell us that in 1663, the occupants of 15 out of the 40 properties in the parish were not taxed on account of poverty. Table 2 has shown that several people left money or corn for the poor in their wills and some left money to the church; it will be noted in the following chapter that these charitable bequests become much rarer in the 18th century. To allow for inflation between then and now, the reader should consult the National Archives Currency Converter from which the following are brief extracts:

> £1 in 1500 would have the same purchasing power as £486 in 2005
> £1 in 1600 would have the same purchasing power as £100.64 in 2005.
> £1 in 1700 would have the same purchasing power as £78.09 in 2005

In the late 17th century a Herefordshire farm bailiff could earn £3 10s. a year plus his food and a living-in farm servant could earn £2 10s. a year.[43] A cow on average was worth £2 - £3 in the 17th century compared with today's average of very approximately £1000. And a sheep was worth between 2 and 6s. compared with today's average price of £100 for a ewe and £60 - £70 for a fat lamb. But it is almost impossible to make comparisons with today's prices because our expectations and requirements for modern living are so very different. Farmers in the 17th century were almost self-supporting. They fed and clothed themselves and their workers almost entirely from the produce of the land. They had their own milk for themselves and their workers and also for calf rearing but before the advent of refrigeration and better transport, milk could not be sold in any large quantity, any surplus being made into butter and cheese. The better off farmers had meat which they salted but the poor ate mostly cheese with occasional mutton and most people kept a pig and poultry. They could catch fish in the Sapey Brook and might have had hares and rabbits which may have been poached. Timber from the farm was used for buildings and repairs and the brash for firewood. The roofs were made either from stone quarried locally or were thatched. The majority of the farm buildings and cottages were still thatched before the 19th century. Furniture was basic; table boards on trestles and benches were probably home made. Tools were made by the local blacksmiths. People took their corn to one of the two mills to be ground into flour or feed for their small numbers of stock. They grew their own vegetables and they had fruit and by about 1600, one or two farmers were growing hops in the parish. Even the poorest farmers made cider and most made beer which they drank with every meal including breakfast. Tea was then an expensive luxury. We have already mentioned flax and hemp being grown and processed in the farmhouse and they used their own wool for their clothes. In the summer months, farmers' wives would go on market days to Bromyard, Clifton (when the market there was functioning) and even to Worcester with eggs, fruit, vegetables and other produce and the cash could be used to pay the rent and to purchase the few small items they might need. The roads in the winter were more or less impassable making travelling then very difficult. People did lend small sums of money and widows and others, particularly the elderly, regarded this as an investment providing them with an income. Larger sums might be invested in property as mortgages.

CHAPTER IV

The Eighteenth Century Manor and Tenants

We read in Chapter II how the Mason family who were lords of the manor in the 1600s were in increasing financial difficulties by the end of the century. In 1713 the manor, Tedstone Court and estate were sold by Robert Mason III to Richard Brompton of Chester Castle for £3031-3s-6d.[1] The fields were listed but no acreages were given; the various farms and cottages included Wooden End House (Woodend), Tidbatch, the Old House or Gabbes, Charletts and the water corn mill. (These seem to have been Demesne farms). It also listed the 'chief fee farms' of the manor (see below). Unfortunately, in order to scrape together a bit of extra cash, the Masons had sold off the advowson↔ and the parsonage house to the rector, George Hay, so that future owners of Tedstone Court would no longer be patrons of the living.

Chief Fee farms
The tenants held their land according to the customs of the manor which, as explained in Chapters II and III, originally involved rendering services to the lord by working on the demesne farm at busy times of the year but had long been commuted to a money rent: a fixed rent which at one time may have represented the value of the property. The holders of these, to all intents and purposes, freehold farms, owed these by now very small annual rents called 'chief rents' to the lord which seem to have been similar to ground rents; they might bequeath or sell their property to others in the same way as would a freeholder today but the heir or new 'owner' had to be admitted to the manor at a meeting of the manorial court and he had to pay a 'relief' to the lord: a sum of money that seems to have been equal to the annual chief rent. At each transaction, the outgoing or deceased tenant's best beast or perhaps a horse had to be paid to the lord as a 'heriot', usually now commuted to the equivalent in cash. These rents and reliefs only increased if a tenant's acreage increased so inflation lightened their significance over the years but the heriots remained quite a burden to farmers.

One of the last surviving rolls of a Court Baron is that of Richard Brompton, gent. in 1715. Thereafter, the manorial records consist mostly of numerous lists and memoranda, mostly undated, of tenants who had paid, or who owed chief rents, heriots and reliefs, frustratingly many without the names of their properties.

↔ Advowson - the right to present a priest to the parsonage or living

HRO

Impr.   We present all those ffreeholders that have made default heare this day and we merce them in 2d a peeice
Itm.   We present the death of the wife of John Best who dyed sence the Last Court possessed of a messuage called Ryley heariatable and that John Sallway Esq is next heier
Itm.   We lastly present all those Cottagers and others who have made any Inclosiers upon the Lord's wastes or Commons and paine them in three shillings and 4d apeeice

The new lord of the manor: George Webb

Richard Brompton lived at the Court for a short time but in 1726 the whole property was again for sale and was bought by George Webb, the younger, of Upper House, Shelsley Beauchamp. The sale included seats in the church, the farms as listed in the previous sale together with 'all that water corn mill … and all going and running gears, utensils and implements and tools belonging to the mill'.[2] The manorial mill was on the Sapey Brook, field names indicating that it was near Whitehall.[3] The following fields were included in the sale:

Upper House, Shelsley Beauchamp as it is today. Now re-named the Manor, this was the home of George Webb, followed by his Moore descendents.

The Wheatcroft	Binefield	three pieces called Small Stye
6 acres in Small Stye Field	Bare Croft	15 acres in the Church Field
Bach Meadow	the Little Orchard	Woefeilds Meadow
Great Meadow	Pigeon House Meadow	Orchard by Churchyard
The Bind Ox Leasow	Cow Pasture	Hamstall
The Bach	Quarry Piece	Hawks Bank
Ash Meadow		

Small Stye, Hamstall, Binefield, Bind Ox Leasow, Church Field and Hamstall were once part of common fields of the manor but by this date enclosure by exchange and purchase was well underway; 'Woefeilds' may be derived from the Old English *woh* meaning 'crooked' but the 'Church Field & Woful Meadow' on the tithe map of 1841 (Map 4, page 46) is just east of the Court and there is nothing crooked about its boundaries.[4] The lord's dovecot must surely have been in Pigeon House Meadow which may have been just north of the church. There are today plenty of buzzards over Hawks Bank.

With his purchase, George Webb only gained the freehold of Tedstone Court, Woodend, Tidbatch and two or three cottage holdings (the demesne). He started buying up more properties as they became available and, as we shall see, the pace of purchasing was later to be increased by his son-in-law, Robert Moore, and his grandson Robert, so that by the end of the century, the Moores owned most of the parish. Neither George Webb nor his descendants ever lived in Tedstone but continued to reside at Upper House, Shelsley Beauchamp or in Birmingham.

In 1736, a useful list of the inhabitants was compiled for George Webb and is recorded as follows:

> A true list of all and Singular the names of inhabitants lying within the parish of Tedstone Delamere in county of Herefs both freeholders in possession & those at present lett to tenants alsoe all cottagers living upon the waste with enquiry to the Estates that are Heriotable & pay or ought to pay Chief Rent to the Lord and owe suite & services to George Webb Gent. Lord of the said manor whose court is to be held at … Court House in Tedstone on Tuesday the 2nd of November by … forenoon.[5] [This may well have been the last court ever held.]

All freeholders in possession
The Rev. John Hays, Rector [Line House]
Benjamin Lane, Gent [Hill Cross]
James Bateman, Gent [Woodham]
John Barnes, [Winley]
John Phillips
Willm. Creece [Burbage]
James Yapp
Richard Brazier
Thomas Brazier [Brierley]
Thos. Norman for late Caswels [Gate House]
Unett Hodges Gent [Horners Mill]
Richd. Cooke Gent [Woodhall]
William Acton
John Price
William Smith

Cottagers
Susannah Hill
Tho. Sanders
Francis Parsons
Susannah Busso?
Rich. Rowley
Frances Smith, wid [deleted]
John Long
Ann Williams
Anthony Moore
Richd. Eaton
Elizabeth Caswal
Ann Soul?

Lands tenanted with names of owners
Richard Brazier for Mr. Higgins Lands [Thrift]
Thos. Brazier for … Adams Lands
Benjamin Baugh for 3 messuages held under the lord of the Manor
The Wid. Philpotts for Turners Land
Aaron Cooke for ? Land
Mary Ford & ? Goodacre
Thos. Creese for … Land
Joseph Somers for Ld. Foleys Land [Hedge House]
Tho. Baldwayne for   ditto
Wm. Bufton for Mr. Yapps Land
Peter Broome tenant to the Lord [Tedstone Court?]
Richd. Cony for Fra. Griffiths Land

An account of chief rents and reliefs 1736. HRO

We can't equate these lists of 41 holdings (pages 79 & 80) with households because one or two of them may have been land only. There are 12 cottagers living 'upon the waste' and some of these appear in an earlier list of people who were presented at the manorial court in 1713 for illegally 'erecting cottages and for enclosing commons within the manor. In order to get the most out of his new investment, the lord would need to know all the holdings of his manor, the names of the holders, the rents paid and any heriots and reliefs that might be due. The majority of the eighteenth century manorial records consist of lists of tenants together with rents, heriots and reliefs paid or pending and the following is a typical example:

1st May 1739. Memorandum of Rents received for George Webb Esq Lord of the Manor of Tedstone Delamere[6]

Recd of Widow Philpotts twenty shills being for one whole years rent	01	00	00
Recd of Mr. John Huck twelve shills for 3 years Cheife rent from Pixall	00	12	00
Recd from [ditto] two shills being one years Cheife rent from Grays Farme	00	02	00
Recd of Tho. Brasier one pound fower shills for three years Cheife rent …from Bryalls Farme	01	04	00
Recd of Benjm. Baugh twenty shills for 3 years Cheife rent for Woodham farme late Mr. Batemans and also recd at the time five shills due at ye decease of Mr. Bateman … for a Relieff	01	00	00
Recd of Mr. James Yapp for 3 years Cheife rent	01	07	06
Recd of Thos. Norman fifteen shills for 3 years Cheife rent [Gatehouse]	00	15	00
Recd of Wm. Crees … 3 years Cheife rent [Winley]	00	17	06
Recd of Edward Hawker one pound for 3 years Cheife Rent from Richd Cooks estate and for a Reliffe due at ye death of ye sd Mr Cooke [Woodhall]	01	00	00
Recd from Mr. Lane for 3 years Cheife rent for Yelds Cross [Hill Cross]	00	01	06

Widow Philpotts who heads the list paid a 'rent' for a property which was probably part of the demesne. All the others were 'Chief Fee Farms' held according to the customs of the manor as explained above. It seems that the chief rents for the latter had not been collected very regularly and it may be that by this date, the annual sums seemed comparatively insignificant and so perhaps it was easier to let them build up.

There is an interesting double entry account agreed and settled between John Ingram, on behalf of George Webb, lord of the manor, and Charles Holland, administrator of the late rector, Rev. John Hay: Mr. Webb is billed for the tithe of three acres of coppice, for a year's rent of an acre of glebe land due Lady Day 1739 at 5s. a year and for 'Damages and costs agreed to be paid for seizing the horse for a heriot'! The rector's administrator is billed for four years chief rent due Lady Day 1740 for the Line House at 14s. 2d. a year and for a relief on Mr. Hay's death of 14s. 2d. One wonders what on earth the damages were for in connection with the taking of the horse, presumably by an over zealous bailiff![7]

TABLE 4
Eighteenth Century Wills and Inventories[8]

	Date	Name S = signature	Will / Inventory	Status or occupation	Money to church	Bequest to poor	Value £	House L = likely P = possible
1	1700	Thomas Lane	I				209	Tipton
2	1714	Elizabeth Lane	W & I	widow		£1	194	
3	1719	William Creese	I				13	
4	1726	Moses Perkins	I				31	
5	1728	Sarah Brazier	W & I	widow			10	
6	1728	George Hay S	W & I	rector			109	Rectory
7	1729	Richard Ford S	W & I	gent			31	Tennall - P
8	1729	William Kerry	I				189	
9	1730	Jeremiah Postans	I				54	Gate Hse - P
10	1731	Thomas Lane - S	W & I	gent			231	Tipton
11	1731	Catherine Perkins	I	widow			20	
12	1731	Humphrey Postans	W & I				158	Gate Hse - L
13	1735	Elizabeth Kerry	W & I	widow			423	
14	1736	Robert Mason S	W & I	gent		£10		
15	1737	John Phillips	I				153	Woodend - P
16	1737	Richard Cooke S	W & I				141	Woodhall
17	1738	Richard Hill	I				10	
18	1742	Thomas Brazier	W & I				7	Lee Lay - L
19	1771	Peter Branch	W	mason				
20	1781	Edward Price	W	yeoman			20	New House
21	1782	William Chrees	W	yeoman				Winley

Notes
1. Thomas Lane. £60 in inventory included hay, a large sum
2. Elizabeth Lane. Wid. of Thomas Lane of Tipton. Lived with daughter at Tedney in Whitbourne. Inventory included a 'desperate debt' of £156 owed her by her son for arrears of rent at Tipton
6. George Hay. Bequests included advowson purchased from Robert Mason, lord of manor
7. Richard Ford. Bequests included land in Lower Sapey & Clifton
8. William Kerry. Inventory included 65 acres of corn, a large acreage, but where?
9. Jeremiah Postans. Inventory included £53 due upon Speciality, probably providing income for his old age. Inventory total was only £54 (see above table)
12. Humphrey Postans. Inventory included £96 due by bond
13. Elizabeth Kerry. Sister of late rector, G. Hay. Inventory included £294 in bonds
14. Robert Mason. PCC will. Former lord of manor
15. John Phillips. Inventory included £18 worth of hops at Worcester
20. Edward Price. Also held ½ Little Riley in occupation of W. Long
21. William Chrees. Also held Burbage

Only five of the 10 people who made wills were sufficiently literate to write their names. This compares with four out of 24 from the 16th and 17th centuries. Of those five above, one was a rector, three were gentry and one was surprisingly styled as 'husbandman'; this was Richard Cooke who farmed Woodhall. It is noted that

Thomas Lane was styled as 'gent' although previously the family had been 'yeomen'; but Thomas was educated and upwardly mobile. It does though appear that there probably had been no school in the parish.

As in the 17th century, nobody left money to the church although there had been several such bequests in the 16th century (see page 21) for possible reasons for this). It is also noted in Table 4 that only two people left money for the poor, one of whom was Elizabeth Lane, a widow, formerly of Tipton, who left £1; and Robert Mason, former lord of the manor, who more generously gave £10. It does seem though that people were tired of giving money to the poor and probably thought they had paid quite enough already through their poor rates. Nationally, during the 18th century, the numbers of poor were becoming an ever increasing burden for parishes to maintain. The only record found concerning the poor is a list of ratepayers entitled 'A Lewne made by the overseers of the Poore of the parish of Tedstone Delamere for Collecting Money for the poore at 2d. in the pound to be Collected monthly as oft as needful in the year 1739' (see Appendix E). The significant words are *as oft as needful*! There were 33 properties assessed for amounts ranging between 4s. 2d. for the Court, to 1½ d. for Held Cross (Hill Cross); not only farmers but smallholders and some cottagers were included. It is therefore understandable that there were only two bequests to the poor during the 18th century. To read more about the parish poor, see Chapter XI entitled 'The Cottages'.

Land Tax
The land tax was another unpopular tax, first levied in 1692; at that time it was not only on land but on other property as well including shops, carriages, wagons and servants but these proved difficult to collect and it later became restricted to land. Land was taxed on income; the other categories were presumably taxed on capital values. The tax records available to us are 1777 – 1831 and are on land only;[9] they can be a useful link between earlier records and the tithe survey in 1841. Between 1779 and 1832 the assessments were used as the record of qualification to vote in parliamentary elections; the returns were made by local assessors who were nominated by special Commissioners appointed for that purpose; a copy of the assessment was pinned to the church door to give an opportunity for appeal.[10] An assessment consisted of lists of names of the landowners, their tenants and the sums assessed; occasionally the name of the farm was given as well:

TABLE 5
Land Tax Assessment made in the Parish of Tedstone Delamere in the County of Hereford for the year 1790 at 4/- in the Pound

Proprietors	Occupiers	Property	Sum Assessed £	s	d
Lord Foley	John Lawrence	[Hedge House]	3	13	0
Wm. Norman	Anthony Norman	[Gate House]		16	8
Rev. Mr. Tomkyns	Wm. Smith	[Glebe]	3	19	8

Proprietors	Occupiers	Property	Sum Assessed £	s	d
James Lane	James Lane	[Hill Cross]		2	8
John Chrees	John Chrees	[Winley]	1	9	10
Ditto	Ditto	Burbage		6	8
Rev. Mr. Broome	Thos. Wood	[Line House]	2	3	0
Thos. Haynes	Thos. Haynes	[Homs]	1	9	10
Martha Brazier	Martha Brazier	[Upper Line House]		1	9
Philip Griffiths	Philip Griffiths	?		1	9
Edwd. Price	Edwd. Price	[Stone House]		5	8
Benjn. Birch	Benjn. Birch	[Horners Mill]		16	8
James Moore Esq	Rich. Wight	[Tedstone Court]	4	4	0
Ditto	John Craddock	[Woodend/Primrose]	5	1	6
Ditto	Thos. Grubb	[Woodhall]	2	12	0
Ditto	Mary Mortiboys	[Dones]		4	0
Ditto	Jn. Beddinton	[Brierley/Thrift]	3	16	0
Ditto	Jn. Caswell	[New House?]	2	4	0
Ditto	Ditto	Mazer		8	8
Ditto	John Berry	[Riley]	2	14	0
Ditto	Thos. Corbett	[Lee Lay?]		1	9
Ditto	Jos. Barnbrook	[Pixhill]	1	19	10
Ditto	Ditto	Grays Farm	1	3	4
Lord Foley	Ditto	Farm Meadow		10	0
James Moore Esq	Ditto	Mill Land		5	0
Ditto	Richd. Portman	[Lower Tidbatch ?]		1	9
Richd Jones Esq	Thos. Knill	[Tipton]	3	19	8
James Moore Esq	late Turner	?		3	6
			41	19	4

Notes
The property names in square brackets are not recorded in the Assessment but have been gained from title deeds and other documents. The property names without brackets are in the Assessment. The Assessment is chiefly notable for showing the extent of the Moores' acquisitions by 1790. The Court is in the tenure of Richard Wight to whose son, Richard, the property was eventually bequeathed in 1805. Woodend appears to have been merged with Primrose which was a farm assessed at 19s. in a 1777 twice yearly assessment, thus making Woodend the largest holding in the parish, see Map 11, page 225 showing the whereabouts of Primrose Cottages, the old farmhouse. Dones is a lost smallholding that was probably near the Thrift. John Berry farmed Riley which still maintained its separate identity as a farm. John Barnbook farmed Pixhill and Grays, still separately listed.

In 1798 the tax was fixed perpetually at 4s. in the pound. Provision was made for landowners to redeem their tax by paying a lump sum and Tedstone Delamere landowners took full advantage of this. By 1818, the Rev. Mr. Broome had redeemed the tax on the Line House as had John Chrees on Winley, James Jones on Tipton, and the two major landowners, Edward Moore and Richard Wight had redeemed tax on all their properties. By 1819, the only people still being assessed for land tax were the following:

Proprietors	Occupiers	Sums Payable		
		£	s	d
Glebe Land	Rev. Mr. Darcy	3	19	8
Lord Foley – Hedge House	John Lawrence	3	13	0
Ditto – Farm Meadow	Richd. Wight		10	0
Anthony Norman – Gate [House]	Anthony Norman		16	8
Winwood – Prices	Tomkins		5	8
Thos. Haynes – the Homes	Thos. Haynes	1	9	10

The Homes or Hams was a holding near the Whitbourne boundary and south of Whitehall, shown on the tithe map as fields: Ham Field, Ham Hopyard, Little Ham Meadow, Ham Meadow, the Hams etc

The Moore family who enlarged the estate

George Webb, lord of the manor, died in 1757. In his will proved 1759, he left his wearing apparel, both woollen and linen, to his servant Thomas Jones, 'to be delivered to him immediately after his decease'; his servant John Fisher was to get a small annual pension of 10s. As his son had predeceased him, George left his estate jointly to his wife, Mary Webb, and his daughter, Ann Moore, 'and because it is my mind that the husband of my said daughter should not intermeddle or have anything to do with my estates or effects', he arranged for the appointment of trustees.[11] Future records show that her husband does seem, though, to have had a pretty free hand in the estate management. Ann Webb had married Robert Moore who was a wealthy edge toolmaker from Birmingham.

Tools by Robert Moore of Birmingham, lord of the manor. *The Colonial Williamsburg Foundation*

> Early in the eighteenth century, Birmingham was an important producer of edge tools. As transportation throughout England improved, London tool retailers came to rely on products from Birmingham, Sheffield and Lancashire .... The name of Robert Moore (possibly father and son) is to be found on blades dating from 1721 – 1776 in London planes.[12]

The early date of 1721 suggests that Robert's father started the business. The business is mentioned in Birmingham Directories as being at Cherry Orchard in 1767 and his son, Robert, as working from 9 Cherry Street from 1770 – 1791 and his second son James was mentioned in the business in 1788.[13]

Robert and Ann Moore and their son Robert were to have a great impact on Tedstone Delamere. During the 18th century, it was they, like many others at this time who had made their money from industry, who invested in land. Farmland at this time was a very good investment. The Moores bought up farms, smallholdings and cottages and once in their ownership, they were able to reorganize the land into larger and more viable holdings. They bought almost all the land to the east of the Sapey Brook together with Pixhill, Gray's farm and Cullets Hill on the west side and this is covered in subsequent chapters.[14]

The Tedstone Delamere estate is split in two
In 1777 Ann Moore willed the estate to her daughter Mary,[15] who made it over to her elder brother Robert, earlier provision having already been made for her. James, the younger son, had been left the business in Birmingham. Robert Moore died a bachelor 16 years later and the property passed in 1793 to his brother James (see the Moore family tree, page 115). James Moore was also childless and on his death in 1805 came the break up of his estates, for as well as Tedstone Delamere, he owned property in Birmingham, Kings Norton, Alvechurch, Lower Sapey and Shelsley Beauchamp; Tedstone Court and Manor, together with Pixhill, Grays Farm and Cullets House were left to his cousin Richard Wight who, following his father before him, was already the tenant of Tedstone Court. James Moore had also owned the Hill Farm, Lower Sapey;[16] its land adjoined the Thrift and would have 'marched' well with his Tedstone Delamere estate; he left the Hill to the family of his friend, Joseph West, of the Homme, Clifton-on-Teme, who was one of his executors. He left his property in Tedstone Delamere lying to the east of the Sapey Brook, together with his interests in Shelsley Beauchamp, to another cousin, Edward Moore, who had been farming at Alvechurch.[17] Thus the Sapey Brook again divided two estates as it had in Anglo-Saxon times. The farms and cottages on the east side of the parish subsequently became part of the Whitbourne Hall Estate in the 1860s.

CHAPTER V

Farms and Smallholdings to the West of the Sapey Brook - before 1841

For convenience of handling, farms and smallholdings have been divided into chapters before and after 1840, the date of the tithe survey. This invaluable survey provides us with the earliest large scale map of the whole parish and for the first time, the names of the landlords and tenants of all the farmsteads, cottages and fields together with the field names and their use. From this base, it has been possible to work backwards and forwards in time. The farms have also been divided by location west or east of the Sapey Brook. This chapter traces the owners and occupants of farms and smallholdings to the *west* of the brook from earliest times until 1841, and are in order of their size in the tithe survey of the same date.

The Sapey Brook
The name 'Sapey' may be derived from the Old English *saepig* meaning 'sappy' or 'full of sap'.[1] The Sapey Brook rises in Upper Sapey, flowing down through Lower Sapey, entering Tedstone Delamere just to the north of Winley by Waste Common and continues through the parish, dividing it in two from north to south as will be seen from Map 1, inside front cover. The land rises steeply from this brook on both sides and the crossing places are difficult especially in wet weather. At the Conquest, when there were two manors in what was to become Tedstone Delamere, it seems almost certain that the natural division of the brook was the boundary between these two estates. Again, approximately 740 years later in 1805, the brook once more became the boundary between estates when James Moore bequeathed his Tedstone Delamere property, splitting it between two cousins, Richard Wight, who inherited the part of his estate to the west of the brook, and Edward Moore who inherited that part of the estate to the east of the brook (to be covered in Chapters VII and IX). The brook is a significant barrier dividing the west from the east. Surprisingly, there are people today living on the west side who have no idea that almost half their parish lies the other side of the brook! To walk beside the brook, particularly at the time of year when the bluebells are out, is something not to be missed and the brook-side cottages known as 'Paradise' were aptly named. Duncumb, writing in 1812, takes up almost as much space romancing about the brook as he devotes to his factual history of the parish:

> Through this parish flows also the brook from Sapey, remarkable for its finely flavoured trout and its romantic beauties. It is also remarkable for a traditionary account of a miracle which is still implicitly credited by the common people: According to this account, a mare and her colt having been stolen in the night from a neighbouring farmer, some centuries past, his daughter (with whom the mare was a great favourite), prayed that she, attended by some of

the servants in the family, might be enabled to trace the retreat of the thief by the footsteps of the animals stolen. These footsteps were discovered without difficulty until the pursuers reached the brook, but on the opposite side no vestige whatever was discernable. It then occurred to the damsel that the robber might have taken his booty down the rocky channel of the stream, in order to evade detection. She had not proceeded far along its bank, before she exclaimed, "My prayers are heard: for see, here are the marks of the hooves in the solid rock." Directed by these supernatural impressions, it is understood that she and her attendants proceeded and discovered the robber in a most romantic spot called "the Witchery Hole," or as some contend "the Hoar Stone" .... Many pretended vestiges of the mare and colt are still pointed out in the channel of the brook by the credulous peasantry, and many more have been cut away by the felon chisel to deck the simple mantle-piece of the rustic naturalist.[2]

A variation of this story is that the horse thief was a man named Gray; he reputedly hid for several days in a barn a short distance from the brook which became subsequently known as 'Gray's Barn'.[3] In fact, Gray's Barn was part of a small farm that was amalgamated with the Pixhill estate in the late 18th century (see page 103). In 1353, there was a grant by John de Grye of Tedstone Delamere to Miles alte Walle of Clifton of all his lands ... in Tedstone, except two messuages, one of which was called 'Le Grye Place'. Surely this personal name is the less romantic but factual origin of the name 'Gray's Barn'? All now remaining of Gray's Farm is a ruined farm building buried in the wood.

THE FARMS

Tedstone Court is covered in Chapters II, IV, VII and XIII and the Glebe Farm in Chapters I and VIII.

1. Tipton Hall

Tipton lies on the west edge of a small concentric field system and in the centre of a larger concentric field system (that encompasses the smaller one) delineated on the north side by a stream. It is suggested that it may therefore be the focus of an early settlement.[4] Of the various early spellings of the name 'Tipton' place-names expert John Freeman considers that the name, *T(h)wypelton,* recorded in an Assize Roll of 1292[5] is probably the nearest approximation to the original form, the first element *Twi* or *Twy* probably means 'double, two'. It is possible that the next element beginning with 'p' might be Old English *pol* or *pull* 'a pool, pond'. If this was the meaning, we are looking at a 'double pool' to which the element *tun* 'farmstead' was added later. Satisfactorily, there were until recently two pools to the front of the house. Field name evidence from the tithe survey of 1841 indicates the presence of a moat; this is remembered but signs have now disappeared under the concrete yard and buildings.

This pool at Tipton is no longer there; there were two further pools at the front of the house. The lower of the buildings on the left was one of the buildings destroyed in a serious 20th century fire.

Benbow Family

Another early record of Tipton is in 1324 when a man with the interesting name of 'Pagan' of Tipton granted a rent to John of Wysham and Hawis his wife:

> By deed poll Pagan of Twypton [Tipton] grants to John of Wysham Knight and Hawis his wife 3s yearly rent issuing out of lands in Tedeston de la Mare viz. 2s out of a tenement which Richard de Bruton and Cicely his wife held for their lives & one shilling which William of Pykeshale [Pixhill] held for his life and the reversion of the said tenements after their deaths to hold to the said Sir John of Wysham and his wife and the heirs of Sir John in fee.[6]

In 1440, John Boteler was presented to the manorial court for non-payment of rent;

> Homage present that John Boteler, free tenant of lands and tenements ... called Twypperton, through John Grye, John Massy and John Stalleward his tenants of the property used to pay to the lord, without being forced to do so, 2s as well as 6d rent for the land. And Hugh Hakeley, former parson who obtained the property later paid the same to Richard Wysham who was then lord of the manor. This 2s has been withheld for the last 16 years.[7]

In 1600, Tipton was sold by John Hopton of Bitterley, Shropshire, gentleman, to Arthur Jarvis and the tenants were John and Joan Lane and George Lane. The Lane family had been tenants here for some time: under the 1543 Subsidy Act, William Lane was assessed at £9 18d., the highest band in the parish and we know from the following extract from a 1588 court roll that William was almost certainly living at Tipton:

Tipton, view of north side, 1931.   *Reproduced by kind permission of English Heritage*

> Richard Hopton esq has not come to court to show evidence to excuse his non-payment of 2s 6d annual rent for lands in Tedstone called Tippton late in the occupation of John Lane and now of Joan Lane widow. He was ordered to do so by a court held 16th April 1583 and a pain of 30s was laid on him which he incurred, but it was respited. Furthermore the homage say that Richard Hopton withheld the said rent since before the death of William Lane right up to the present time, as appears more fully in the court rolls. The bailiff is ordered to distrain on him for the back rent and to answer to the lord for the arrears.[8]

Richard Hopton lived in Shropshire and perhaps it wasn't easy for him to make the payment. There was a kind of banking system then but it would probably not be used for paying small sums like this. He would have had to ride over with the cash or else send a servant. This is the same small fixed rent of 2s. 6d. paid for Tipton in 1440 by John Boteler (see previous page). In 1623, George Lane purchased the property from Jarvis.

The Lanes and their important house
As the property was moated, it was clearly of high status; in the deeds, the property is described as a manor; this would have been a sub-manor to the main manor of Tedstone Delamere. In the very early days, it may have had its own field system but this does not appear in the records where there are references only to rents being paid for it to the lords of Tedstone Delamere. Part of the house dates back to medieval times. We are fortunate that Jim Tonkin carried out an investigation of this house in the 1970s and his report is as follows: [9]

> This is an interesting example of a medieval house which was largely rebuilt during the 17th century and added to again in the 18th and 19th.
>
> There is little evidence of the medieval house left today but there is sufficient evidence to show that there was such a building and to give some idea of its size. In the attic over the central block are two posts about 6 feet from the east wall. They are in the position of spere posts marking the line of the screen between the entry passage and the hall. If these are spere posts it means that the present east (kitchen) wing is probably still fulfilling its original function of a service wing to the hall.

Spere posts were part of a spere truss, a screen that projects from the side walls to block off the view into the medieval hall from the crosspassage doorways. In a high status building, they were sometimes quite elaborate.

> The other cross-wing (parlour wing) seems to be later. It probably replaced an earlier wing, but it is possible that there was not a wing at this end in the original building. Thus it seems likely that there was a medieval house with a hall about 20 feet by 15 feet with a service cross-wing with kitchen and pantry downstairs and two chambers up and possibly a parlour wing at the other end. A glance at the back of the house shows the big, square panels in the service wing and the smaller, later panels in the parlour wing.
> The original hall probably had an open hearth somewhere in the middle and the smoke got out through a louvre in the roof.
>
> Unfortunately, this original roof, which was probably well carved, has been entirely replaced by one in the 17th century.

A year after the Lanes purchased Tipton, it was the subject of a marriage settlement between George Lane the Younger and Sarah Hill; the house and fields were split between the parents, George the Elder and Joan, and the young couple, and how they were to do it is carefully laid down in the deeds: the newly-weds were to have the parlour and buttery and two chambers over the said buttery and parlour and the two cocklofts over the chambers. So often, as happens today when a family purchases a house, the first thing they do is to spend money improving it. This parlour crosswing, which may have replaced an earlier one, was probably built, according to Tonkin, early in the 17th century so it was most likely built specially for the young couple. The newly-weds were also to have the stable and lower barn and the following fields: Upper Croft 4a, Pool Close (pasture) 2a, Hill Croft (arable) 8a, Upper Smallflies[×] (arable) 7a, Smallflies[×] (meadow) 1a, Hillgrove (meadow) 4a, Birchey Leasow (arable) 8a, Bromylands (2 parcels of arable and pasture) 9a, Stocked land alias the Squire 8a, West Field (pasture) 2a, Hallow Batch[1] and Hallow Batch Bank (pasture) 3a, Hopyard ½ a (this is quite an early date for the production of hops), Hollands (pasture) 8a, totalling 64 ½ acres. The parents were to have the residue of the property for life.[10] An interesting field name, which was probably included in the part retained by the parents, is mentioned in the court rolls of 1621 when George Lane was ordered to repair a hedge in a field called *Dedman's Furlonge*. This is marked on the 1841 tithe map as being immediately NE of the Tipton farmstead. This field name is often connected with a bad death, perhaps where there had been a gibbet, and was often situated at a crossroads, beside a road or on a parish boundary.[11] This particular field is beside the road leading from Tipton to Winley and beyond.

So once they had bought the farm, the Lanes had set about modernising their medieval house. George, senior, died in 1633 and his will tells us that he was then living at the Gate House. Tipton was later to pass to George and Sarah's son, Thomas. By 1702, Thomas had died and there was another settlement on the occasion of the marriage of Thomas the younger to Joyce Wright who came with a marriage portion of £300. There was to be an annuity of £18 paid to Thomas's mother, Elizabeth (formerly Rumney) and the provision that if there be more than one child of the marriage, the estate was to be charged with the sum of £300 to be divided between the younger children. Elizabeth died in 1714. She had been living in retirement with her daughter Elizabeth, the wife of John Collins of Tedney in Whitbourne. Her inventory lists her possessions which are typically small for a person living in another person's house.[12] What is not typical is the amount of 'desperate debts'. Desperate debts were ones for which there was no hope of them being paid. One of these was for £156 unpaid rent that her son Thomas owed her:

> A true and perfect Inventory of the Goods & Chatels of Elizabeth Lane late of Tedstone Delamere but now of Whitbourne

---

[×] part of former open field
[*] There is a field called *Hollowbache* in the glebe terrier on page 20

Impr. Her wearing apparel Books and Money in purse	07	00	00
One bed & bedstead with the appurtenances thereunto belonging	03	00	00
Two chests and one trunk	00	12	00
Linen of divers sorts	05	05	00
Money due upon her bonds	14	11	00
Money due upon a Desperate Debt	01	00	00
Arrears of rent due from Thos Lane a Desperate Debt	156	00	00
Old chairs & lumber	01	00	00
Sum Total	193	19	06

Elizabeth made legacies to the poor of both Tedstone Delamere and Whitbourne and made small gifts to members of her family, the children of her daughter Elizabeth Collins getting larger sums of £10 each and the remainder was to go to their mother with whom she had been living, which would have been very little if the 'desperate debts' were taken into account!

But as we shall read on the following page, a great deal must have been spent throughout the century on modernisation of the house. Thomas Lane of Tipton died in 1731 and his particularly interesting inventory listing the items in each room in his house is reproduced in full:[13]

Imp[rs] his wearing apparell and money in purse valued at	10	00	00
It. Goods in the Parlour	13	00	00
It. In the room over the Parlour two beds and all appurtenances to them & the other ffurniture in the same room	10	00	00
It. In the Hall chamber two beds & appurtenances & the rest of the ffurniture in the same room	05	00	00
It. Cheese in the Cheese chamber	01	00	00
It. In a little room over the Hall one bedd & bedsteads	02	00	00
It. In the Maids Chamber one bedd	01	00	00
It. In the topploft a small parcell of ffeathers One grate & some lumbar	00	10	00
It. In the Servant Mens room two bedds & a todd of old hopps	02	00	00
It. In the Hall one Clock & other goods	03	00	00
It. In the Kitchen Brass & Pewter of all sorts & all other ffurniture there	07	00	00
It. In the Back Kitchen two ffurnaces & other lumber	02	10	00
It. In the Killhouse two killhares one maltmill two Grates & other things there	02	00	00
It. One Wagon three Tumbrills two Drays & three pair of Harrows	10	00	00
It. The Implements of Husbandry of all sorts & tack of teem	04	00	00
It. Cidermill Screws & Hares & all appurtenances thereunto belonging	03	10	00
It. Hogsheads Tubbs Sceels Coopers ware together with the Cider & malt drink in them	13	00	00
It. In the Dayryhouse Utensils	01	00	00
It. Three yoke of Oxen	30	00	00
It. Nine Cows & one Bull	30	00	00
It. Eight young Beasts Six Yearling Calves	20	00	00
It. Three Horses & one Colt	12	00	00
It. Thirteen Piggs & Fifteen Sheep	10	00	00
It. Thrashed corn in the house & corn growing upon the ground	20	00	00
It. Lent grain growing upon the ground	15	00	00
It. Linnen of all sorts	01	00	00

It. Timber & cordwood fill upon the ground	02	00	00
It. Lumber & things omitted and fforgotten	00	10	00
	231	00	00

Major changes to the house

Jim Tonkin's description of the alterations to the house which would have been carried out by the Lane family are particularly interesting as they seem to describe the same rooms that are listed in Thomas Lane's inventory on the previous page:

> This timber-framed, medieval house was much altered in the 17th century. It seems likely that this was done at two different periods. The parlour wing with its quite small, regular panelling looks as though it was built early in the century. It is quite big and originally contained two rooms on each of three floors and also a cellar running its full length. A stairway ran from top to bottom above and including the present cellar stairs; part of this is still in use but it has been extended. [*This is the wing that may have been built for the young George and Sarah on their marriage in 1624.*] It seems that this wing may have replaced an earlier one but if so the latter was taken down completely, for the carpenter's marks on the hall side of the framing are of a 17th century type and are a remarkably complete and intricate set. The beams in this wing have simple run-off stops entirely different from those in the hall block. The bigger, front room would no doubt have been known as the great parlour and the smaller room behind as the little parlour.
>
> It is probable that the big fireplace in the hall and the great stack that now hides most of the back wall of the hall block were built at this time, but it seems that the hall remained open to the roof for another 50 years or so. Also the through passage from front door to an opposite back door remained.
>
> Later in the century, towards the reign of Charles II, the hall was ceiled to make a first floor and attics and probably it was re-roofed at the same time. The distinctive feature is the highly ornate type of stop at the ends of the beams. It is unusual and seems to date from about 1680. [*In the 1731 inventory above,*] the rooms were: Hall, Hall Chamber, a little room over the hall, Parlour, Room over the Parlour, maid's chamber, topploft, servant men's room, cheese chamber, kitchen and back kitchen. The little room over the hall was probably over the entry passage, the maid's chamber may well have been the parlour attic, the topploft was probably the hall-block attic and the men's room and cheese chambers were quite likely over the kitchen and back kitchen. The greater number of rooms today is the result of later sub-divisions.
>
> In the 18th century there were two more additions, the stairway extension between the hall stack and the parlour wing and the little room between this stack and the kitchen wing. The latter was built outside the old back doorway using this as an entrance, and has a corner fireplace typical of the time with a contemporary lintel. The stairway may have been added earlier in the century, perhaps even before the 1731 inventory. Its thinner timber-framing shows up clearly at the back of the house. In the 19th century a brick china pantry was built on to the parlour with a room above it.
>
> Thus the house, while keeping its shape and size almost unaltered has been adapted for changing conditions and uses over a period of perhaps almost five hundred years and is a good example of the way houses have changed in this way.[14]

Thomas Lane in his will mentioned 'all that my capital messuage wherein I do nowe inhabit called or known by the name of Tipton alias Tupton'; he left £20 apiece to his daughter Jane, the wife of Thomas Deakin and to his sons Thomas, Richard, James and George. There is reference to the marriage indenture of 1702 in which it was laid down that the estate of Tipton was to be charged with the sum of £300 to be paid by Benjamin, the eldest son, and divided between the younger children. These were all to be given £60 which was to be paid within one year. Everything else was left to Benjamin. Trying to be fair to all the children was the downfall of many farming families. Indeed this was probably writing on the wall for the Lane family continuing at Tipton. Benjamin mortgaged Tipton for £300 in 1736, in 1743 the mortgage was increased to £500 and in 1746 there was a further charge thereby increasing it to £600 plus unpaid interest. In 1748, Benjamin Lane sold the manor and messuages, which included the blacksmith's shop at Hill Cross, to his younger brother, James. Later Tipton passed to Richard Jones of the Hope, Edvin Loach, who had married James's youngest daughter, Elizabeth. It is unknown whether James Lane actually lived at Tipton after he had bought it but by 1777 Thomas Knill was the tenant there.[15] The Knills went on to purchase the property.

Tipton's famous grandson
Thomas Knill was born in Lower Sapey. He and his wife Elizabeth settled at Tipton and had a large family of eleven children. His second son, John, left Herefordshire and became a wharfinger in London where he made his fortune. He came to own docks near Tower Bridge. John's son Stuart, who took over the business from his father, became Lord Mayor of London and was made a baronet. The Knills also bought Winley. In 1841 James Blissett, the Knills's tenant, was at Tipton and the farm was then 185 acres.

2. Hedge House – puzzles and problems
Hedge House is not recorded in early documents except for a cottage mentioned in title deeds of Tedstone Court and Manor in 1628 when it was recited that in addition, the property to be conveyed included 'one cottage called ye Hedgehouse then in Ford's possession' but no mention of a farm.[16] Records seem to suggest that today's Hedge House land north of the Whitbourne road was once part of a much larger Gate House Estate, then known as Gatley, an important property in the 16th century. Interestingly, in the nineteenth century, part of Hedge House, probably the Hedge House fields lying south of the Whitbourne road, was part of the very large manor of Bromyard held by the bishop of Hereford, but Gatley was part of the manor of Tedstone Delamere. Research by Martin Toms into the history of the Mortimer family who held the manor of Tedstone Wafre proves that a medieval deer park belonging to the Mortimers straddled today's B4203 road, incorporating a small area of Tedstone Delamere land in the north-west of the parish above Hedge House Lane. The deer park is shown on Map 2, page 5 and an aerial photo showing the deer park on page 8. Two field names, *Park Head* and *Park Head Field,* are marked on the Tedstone Delamere tithe map, see page 4. It is unusual to have a deer park straddling a main thoroughfare that has been important from at least the Iron Age, providing an essential route between the Midlands and the Welsh Marches.[17] An explanation could be that there were two adjoining parks here, the larger one to the west and the

smaller to the east side of the road. It was quite usual in Tudor times [and probably before then] to have two parks, one for red deer and one for fallow.[18] Parkhorn Farm is situated on the northern boundary of the park just east of the road and its interesting name could be significant: 'horn' may be derived from *hyrne* 'a nook, a corner'. Another related element is *horning* 'a bend, a corner, a spit of land' which topographical names only make sense if they are describing the pointed corner of a separate eastern park.[19] There are other theories and research may one day come up with a positive answer. A gate or gates with somebody to operate them would have been necessary. There is plenty of food for thought here, but the intriguing story continues:

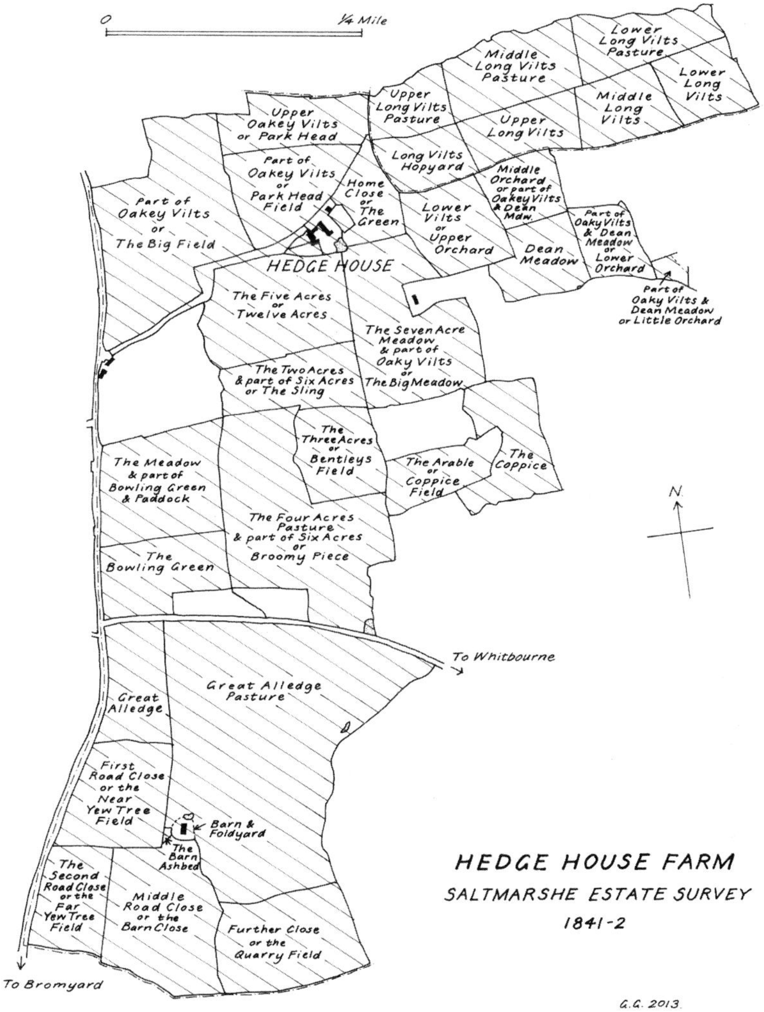

HEDGE HOUSE FARM
SALTMARSHE ESTATE SURVEY
1841-2

MAP 5.

The Manor of Burton and the Witley Court Estate

The Militia Assessments of 1663, in which the names of farms aren't given, only those of the owners (see page 56), list William Acton Esq as being assessed for £12 in Tedstone Delamere, one of the largest sums. Purely by a matter of elimination, as we know which land the other large assessments were for, Acton must have held land that is now Hedge House but formerly seems to have been Gatley.

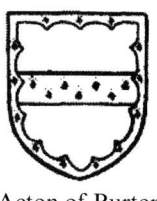

Acton of Burton

Neighbouring Gate House was certainly held by the Acton family (for the full story see pages 110 & 111). who were lords of the manor of Burton (Burton Court in Lower Sapey). In 1669 William Acton conveyed Burton to Thomas Tyrer and Richard Avenant[20] who were probably acting for Lord Foley.[21] It is suggested here that the sale included Hedge House/Gatley land, for towards the end of the 18th century, Hedge House, by then a sizeable farm, is recorded in 1792 as belonging to Lord Foley.[22] Richard Foley was a prominent 17th century Midlands ironmaster; his son, Thomas, took over his father's business and made great profits from it in the 1650s and 1660s which he used to buy estates; he built Witley Court. His grandson, Thomas, became the first Baron Foley in 1712 and it was his son, the second baron, who built the amazing baroque church there, mould-makers reproducing the plasterwork of the chapel at Cannons, Lord Chandos's palace at Edgware, Middlesex. Foley never married and on his death in 1776 his estates passed to a distant cousin, Thomas Foley of Stoke Edith, for whom the title was revived in 1776.[23] At the beginning of the 19th century, c1811, Foley's grandson had gambled away the family fortune and Lord Foley went bankrupt. In a list of Tedstone Delamere's inhabitants, dated 1736, Joseph Somers appears as a tenant of Lord Foley's land[24] which one must assume was Hedge House. Records seem to show that Hedge House was held by the Foleys through the 18th century and remained with them into 1831.[25] Witley Court and the heavily encumbered Great Witley Estate were sold in 1837 to the trustees of Lord Ward, heir to the Earl of Dudley,[26] but this didn't include Hedge House which had already been sold in 1832 to Edmund Higginson, thus becoming part of the Saltmarshe Estate.[27]

Sale particulars dated 29th June 1831 include Hedge House, then a farm of 191 acres.[28] There is no plan although the fields are listed but fortunately some of the older field names, which are not present in the tithe survey, appear in the plans of the Saltmarshe Estate surveyed 1841-2, enabling the position of these fields to be plotted[29] and are shown in Map 5 (p.95). Some fields have interesting names including 31 acres of pasture called *The Great Alledge,* a good size for a field at that time. This large field was south of the Whitbourne road, the name is a form of Middle English, *alange* meaning 'remote, lonely' which fits well this land at Hedge House that is on the edge of the parish bordering Tedstone Wafre and Norton;[30] the tithe survey records the name of this field, not as *The Great Alledge,* but as *Old Hedge House Ground,* see Map 4 on page 46; it is possible the name 'Hedge House' is a corruption of *Alledge.* There were over 80 acres of land listed in the 1831 sale particulars called *Vilts* in twelve fields, partly in Lower Sapey and partly in Tedstone Delamere; this was possibly cleared woodland. The name could mean 'clump of felled trees'.[31] Today, 'Vilts Plantation' is a wood over the county boundary in Lower Sapey. A field called *The Bowling Green* is at the corner of the Whitbourne road with the B4203; it may once have been a bowling green or sometimes the name refers merely to land that would be suitable for such, on account of its dimension, shape, and level surface.[32] The 1831 particulars do not refer to a farmhouse, only farm buildings and a cottage. A cottage on the site of today's farmstead is shown on an 1831 map as 'New Cottage'.[33] It is clearly marked on the 1841-2 Saltmarshe Estate map and seems

The Clifton-on-Teme Hunt meet at Hedge House. The photo shows the cottage refered to in the 1831 sale particulars. Following their purchase, the Saltmarshe Estate enlarged the cottage with a very substantial extension at its rear, creating a roomy farmhouse.

to be the front of the present house which was greatly extended by the Estate in the later 19th century. It is suggested that the old farmhouse may have been south of the Whitbourne road: deeds relating to various properties along the Whitbourne road refer to this road as 'the highway leading from Hedge House to Worcester'[34]; a description that could not possibly relate to the position of today's farmhouse (see Map 1, inside front cover) unless the approach was off this road. South-west of the road is a field marked on Map 4 and called, as mentioned above, *Old Hedge House Ground,* (formerly the 'Great Allege') which adjoins an isolated barn and fold-yard, where now the new house, Oldridge stands. A smaller field, adjoining, also formerly called the 'Great Allege' is no. 23 on the tithe map where it is called *Old House Field.* One asks oneself whether this was the site of an earlier Hedge House farmstead?

The tenants of Hedge House from 1777 – 1826 were a family called Lawrence. John Lawrence was followed by his son, William. In 1828, William Beavan was the new tenant.[35] He was farming 167 acres in 1841 of which 32 acres were in Lower Sapey. In 1855, Maria Beavan was granted her free-bench* at Hedge House by Bromyard and Bromyard Foreign Manorial Court.[36] It seems likely that the land in the Manor of Bromyard was the part of Hedge House land south of the Whitbourne road. There seems to have been a connection with Middle Norton Farm in the next parish in the late 18th / early 19th centuries as this farm, sometimes known as a manor, was also owned by Foley and its tenants too were Lawrences.

---

* A 'free bench' is copyhold property which a widow has for her dower after the death of her husband

3. The Line House

William *de La lynde* is mentioned in an Assize Roll of 1292;[37] *Lynde* comes from OE *lind* 'lime-tree'.[38] The name 'Line House' probably means 'house of a man with the byname or surname *de La lynde'*. In 1500, lands listed amongst the property of the late Humphrey Dore included:

> a messuage in Tedstone Delamere called *Catley* worth 30s, held of John Wisham as of his manor of Tedstarn Delamere by service of a ¼ of a knight's fee⁎⁎, a messuage in Tedstone Delamere called *Lyndehouse* held in socage◻ of John Wisham, as of his manor of Tedstone Delamere by 3s. 4d. rent to be paid to the said John ....
> 40 acres of land and 10 acres of pasture in Tedstarn aforesaid called *Ballescote* held in socage of John Wisham and by 10s rent to be paid therefore ....[39]

Humphrey Dore held the manor of Burton Court in Lower Sapey. His heirs were his sisters: Margery, wife of John Acton, and Joyce, wife of Humphrey Saunders. Humphrey Dore's mother was a member of the powerful Mortimer family who held the manor of Tedstone Wafre. Ballescote was held with the Line House subsequently.

An ancient oak at the Line House Farm.   *Rosemary Keep*

In 1615, John Capper died holding the Line House by indenture, at 26s. rent p.a.; his widow Margaret was to hold it for her life; as explained in Chapter III, after a land transaction, a 'heriot' or best beast would be claimed by the lord of the manor; in this case a black ox worth 50s. was seized by the bailiff for this purpose. In 1622, Lynne Farm and Ballescote, with one and a half yardlands belonging (a yardland was the same as a virgate), passed to John Barnes of Winley, the Capper's son-in-law.[40] It seems that contrary to the agreement, Barnes had been repeatedly asked 'in gentle manner' to pay heriots and services and William Wysham was ordered to appear before the High Court of Chancery to answer to the premises.... It is doubtful if this was sorted out to Barnes's satisfaction because in the 18th century the Line House appears in lists of farms and their tenants subject to payment of chief rents, heriots and reliefs to the lord of the manor. It is suggested that the two fields on the tithe map, (see Map 4, page 46) near the Line House called *Over Boss Croft* and *Lower Boss Croft* may represent part of the former 'Ballescote'.

In 1663, a John Barnes was assessed at £4 10s. for the Militia Assessments.[41] Owners rather than tenants were subject to this tax. A year later he was taxed for one hearth and at the same time Richard Barnes paid tax on two hearths but was not mentioned in the Militia Assessments so must then have been tenant of his property (this is

---

⁎⁎ A knight's service is explained on p.34 Catley (alias Gatley) is thought to be the present Gate House
◻ Tenants by socage were free farmers usually holding farms of a virgate or half a virgate in exchange for a money rent as opposed to customary tenants (the majority) who in the early days were tied to the manor and owed either a money rent or work on the lord's lands and could not freely dispose of their holdings. A virgate or yardland in this parish was about 40 acres

explained on pages 56 & 57).[42] John Barnes died in 1670; he may have died at the Line House or possibly at Winley which was also owned by the Barnes family in the early 18th century. In his will, he gave £20 to his son Thomas that was to be paid him within ten years of his death together with 'one bedd and boulster, two blanketts and two paire of sheetes' that were to be delivered to him within the space of one year. Beds and bedding were then highly valued items and important enough to be bequeathed in a will. His two younger daughters, Mary and Anne, were to get £50 apiece and half of the pewter, brass, beds, linen and furniture, to be divided between them. Everything else was left to his youngest son, William, who presumably had remained at home doing the farming. William and his sister Elizabeth were made joint executors. The inventory made of John's possessions lists the contents of his house and farm and there seem to have been five rooms: hall, kitchen, chamber, copp loft and chamber over the kitchen. It is not absolutely certain whether this was Winley or the Line House as the Barnes owned both but the description does fit the Line House. This inventory is reproduced on page 65.

In 1713, Francis and Anne Barnes sold 'Lynde Farm and Barnscott' to the rector, George Hay for £500 (both signing their names with a mark).[43] Later in 1713, the Line House was listed amongst the farms of the manor owing rent, George Hay, clerk, being subject to the payment of 14s. 2d chief rent.[44] In 1728, Hay bequeathed the Line House, let to Richard Collins at a yearly rent of £30, together with all that part of the farm in his own possession, to his wife Elizabeth. Their daughter sold the property to a later Tedstone Delamere rector, John Landon, who in turn sold it in 1755 to Robert Butler of Tedstone Delamere for £870; it was then in the tenancy of Francis Foulk. For the next 200 odd years it was occupied by tenants: in 1777, John Chrees of Winley was paying land tax for the Line House (as a tenant) and by 1801, the tenant was Thomas Wood. In 1819, Rev. John Broome of Forthampton, Gloucestershire left the property in trust for his wife and daughters and their descendents. After Mr. Broome's death, it passed to his daughter Isobel and her husband Slade Baker.[45] See Map 8.

In 1841, Slade Baker still owned the Line House and Thomas Wood jun. was the tenant farming 108 acres. From 1853 until his resignation in 1875, Rev. Slade Baker was the incumbent of Clifton-on-Teme. The Line House remained with the Baker family until 1891 when it was purchased by Edgar Wight, see Chapter VII.

The Line House has always been a property of some importance. It was one and a half virgates, one of the largest farms in the parish. There are two fishponds.

The Line House. *Rosemary Keep*

4. Pixhill

An early reference to Pixhill is recorded in 1324, Pagan of Tipton paid a three yearly rent to John & Hawise of Wysham for land which included one shilling 'out of lands which William of *Pykeshale* held for his life and the reversion of the said tenement after their deaths …'. 'Pixhill' probably means 'nook or corner of a man named *Pic*', from the OE personal name *Pic* + OE *halh* 'nook, corner of land'. The change to – *hill* is 19th century. (The same personal name seems to occur in *Pixley*, near Ledbury.) [46]

As recorded in Chapter III: in 1510, Richard Capper purchased one messuage with a noke (about 12½ acres) of free land called 'Pixhall' from Thomas Hall. Richard's death was reported at the manorial court in 1550 when a heriot was owed of one ox coloured 'valowe' (yellow?) worth 16s. and a relief of 4s. John Capper was his son and heir.[47] In 1588, John was in trouble for enclosing a piece of land adjoining the end of Badley Wood and the road leading to Hill Cross. He had apparently kept it enclosed for the previous 15 years 'to the damage of the lord'. He was ordered to open it up before Michaelmas and let it lie open as it used to be on pain of 10s. Almost a year later, he hadn't opened up the land so was fined 10s. At the same court, he hadn't appeared to give his verdict about a road, as he was supposed to have done, so for that he was fined 3s. 4d. And, as if that wasn't enough, he and William Capper and John Sheare had pastured their beasts and trampled down the grain and herbage in Bine Field (one of the common fields) ….[48] So clearly John was not being a very good member of the community! Anne Capper, presumably the mother of John and William mentioned above, died in 1605 and left an extraordinary will which has been reproduced on page 62.

Pixhill. *Sue Haffenden*

The RCHME says that the greater part of this delightful timber-framed house dates from the early 17th century with a large early 18th century addition at the rear.[49] The main part of the house was built by the Cappers who had held the property for 200 years, a long time!

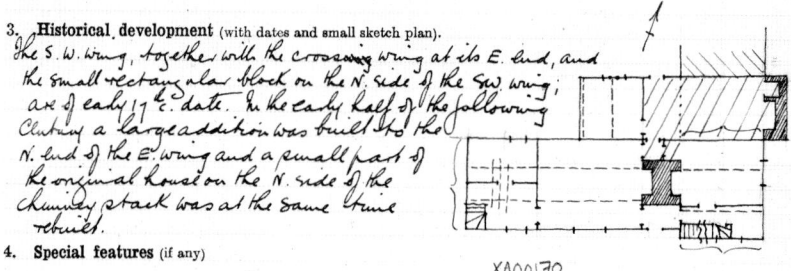

Pixhill. RCHME surveyor's report 1931. *Reproduced by permission of English Heritage.*

In 1710, Edward Timmings of Bishops Frome, yeoman, purchased the property for £379-18s from John Capper for the benefit of himself, his daughter Elizabeth Nicholls and his grand-daughter Elizabeth. It was then in the occupation of Elizabeth Harris, widow. In 1736, John Huck of Whitbourne bought the farm for £410. It was described as:

> All that messuage or tenement called Pixhall or Pixall with barns … belonging. Two pieces of arable land containing 10 acres lying on the Upper side of the roadway leading from Tedstone to a common called Badley Wood. Also all that piece of arable land below a cottage of one Davies containing 5 acres, all that piece of rough pasture ground called the new leasow containing 3 acres. All that orchard called Low Croft containing three acres. All that orchard called Pigscoat containing 3 acres. All that meadow near the messuage called Pixhall containing 1 acre. All that piece of meadow ground called the Broad Meadow containing 2 acres. All that parcel of ground part pasture and part hop ground called Old Pixhall containing 3 acres. All that piece of arable called Wheatly Bank 3 acres. All that rough pasture called the Horse Pasture containing 1 acre. All that orchard called Road Orchard, 1 acre. All in Lower Tedstone, al. Tedstone Delamere, now in the possession of John Huck and Richard Baker.[50]

The land totalled 35 acres. The Hucks were a well established Whitbourne family from Poswick Lodge. They also owned Redhill at Badley Wood so it would make sense to farm Pixhill as well as it is just across the road. John Huck died in 1759 leaving Pixhill to his wife Elizabeth and his Whitbourne property together with Bastonhall Farm, Suckley to his daughter Susannah, his widow receiving the rents until Susannah was 21. In 1776, Mrs Huck mortgaged Pixhill for £400.

Mortgages
A large portion of title deeds are mortgage documents. Nowadays many people have at one time or another bought their property with the help of a mortgage from a building society. Mortgages were just as common in the past but instead of a building society, money was borrowed from private individuals. Most mortgagees (those who lent the money) were fairly local to Tedstone Delamere or perhaps might come from neighbouring counties and presumably were found by the lawyers. There never seemed to be a shortage of people willing to invest and this investment in a property might be bequeathed in wills or assigned to another person. Interesting as mortgage documents are, including as they do, much family history, it is not proposed to mention them all here as the book would become far too long. But one unusual one coming from the far side of the world is of particular interest. Captains of naval ships could become very rich by capturing vessels and bringing them into port, and then of course they would need to invest their prize money. When Mrs Huck mortgaged Pixhill and the Grey House, she borrowed money from James Vasbon, late of Ludlow, but now of the Royal Navy, Captain of H.M. Sloop Alert. Mortgage documents for Pixhill went to and fro via the lawyer from Whitbourne to Jamaica so enabling Captain Vasbon to collect his post.

Lease of Pixhill and Gray's House
In 1788, Mrs Huck leased Pixhill and the Gray's House to Joseph Barnbrook for £50 per annum. The lease was for seven years, one or two clauses of which are worth

repeating: the timber was not included in the lease except such underwood as the tenant might need for 'hedgeboot, fireboot and hop poles' which was to be used on the premises and not elsewhere, and the tenant was not to 'dig, delve, search for & carry away stone'; he was to farm in a good and husband-like manner etc. He was to 'find a sufficient quantity of straw, lugs and twigs and other thatching stuff for repairing the thatch of the buildings'. At the end of the lease, he should leave seven acres in hop ground (two at Pixhill and five at the Grey House) and such hop ground was to be well stocked and planted with hops and the ditches there well scoured and cleansed and he should leave 'upon such hop ground all the poles ... thereon well striped [stripped?], sharped, piled and tied for the use of the said Elizabeth Huck'. Elizabeth Huck would allow out of timber growing, wood 'for wagon boot, cart boot and plow boot'. These were relicts of typical perks which came the way of villeins as 'customs of the manor'. *Fyrebote* was the right to gather dead wood for fires, *hedgebote* was a similar right for mending fences. Wagon boot, cart boot and plow boot are further similar rights.[51]

In 1789, Mrs Huck sold Pixhill and the Gray's Farm to Robert Moore of Shelsley Beauchamp, lord of the manor of Tedstone Delamere, for £864-8-0; they remained with the Tedstone Court Estate until its break up and sale in 1996.

Mr Robert Moore bo^t of Eliz. Huck
To a ... frame & dresser in the kitchen
at Pixall farm, Dog Wheel**, bacon cratch[□]
Long table, five benches   £10   10
In the dairy five shelves & a safe
A cider mill & press & skrew &
all the Hop poles on the farm

Account for extras at sale of Pixhill in 1789.   HRO

** A small short legged dog was used for turning the spit, a *turnspit* dog. A wheel was fixed at the side of the fire which the dog turned
[□] In this context, a *bacon cratch* is probably a rack or wooden frame

In 1841, Pixhill was owned by T. P. P. Wight (as trustee) and was in the tenure of John Hill. There were 82 acres which included land from the former Gray's Farm and from a smallholding known as Cullets; there is no further reference to a separate existence of these two properties.

5. Gray's Farm

This farmstead, which has now disappeared, apart from foundations and a collapsed building buried in the woodland, is probably (as related on page 88), the holding recorded in 1353, when there was a grant by John de Grye of Tedstone Delamere to Miles alte Walle of Clifton of all his lands … in Tedstone, except two messuages, one of which was called *Le Grye Place*. Gray's Farm or the Gray House was once one of the larger farms, a holding of one virgate. An entry in the court rolls in 1493 is interesting:

They [the Homage] present the death of John Helme who held one messuage and one virgate of land called Greyslond for which a heriot is due to the lord. And Joan Helme is his daughter and nearest heir and she is aged 13 so her ward and marriage belong to the lord. And he has sold the said ward and marriage to John Pechar.[52]

Selling the marriage of a ward was a fairly common occurrence. How it worked was that the chap who bought the wardship, in this case John Pechar, had the right to marry her off to whoever he wanted, and also managed her estate until the marriage, so both ways, it was a profitable thing to do. We don't know whether John Pechar married her to his own son but this was a common outcome thereby getting her property into his own family on the cheap, as it were. A similar case was described in Chapter III.

Sale by Mrs Huck of Gray's Farm. Also listed is Holder's cottage near Whitehall Common and land called Team Side where there was a timber frame intended to be made into a house. *HRO*

In the mid 18th century, Richard Huck the elder of Poswick gave the Gray House to his younger son John, a baker and maltster in Worcester, mentioning 'the love and affection he had for his son and for making provision and maintenance for his livelihood'. As recorded, John Huck bequeathed Pixhill and the Gray House to his wife Elizabeth who sold them in 1790 to Robert Moore, lord of the manor. The purchase money for the Gray House with 38 acres was £855. Included were Holder's cottage adjacent to Whitehall Common and a two acre piece of land called *Team Side*[53] where there was 'a timber-frame intended to be made into a house'. It is interesting that timber-framed houses were still being built at this late date. The Gray House does not appear in the tithe survey of 1840 but Gray's Farm Croft & Orchard together with Flat Meadow & Burlip Hill (both formerly part of Gray's) were included then amongst Pixhill fields. All that now remains to mark the site are a couple of small dilapidated buildings buried in the woodland.

6. Winley

An early reference to Winley is when *Ric(ard)us de Wynele* is mentioned in an Assize Roll of 1292.[54] The name means a 'wood or clearing of a man named *Wina* or *Wynna*', from either of the OE personal names *Wina* or *Wynna* + OE *lÂah* 'wood, clearing'.[55]

A distant view of Winley; note the heaps of muck waiting to be spread by hand.   *Kathleen Harris*

Another early reference to Winley is found in a court roll of 1428 when the homage presented the death of John Caluhull who held *Wynleslond*.[56] At the same court, William Calluhull was fined for trespassing in the woods with his cattle and was fined 6d. At the next court, the wood bailiff presented William for trespassing with his beasts twice in the wood and he was fined 4d then at a court the following year, he was ordered to 'put up a hedge between himself and a wood called Caluhulle'. Clearly he had become a bit of a pest. Another early reference to Winley of 1451 is found amongst the manorial records after Alice Callowhill, John's widow, had died:

> They [the tenants] present the death last December of Alice, the relict of John Calowhill who held 3 messuages and 3 nokes of land called Calowhill, Morehous and *Tyboirys* [or Tybouys?] *Wynley* by rent of 12s 8d pa. Two bullocks are owed as heriots and William Calowhill, John's son, produced in court a deed showing that he was freed from paying the third heriot. And William acknowledged tenancy of the said properties for the said rent, suit of court, relief of 11s, heriot when due and the accustomed services. And he did fealty. Then the lord claimed that he should have 2s 8d from the said William in annual rent for the messuage called Morehous but William said he should by right only pay 7d pa so he was ordered to produce evidence of this at the next court.[57]

Callowhill and Morehouse are lost places although Morehouse is remembered in the name of a field south-west of the Thrift called *Moorehouse Meadow,* (see Map 4, page 46). The Callowhills were quite an important family and were related to the Wyshams, the lords of the manor. They bought Woodmanton, Clifton-on-Teme, from John Croft in 1540 although it has been said that it passed to them in the female line from the Wyshams. John Callowhill of Tedstone Delamere presented four clergy to the living of Clifton between 1556 – 67. John Callowhill of Worcester, a clothier, who could have been the same person, died in 1573 and mentioned in his will, is 'one great pott which was brought from Tedstone' and also 'standing timber at Ladie Wood' (see Chapter III page 60. Ladywood is in S. E. Tedstone Delamere.) Thomas Callowhill held Winley in 1510 following the death of his mother Joan. By 1534, Edward or Edmund Perkins or Perkyn was tenant here but the Callowhills continued elsewhere in Tedstone. It is very likely that it was Edward Perkins who built the present Winley farmhouse. In 1550, Matilda, daughter and co-heir of John Mylwood held the fifth part of half a virgate of land at Winley, so is this evidence of there being a small settlement at Winley? There is an entry in 1551 when clearly the Perkins family were still there:

> Edward Perkyn who held certain lands called Wynley has died since last court and Richard Perkyn is his cousin and nearest heir as appears by deed of foeffment produced in open court. Richard is 19 years old and they don't know whether a heriot is due. Richard is ordered to bring his deeds to the next court as it is not certain by what tenancy he holds the property and his fealty is respited until then. They also say that Edward Perkyn holds part of the said lands called Wynley by right of his wife Anne but they are completely ignorant about what services are due. He is present in court and is admitted to the lands.[58]

Above is a fairly typical entry at this time. When an heir claimed a property, care was always taken as to how the tenancy was held and Richard was told to bring his deeds to the next court. Winley at this time was half a virgate (about 20 statute acres).

Richard died in 1615 and his grandson, John, inherited but it was then sold to John Capper for his daughter, Cristiana Barnes, wife of John Barnes. The bailiff was ordered to seize a red ox as heriot and deliver it to the lord's store. Both the Cappers and the Barnes were important families in Tedstone at that time.

The house

The RCHME date the house as being from the second half of the 16th century.[59] Roy and Vera Perry, prominent members of the Woolhope Club, who visited the house in 1996, suspected that the house could have had a smoke hood, a timber chimney, to carry the smoke up and out through the roof.

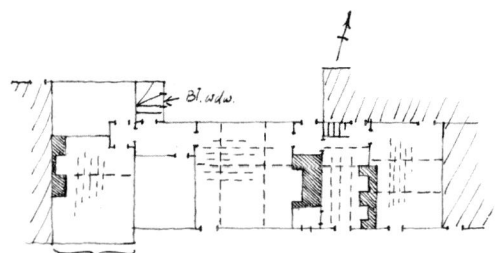

Winley. RCHME surveyor's plan.
Reproduced by permission of English Heritage

The house is laid out on an east-west alignment with the 'upper' end towards the west; the site slopes down towards the east. It has recently been visited by vernacular-buildings expert, Duncan James, who says that the primary structure is a timber-framed, two storey house of four bays. On the ground floor it has been almost completely under-built in stone but much of the first-floor framing survives. For this description the primary bays of the main range are numbered west to east, 1 to 4, and the secondary bays of the main range numbered west to east, 5 and 6. At the west end is a two-bay crosswing and a later two bay wing has been built against bay 6, extending north.

Duncan James finds that the primary, main range is constructed from pit-sawn timber, which indicates a post-1530/40 date. This is a transition building erected at a time when the open hall was going out of fashion yet before the chimneystack had arrived at the vernacular level as a replacement for the open hearth. Winley was built with a hearth at the lower end of the ceiled hall and did indeed employ a smoke hood. This was constructed in the ceiled hall, against the framing between the hall and the crosspassage. The ceiling in the hall has been built to stop one panel short of the crosspassage framing and in the south side of this space the hood was built. At least four primary mortices in the west face of the crosspassage screen indicate where it was fitted and there is a mortice in the soffit at the centre of the ceiling beam for a corner post to this structure. In addition, a heavy accumulation of soot is high up on the west face of the crosspassage framing at first floor level.

Duncan James says that the present chimneystack has been built into the two-panel-wide crosspassage bay. The north doorway of the crosspassage survives in use. Here the west door jamb is a storey

Winley 2007.

post that has been hacked back at ground-floor level but the bottom of the doorhead mortice survives to indicate that this was a doorway. In addition, there is no mortice for a midrail. On the east side of the opening there is a peg hole in the girding beam that indicates the position of the door jamb on that side. (Now underbuilt in brick or stone).

To the east of the crosspassage, the service bay survives. All the five primary trusses are in place, more or less intact within the house. A further two bays have been added to the east end. Bay 5 was a 1½ storey timber-framed structure (i.e. with a lower wallplate level than the main range). Bay 6 appears to have been added to create a hop kiln, at which time bay 5 may have been raised to the same height as the rest of the range.

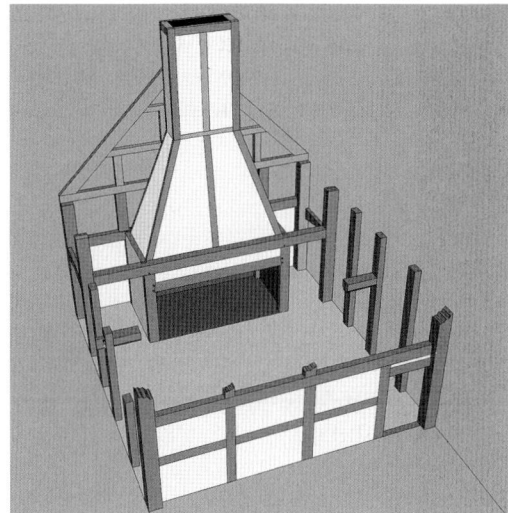

Sketch of a similar smoke hood to that at Winley. Note, though, that this one is central whereas the one at Winley was off centre. *Duncan James*

The crosswing at the west end was added to the range after a considerable length of time evidenced by substantial weathering on the west face of the west end primary truss and crossframe. The wing appears to have been built in stone, with timber cross-frame and roof structure. A later addition is the winder staircase built within a stone staircase tower in the return on the north side between the wing and the main range.

Vent for the former hop kiln in bedroom ceiling. *Duncan James*

To summarise, Duncan James considers that the date for the primary range, on the evidence of saw marks, must be later than 1530/40 but the ceiling beam chamfers are not particularly wide, as would be usual for the late 16th century. It seems likely that the date of the primary range may be *c*1540-75 and that the inserted stack belongs to the late 16th or early 17th century. The west wing is very probably of mid-to-late 17th century date. The ceiling beams have scroll stops.

The east end additions are difficult to date but the kiln may well be late 18th/19th century in date and the brick addition to the north is probably of similar date.

Duncan James did not carry out a detailed study of this interesting building so dates are provisional. However, what is certain is that this was a ceiled hall house built with a primary smoke hood. It is not a converted open hall into which a smoke hood was inserted. The date of late 16th century suggested by the RCHME is likely to be a little late.

The Chrees family
In 1709, the burial of Thomas Barnes of *Winley* was recorded in the parish register, followed in 1711 by that of William Barnes of *Winley*.[60] In 1713, John Barnes was in possession.[61] In 1736, he was paying 5s.10d. chief rent for Winley but by 1739, William Chrees was the new owner. William and Mary Chrees brought up a family of six here. In his will, he left £12 to his wife Mary to buy mourning for herself and their children. He gave Mary the household goods, linen and furniture (all the hogsheads and casks excepted); she was to have the use and enjoyment of the parlour, the room over the same middle room and the garret. She was also to have that part of the garden facing the back door called the 'Cabbagepane' together with the liberty to fell, top or lop firewood as she shall reasonably have occasion for during her residence at Winley. Also provision was to be made for her, over and above that made by their marriage settlement out of the Burbage estate, of £10 per annum out of the Winley estate. His children Mary, Elizabeth, and Benjamin were each to get £100, William being already provided for. Benjamin was to have £5 for clothes and other necessities during his apprenticeship. Their eldest child, John, inherited the farm and the second son, William, became an attorney in Worcester. The family were clearly educated at this date, John taking a leading role in helping Robert Moore, the lord of the manor, to solve the dispute between the parishioners and the rector regarding the commutation of tithes (see pages 26-29), his brother, William, acting for the parishioners. John remained a bachelor living with his mother who seems to have been a powerful lady.

John Chrees died in 1815 at the age of 75. His will contains much of family history interest, his estate being divided between members of the family, his surviving brother Benjamin and nephews Benjamin Birch and Patrick Drummond being the executors. But the most interesting is a little human story that emerges and the reader is left to make of it what he or she will:

> I give and bequeath unto Mary Eaton, spinster, now living in my service the sum of three hundred pounds to be paid to her within twelve months next after my decease Also I give & bequeath unto the said Mary Eaton the bed on which she sleeps together with a pair of sheets and blankets also the Corner Cupboard in the parlor the small writing desk and drawers two round tables Also my tea Spoons & China .... And whereas I am desirous of making some provision for John Eaton the natural son of my servant Mary Eaton Now therefore I bequeath unto the said Benjamin Chrees Benjamin Birch and Patrick Drummond the Sum of nine hundred pounds upon trust that they ... apply the interest towards the maintenance and education of the said John Eaton until he shall have attained the age of twenty four years when I direct that the principal sum of nine hundred pounds be paid to him.[62]

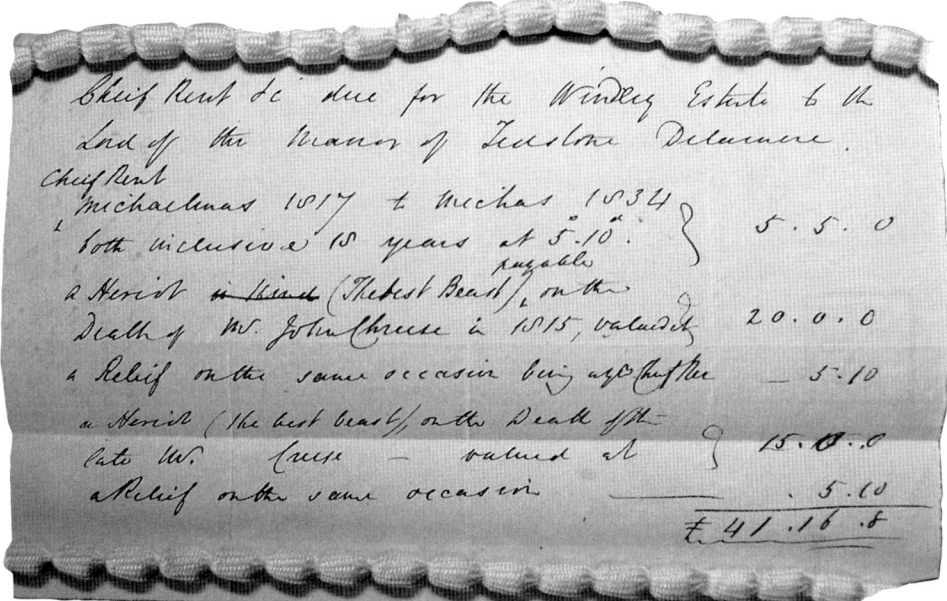

An account for chief rent at Winley 1817-1834. HRO

Mary could have the care and education of her son for the first nine years if she should so wish and be paid £30 per annum for that purpose. She was also to have the mahogany table. Two months later, John Chrees was having further thoughts about distributing his valuables and wrote a codicil giving his sister, Elizabeth Birch, a silver tablespoon marked 'M.C.' (his mother's?) and a pair of silver mounted spectacles; to Benjamin Birch he gave his jug topped with silver. He gave to Mary Eaton a small silver pepper box and a mahogany card table which stood in the parlour. He also gave Mary, to keep for her son John, a metal watch and a silver tablespoon marked 'J. C.' The codicil was not witnessed but was allowed on deponents swearing on oath that the handwriting was that of John Chrees.[63]

In 1834, when T.P.P. Wight was acting as trustee for the young James Lane Wight, and was endeavouring to find out what chief rents were due to him, an elderly woman was asked what she could remember about payments from Winley and made the following affidavit:

> Mary Caswell says she is about 80 years of age that she lived at two different times with Mr. Chreese & his mother as much as 6 years and worked for them after she was married 15 or 16 years. She has frequently heard Mr. Chreese & his mother talk of paying 'Chiefage' to Mr. Moore she also remembers Mrs. Chreese grumbling very much about paying it she did not like to part with the money.
> Mary Caswells Mark [64]   X

In 1841, Winley was owned by John Knill, (a London merchant) who also owned Tipton and his tenant at Winley was Edward Jones. The farm was then 50 acres.

7. Upper Grounds

This land of 70 acres on either side of the road to Whitbourne part of the Tedstone Court estate in 1824.[65] It was owned by Philip Wight (as a trustee) in 1841 and, together with Pixhill, was in the tenancy of John Hill (see Map 9). There is a farm building marked on the tithe map but no house. This is the land which became the farm of Upper Grounds.

8. The Gate House

This small farmhouse dating from the 17th century is situated in the fork between the B4203 and the old road that now goes as far as Hedge House but used to continue to Lower Sapey and beyond. It has a very interesting early history: *Gat* or *Gatt* is OE for 'gate' and this property must surely have been connected with gates to the Mortimer's deer park, see pages 94-96 relating to Hedge House. The Gate House was the messuage and lands called Catley [alias Gatley] held by Humphrey Dore in 1500 (see below). At this date it seems likely that it included some, if not all of the land that is now Hedge House Farm. It seems to have been a sub-tenancy, held under the de la Mares, lords of the manor, and had been created by the end of the 12th century.[66] In 1500, Humphrey Dore's Gatley, mentioned above, was 'worth 30s., held of John Wysham as of his manor of Tedstone Delamere by service of a quarter of a knight's fee'. Humphrey also held the Line House. He had inherited the manor of Burton (Burton Court in Lower Sapey) from his brother William, yeoman of the pitcher house to Henry VII, together with a casket containing all the deeds relating to the manor.[67] Humphrey Dore was a member of the powerful Mortimer family (his mother was a Mortimer) who held the manor of Tedstone Wafre and this is significant because field names show that a large deer park there of the Mortimers stretched across what is now the main B4203 road onto Tedstone Delamere land and the fact that a relative of the Mortimers held the Gate House, which is in this significant position relative to the management of the former deer park, is interesting.

Farm buildings at the Gate House; Donald Boughton is standing to the right of the picture. *B&DLHC*

Humphrey was not a particularly good tenant in Tedstone Delamere, in fact, as you can read on pages 52 & 53, he could be described as a 'neighbour from hell'. He died in 1501 leaving Burton to his sister Margery, wife of John Acton. In 1551, John Acton senior owed suit for certain lands called *Gatteley*.[68] It seems very likely that land now part of Hedge House was included with Gatley in the Burton bequest.

Recent extensions to the house have unearthed foundations of a large building here and there are signs of a fire at some time in the past.[69] The suspicion therefore is that the Gate House was once a more important property, and probably most of the 1840s Hedge House land went with it.

George Lane died at the Gate House in 1633. By this time, the present farmhouse may have been built. He had moved there from Tipton, formerly shared with his son. The move was probably to make room for his son's increasing family at Tipton. His interesting will shows how farmers seemed to have very little cash in hand and instead of cash, livestock were left as legacies: he left a sheep to George Jones, another to Judith Corbet, his servant. These sheep were in the possession of Roger Colley, their price was to be bargained. Twenty more sheep were to be sold and the proceeds divided between various members of his family. He gave four pewter dishes to his daughter Bridget. His son-in-law William Woode was to get 20 sheep, his son William was to have the bedstead in the inner chamber, a joined press in the outer chamber, his son George was to have the great tester bed in the outer chamber, and the table frame, forms and benches in the hall, various household items such as a kneading skeel and outside, the tack of the team, but they were only to have the furniture etc after the death of his wife Joan. He gave one strike (a measure, usually identical with a bushel) of corn to his sister Margaret Jones, half to be presently delivered and the other half after the next harvest.

Inventory of George Lane 1633

Imprimis fower oxen priced	12	00	00
It six kine five wth calves and one without a calf pric	11	00	00
It three heifers and five yeare-old beasts pric	5	00	00
It one mare and colte pric	2	13	04
It one score of old sheepe and 12 other sheepe pric	5	06	08
It five small swine pric	1	00	00
It corne in the field by estimacone twentie acres or there about	5	00	00
It oats, pease, poulse and barley in the field by estimacone	4	00	00
It corne and hay in the barne and malte in the house pric	4	00	00
It poultrie about the house as turkies, geese, ducks and hens pric		03	08
It fower fetherbeds and two flocke beds with the furniture to them belonginge pric	2	00	00
It the linens in the house and napery wares pric	3	00	00
It brasse and pewter of all sorts pric	2	00	00

It table board, benches, formes, stooles, coffers and one presse, bedsteeds, spinning wheeles and cardes and one sack pric	2	00	00
It hogsheads, barrells, vessells and other treene ware		13	04
It beef and bacon	2	00	00
It two broaches and cob irons and one driping pan and iron wares for house keepinge pric		10	00
It one corne waine, one dunge waine, and all the tacke and furniture of the teeme pric	1	10	00
It axes and bills, shovels and tooles of husbandrie		10	00
It the wearinge apparel of the deceased pric	2	00	00
Suma huius inventore	77	15	00

The Gate House seems to be the property mentioned in 1729 then 'near unto a place called the Hedge House now in possession of Humphrey Postans' purchased by Edmund Caswell and which his son Edmund mortgaged. In 1739, it was purchased by Thomas Norman, a wheelwright of Lower Sapey, for £288 8s.[70] Land tax records show that the Gate House was just a modest sized holding in the late 18th / early 19th centuries.

Land Tax payments for the Gate House:
1777	Mr Norman	half yearly payment of 8s. 4d.
1790	Wm. Norman proprietor; Staples occupier.	annual payment of 16s. 8d
1819	Anthony Norman prop. / occ.	ditto
1831	late Norman prop; Thos. Holland occ.	annual payment of 15s. 5d.
Ditto	John Stallard occ.	annual payment of 11d.

In 1831 above, the property was split and it is probable that John Stallard occupied Gate House Cottage. In 1841, the Gate House was a small farm of 21 acres, Thomas Holland was owner/occupier; sometime after this date, it became part of the Saltmarshe Estate.

Oddments of land
Lord Ward owned a couple of fields near the church in 1841: Farm Meadow and Coppice Meadow which together with a cottage near Whitehall totalled *c*10 acres. His trustees had purchased the Witley Court Estate after Lord Foley's bankruptcy. As we have seen, page 96, Foley had owned the Hedge House which was sold to Edmund Higginson of Saltmarshe in the early 1830s. It seems that this small remnant of 10 acres and a cottage, away from the main block of Hedge House land, had somehow been missed from the transaction. But this bit of land is particularly interesting. The ownership can almost certainly be traced back to the very tiresome Humfrey Dore who, amongst his other misdemeanours, was presented at the manorial court in 1498 for enclosing 'the common church way to the harm of all the parishioners'. The tithe map of 1841 shows this land of Lord Ward's as being adjacent to the churchyard, (see Map 8 on page 164).

A three and a half acre field on the tithe map called 'Dr Booker's Land' near Tipton is interesting. Dr Luke Booker was rector 1805 – 12 and in 1840 the field was owned by his son, Thomas Booker who was Member of Parliament for Hereford, see page 146.

In 1841, land in the west of the parish, unlike that on the eastern side, was in the hands of several landowners. As we have read, James Moore had split his estate between two cousins, Richard Wight who inherited his land to the west of the brook which included the Court and the increasingly unimportant lordship, and Edward Moore who inherited the land to the east of the brook. The Moore family had been less acquisitive on the west side and some significant farms which included Tipton, Hedge House, the Line House and Winley remained firmly in other hands. This was not the case on the eastern side and we read in the next chapter how the Moore family gradually acquired almost all the land there creating a significant estate.

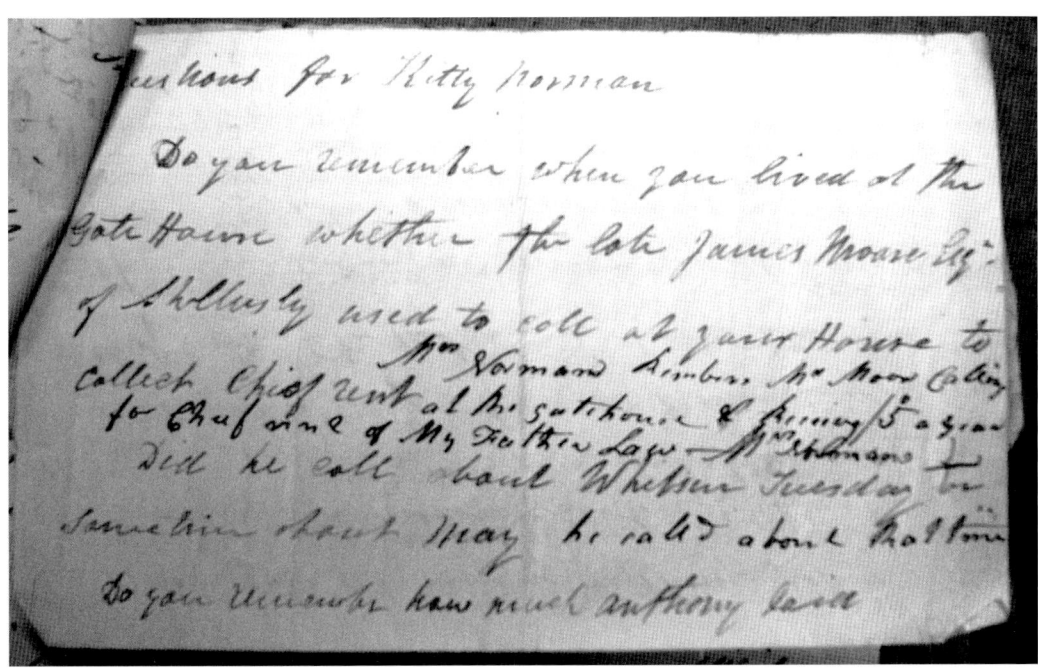

In the 1830's, T.P.P. Wight was trying to find out what chief rents were paid by Kitty Norman's father-in-law to the lord of the manor. By the 19th century, chief rents had been collected very infrequently and no proper records had been kept.

HRO

CHAPTER VI

Farms and Smallholdings to the East of the Sapey Brook and the Development of the Moores' Estate - before 1841

> What a pity that these ancient humble farms should be destroyed and thrown into the great farms, thereby taking away all the poor man's prizes and the chance of his rising in the world.
> *Kilverts Diary 1870 – 1879, Selections from the Diary of the Rev. Francis Kilvert* ed. William Plomer, (1999), 228

We have read in Chapter IV how in 1726 George Webb of Shelsley Beauchamp bought Tedstone Court, together with the lordship of the manor, and farms and cottages that included Woodend and Tidbatch on the east side of the Sapey Brook. The estate was subsequently enlarged by Robert Moore of Birmingham, an edge toolmaker, a wealthy industrialist who had married Webb's daughter, Ann. He added to the western side of their Tedstone Court Estate in the late 18th century by purchasing Pixhill and the Grey House. The 18th century is known for the growth of large estates and the demise of the small landowner and in this chapter about the eastern side of the parish, we shall find that a number of owner-occupied smallholdings virtually disappeared. The chapter tells how the Moore family gradually acquired almost all the remaining land to the east of the Sapey Brook, then reorganised it into fewer but more viable holdings.

Going back to the end of the 17th century, most of the land then was no longer in strips in the common fields; enclosing the land by negotiation with one's neighbours was a long and gradual process and for some time it remained in small parcels dotted about the parish. During the 18th century, Robert and Ann Moore and their son Robert, like many others who had made their money from industry, invested in land. It was Robert and members of his family who did much to change the farms and smallholdings by creating larger units. A map of the Woodam Hall Estate at the time of its purchase by Robert Moore in 1787 shows this farm of 53 acres in as many as five separate blocks. The interesting story of how Robert Moore reorganised this particular farm is told on page 120.

The descent of the Moore family
Robert Moore junior, the son of Robert and Ann, died intestate in 1793 and having had no children, the estate passed to his younger brother James. James Moore also had no children and on his death began the break up of this now large estate which is recorded in Chapter IV. He left his property in Tedstone Delamere lying to the east of the Sapey Brook, together with his interests in Shelsley Beauchamp, to a cousin, Edward Moore, who had been farming at Alvechurch.[1]

The names of Edward Moore of Alvechurch, farmer, Robert Moore Esq and James Moore appear in a list of people who had taken out certificates for killing game published in the Berrow's Journal of 1790; to this day, shooting is a valuable part of the rural economy here. One can understand why the family made the Upper House at Shelsley Beauchamp their home. Now known as the Manor, it is a fine house with wonderful views looking out over the Teme Valley and must have been a welcome change from the expanding industrialisation of Birmingham. Edward died some 27 years later in 1838 at the great age of 85 years. There is an imposing box tomb to Edward Moore and other members of his family just inside the gate in Shelsley Beauchamp churchyard.

The Moore family tomb to the left of the gate into Shelsley Beauchamp churchyard.

He and his wife Mary having had no children, their Tedstone Delamere property passed to a nephew, Charles Edward Moore.[2] Charles Edward was the fourth son of Edward's brother John. His three elder brothers had each been left the estates in Alvechurch and Kings Norton by James Moore in 1805 so clearly Edward was rectifying this omission by leaving property to this particular nephew.

Moore family tree

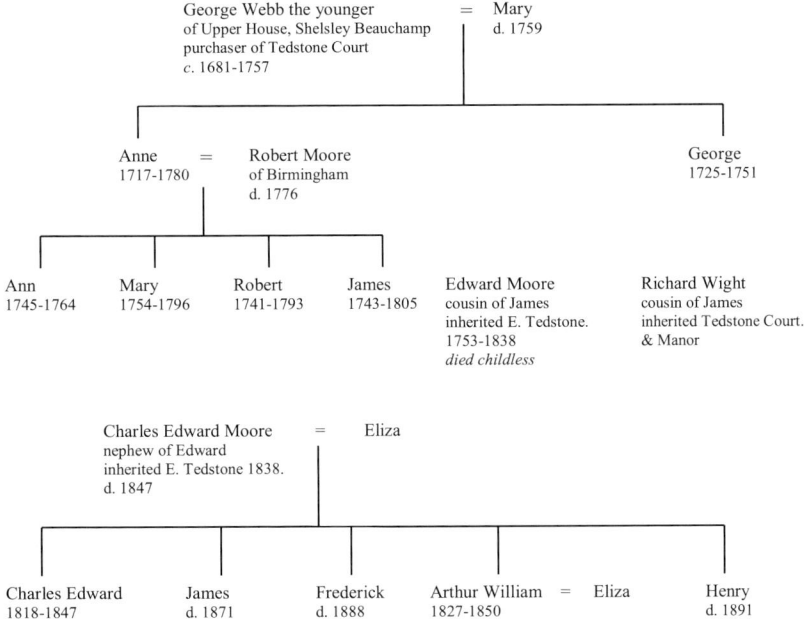

The story of the Moores' estate in Tedstone Delamere in the 18th century is an important one because it was a period of immense change in the parish. This was a period of expansion and acquisition by Ann and Robert Moore and their son Robert and once the land was in their hands, a reorganisation of the farms on the eastern side of the parish began. As explained, after Robert's brother James's death in 1805, the estate was split between his two cousins, Richard Wight and Edward Moore. Edward Moore and his nephew, Charles Edward Moore who succeeded him, continued with these changes: farms and smallholdings were amalgamated, one or two farms and a number of smallholdings entirely disappeared and remaining ones became larger. This major reorganisation carried out by the Moores created a very different estate, eventually to be purchased by Edward Bickerton Evans of Whitbourne Hall in 1866 and we read of this in Chapter IX. Some of the now surplus smallholder's dwellings remained, for a while, becoming homes for labourers. With later generations came the disappearance of many of the now landless small farmhouses and cottages and this trend continued right up to the end of the 19th century and beyond (see Chapter XI, The Cottages).

THE FARMS

The Thrift

The Thrift (also Freeth) is an unusual name that generally means 'woodland'. It can in certain cases mean land overgrown with brushwood or scrub on the edge of forest and this description could well apply to this particular farm being, as it is, on the edge of the wooded area beside Waste Common and the Sapey Brook.[3]

The Thrift was the subject of a marriage settlement in 1657 between Richard, the son of John and Mary Hill of Tedstone Delamere and Elizabeth, daughter of Martin Hay, Elizabeth bringing with her a marriage portion of £200.[4] Three other houses in Tedstone Delamere were included in this settlement, namely Howan, Whitewoods Croft and Showley Heath, all properties that have frustratingly disappeared although Showley Heath is remembered by the field names Shoals Heath Bank and Shoals Alders Wood which lie next to the southern parish boundary near Ladywood and are marked on the tithe map of 1841 (see Map 4, page 46). As early as 1443, the death of Agnes Porter was reported at the manorial court; she had held one messuage and two nokes of free land called *Sewalles/Shewells* for which a cow worth 8s was due as heriot. Her heirs were John Wyse and William Welonde.[5] *Whitewoods Croft*, mentioned above, is another disappeared property. In 1558, the death of John Dee who held a messuage and one virgate at Whitwoods Croft was reported at the manorial court. John's heir was his son, Richard.[6] One virgate (approximately 40 acres) in Tedstone Delamere would have been one of the larger farms, an average sized holding consisting of a noke (10 acres).

Ten tenements in Clifton-on-Teme were also included in the Hill's marriage settlement. This family seems to have been quite important in the parish, for John Hill was one of the Raters for the Militia Assessments in 1663 (see page 56), himself being assessed at £2 10s. and his son Richard at £6 10s. John was assessed for four hearths in the Tedstone Delamere Hearth Tax records of 1664, only second in number to Robert Mason gent of Tedstone Court. The only other house with four hearths was Tipton, so John's house was a substantial one and to date its whereabouts remain a mystery;[7] it seems too large to have been a former house at the Thrift which was a much smaller farm than it had become in 1840. But back to the Hill family, Richard and Elizabeth had four sons: John and Robert, who died without issue, William who succeeded to the property and Richard who died later in Tedstone Delamere.

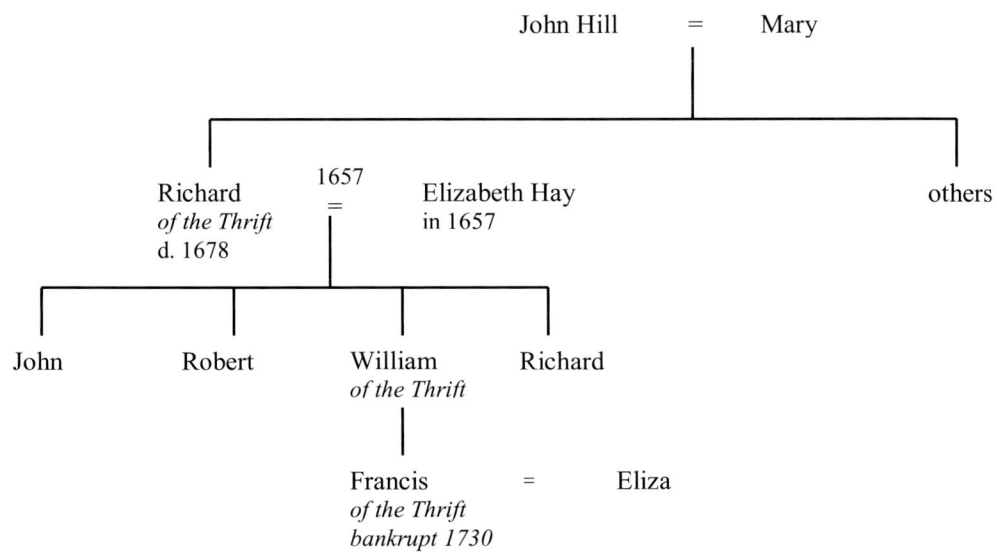

Descendents of John and Mary Hill of Tedstone Delamere

In 1724 Richard's son, William, was seriously troubled by debt, part of which had been incurred by his brother Robert. The property had been left to William and Richard Hill for their lives and then was to go to William's son Francis who was to have £15 a year until he was 21 and the remainder of the rents were to pay off the debts. But Francis inherited a poisoned chalice. He borrowed to pay off his father's debts. George Webb, the lord of the manor, bought a part of the estate but this did not include the Thrift. Francis was never able to get clear of his creditors. In 1727 the Thrift had been let to Richard Ffisor at an annual rent of £18 and by 1729 was let to Richard Brazier and this property together with Clifton property was the subject of a settlement made by Francis on his wife Mary should she survive him. Francis was finally declared bankrupt in 1730. He had for the previous six months exercised the trade of victualler and chapman at his house in Clifton and bought and sold wines, brandy and other goods.

The Thrift, still in the tenure of Richard Brazier, was sold in 1731 to James Higgins for £300; the land was then divided into 16 small fields which were listed and totalled

42 acres. Field names: Hopley and Collins Hill, which were once parts of common open fields, survive into the 19th century and are recorded in the tithe survey of 1841. In 1739 the occupant of the 'Frith' was assessed at 10d. for the Poor Rate and in the general pecking order this is way down the list, one of the closest to it being the occupant of Tidbatch who was assessed at 7d. Larger sums assessed were for the Court at 4s. 2d., the Rectory at 4s., and the Hedge House at 3s. 8d., see Appendix E. The occupier of the now disappeared farm of Riley next door to the Thrift was assessed at 1s. 4d.[8]

In 1762, lord of the manor, Robert Moore, purchased the Thrift from James Higgins for £585, on behalf of his wife Ann. The tenant was Edward Price, who paid a rent of £22 10s. p.a.

> I Robert Moore of Birmingham, gentleman have this day purchased an estate called the Thrift ... which money was my loving wife Ann Moore's money which was left her by her late father Mr George Webb deceased as executrix to him. Though the above estate was purchased in my name I do hereby declare that the above estate is my wife Ann Moore's and do authorise and give her full power to dispose of the above estate by will or otherwise to any or all of her children that she hathe now living or may hereafter hath by me.[9]

In 1777, Mr Price was paying 16s. 6d. half-yearly land tax for the Thrift, 1s. 10d. for New House (probably part only) and 8s. 4d. for Impy, another 'lost' farm[10].

It was probably Robert Moore, the son, who carried out the major reorganisation to enlarge the Thrift at the expense of some of these other mostly small farms and at the same time building a new house suitable for this now much bigger farm. Significant amongst these disappeared holdings in the area were Brierley, Riley, Impy, Little Riley and Mazer. These farms appear in the court rolls and are covered in Chapter IV. Brierley was a farm of half a virgate which, frustratingly, it has not been possible to place, but we know it was on the eastern side of the brook. In 1780 it was farmed by John Bedington. Land tax assessments are as follows:

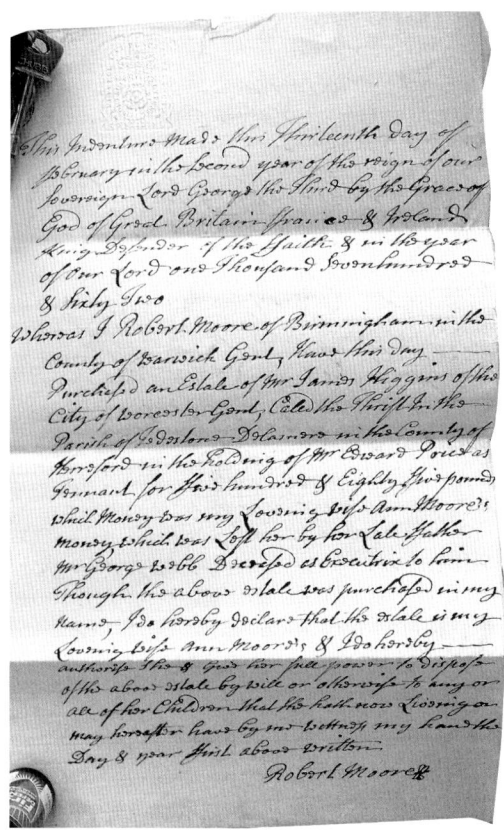

1762 . Purchase of the Thrift by Robert Moore for £585. *Whitbourne Estate*

Mr Price	1777	The Thrift	£1	13s.	0d.
Jn Bedington	1777	Brierley	£1	10s.	10d.
Jn Bedington	1790		£3	16s.	10d.
Jas. Bedington	1817	The Thrift	£6	10s.	0d.

The assessments tell us that the Bedington's property greatly increased in size. In 1816, we learn from the parish registers that James Bedington, son of John, lived at the Thrift. To understand the above, one should realise that the land tax assessments remained the same throughout the period, only increasing if the acreage increased. They appear to show the growth of the Bedington's land as properties were merged with it and with the addition of the enlarged Thrift sometime between 1777 and 1817. The small farms mentioned above may also have enlarged New House, Woodend and Woodhall as these farms also increased in size. In the tithe survey of 1841, the Thrift was 240 acres, a substantial increase from the 42 acres of 1731.

The Thrift farmhouse appears to be late 18th century and is a warm red brick house with large, light airy rooms and accommodation for the family and a number of living-in house and farm staff. This was a fine new house built by the Moores with the Bedingtons as tenants and one must assume that Brierley farmhouse and the old house at the Thrift were inferior in some way, perhaps pokey or in a bad state of repair and were abandoned. There are very substantial vaulted cellars for the cider and beer produced, and a large dairy at the Thrift.

The Thrift farmhouse was built in the second half of the 18th century.

In 1841, Thomas Roper and his wife Ann were tenants here. They had 20-year-old twin sons, George and Sandy together with living-in farm staff: Joseph James aged 25, two 15 year old lads Francis Griffiths and James Jones and a 15 year old farm servant Martha Nottingham. The farm included the now landless farmhouses of Riley and Stone House as homes for the workers.[11]

King post roof at the Thrift.

The Woodhall, Woodend, Wooden End confusion
These seem to have been three farms that became two. Nineteenth century people were confused, maps were giving varying names for the farms as were the landowners and parishioners. Research appears to show that until the late 18th century Woodhall, Woodend and Wooden End were at least *three* individual farms. In the 1713 sale of

Tedstone Court and manor, *Wooden End* was included in this sale to Richard Brompton as part of the demesne, the farm then passed to the succeeding owner, George Webb in 1726 and was subsequently bequeathed to the Moores through Webb's daughter, Ann.[12] On the other hand, at the time of the same 1713 sale, the freeholds of *Woodend* and *Woodham Hall* were 'owned' by Mr. Cooke and James Bateman, the latter two farms being included as part of the manor and were referred to in the deed as *'chief fee farms'*. Once the freehold of both Woodend and Woodham Hall were purchased by Robert Moore towards the end of the 18th century and all three properties were in his ownership, a reorganisation took place. It appears from a study of (a) the 1787 map made for the sale of Woodham Hall to Robert Moore, see Map 6 on page 121, and (b) the 1848 estate Map 7 on page 122, that the farmhouse & buildings of Woodham Hall shown in (a) must have been demolished or allowed to fall down at some stage before the creation of map (b). The land that was dotted about in five parcels in (a) later enlarged other farms. During the 19th century, probably because of the confusion with the names of the farms Woodend and Wooden End, Woodend became Woodhall and Wooden End became Woodend but the old names still continued to be used by some people. It is likely that this area was the site of an early hamlet.

1. Woodend

Earlier spellings refer to this property as 'Wooden End House',[13] which is a name that doesn't occur often; it might have been a description of the house itself which would have been unusual at the time for it to become the subject of the property name. Another similarly descriptive name for a property not too far distant is Bredenbury or 'Briden burg' meaning a boarded manor house.[14] But in the same way as with other names on this eastern side, it very probably relates to woodland. There are signs of former fish ponds just east of the house. Fish was an important part of the diet in medieval times when numerous fast days were called for by the church. The death of a tenant, William Elt, was recorded at the manorial court in 1558:

> Death of William Elt who held 1 messuage and one noke of land called Woodenend. No heriot is owed because the property was in the jointure of Margaret, William's wife. Because Margaret hasn't brought her jointure deed into court she is ordered to produce it within 1 month Richard Elt is son and nearest heir but don't know his age because he was not present in court so was not admitted nor did fealty.[15]

A noke is not always a set amount of land but is usually about 10 acres in this area; it does not sound as if this was the principal estate. We cannot be certain that the above entry refers to Woodend. It could refer to Woodhall. A further entry in 1621 is as follows:

> Death of Roger Hunt who held for the term of his life 1 messuage called Woodend and one virgate of land. His best beast is due as heriot in accordance with his indenture and a red ox worth 50s has been taken and delivered to the lord's store.[16]

This being one virgate, about 40 acres, probably is the principal estate. Very often by this date, heriots had been commuted to cash and it may be that why this hadn't

FARMS AND SMALLHOLDINGS EAST OF SAPEY BROOK

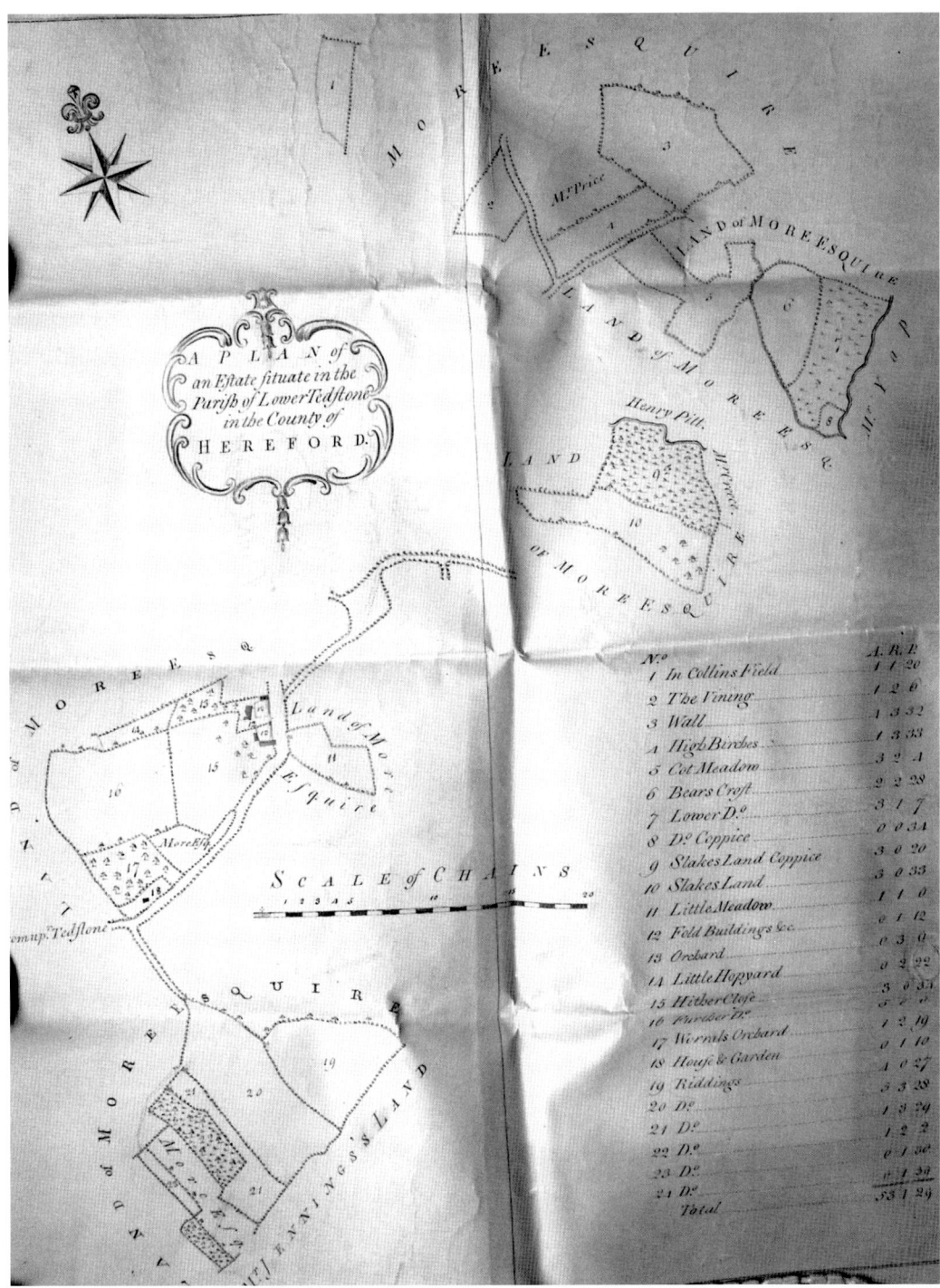

MAP 6. A plan of the Woodam Estate 1787. *Whitbourne Estate*

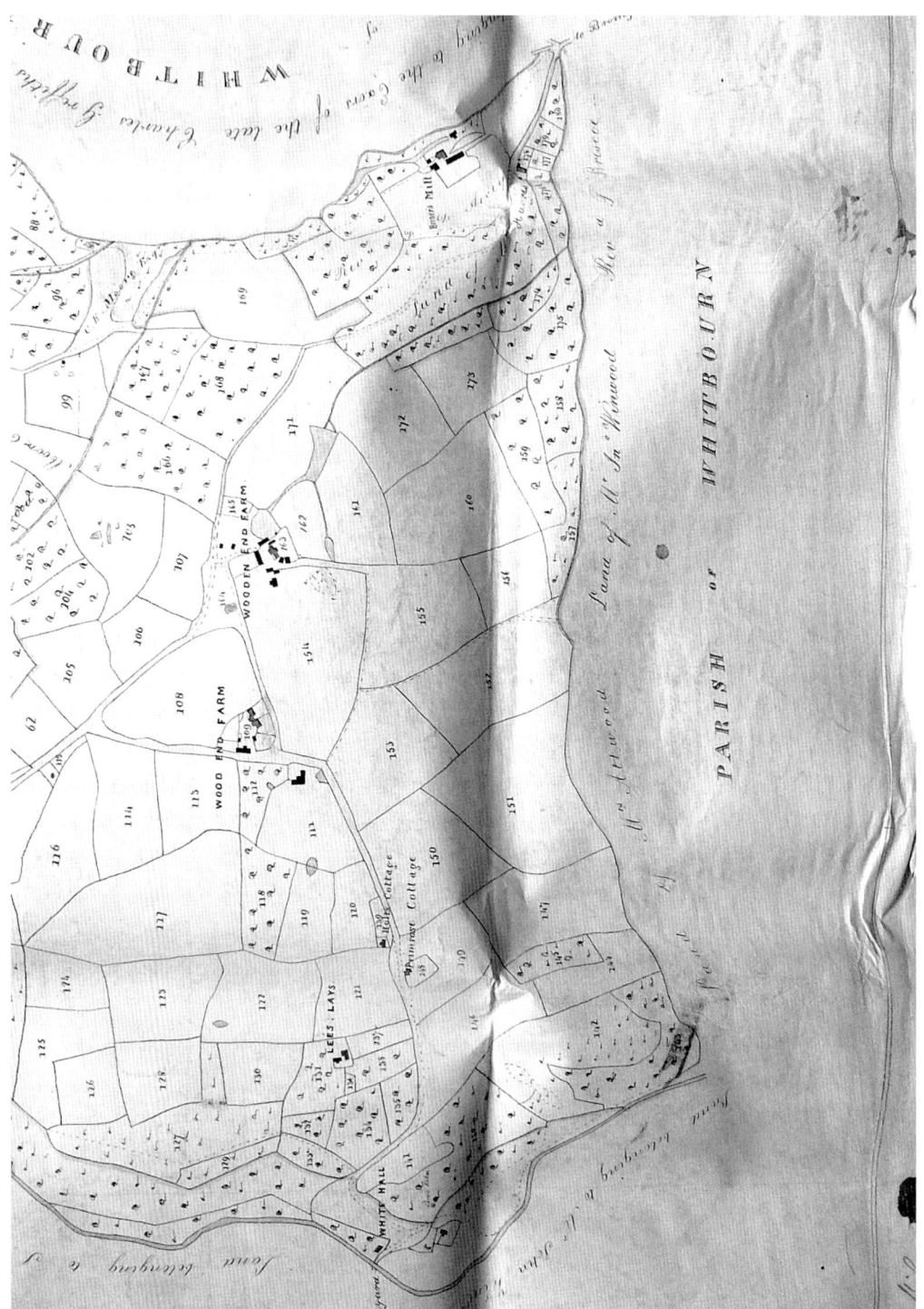

MAP 7. Plan of the Moores' estate in Tedstone Delamere 1848 (southern part).

happened here was because the lord actually lived and farmed in the parish and could cope with these livestock. In 1657, the manorial court was to meet here: 'day is given to the homage till the twenty seaveenth day of May next to yeelde their verdict at Woodenend…'.[17] One would have expected them to meet at Tedstone Court but it may have been more convenient to meet closer to the various places in dispute thus enabling the jury to walk out and view them first:

Woodend farm from the road.

> And we have likewise viewed one other difference between John Hill and James Bateman concerneing one Crab tree and one Apple tree doe likewise conceive the said trees to belonge to the meare** in Collins hill aforesaid
> We doe present Daniel Collins of Tedney for stankeing up one brooke at a leasowe of his the said Daniel Collins called Mazor and for barring of a briddleway over the said brooke whereby travellers are in greate danger and we enioyne the said Daniel Collins to cause a bridge or sufficient way to be made… over the said brooke before the Feast day.[18]

John Hill lived at the Thrift and James Bateman was from Woodham Hall, just a stone's throw from Woodend. Tedney, where Daniel Collins lived, is just over Tedstone Delamere's eastern boundary in Whitbourne but Collins held land in Tedstone Delamere. In 1639, he was mentioned in the Worcestershire Quarter Sessions Rolls when Humphrey Salway of Clifton, husbandman, and his wife Frances were charged with stealing faggots of wood from him.[19]

In 1713, Woodend had been held by the Masons, the lords of the manor, as part of their demesne. An interesting possibility arises: as one of the courts was held here, did Wooden End represent the manor house of the ancient Saxon manor of Lower Tedstone, or perhaps more realistically, the site of the demesne farm of that manor? In the 1713 conveyance documents, it was described as:

> All that messuage called the Wooden End House, now or late in the possession of John Landers … with all edifices, orchards and gardens belonging, the Birch Field, two New Fields, Black Furlong, Barley Close in Dunley Field, 4 acres Lye Croft, Dones Close, the Riding Quist Furlong, Bridry Furlong, Ton Pasture, Dunley Plock, Norchard Field, Grove Meadow, Barne Meadow, Lady Wood, Orchard Poole Meadow, and Morehouse Meadow and … Barne Closes.[20]

Dunley and the Ridings were former common fields.

In 1793, John Price seems to have been the owner. He died and left the farm known as 'Woodeninn' to his wife Ann and grandson John Craddock. But was this the main estate?

** *meare* is probably a boundary hedge or fence. Collins Hill was one of the common fields of the manor

The farmhouse is a 17th century building. The RCHME surveyor's report follows:

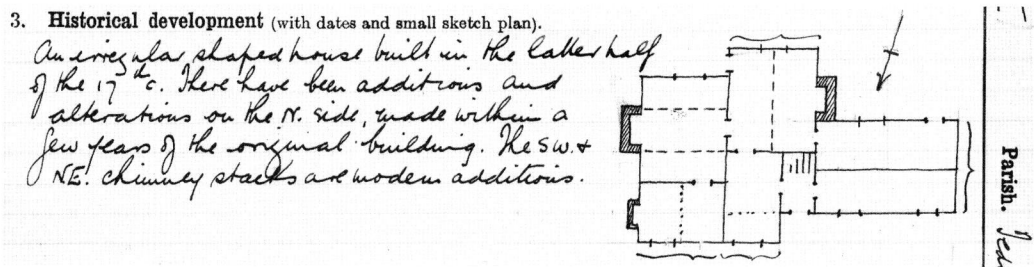

Woodend. RCHME surveyor's report. *Reproduced by permission of English Heritage.*

In 1841 Woodend, in the ownership of Charles Edward Moore, was farmed by Daniel Davies whose household consisted of two young children, two female farm servants and two farm labourers aged 25 and 13. The farm had been enlarged to 155 acres and included Primrose Cottage, on the opposite side of the road to the present cottage of that name, a double dwelling where the two farm workers lived.[21] (Primrose had formerly been another small farm.)

2. Woodham Hall – now disappeared

'Woodham Hall' Farm (sometimes called just Woodam) was referred to in the 1713 deeds as follows: 'a chief fee farm or other rent of 5s issuing out of a house and lands called Batemans or Woodham Hall now or late in the possession of James Bateman'[22] meaning that it was a freehold property of the manor paying a chief rent of 5s. James Bateman gent, possibly the father or grandfather of this James, was mentioned in the 1663 Militia Assessments and he was also assessed for one hearth in 1664; so he was an owner-occupier (see page 57). The burial of Frances Bateman was recorded on a flat stone in the aisle of the parish church:

> Frances Bateman, died May 28th, 1708
> Heav'n took her soule: the earth her corpse did seize,
> Yet not in fee; she only holds by lease,
> With this proviso – when the judge shall call,
> Earth shall give up her share, and Heav'n take all.[23]

This stone is sadly no longer visible. At the time of George Gilbert Scott's restoration of the church in 1856, memorial slabs inside the church were used to cover his new heating pipes and were overlaid with tiles![24]

In 1739, a Mr. Wheeler was assessed at 1s. 9d. poor rate for Woodham Hall.[25] In 1780 Woodham Hall, a 59 acre farm, was in the tenure of Sarah Bayliss. And then in 1787 Robert Moore, the Younger, bought Woodham Hall, Showells and a cottage called Whounall, from one of Wheeler's daughters. In 1787, some progress had been made, probably over centuries, in enclosing the land in the common fields but this farm was still in five separated blocks dotted about the parish. There was an acre 'in Collins

Field, and six small fields amounting to about 15 acres in 'Riddings' common field. From the plan (Map 6), Whounall or Worrall appears to be the present day Primrose Cottage. The plan marks the eastern side of the parish as being 'Lower Tedstone' and the western side as 'Upper Tedstone'.

3. Woodhall – formerly Woodend (modern name used below)

Another name referring to woodland, Woodhall is a most attractive farmhouse. John Cooke, a tanner, died here in 1686; he inherited the property from his grandfather, another John Cooke. It is possible that the tannery was at Woodhall. In 1736 Richard Cook paid 5s. chief rent for Woodhall to the lord of the manor.[26] The Cook family seem to have been in Tedstone Delamere for some years, John Cook being assessed for £6 in the Militia Assessments of 1663 and for one hearth in 1664 and was one of the more substantial inhabitants.[27] In 1739, Woodhall was assessed at 3s. for the Poor Rate, one of the higher payments. Richard Cook died in 1738. In his Will, he named his kinsman, Samuel Parkes of Great Shelsley, his executor and he left his household goods, corn, hay, cattle, farm implements, stock and personal estate in trust to pay his debts and funeral expenses and 'the overplus if any' was to go to his 'dear wife Elizabeth'. He must have feared there would be no 'overplus' because the will continues 'if My Personall estate shall not be sufficient to pay all My Debts and Funerall Expenses then I doe hereby Charge My Lands & reall Estate in Tedston', it being subject to his wife's life in such part of his real estate that was settled on her before her marriage. It was his wish that the land and real estate should go to his nephew, Adam Parkes, eldest son of his late sister, Ann. His wife, his brothers Joseph, Samuel, Thomas and his sister Ann were all to get £5 apiece. One can't help feeling somewhat sorry for his wife!

Woodhall in 1931. *Reproduced by permission of English Heritage*

		£		
	A true and perfect Inventory of all the Goods Cattells and Chattells of Richard Cooke late Deceased of the parish of Tedstone Delamere in the County of Hereford takin And Apraised this 30th of December 1737 By William Arden & Peter Broom			
Impr[im]s	Wearing Apparel and Money in purse	05	00	00
	One Ox four Cows One Horse 10 Sheep Three Piggs 2 Calfs and Corn pease & Oats in the Barn	34	11	00
	Hay £7 7s, Two Wains One Wheel Dray and all other Tack of Team	16	10	00
	Cyder & perry in the casks and Empty Casks	25	17	00
	Corn on the Ground and One Bagg Hops	14	00	00
	Cyder Hairs Kiln Hairs, all Sorts of Utensils for Husbandry etc	04	19	06
	One Clock and all Sorts of Linnen	08	08	03
	Corn and other Grain Thrasht Beef & bacon & Cheese &c	10	11	06
	Bedds Brass and pewter Chairs Tubbs Tables and all other sorts of Household Goods	20	00	00
	Odd things unseen and forgotten	00	19	00
		140	16	09

This Inventory was exhibited at Ludlow the 11th day of December in the year of our Lord 1738 by Samuel Parkes the Executor named in the Will of the deceased for a true and perfect Inventory of all and Singlar the Goods Chatells And Credits of the said deceased but under a protestation of adding hereto if he shall discover anymore hereafter

One is always surprised at how few livestock the farms were supporting at that time compared with today. Probably livestock had been sold before the winter but our ancestors made sure they were never short of something to drink for the valuation of cider and perry was quite a large proportion of the whole! The clock and the linen would be items that would only be found in the more superior households.

It is not known whether Adam Parkes ever farmed here himself but in 1760, Joseph Parkes, late of Worcester, a hop merchant, bequeathed Woodhall to trustees to maintain his brother Sam Parkes for life. Sam was a Worcester mercer and manufacturer. But Sam went bankrupt and so the very next year, the farm was advertised for sale in the Berrow's Journal as a convenient farmhouse with useful outbuildings and about 90 acres together with a small tenement (probably Primrose). But it can't have sold for in 1772 Robert Moore paid £1505 5s. to purchase Woodhall from the assignees of the estate of Sam Parkes, who had died a widower without children. The farm had for sometime past been in the occupation of Edward Hawker at a yearly rent of £44. It was then 87 acres, the fields being listed: some of the field names are relics of the open field system e.g. Shortland Furlong; Dunley was one of the common fields, the name perhaps referring to the colour of the soil; Castle Field is an interesting one but unfortunately does not appear in the tithe survey so we can't pinpoint it; there are fields which must once have been part of the lord's demesne land eg Lordsfield Meadow and a close of pasture in Lords Field; Redding [*ryding*] means a clearing from woodland.[28]

In 1780, the tenant was Thomas Grubb. Woodhall was 103 acres in 1841 and the tithe map (see Map 9, page 175) shows the whole within a ring fence and clearly illustrates the great changes that could be made by the landowners once all was in their ownership. In 1841, Ben Grubb, the son of Thomas, lived at Woodhall with his wife, Sarah, and his children, Ben junior and Hariet. There were two living-in farm labourers: Ben's brother, William, and a 15 year old lad. The farm then included Dunley Cottage where another farm worker was housed.[29]

New House
This attractive farmstead with house of stone and plastered-timber-framing comprises house and buildings that used to form a courtyard. There is an old quarry just south of Riley Cottages (see map on page 46) and it is possible that this stone was used for building the clutch of stone buildings in this part of the parish, namely New House, the two Stone Houses and Riley Cottages. The house is built on a modified L shaped plan and the RCHME dates it from the latter half of the 17th century. Early in the second half of the 18th century it was enlarged by an L shaped addition built round the north-western angle. Later a chimney was added at the western end of the north side, and the south range extended to the east. The east wall of the south range has a three light original moulded frame window.[30] There are two blocked windows in the south wall, probably to avoid paying window tax.

In 1777, New House was in the tenancy of Mr. Baylis who was assessed at 13s. 8½d. for land tax and a second property called New House was occupied by Mr. Price who was assessed at 1s. 10d.[31] Was the property divided or what seems the more likely option: were there two properties of the same name? The larger property was tenanted by John Caswell in 1790 (see Table 5, land tax assessments, page 84).

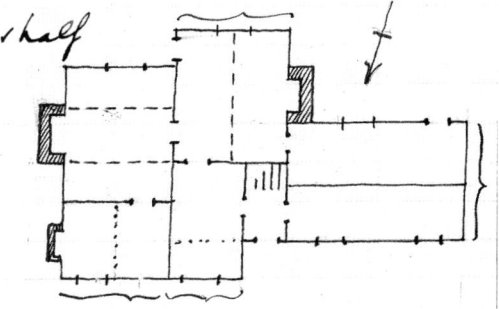

New House. RCHME plan 1931.
Reproduced by permission of English Heritage.

The Price property – (the smaller one)
In 1781 Edward Price left to his son, Edward: 'the messuage and lands wherein I now dwell called the New House'. (It was probably Edward Price, senior, who was farming

New House. Anne and Sheila Jones with members of the Bromyard Local History Society. *B&DLHC*

the Thrift as a tenant in 1762.) New House was charged with the following payments within six months of the death of his wife Mary: £60 to his daughter Ann who was the wife of William Burraston of Whitbourne, cooper, and £60 to another daughter Mary, wife of William Mann of Great Shelsley, yeoman. He left his wife all his goods and chattels making her his sole executrix. It seems it was possible to pay off debts by using promise of legacies yet to come for in 1782 William Mann owed £84 to Rev. Thomas Jennings of Whitbourne and Thomas Smith of Lower Sapey and he persuaded them to take the promised legacy of £60 in part payment! This will is another example of the hazards associated with trying to be fair to all one's children; Edward's children must have had a long wait for their money because it wasn't until 1799 that Edward Price the Younger managed to pay off his father's legacies by mortgaging the Stone House where he was then living.

In 1841, New House belonged to Charles Edward Moore and was farmed by Daniel Davies of Woodend; it was then 133 acres. The house was inhabited by a farm labourer, Joseph Passey together with his wife and family.[32]

Horner's Mill

Sited on the Whitbourne Brook, on the far south-eastern boundary of the parish, Horner's Mill is a delightfully situated property in a sheltered valley, the brick house has a Georgian flavour to the interior; another wing makes the house L shaped. There is a well-proportioned central hall with parlour one side and kitchen the other. The cellar has a vaulted roof. The mill has gone but the leat is still visible, remains of the dam can be seen on the brook and there is a flood hatch. A long timber-framed barn of stone, brick and weatherboarding, incorporates a pair of crucks; it has been much altered and renewed.

Farm buildings at Horner's Mill. One of the buildings contains a pair of crucks. *Rosemary Keep*

Horner's Mill was formerly known as Peck Mill. A rather pathetic entry in the Patent Rolls of 1481-5 may relate to a former inhabitant of the mill:

> Pardon in consideration of the poverty of Lucy Porter, who has long since been sued thereof in the king's court in great misery, to John Pecke of Tedstone Delamere, county Hereford, and the said Lucy his wife for the death of John Kyng, and of any consequential outlawry and waivery, and restitution to them of their goods and chattels seized thereof to the escheator.

A family by the name of Hornar/Horner gave their name to this property at a later date. It was reported at the manorial court in 1532 that John and Joan Hornar had granted to their son, Edward, 'tenements with one mill in Teddeston'. He was admitted as tenant and did fealty.[33] In 1558, the death was recorded at the manorial court of Edward Horner, a free tenant:

> … who held 1 messuage and 1 noke [10 acres] of land and there is due to the lord as heriot one red cow worth 20s. Augustine Horner is his son and nearest heir and he is of full age and a relief of 3s 1d is due to the lord. He came to the court and acknowledged tenancy by rent of 3s 1d pa and heriot when it should be due and did fealty and was admitted.[34]

Augustine died in 1591. He was buried at Whitbourne Church to which he left 3s. 4d. and he also left two bushels of corn to the poor people in Tedstone Delamere. He left £10 each to his two daughters, Joane and Elizabeth, together with the usual feather beds and bedding. He left 'one bullocke Collo blacke called gilberte' to his son-in-law, George Coombey. He left his dwelling-house, then still called 'Peckmill' with the barn, mill and lands to Joan and to Elizabeth he left his messuage called Middlefield, a leasowe of pasture called the Impe and three crofts adjoining. It is interesting that Augustine is described as 'yeoman' rather than 'miller' so perhaps the mill wasn't then working. He signed his will with a rather distinctive letter A which appears on other documents such as a glebe terrier. In 1599, Augustine's family sold Peck Mill to Thomas Eckley. In 1630, Thomas Eckley died and in 1697, the death was recorded at the manorial court of a subsequent owner, George Unett and the mill passed to James Hodges. Horner's Mill is recorded in 1713 when the manor of Tedstone Delamere was sold by Robert Mason, as 'a chief rent of 2s.1d. issuing out of house and lands called Horner's Mill'.[35] It was then still in the possession of James Hodges. Horner's Mill deeds date back to 1714 when the property was bought by James's son, Unett Hodges for £200. It included a tenement called the Perke (Peck) House, pasture lying between the old brook and the mill pound, a plock of ground lying at the Mill House of half an acre, an acre of ground lying above the mill between the old brook and the mill pound and other lands totalling 31 acres. In a marriage settlement of 1740, when Unett and Jane Hodges of Whitbourne were making provision for their son, another Unett, Peck House was in the tenancy of William Caswell. William Caswell had been assessed at 10d for the poor rate in 1739, so very likely it was this property that was rated.

Unett Hodges, the younger, yeoman and chapman, was declared bankrupt in 1756 having fallen out with his father! The Commission of bankruptcy found that 'Unett Hodges, the younger, had within the last three to four years dealt in buying and selling wheat, peas or grain and had during this time become indebted to his father for £200. A notice was placed in the London Gazette for a sitting under the Commission to meet at the home of Thomas Taylor known by the sign of the Kings Arms in Bromyard. The creditors there elected Unett Hodges the elder and John Yapp to be assignees of the estate. Perk House was then given a yearly value of about £7 per annum. There are further documents of 1756, 1776 and 1778 when Thomas Caswell was the tenant but it is noted that during this whole period there is neither a reference to a working mill nor is the tenant referred to as a miller so presumably the mill had fallen into disrepair. The fields are listed and include 3 acres in the Stockings Common Field.

In 1783, the property was sold to Ben Birch of Clifton-on-Teme, maltster, for £300. In 1802, Ben Birch of Tedstone Delamere, *miller*, and his wife Elizabeth, sold the property to Richard Whettall of Linton, miller:

> 'all that messuage lately erected with the newly erected water corn grist mill and malt house commonly called the Peck House with lands belonging for £1684'.

The large price inflation reflects the new house and mill. In 1803 Richard Whettall was clearly in some financial difficulty owing money to several people and he granted the property to Thomas Whettall, miller and John Best, both of Linton, in trust with provision for them to sell when necessary to pay these debts. At this time it was also known as 'Arnolds Mill'. In 1813 it was sold to Rev. John Darcy of Morton, Cheshire for £2100. Mr. Darcy was the Tedstone Delamere rector at the time but appears to be living elsewhere. In 1841, two very young men were living alone at the mill, Edward Starling aged 15, described as miller, together with his 14 year-old brother John.

Horner's Mill is unusual in that it never belonged to the Moore family.

Tidbatch (alias 'the Shop House')
This property was recorded as early as 1349:

> By deed poll William son of John Titbach grants to John son of Hugh Titbach all his lands in Tedstone Delamere called Titbach in fee.

Titbach probably means 'the tit's stream or valley' from OE *titta* 'a tit or small bird' + OE b^3ce 'stream, valley with a stream'[36] which meaning seems exactly right. It was included in the sale of the Tedstone Court Estate by Robert Mason in 1713 as part of the demesne land.[37] It then passed with the estate to George

Tidbatch 1977. *Kathleen Harris*

Webb and then to the Moore family. In 1739 it was assessed at 7d. for the poor rate, typical of a cottage with a small amount of land.[38] Formerly Upper Tidbatch in 1841, this property was the blacksmith's; nearby Lower Tidbatch which was let with it housed a carpenter who perhaps operated from Upper Tidbatch and may well have worked for Richard Powell, the blacksmith. This little farm is situated on what was once a very well trodden track. Before the advent of the motor car, it was the shortcut to many places and would have been much used. Now isolated and, at the time of writing, buried in deep undergrowth, it was once a busy place with horses being brought to be shod and carts, implements and tools repaired. A visit to the blacksmith was a social event where one caught up with all the news. In remote parts of the countryside with no pub and no rapid means of transport, visiting the blacksmith was a day out to be looked forward to. The once attractive property has the most wonderful view but it is now completely overgrown and has become a sad ruin.* It is situated just above steeply falling banks down to the Sapey Brook. This late 17th century two-bedroomed timber-framed small farmhouse has a raised roof and a later addition at the end with stone shelves serving as a dairy. Between the house and dairy is a scullery complete with copper boiler, sink and a bread-oven, un-restored and all just as it was. Taken alone, the house is probably not of any particular value as there are many more like it but taken as a group, together with its farm buildings, it seems a rare survival. There is a small two-bay timber-framed barn with a pair of wagon doors on the yard side. One bay is floored and the other is designed for the storage of hay or straw. An early-19th century cider house is set between the cottage and the barn and is built of local red sandstone; one can imagine blacksmith Richard Powell sampling the cider with favoured customers. The tiny cider mill is still in situ and a two-bay stone cow-house, originally for six cows, has been slightly altered to cope with the housing of horses and pigs. The forge adjoins the house at its other end. Flax was once grown here, a small field shown on the tithe map is called 'Flax Ground'.

At the time of the 1840/41 tithe survey, the farm was 17 acres. In 1841, Richard Powell, blacksmith, aged 65, who was the first of four generations of blacksmiths operating in Tedstone Delamere, lived there with his wife Elizabeth and was assisted by a 25-year-old son, also called Richard.

Lee Lay
The name probably means 'wood clearing'. Lee Lay is most likely the property mentioned in the will of Thomas Brazier in 1742 when he left his brother Richard: 'the tenement I lately purchased of William Acton …with all the rest of my goods and chattels'.[39] In 1739 Thomas Brazier had been assessed at 1s. 6d. for the poor rate seemingly putting Lee Lay on a par with Winley and Pixhill, both rated for very similar amounts. Thomas died in 1742.

---

* Since writing this account, the house and buildings at Tidbatch have been demolished.

A true and perfect Inventory of the Goods and Ch[att]ells of Thomas Brazier of the parish of Tedstone Delamere and County of Hereford

	£	s	d
Twelve Hogsheads and Barells	1	08	00
Eight Sheep	1	07	00
A Skeel* and three Tubbs	0	08	06
A bedd and Blankets	0	15	06
A Pigg	0	10	00
A Cupboard	0	02	06
A Coffer	0	01	00
Wearing Apparel	0	12	00
All other Smal Tools	0	02	06
Wheat and Grain in the Barn	1	02	00
For Cyder and Perry	0	18	00
	7	04	00

Richard Brazier)
the marke of   ) Appraise[er]s
William Gaskins)

In his will, the eight sheep were to go to his kinsmen, Thomas and Richard Brazier, the bed and furniture were to go to his kinswoman, Ann Brazier, and his sister, Elizabeth Acton, was to get one guinea and a bag of wheat.

In 1765, brother Richard, a cordswainer, died and as well as Lee Lay, where he lived, he owned another property called **Bearcroft** and he had clearly put considerable thought into what happened to this after his death, for after leaving his wearing apparel and £5 to his son Richard, he also left him:

William and Mary seal, the size of a 50p piece, found in the foundations of the house. The late 17th century seems a likely date for the building.
B&DLHC

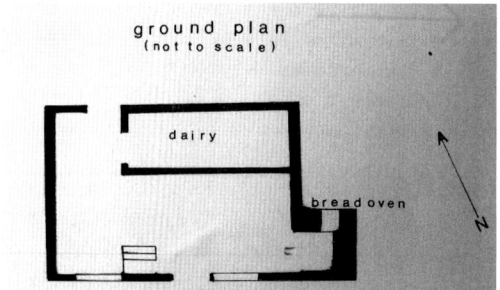

Lee Lay - south elevation.   *Rosemary Keep*

A sketch of Lee Lay before restoration.
Rosemary Keep

---

* Wooden bucket, pail or tub for holding milk or water

> 'that part of my messuage in Tedstone which he now uses and occupies called Bearcroft and also the bay or building that he likewise uses to put his drink in with the chamber over it and also the garden used by my said son adjacent to the messuage. Also all that orchard adjacent to this garden on the south side and also the upper part of the land that I have marked out, being part in an orchard and the other part coppice …. To my daughter Ann wife of Philip Griffiths, all that part of the messuage wherein they now dwell and the garden and land … which they now occupy and use and to enjoy free use of the oven in the kitchen, kiln and mill and liberty of the kitchen fire for baking and brewing as often as they require without interruption from my son Richard. Also my wish is that my daughter Ann shall have the staircase to her and her heirs for ever. Also my will is that a partition be made between my son and daughter at the joint charge of mason's and carpenter's work and the timber to be used is to be felled off my son's land.'[40]

Sadly Bearcroft is one of the many properties in Tedstone Delamere that have disappeared. At a meeting of the manorial court in 1532, a 'church road from Barcrofts Glatt to le stable' (a *glatt* is a gap without a gate) was said to be out of repair. Four men were ordered to repair it on pain of 20p. including the lord of the manor, Thomas Wysham gent. but it was noted that his pain was to be forfeited to Tedstone church.[41] Perhaps he was too posh to man a shovel with the rest. A small field No 452 on the tithe map and south of New House farm is called Bearcroft Close. The name may relate to *bear* or two-rowed barley grown in the Midlands.[42] Richard Brazier's will continues: to his daughter Sarah, wife of Frederick Richards, a weaver, he left:

> 'all that my messuage wherein I now dwell called Lea Leys together with all buildings, gardens, orchards, lands thereunto belonging and in my own possession to hold to Sarah for her life and also paying to John Harris £20 and also paying to my daughter Susannah Stephens £7 when she reaches the age of 21 years'

To son Richard he left one large hogshead containing about 110 gallons. Sarah Richards was to have the residue of goods, chattels and personal estate and was to be his sole executrix. Richard Brazier Richards, the son of Sarah & Frederick, inherited Lee Lay and in 1791 it was bought by Robert Moore for £262 10s.

At that time it was let to Thomas Corbett whose descendants continued to farm at Lee Lay for over 100 years and indeed direct descendants of Thomas Corbett are still in the parish today farming at Woodend and Lower Thrift. Thomas and Ann Corbett's daughter, Amelia, married Thomas Jones and they lived at Lee Lay, bringing up their family there. In 1841, Mrs. Amelia Jones lived there with her six children; Charles Edward Moore was the landlord. It was then nine acres.

Stone House A
It is referred to as A because there was another Stone House referred to as B, see Map 4, page 46. Stone House A is marked on the tithe map and was approached by a track going south-west from Lambs Green. It is also marked on the OS map of 1904 but has since disappeared. The first mention we have of Stone House is in 1737 when John Price left it to his wife, Ann. His eldest son, Edward, who had been living with them, was to have the smallholding after his mother's death and after legacies of £25 each had been paid to John's other children, Ann and Joseph. John's

grandson, Edward Price, mortgaged Stone House for £280 and then in 1804, Thomas Winwood of Whitbourne, a cooper, purchased the property known as the 'Stone' for £500 with the help of a mortgage from Edward Freeman.[43] On the back, the indenture reads as follows:

> Be it remembered that on 9th Oct.1804 possession and seizure of all the within mentioned hereditaments were delivered by … by delivery to said Thos. Winwood and James Wormington of *one twig* in the name of possession and siezen thereof ….
>
> 23rd Jan. 1810 An inventory of household goods and other effects of late Thomas Winwood [of Stone House]
>
> | | |
> |---|---|
> | Feather bed & bolster. Covers | Large Sked |
> | Quarter cask. Frying pan. Spade | 4 pr. Sheets |
> | Oak chest. Do. Box oak | 4 post bedsteads |
> | 2 leaved oak table. Clock | Old chest. Skeel |
> | 2 Pikes. 2 Rakes. Dung fork & Hook | Hacker & Bill, cutting knife |
> | 3 chairs. New Pail | Brass kettle. Copper tea do. |
> | Hop bar. Axe, saw & bagging bill. | 4 wood trenchers |
> | 4 wood trenchers | Cheese ladder[?] & strainer |
> | 2 bee hives. Corn tub | Lot old iron. 2 bean hooks |
> | 3 sickles and … band | Rick hay about 30 cwt. Scythe |
> | The family cider. ½ the perry | 2 oak shelves in frame |
> | Bacon rack, oak dresser, Sway & sinks | Shelf over mantelpiece |
> | 6 hogs heads. | 2 benches Shelf, small table |
> | 5 cider hairs. 2 kiln do. | Cyder Mill & press |
>
> Total amount £43. 19. 6
>
> Strickland & Horsley, Appraisers

This seems a much fuller inventory than earlier ones but all of the items appear the kind of necessities that smallholders would have needed in the previous centuries although the clock is rather special. Perhaps the reason for the fullness of this one is that it was carried out by a firm of valuers rather than two or three of the bereaved's neighbours who would be trying to limit the amount of tax payable by their friends. A second inventory is a valuation of the Stone House with five acres of meadow, orcharding and hop land together with the furniture in the first inventory and it totalled only £143 19s.6d. so remembering that Thomas had paid £500 for the property in 1804, one wonders what had happened? It is likely that some land had already been sold to the Moores. Although Thomas was clearly living at Stone House in Tedstone Delamere, he was buried in Whitbourne.

In 1840/41 John Winwood, almost certainly Thomas's youngest son, owned this smallholding but John Smith, an agricultural labourer, occupied it; it was then a small isolated property with the land on all sides belonging to Mr. Moore. John Winwood also owned the smallholding known as Hams (on the following page) on the parish's southern boundary. In 1839, Winwood owned and lived at Rosemore in Whitbourne, a 255 acre farm.[44]

The Homes or Hams

The name 'Hams' is from the OE *hamm* meaning 'land in the bend of a river' or 'stream-side meadow'. This smallholding situated at the most southerly point of the parish occupied the level land beside the Sapey Brook below Whitehall; the holding has now gone. The death of a person by the name of Yeomans, who held a messuage and certain lands called *le Homm,* was recorded at the manorial court in 1689 when they did not know who the heir was.[45] In 1713, William Wynne paid 8s chief rent for *Homs*.[46] Land Tax records tell us that from 1777 until almost 1801, Thomas Haines was owner-occupier. By 1801, John Winwood, who also owned Stone House above, was owner. In 1841, John Winwood had this 23 acre holding in hand; there were then nine small fields all incorporating the name 'Ham': 'Ham Orchard', 'Ham Hopyard', 'Ham Meadow' etc and a tenth field called 'Lime Kiln Coppice'. Lime was an important resource and used from the medieval period for both mortar and limewash in buildings and was added to the fields as a useful fertiliser. It was extracted from limestone by burning.[47] There was no farmhouse at the Hams but Winwood owned a cottage there which was let to John Palmer. Today this cottage is the only one still standing at Whitehall (see page 231).

This chapter ends in 1840/41 with Charles Edward Moore in possession of all of Tedstone Delamere to the east of the Sapey Brook except the smallholdings: Horner's Mill, The Hams, Stone House A and Ladywood. The last 100 years had been a period of immense change when the map of this side of the parish had been substantially redrawn. The Robert Moores, father and son, followed by James, Edward and then Charles Edward Moore had gradually bought up property as it became available. This included not only the farms of the Thrift, New House, Woodhall and Woodend but many smallholdings. They then reapportioned the land, enlarging the farms but losing a number of smallholdings, most now having gone without trace.

The period in history that is to follow is one when local historians are truly in clover for there are for the very first time two new sets of records which taken together provide an overwhelming amount of information. The tithe map and apportionment of 1840/41 tell us who owned and who occupied every acre of the parish, see Maps 8, 9, 10 and 11 on pages 164, 175, 216 and 225. Fields mentioned in the text are recorded on Map 4, page 46. The fields are all named, together with their acreages and uses. The census of 1841 is particularly useful coming, as it does, so close to the tithe survey. It lists the inhabitants and where they lived. Their approximate ages and relationships to the heads of household are given along with occupations. Together these documents provide a firm base from which to work backwards and forwards and subsequent ten yearly censuses are of even greater use giving more accurate ages along with the name of the parish where each member of a household was born and the number of people a person employed. The later story of these farms on the eastern side and the people who lived in them, and importantly, the new landowner, continues in Chapters IX and X.

Haymaking at the Court.

CHAPTER VII

The Wight Family and their Tedstone Court Estate

The new mansion house

Richard Wight had followed his father, Richard, as his Cousin James Moore's tenant at the Court (see Chapter IV page 86). His father died in 1800 and his mother three years later[1] leaving Richard looking after the farm and a household of six younger brothers and sisters at the early age of 23. A couple of years later he was to inherit the Court and manor from his cousin James but according to the will, he was not left any cash.[2] It seems probable that the old house was then in a poor state of repair: for the past 150 years it had been lived in firstly by the poverty stricken owners, the Mason family, then by a series of tenants. In 1809, Richard Wight married Maria Shelton from nearby Upper Norton.[3] Maria's father, Brown Shelton of Eastham was a ne'er-do-well; he was made bankrupt 8th July 1781 and had to sign over his Eastham Estate in trust for the sole and separate use of his wife, Mary Lane, Maria's mother, for life and then to their issue in male tail. He was later divorced by his wife which was unusual for those times. By all accounts he was not a pleasant person; he tried to have his wife certified as a lunatic and gain control of her property.[4] Mary, poor woman, died in 1821 aged 73 and is remembered on the Wight family tomb in Tedstone Delamere churchyard by the following inscription;

> Mary Shelton late of Norton died 1821 aged 73
> She sustained a life of many and great trials with Christian resignation & died in the hope of a blissful immortality

WIGHT FAMILY OF TEDSTONE COURT

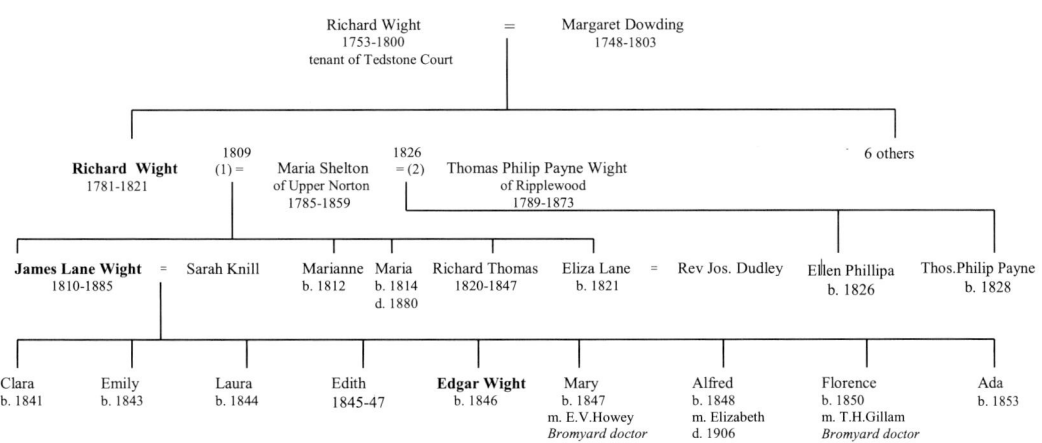

In Mary Shelton's will of 1816, Brown was left an annuity of £30 a year; he was described as her former husband from whom she had been divorced for many years. Her daughter, Maria was left £1,500, plus another £300 and £200 for her granddaughter, Mary Ann (Marianne?) Wight. She seems to have been a woman of considerable wealth. Maria brought £5000 to the marriage when she married Richard.[5] It seems probable that it was Lane money which largely contributed to the building of the new Tedstone Court. Maria's brother, Brown Shelton the Younger, was a Bromyard surgeon and had built 32 High Street in 1794.[6] This house, now a dental surgery, unassuming from the outside, contains an extremely fine interior with richly moulded plasterwork, panelled doors and a fine staircase.[7] Brown's son, John Brown Shelton, continued with a remarkable refurbishment of the Bromyard house and it seems clear that this was a family keen to be at the forefront of fashion. Maria may well have been largely instrumental in the plans for the new house at Tedstone Court and it could be that the same craftsmen were employed. This was a time when a number of gentry houses were being built. The new mansion house at Bredenbury Court was built in 1810, later to be enlarged, and Birchyfields in Avenbury was also built at around this time.[8] A century later, Tedstone Court with 322 acres was described as:

> ... the commodious manor house, a residence standing on an eminence commanding unrivalled views over a great extent of some of the most beautiful country in the kingdom with the conservatories, horticultural buildings and vineries, pleasure gardens, park like grounds, flower, fruit and vegetable gardens, productive orchards, stabling, ample farm buildings, 7 cottages, four of which are modern and woodland and covers, with excellent sporting in the way of shooting, hunting, trout fishing and golf.[9]

Alterations were made later: the bow window to the front looks Victorian and the rather fine looking conservatories were probably also added at a later date.

Tedstone Court, built c.1809 for Richard & Maria Wight, replacing an earlier house.
Bellville Collection

The fine staircase at 32 High Street, Bromyard (the dental surgery). This house was built by Maria Wight's brother: Brown Shelton. *Duncan James*

The Wight family

Maria and Richard had five children but tragedy struck this family for in 1821 Richard died at the age of 40 leaving Maria having just lost her mother, with a new baby and young family to bring up and an estate to manage. His memorial in Tedstone Delamere church reads:

> this truly excellent Man
> was snatched in the prime of life
> from a wife and family to whom his virtues rendered
> him a most inestimable blessing

Five years later, Maria married Thomas Philip Paine Wight of Ripplewood, Collington.[10] He was Richard's first cousin, both being the grandsons of Thomas and Margery Wight of Bishops Frome. He took over the running of the estate for her. Maria and her second husband, Philip, had two children, one a son: Thomas Philip Paine (the Younger). They only employed a couple of living-in house servants at the Court, much like any other farmer, but they did have a groom, Isaac Coterel, quartered in the house. In the 1851 census,[11] Philip Wight was described as a 'farmer of 217 acres employing 5 labourers'. Pixhill was then in hand, and Daniel Clews, farm bailiff, lived there. Land that subsequently became Upper Grounds Farm was part of the Tedstone Court farmland.

In memory of Richard & Maria Wight.

The last gasps of the manorial system

By the 19th century, chief rents and heriots were becoming increasingly hard to collect. Inflation had played its part and these now very small rents had been allowed to build up year after year uncollected. Twelve years chief rent was included in the following very varied account sent to Mr. Wood of the Line House:[12]

Mr. Wood Debtor to R Wight

1811			£	s	d
March 7th	To two bushels & half of beans @ 7s per bushel			17	06
11th	two and half of beans			17	06
12th	two bushels of beans			14	00
13th	one ditto			7	00
	Two gallons of Brandy @ 28s		2	16	00
	Cash			4	00
	12 yrs Chief rent to Michaelmas 1818 @ 14/2		8	10	00
			14	06	00
	a bushel of oats			15	00
	Mr. Wood's bill		4	15	00
	halling 3 bags of hops			4	06
			14	14	06
	Mr Wood's bill		4	15	06
			9	19	00
1817					
June 24th	a Cow bulled			10	06
25th	ditto			10	06
July 15th	ditto			10	06
			11	10	06
1819					
January 1st	Settled R. Wight				

The reader must make what he will of the figures and odd calculation! The bill is a mixture of all sorts! The brandy is an unusual one; had he been making it? It seems that accounts were not paid very frequently. The affidavits recorded below were produced in later years for T. P. P. Wight (Philip), Maria's second husband, who rode round collecting statements from local people to try to prove the almost forgotten manorial customs and so help his cause; a statement by Thomas Wood said:

> I remember the late Mr. James Moore and his bailiff coming to Linehouse and sitting on their horses backs at the Horse Block to receive Chief rent of my father. I have some receipts of Mr. Moore for chief rent up to his death and some of Mr. Wight's for chief rent the same. Thos. Wood junr.[13]

He also collected an affidavit regarding chief rents at Winley:

> Mary Caswell says she is about 80 years of age that she lived at two different times with Mr Chrees & his mother as much as 6 years and worked for them after she was married 15 or 16 years. She has frequently heard Mr Chrees & his mother talk of paying 'Chiefage' to Mr Moore, she also remembers Mrs Chrees grumbling very much about paying it, she did not like to part with her money.   Mary Caswell's mark X[14]

Another affidavit was taken after a change of the lord of the manor who Mrs Chrees appears to approve of:

Mrs Tombs well remembers the late Mr Richd Wight calling for chief rent & Mrs Chrees was much pleased of having Mr Wight for a landlord & paid his chief rent 5s 10d the same time.

There was also great difficulty collecting heriots from executors and their lawyers, and sometimes the lord of the manor was the last person to get a look in: in 1834, Philip Wight did his best to find out what heriots had been paid for Winley following the death of old John Chrees in 1815. The second part of this extract taken from a letter from his solicitor illustrates the point:

Chief Rents, heriots and reliefs due for Winley.   *HRO*

> ...but for the Heriots, the one due on the death of John Chrees, there was a horse which was sold to Mr. Jones [new tenant] for £21, the money received and paid in a due course of administration and for the heriot on the death of William Chrees ... there were two horses one sold for £15 the other for £10, ... the Executrix (Mr. Chrees's sister) refused to prove the Will & it was proved by Mr. Holyoake the Banker a creditor who sold the horses and took all there was.[15]

The manor has never actually been abolished but it finally lost any vestige of importance after the Law of Property Acts (1922-25) were passed; these provided for the immediate abolition of copyhold tenure.[16] In the 1841 tithe survey, Tedstone Court Farm was 'owned' and occupied by T. P. P. Wight and was 146 acres. Pixhill and Upper Grounds were part of the estate and at that time were both let to a tenant. Philip Wight ran the estate which was in trust for the benefit of his wife and her eldest son, James Lane, by her first husband Richard.

James Lane Wight made a career in London as a wharfinger having joined the business of John Knill & Co, Wharfingers, Fresh Wharf, London Bridge. John Knill was Tedstone born and the owner of Tipton and Winley and James married his daughter, Sarah. Sarah's brother, Stuart Knill, later took over from his father and subsequently became Lord Mayor of London and was made a baronet. In 1851, James and Sarah Wight were living at 57 Nottinghill Square, 33-year-old James being described as 'wharfinger & farmer of 150 acres'. They had seven children, the three elder girls and little Edgar, aged five, being educated at home by a governess, the three smallest

The Wight Family Grave

looked after by their nurse. Within three years, these children had lost their mother: Sarah died in 1854; a stained glass window in the church is dedicated to her memory.

The base of a window in the church dedicated to Maria Wight.

James's mother, Maria Wight, died in 1859, just after the restoration of the church; the east window in the chancel is dedicated to Maria's memory. By the time of the 1861 census her widowed husband had moved back to his former home at Ripplewood in Collington, where he was farming 218 acres in 1861, and James's teenage family was installed at the Court. Four of James and Sarah's children had been born in London but the youngest, seven-year old Ada, was born in Tedstone Delamere. One gets the impression from the 1871 census that the family had gone up in the world. This was not a farmer's household; seven indoor staff were employed including a lady's maid, a butler and a footman. It is noticeable that the majority of servants came from afar, not from Tedstone or neighbouring parishes.

1871 census for Tedstone Court

Name	Relation to head of family	Condition	Age	Occupation	Where born
Emily Wight	daur	Unm	28		Middlesex, London
Mary Wight	daur	Unm	24		" "
Alfred Wight	son	Unm	23	Undergrad. New College, Oxford	" "
Florence Wight	daur	Unm	21		" "
Ada Wight	daur	Unm	17		Tedstone Delamere
Maria Upfill	niece	W	35		Bromyard
Annie Upfill	daur of niece		8		Bromyard
Anne Stevens	serv	Unm	41	Cook	Dossington, Glos
Eliza Pardoe	serv	Unm	40	Ladies Maid	Arley Kings, Worcs
Harriet Edwards	serv	Unm	23	Housemaid	Stourport, Worcs
Anne Childs	serv	Unm	16	ditto	Upper Sapey, Herefs
Agnes Powell	serv	Unm	18	Kitchenmaid	Hallow, Worcs
James Gough	serv	Unm	42	Butler	Llanfair Waterdine, Salop
Thomas Freeman	serv	Unm	17	Footman	Whitbourne, Herefs

Estate Farms
These are covered in Chapter X, pages 183-188.

The lodges and new cottages (see also pages 219, 220 and 223)
Between 1851 – 61, a pair of substantial gabled brick cottages were built near the Pixhill drive entrance, one housing farm workers and the other occupied by a gardener, James Merrick, and his large family. The cottages replaced two dilapidated ones nearby. The two lodges were also built between 1851 – 71 when the lodge to the principal entrance was occupied by the coachman, Charles Gouge, and the lodge

Lodge to the principal entrance.

South Lodge.   *HRO*

guarding the back drive was inhabited by a gardener, Charles Hill. The last cottages to be built by the Wight family were Diamond Cottages in the Line House Lane, sometimes called Jubilee Cottages, presumably erected at the time of the Diamond Jubilee.

Water, gas supplies and the gardens
The water supply to the Court and buildings was from a spring in Pixhill Orchard from whence it was pumped by a 2½ H.P. Oil Engine through pipes to a reservoir at Upper Grounds with an alternative supply there by means of a 105ft well with wind pump. This reservoir supplied the water by gravitation. A ram in Enclosure 72, first installed in 1889 pumped water from a spring and pond adjoining, to two big tanks over the stables, supplying the servants' quarters, farm buildings and stables. It kept working until the mid-1920s when the dam started leaking. This small ram can now be seen pumping water in the Hereford Waterworks Museum.[17] Fire extinguishing apparatus was installed at the Court and there were hydrants up to the top floor. Acetylene gas was laid on to the office, staircase hall, servants' hall, work kitchen, back kitchen and stables. The back corridors on the ground floors had hot water radiators. The cider house with the mill became a gas house with Cel… Illuminating Co's Gas Making Apparatus. There was apparently a well with force pump in the kitchen. A description of the gardens is interesting: There was an ornamental lawn, tennis court, flower gardens, a rosary frame yard, ranges of six-light and seven-light cold and heated frames, span peach and nectarine houses, a plant house and propagating house. There was a one acre walled-in fruit garden across the Whitbourne road with plum, pear, cherry, apricot and fig trees and two vineries. A well with horse-gear pump supplied water to the gardens.[18]

Mrs. Wright, the daughter of the Rev. Simcox Lea who was rector here 1873 – 93, remembers the Wight family:

> Mr. Wight [*ie* James Lane Wight] … had five daughters and two sons, all much older than any of us when we came as children to the rectory. Miss Wight, the eldest, managed the house and the gardens, and took an interest in all the tenants on the estate; Mary Wight devoted her energies mainly to the hunting field; Laura worked on behalf of the Girls Friendly Society; Ada was the one we relied on for church decorations; Florence married the newly-arrived

Bromyard doctor, Dr. Gillam. The son, Edgar, was in the Knill family (his mother's family) business in London; Alfred was a clergyman. Mr. Wight had built a large reservoir in the hollow below the Line House Lane. It was very deep at one end, so it was only after a severe and prolonged frost that the ice was considered safe enough for the Rector's large family to be invited to skate on it. From this reservoir, the Wights drew plenty of water for domestic use, as it never ran dry, but they liked to have their drinking water fetched from a spring in the field below our Rectory 'dingle', beside the footpath to Tipton.[19]

Harvesting apples and hops

Further memories of Mrs. Wright include the following:

> Chief among my memory pictures of autumn at Tedstone are those of the apple orchards. At Tedstone, I remember them best lying in heaps under the fruit-stripped trees; they were lovely to look at – red, yellow and green, mingled with the russet of fallen leaves – waiting for the wagons which would carry them away to the cider-press. The Court cider-press was in the backyard, close to the hop kiln. I remember seeing the dark brown straining-cloths hung out to dry, after their work was done …The hop-yard belonging to the Court was at the far end of the Line House Lane, on the right sloping down to the Sapey Brook. Here the parish folk came to work for Mr. Wight, the squire. It was a sort of picnic time for them. Mothers of families thought the smell of the hops was good for the children, and for themselves too…. There were wooden tallies, notched for every bushel emptied from the crib by the tally-man. We used to go and help the Powell family at their crib.

By 1881, James Lane Wight was at the Court, presumably retired, with two spinster daughters, Emily and Mary. As we have read, Florence married a Bromyard doctor, Thomas Henry Gillam, who bought 32 High Street in 1881 after the death of John Brown Shelton, and so the association between this property and the Wights continued. We know that Gillam was rather straight-laced for when a discussion was going on about re-pewing Bromyard church, he thought that the seating of men and women should be separated, perhaps he was referring only to the 'lower orders'![20] James Lane Wight died in 1885 but Emily, Mary and Ada continued to live at the family home. Their elder brother Edgar, a London barrister, inherited the property; he was a bachelor and retired at an early age to live the life of a gentleman at the Court.

The Wight family was at the Court for over 100 years; their time is marked by the many buildings they erected. The new mansion house was built by Richard Wight in about 1809. His father had been a tenant at the old Court, Richard was born in the parish and was a Tedstone farmer born and bred, but his son James Lane, and grandson Edgar made their careers outside farming; they seemed to have been prosperous which enabled money to be invested in the estate: creating the new farmstead at Upper Grounds, building the smith's cottage and forge, buying cottages in the dingle, building the Brick Cottages by Pixhill, the two lodges, and the pair of Diamond Cottages in Line House Lane. An important later purchase was the Line House Farm in 1891. Edgar had no family and so in 1908 the property was put up for sale.

CHAPTER VIII

The Church of St James

Part II
The Nineteenth Century Rebuilding of the Rectory, Restoration of the Church and Stories about some of the Parsons⁂

Sometimes I dream I am at church, but it isn't an Oxford church, it is the little church in the meadow beyond the Court, where I heard my father pray and preach, for over 20 years. And the country folk are there too, who used to sit in those same pews.
Recollections of Tedstone Delamere, 1873 – 1894
Mrs. E. M. Wright, the daughter of the Rev. F. S. Lea, (1952), 32

Rev. Dr. Luke Booker

The nineteenth century was a period of great change in the parish but we start the chapter with one of the parsons: the rector, Mr. Packington-Tompkins, whom we met in Chapter I, resigned in 1805 and was followed by Luke Booker who was a poet and author of a number of published books and sermons but he was a sad man and with reason. He was fascinated by the beautiful Tedstone scenery and in particular, the Sapey Brook; a poem is published in Duncumb's *Collections*: the rector, 'under the anguish of affliction', found comfort by the brook. He asked an 'aged peasant' about the name of the brook and his answer is given in a lengthy poem, the fourth verse of which is given here: the poem starts 'Thou lovely brook, without a name:

Rev. Dr. Luke Booker.
Dudley Museum & Art Gallery

> Yet tho' no verse of mine may live,
> A name to thee thy bard will give,
> Through Tedstone *Delamere's* rich plains,
> Where crown'd with hops Pomona reigns,
> Thou musically flow'st along,
> In concord with the woodman's song;
> Still flowing, grace those plains so fair,
> And hence be called, THE DELAMERE.[1]

⁂ For full list of the rectors, see Appendix D

However, despite the 'aged peasant', the stream today is always called the Sapey Brook. In 1811, Booker married Phyllis Ann Moxam, daughter of Edward Moxam gent. as his second wife; her family came from Bromyard and owned property including 23–27 High Street, a large block of two messuages in the town centre; but they also owned property in London and Kent. This all passed to Luke's wife and when she died in 1817, it was to go to their eldest son, Edward, who very sadly drowned whilst at school at Eton. Dr. Booker resigned in 1812, moving to a larger parish, namely Dudley. Dudley was a very poor place at that time and going through a period of considerable political turmoil. Dr. Booker is said to have sided with the Conservative faction. He was apparently a prominent opponent of Reform. The Reform Act of 1832 was the first of a number of acts designed to reform the franchise; at that time, the only people who had a vote were those who owned land. He purchased a small field in Tedstone Delamere, still known as 'Dr. Booker's Field' in the 1840 tithe survey although it was many years after he had left. It was then owned by his son or stepson, Thomas Booker, later to become MP for Herefordshire. This 3½ acre field would have entitled him to a vote in Tedstone Delamere although he lived in Cardiff.

A picture postcard depicting Dudley church bears the following inscription:

> St. Thomas' Church replaced the medieval church which had fallen into disrepair and was demolished in 1815 by order of the vicar, Dr. Booker.[2]

Clearly he was somebody to be reckoned with! But Booker had great sadness during his life as we know from a memorial inscription in Dudley church:

TEDSTONE DELAMERE PARISH

No. on Register	Name of Voter	Place of Abode
590	ARDEN, William George	Tedstone, Delamere
591	BAKER, Slade	Bowdley, Worcestershire
592	BOOKER, Thomas William	Velindra-house, near Cardiff
593	CRADDOCK, Edward Hartopp	Tedstone, Delamere
596	DAVIS, John	Sapey Upper
598	GREENWOOD, Thomas	Line-house
599	KNILL John	20, Addington-place, Camberwell, London
601	MOORE, John	Tedstone, Delamere
602	MOORE, James	Bedford-row, London
603	ROPER, Thomas	Thrift
604	TOLLEY, Francis	Tipton-Court
605	TAYLOR, Samuel	Woodenend
607	WIGHT, James Lane, Esq.	52, Nottinghill-square, London

Electoral Roll 1852. The only people who had a vote where those who owned land; half of these lived elsewhere. *B&DLHC*

> To the memory of Anne / who died May the 10th 1806, aged 35; & of Phyllis Anne / who died May 17th 1817 aged 28 & of Elizabeth who died Jan 6th 1827 aged 33 / The beloved wives of Luke Booker LL.D; F.R.S.L. Vicar of this parish / Eight of their children, like vernal flowers / Blossomed and died / An affectionate husband and father consoled by the faith and hope of the Gospel / dedicates this to worth and innocence 1827 / Also to the memory of the said Luke Booker / who died October the 1st 1835 aged 73.

Rev. Edward Hartopp-Grove and the rebuilding of the Rectory

In 1811, the advowson (the right to present a priest to the living) was purchased by Brasenose College, Oxford which must have provided much needed stability after the previous frequent changes, and a number of parsons later to be presented to the living were academics from that College; in 1811, John Darcy, a Fellow of Brasenose, became rector after Dr. Booker. He was at Tedstone for 25 years and was succeeded in 1844 by a gentleman who had grand ideas and ambitions to improve the living.

He was born 'Edward Grove' but in 1809, he had married Emelia Cradock-Hartopp, the daughter of Sir Edmund Cradock-Hartopp, 1st baronet,[3] and adopted the name Hartopp-Grove. By the time he resigned the living in 1854, he was styling himself Edward Hartopp-Cradock;[4] this change of name must surely have been something to do with inheritance of land or money.

On his institution, Hartopp-Grove, in a letter dated 13th January 1885, petitioned the Bishop for a licence for non-residence on account of the Rectory being unfit for him to live in. (He happened himself to be then living in an exclusive area of London, namely Belgrave Square.) He explained to the Bishop that he did not intend to perform the duty in Tedstone Delamere himself but to employ the Rev. F. H. Barber as curate with a yearly stipend of £80 and an additional allowance of £20 with which to provide him with somewhere to live; the curate was at that moment living in the unfit rectory that was to be pulled down, but he was shortly to move to Evesbatch! The Bishop was told Evesbatch was only 6 miles from Tedstone Delamere but surely it is nearly double that distance, so a long ride there and back for our curate. Barber was also incumbent of Lower Sapey so he would have had a very busy Sunday. Poor Lower Sapey and Tedstone! The letter to the Bishop continued, giving the value of the benefice as £280 and saying that though the rectory was in poor repair, the buildings and fences of the glebe land were in good order.[5] An estimate was sought from George Pearson of Ross, builder and surveyor, for firstly merely repairing the existing house:

> Survey made ... of the Rectory House & outbuildings at Tedstone Delamere ... consisting of a dwelling house, barn, stabling & coach-house sheds etc and will require the sum of £39 4s. to put them in repair. The dwelling house is small and inconvenient partly built of stone and partly of brick & covered with stone tiles & slates & in its present state is not a suitable residence for the Rector and his family.

This photo shows the new Victorian rectory with the hipped slate roof and the early 18th century wing with gabled roof, the latter surviving from the earlier rectory.
Barry Phillips

There clearly never was the intention to just repair the rectory and Pearson produced further plans to demolish most of it and build a much larger house in its stead with commodious reception rooms and accommodation for a butler and other staff necessary for the household of a wealthy Victorian rector.[6] A total of £1220 was required and this was made up by: firstly, £35 14s. paid for dilapidations** by the representatives of the previous incumbent, Mr. Darcy; secondly, by £436 6s. paid by the Rev. Hartopp-Grove out of his own pocket; and lastly, by £748, obtained by a successful application to the Governors of Queen Anne's Bounty for a mortgage on the glebe and tithes, totalling a sum of £1220. A part of the early house seems to have been retained and used as stabling and staff quarters. This west wing is gabled, of brick on stone with a tiled roof and casement windows and seems of early-18th century date. (It is today an attractive dwelling semi-detached from the main house.) The main Victorian block is of a quite different larger brick with a hipped slate roof and sash windows.

But Tedstone Delamere was not alone in getting a new Rectory. A survey conducted in 1835 recorded 1728 parsonages as being unfit for habitation and 2878 parishes as having no parsonage at all.[7] It was thanks to the agricultural boom in the mid-19th century that all over England, houses for the clergy arose on a large scale, many much larger and grander than our Tedstone rectory, for Victorian clergy aspired to be gentlemen.

It is uncertain whether, after all this, our rector or his curate ever actually lived in Tedstone Delamere as the 1851 census gave the only occupant of the Rectory household as Mrs Mary Brown with the job description: 'In care of a House'. Hartopp-Grove resigned the living in 1854 and went on to greater things, having been appointed Principal of Brasenose College.

Rev. Gregory-Smith
Hartopp-Grove was succeeded by Isaac Gregory-Smith: another Fellow of Brasenose, a young man of 27 when appointed. The 1861 census tells us that he actually lived at the rectory with his wife and two small children together with a housekeeper, nurse, nursemaid and footman; anyone who has read Jane Austen's 'Sense and Sensibility' may remember that members of the clergy would take in gentlemen's sons for tuition in order to augment their income: also included in our rector's household was a ten-year-old pupil, John Lloyd. Gregory-Smith employed a curate, W. S. Raymond BA, educated at Magdalen College, Cambridge; one does wonder what these two young men found to do all day with just one parish! In 1872, Gregory-Smith moved to a larger parish when he became vicar of Great Malvern where he remained until 1896.

The major restoration of the parish church 1856-57
The 19th century experienced a boom in church building in the countryside. This has been ascribed, not as one might imagine, to an increase in piety amongst

---
** The sum charged to make good any damage to ecclesiastical property during an incumbency

Sketch of the church before restoration in 1856. *Hereford City Library*

parishioners, but to an aspect of estate management during the agricultural golden age between 1850 and 1875[8] and it would seem probable that owners of estates would not wish to be outdone by their neighbours who were busy improving their own churches. Locally, a number of new churches were built during this period including Collington 1856, Edvin Loach 1860, Stoke Lacy 1863, Fromes Hill 1864, Pencombe 1864, Little Cowarne 1870, Tedstone Wafre 1873, Bredenbury 1877; neighbouring Harpley Church was also built in 1877, the new site having been given by the Whitbourne Bickerton-Evans family who had land there. In addition, a great many churches were substantially restored at the same time. Locally, one can say that Tedstone Delamere was leading the way, being one of the first churches in the district to be rebuilt or restored.

A watercolour by Charles F. Walker painted in 1849-51[9] shows the attractive little church at Tedstone Delamere supported by huge buttresses; The church may have looked picturesque but at some stage in the past it had clearly begun to collapse; buttresses had been referred to in 1600 so were not a recent necessity, see page 21. Walker is considered to be an accurate recorder of the churches of his day.[10]

Repairs in 1842
A churchwardens' account book dating from 1842 – 95[11] gives a list of quite substantial expenditure on the church just a few years before the restoration; one must assume that no thought of this great work existed in 1842:

26th December 1842

The Account of William Bevan			
Bills Paide. R.Travil Bill. Mason	10	05	04
Mr. Lewis Bill – Carpenters bill	09	16	07½
Mr. Powell Bill – Blacksmith	02	10	05¼
Mr. Rowlands Bill for Tiles	07	04	06
Mr. Jinks Bill for Hare		15	00
Mr. Hall Bill for Nails		15	09
Mr. Blissell. Bill for Halling tiles	04	00	00
Mr. Winwood Bill for lath	04	04	06
Mr. Roper Bill Halling lime	01	05	00
Mr. Dallow Bill for brick		08	09
Mr. Potter Bill for lime	01	02	00
Mr. Bevan Bill Halling	03	07	06
Mr. Lipscombe Bill for Halling	01	00	00
Mr. Blunt Bill glazing		05	00
	£47	01	10¾

Even as late as 26th March 1856, Mr. Amiss was paid 8d. for repairing church windows. Mr. Jinks' bill for hair must surely have been from James Jenks, the Bromyard tanner.

The restoration
On 19th May 1856, William Green was paid 1s. 6d. by the churchwardens for a day's work cleaning a room at Tipton that was to be used for Divine Service during repairs to the church; and then later in the year, Mary Green was paid 1s. for 'scouring room at Tipton after Hop picking', presumably because it was still being used for services. James Ward of Tipton was churchwarden at the time.

Unlike the building of the Rectory, for which there are plenty of records telling us how the money was raised together with detailed architectural plans of the building, there are apparently virtually no surviving records about the restoration, which was almost a rebuild, of the parish church. One must assume that the Wight family at the Court were probably major instigators of the project, perhaps assisted by James Moore of Shelsley Beauchamp who at that time owned half the parish; they might have been advised by that very important former rector, the Rev. Hartopp-Cradock, now the Principal of Brasenose College and indeed it seems highly likely that the major part of the funding came from the College, the patron of the living. For this great enterprise they chose, not just any old architect, but the best:

The church architect
The man chosen was Sir George Gilbert Scott who was to become probably the best known of all the Victorian church architects; Scott had been inspired by Pugin to join the Gothic revival movement, he later became deeply involved with the restoration of Worcester Cathedral and he was responsible for the restoration of the choir at Hereford Cathedral including the screen that was unveiled in 1862 at the

International Exhibition and was hailed as the 'grandest and most triumphant achievement of modern architecture'; the screen is an extraordinary mixture of wrought and cast iron, copper and semi-precious stones and mosaics. It became unfashionable and had rusted in the Cathedral's damp conditions and in the 1960s was removed, restored, and now has pride of place in the Victoria and Albert Museum. But this was in the future. Locally Gilbert Scott had been responsible for the new church at Eastnor in 1852 and perhaps it was this that had inspired the Wights. He later designed the church at Edvin Loach in 1860. It seems extraordinary that there are no surviving plans or indeed any details of how the money was raised. All we know is that it resulted in the charming little church we have today. The following appears in the parish register:

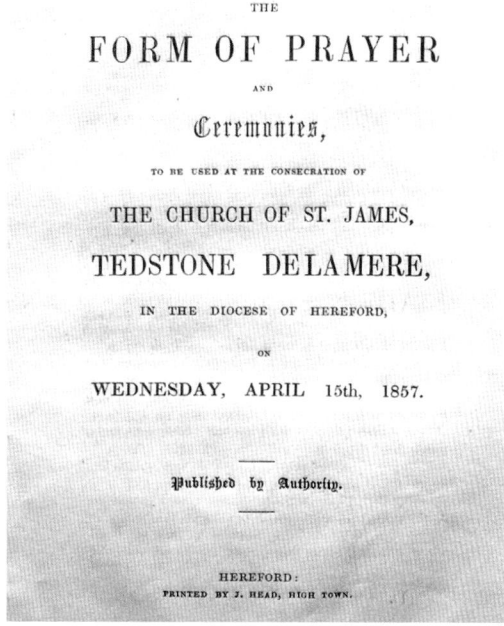

Consecration Service Sheet 1857.　　　　HRO

    Copy of Memorandum on Parchment
    Inserted in the Foundation Stone under East Window
    This stone was laid by Miss Clara Wight of Tedstone Court July 2nd 1856.

    At that time, the Chancel was rebuilt & enlarged, a Vestry was added, the Nave** was repaired throughout with new Porch, Bell turret etc by Voluntary Contributions. Also an Organ & 4++ Bells were given.

	Signed by us
The architect was	I. Gregory-Smith M.A. late Fellow of
G.G.Scott Esq. 20 Spring Gardens	Bras. Coll. Oxford, Rector
The builders were	W.S. Raymond B.A. of Magd. Coll. Camb.
Messrs Pearson & Son, Ross	Curate
LAVS. DEO	DOMINUS BENEDICAT OPERI

This note, written into the parish register by the rector, seems to be the only record of the work carried out! Clearly, Messrs Pearson's building of the Rectory must have been satisfactory as the same firm was entrusted with the work on the church. The new set of five bells which replaced the two old ones was cast by Messrs. Charles and George Mears.[12] 15-year-old Clara Wight, who laid the foundation stone, was the eldest of the children of James and the late Sarah Wight. The restored church was re-consecrated on 15th April 1857 by the Bishop of Hereford. This was necessary

---

** should be 'almost entirely rebuilt'　　　　++ should be '5 in lieu of 2 old bells'

The Church after Restoration. *Hereford City Library*

because the new chancel was larger than the old one and so partly occupied unconsecrated ground.

Sometimes now there is regret that our 19th century ancestors did such *thorough* restorations, sweeping away much that was old and loved, but on the other hand there is plenty of evidence that churches had been allowed to fall into a parlous state after years of neglect and so perhaps we have a great deal to thank the Victorians for. Things that were lost included the carved oak gallery and pulpit which, in 1873, the Rev. Frederick Simcox-Lea discovered had been used for shelves in the rectory coach-house and saddle-room and even door-posts for the open cowshed in the rectory field! A carved board was dated and carried the name of the craftsman. The rector had every bit removed and gave it to Mr. Onslow, the rector of Upper Sapey, who was doing something then to his church. Another 'crime' the rector discovered was that the memorial stone slabs in the church floor were used to cover the new heating pipes, the stones then being hidden under common tiles.[13] The hour glass was probably moved (to the porch) at the same time as the pulpit was moved. In the days of lengthy sermons, when the preacher began, he would set the hour glass running and the congregation could rely on his finishing his exhortations within the hour! We should be thankful that the restorers kept the attractive 15th-century rood-screen.

Church plate
But back to Mr Gregory-Smith who meticulously listed 'things belonging to the church' in the parish register. The contents of the 'large oak chest in the Vestry' included a large prayer book, a large bible, two large altar books, the usual kneeling mats and cushions.

The small deal box contained:

1 flagon silver old
1 chalice silver old
1 paten silver new
1 large paten pewter old
1 altar dish oak

1 water ewer pewter
1 linen cloth
3 napkins

Some of these are described in more detail by Berkeley Scudamore Stanhope, who records what he found during his visit to the church, in his book on Herefordshire's church plate and published in 1903.[14] The 'flagon silver old' is probably the one reproduced here, and recorded by Stanhope as being inscribed 'The gift of Robt. Mason, Gent., to the Church of Tedstone Delamere, 1715'. Robert Mason had been lord of the manor and lived at the Court but had been forced to sell the estate because of financial difficulties in 1713 so this must be seen in the light of a farewell gift, the family having been associated with the parish for nearly 100 years. The 'chalice silver old' is possibly the one that was later copied, Stanhope thoroughly approving of the result:

The Tedstone Delamere silver flagon is inscribed: 'The gift of Robert Mason, Gent. to the Church of Tedstone Delamere, 1715

> The above old cup having become much worn, the Rev. J. Simcox Lea, who was then the rector, had a new cup and cover made as an exact reproduction of the old one. It is hoped that this example will be followed in future, and that we may have more reproductions of a fine old type in the place of 'modern medieaval' cups, of which but too many are now to be met with in country parishes.

The 'paten silver new' in the parish register is probably Stanhope's paten inscribed 'Tedstone Delamere, Christmas, 1854'. The 'large paten pewter old' in the parish register is possibly his 'Plate. Pewter marked on the bottom 'E. L. ex dono 1687' ... The name of 'Cave, 64' on the right side ... Possibly the number stands for '1664'.

The chalice silver old, recorded in the parish register, and also by Stanhope, must be the one which has been the subject of a recent mystery. In about 2002, it was discovered that an old and valuable chalice, apparently thought to be in the safe keeping of the Cathedral, was mysteriously mislaid. It is understood this is still not resolved.

Churchwardens' accounts 1842 - 95[15]
These are the only churchwardens' accounts known to survive. During this time the accounts were prepared by four churchwardens: William Bevan 1849 (of Hedge House), Francis Tolley 1849 – 53 (of Tipton), William Bevan 1853 – 55, and in 1856 James Ward (Tolley's successor at Tipton) became churchwarden and held the post for 34 years being followed by his son Stanley in 1891. The expenditure during each year was listed and was balanced by a levy on the parish ratepayers. The regular

expenditure included such items as bread and wine at Christmas, Easter, Whitsuntide and Michaelmas. Washing the surplice also featured at the same time as the bread and wine, the clerk's salary at £3 rising to £3 10s. by the end of the period was another regular expenditure. Other entries were for maintenance of the building and churchyard; in 1859 George Bullock (the rectory gardener) was paid 2s. for cleaning up the churchyard and Thomas Corbett was paid 2s. 6d. for tidying walks. Until 1873, the churchwardens' meetings were always held in the church porch according to custom, but after the arrival of the Rev. Simcox Lea, they retreated to the comfort of the small vestry where there is a tiny fireplace. In 1869–70, the means of raising the money changed: instead of a levy on the parishioners, it was collected by 'voluntary rates or subscription' and by 1873, 'donations and offertory' appear as part of the accounts and there is no further mention of a levy on the ratepayers. Miss Mary Wight was paid for her work with the choir; it seemed slightly surprising that the squire's daughter should be paid but the rector also saw that his daughter Elizabeth was paid for teaching at Sunday School. He himself was personally generous and made regular donations.

A page from the churchwardens' accounts 1850.   HRO

The Rev. Frederic Simcox Lea and life at the rectory

Mr. Lea was born in 1822, coming from a long line of Kidderminster carpet manufacturers. His only education was at a small dame school and he began his career in the family firm but finding this not to his taste, he saved enough money to pay for his Oxford education and after qualifying, became a clergyman. After two curacies, he spent the next 17 years of his career in an East London parish until advised to move to the country for the sake of his health. On the resignation of Gregory-Smith in 1873, Lea was appointed to the Tedstone Delamere living. His daughter, Mrs. E. M. Wright, as an old lady, wrote many anecdotes for publication in the parish magazine and these paint a charming picture of rectory life in the late 19th century and have been used in this chapter. At that time, the nearest railway station was Worcester; the horse drawn furniture vans containing the rector's belongings got stuck going up Badley Hill and had to wait until more horses could be borrowed from a helpful farmer. If anyone needed to go to the station at Worcester, a cab would be hired from the Hop Pole in Bromyard. Later, when the railway came to Bromyard, trains were within walking distance: four miles across the fields and five by road. During the 20 years the Lea family was at Tedstone, they never possessed a carriage or horse. Mr. Lea used to walk across the fields to Bromyard via the Downs to get his hair cut. There were seven children in the family, Elizabeth (who became Mrs. Wright) was the eldest girl, then eight years old. She recalls plain living and high thinking, thrift and simplicity, being the standards set by their parents.

The rectory garden
The garden was marvellous for children, 'it had a pond, various trees adapted to young climbers of all ages, a spacious orchard where pigs and poultry took their open air exercise, and where stood the stacks of faggots necessary for heating the brick oven wherein the family bread was baked every week'. The gardener:

> who from his youth upwards had belonged to the rectory garden, could neither read nor write. Perhaps that was why his eyesight was so keen that he could see a fox running across a field some distance away on the far side of the brook valley, much too distant for him to shout directions to the huntsman in pursuit, so he had to have the day off to go and help them. His parents had lived in a very small and primitive cottage on Badley Common. He was a wonderfully clever gardener, the pigs were his chief pride and joy but next to them he loved his vegetables. The rubbish-heap was the home of gigantic cucumbers and marrows. We – or rather he, as monarch of the garden – took so many prizes at the Bromyard Flower Show each year that the envious named it 'George Bullock's Show' Our pickling cabbages were surely the world's best! G.B.'s pride in the pigs perhaps reached a climax with their final fattening. Pig killing day was a red letter day, at any rate in that part of Herefordshire. We kept two pigs, one of which was killed just before Christmas and the other one just after Christmas. The usual weight aimed at by G.B. was 20 score. In the Rectory cellar was a broad slate slab whereon G.B cured the huge sides of bacon and the monstrous hams which subsequently hung from the kitchen ceiling. According to local tradition a pig must never be killed when the moon was on the wane, or its flesh would shrink in the pot. G.B. and the professional pig killer of course, always bore this rule in mind.

Mrs. Wright described the great activity in the kitchen after a pig was killed, every member of the household being summoned to make pork pies, their brick oven holding about twenty large pies. The big sacks of flour came from a flour-mill near Worcester. Butter and milk came from Mr. Ward's farm at Tipton. Mrs. Ward would take the rectory household's surplus eggs to Worcester market every Saturday.

> My mother was an excellent housekeeper and years in advance of the century in matters relating to health and hygiene. Many a sick person, or anxious mother of babies and small children was grateful to her for simple homely advice and practical help in a small parish many miles from a doctor or chemist. I can remember the large bottles of castor-oil, and cod-liver-oil in our larder, ready to be drawn upon by anyone in time of need.

Mrs. Wright remembers Richard Powell:

> the Parish Clerk of olden days ... he was one of the real old type that knew all about every grave in the churchyard, and without whose loud 'Amen' no service could be fitly conducted. Some of the verses of the Psalms might be too long and difficult, but with a brave leap he would lead us all in at the finish with fine solemnity. Of course we never tried to chant the Psalms or responses for both Clerk and congregation would have thought that savoured of 'popery'. Seventy years ago, it was still customary in some West Midland districts to decorate village churches on Whit Sunday with sprigs of birch stuck in holes bored in tops of pews. I can remember this being done by Richard Powell in his capacity of Parish Clerk, but when he was gathered to his fathers in the same profession, the custom died with him.[16]

The places where these holes were can be found in some of the pews, now neatly filled with wooden pegs. Richard Powell was also the blacksmith. The churchwarden's accounts tell us that he was paid £3 per annum for his clerk's duties in 1842. By 1895, the sum had increased to £3 10s but by this time, his son Richard had succeeded him as clerk.[17] In churches where there was a 'three-decker' pulpit, with sounding board and reading desks at three levels, the parson preached from the top level, read the service from the middle level, and the reading desk at the bottom was occupied by the parish clerk. His duties were to obey the parson and then 'be able to read the first lesson, the epistle and the psalms ... and that he keep the books and ornaments of the church fair and clean ... and also that he endeavour himself to teach young children to read if he be able to do so'. The Canons of 1603 also included a 'competent skill in singing (if it may be)'. It is not thought that Richard Powell taught children to read.

The tithe-dinner is recalled:

> My father in his study, sat like Matthew at the receipt of custom, and farmers and cottage folk came with their respective tithe dues. I believe my father often returned the two or three shillings paid by some of the parishioners, but in any case, each and everyone could return home fortified by a substantial dinner of roast beef and plum-pudding.

This seems a much more attractive way of collecting the tithe than that described in Chapter I when the Rev. Packington Tompkins let the Rectory, glebe and tithes and his poor tenant had the thankless task of trying to collect the money from disgruntled parishioners!

When the Lea children grew up, they used to receive invitations to tennis parties; the Miss Wights would take them to the more distant places in their large waggonette but they thought nothing of walking to play tennis at Edvin Loach Rectory or Whitbourne Hall.

Elizabeth Lea, later to become Mrs Wright, 1896.
Barry Phillips

When she left school, Elizabeth was promoted organist, hitherto their governess or one of the Miss Wights having performed that function. The choir consisted of a handful of children, boys and girls; Elizabeth went through the hymns with them for half an hour before the afternoon services. Two of the Miss Wights would sit near the organ to help with the singing. Another of Mrs. Wright's stories is about the drama when the furnace went wrong:

> Poisonous coke fumes came up through gratings in the aisle. The gratings did not reach the chancel steps so the air in the chancel, and in the pulpit, remained unaffected. Hence my father was not aware of anything amiss, and continued the service to its normal close. The fumes seemed to concentrate at the West end of the Church where my sisters and I, and two Miss Wights sat together with the school-children. My sister Margaret noticed that one little girl was on the verge of fainting, and with her inborn nursing instincts, she realised what was happening. She took the child out at once into the fresh air and told the other children to follow …. When the service was over, I remember finding it difficult to stand up and walk decorously as one should in church. Together with the Miss Wights, I sat down wearily in the porch, our faces pale, and our heads aching, till our feeble knees were firm enough for the journey back to Court and Rectory.

Mrs. Lea, as the wife of a clergyman, found it necessary to say that no servant of hers might wear flowers in her bonnet on Sundays 'since such tokens of vanity must not be seen in the pew allotted to the Parsonage staff'. But in spite of this her staff apparently stayed with her for many years.

Memorial to Prebendary Lea.

Towards the end of the 1880s, the rector's health was starting to fail and he was assisted by his eldest son Thomas, who acted as his curate. Prebendary Lea died at Tedstone in 1893.

Rev. Charles Williams
George Sandford was incumbent for three years and was followed by Charles Williams.
He had a wife who:

> had a tendency to stand in the church porch dispensing gossip about all and sundry in the parish. In 1906 this brought her trouble when she reported that a Mr. Bowers of Limehouse [Linehouse], Tedstone Delamere – agent to the Delamere Estate – was frequently intoxicated and had young men in his house late at night, playing cards, drinking wine, spirits and beer.

It all sounds like a storm in a teacup to us today. Mr. Bowers sued for slander and was awarded damages of £100, a lot of money in those days.[18] The rector, though, seemed to be well thought of. While preaching a sermon one Sunday his sleeve caught fire on a nearby candle; not noticing this he continued until a voice from the back of the church said 'Beg pardon, sir, Parson's alight'![19] Charles Williams stayed for 42 years (1897 – 1939); as David Annett relates, 'he must have had an enviable life – as is suggested by a brass in the chancel .... The parishioners who erected the memorial added as an epitaph the well chosen text 'Be ye steadfast, unmoveable'![20]

War Memorial.

The Victorian rectory in later years

Only rarely does this rectory seem to have been lived in by the clergy; the Rev. Charles Williams lived in Glebe Cottage; early in the 20th century, Frank Evans and his wife, Fanny, occupied the rectory, presumably moving to Whitbourne Hall after the death of his grandmother in 1910. The rectory was occupied by soldiers during or just after World War 2; Miles and Nan Bellville lived there for a short time after their marriage. In recent years, the house has been divided: the Victorian section is known as Delamere House. The former brick-built stable block, which it adjoins, was part of the earlier rectory and seems to date from the early-18th century.[21] It is now made into a separate house known as 'St Agnes', named after St Agnes's well in the field opposite.

Frank & Fanny Evans on holiday with the Bellvilles. They lived at the Rectory in the early years of their marriage before moving to Whitbourne Hall.

Bellville Collection

Mr. Easton mowing at Glebe Farm.   *Easton Family*

Glebe land

Glebe Farm is recorded in Chapter I on pages 26 and 30 and at this time, in 1792, the farmer lived in the Rectory. In 1844, we know that the buildings and fences of the glebe land were reported in good order: to enable the building of the new Victorian Rectory, the sum of £748 was granted by the Governors of Queen Anne's Bounty by mortgaging the glebe and tithes. In 1841, 34 acres of glebe land was let to James Bevan but there was no house; another five acres was let to James Palmer and consisted of three fields: Big Field is where the 20th century rectory was to be built and the two smaller fields: Far Piece and Little Piece are where council houses were to be built. Later, the newly built Glebe Cottage was let in 1862 to George Bullock, the rectory gardener, who was still in residence in 1897. At this time, 24 acres of glebe land were let to Edgar Wight of Tedstone Court and eight acres to Sarah Bishop.[22] As just recorded, the Rector, Charles Williams, lived in Glebe Cottage for a time early in the 20th century. In 1946, the glebe land was sold by the Church Commissioners to Mr. and Mrs. Easton who were to carry out dairying here. They rented Glebe Cottage from the Commissioners for a short time, purchasing it five years later. Mrs. Easton sold the land in 2000 to Roger Benbow, and the buildings for conversion to a house, now aptly named 'Churchlands'.

Buildings at Glebe Farm before and after conversion. *Easton Family*

Is the church haunted?
No church history is complete without a ghost. Tradition has it that at midnight on mid- summer's eve, ghostly music can be heard coming from the church. One such night, the Bellville children took candles and sat inside the church waiting, but just before the stroke of twelve, courage failed them and they fled![23]

Twentieth-century changes
Falling church attendance and shortage of money must have combined to bring the Diocese and the Ecclesiastical Commissioners to conclude that the only salvation was to merge parishes. The changes leading up to the eventual creation of the Greater Whitbourne parish have been covered in great and careful detail by Allan Wyatt in his forthcoming book on the history of Edvin Loach which interested readers should consult. Only a summary of the main changes, of which there are several, is given here:[24]

1. Locally a commission was set up to join Tedstone Delamere with Edvin Loach and Tedstone Wafre and in 1929, the merger was approved. But neither of the incumbents was interested, so nothing could be done until both livings fell vacant. The first vacancy was at Tedstone Delamere with the death of Charles Williams in 1939; Evan James, later to become rector of Thornbury, was appointed priest-in-charge here until such time as Edvin Loach should also fall vacant; this happened when the rector there died in 1947. The commission had also decided that the new rector of the combined parishes should live in Tedstone Delamere Rectory and the one at Edvin Loach should be sold.
2. Donald Edward Jones, Frederick Massey and Leigh Simpson became successive rectors of the three parishes (see Appendix D). Mr. Massey seems to have been the first to live in the new modern rectory.
3. In 1967, after a lengthy interregnum, Frank Cherrington became rector of the above three parishes but also priest-in-charge of Upper Sapey with Wolferlow.

4. In the late 1970s, there was a new scheme to bring these five parishes together but only four churches (because Tedstone Wafre church had been closed due to lack of support, later to be converted to a house) with the more populous parish of Whitbourne. This created a new single parish with five churches but one PCC, one rector, and one rectory which was to be at Whitbourne. Wolferlow church was later to become redundant, making only four churches.

This charming little church at Tedstone Delamere suffers, along with so many other country churches today, from lack of a congregation except at Easter, Harvest Festivals and Christmas when the church is packed. Recently, an architect's report drew attention to serious dilapidation of the roof. The overall cost to put this right amounted to £90,000 including VAT. It hopefully bodes well for the future that in December 2009 a large grant of £60,000 was awarded by English Heritage which together with further grants from bodies which include a Listed Places of Worship Grant of £13,000, a £5000 grant from the Wolfson Foundation, £4000 from Hereford Historic Churches, £3000 from the Garfield Weston Foundation and £1000 apiece from the Alan Evans Memorial Trust and the Edward Cadbury Charitable Trust. The remainder has been raised by the parish in a range of special fund-raising events and the restoration is now successfully completed.[25]

CHAPTER IX

The Estate to the East of the Sapey Brook and its Owners[1] - after 1841

> The various farms and estates at Tedstone Delamere, ... have from time to time and at different times been divided into different farms and under different names ....
> *Declaration of Ben Grubb, 1851*

Chapter VII has dealt with the 19th century Tedstone Court Estate that lay to the west of the Sapey Brook; that was the property held by the Wights; whereas this chapter is about the Moore Estate that lay to the east of the brook and was subsequently purchased by Edward Bickerton Evans of Whitbourne Hall.

1. The Moore Estate.
Charles Edward Moore of Shelsley Beauchamp owned almost all of eastern Tedstone Delamere in 1840/41.[2] Mr. Moore had five sons and trying to be fair to them all must have been difficult (see family tree p.115).

He lost his eldest son at the early age of 29 and there is a very fulsome memorial to the young man, also called Charles Edward, inside Shelsley Beauchamp Church; his father died a few months later. It is possible that, with the death of the heir, any plans for the future of the estate came to nought, for the other sons appear to have had occupations that were quite unconnected with farming. James, the second son, was a lawyer and member of Gray's Inn; the third son, Frederick, studied medicine; Arthur William BA sadly also died young at the age of 25. Henry, the youngest son, outlived them all, dying in 1891. The estate was advertised for sale in 1844 but had failed to sell. When Charles Edward senior died in 1847, he left Upper House at Shelsley Beauchamp, together with all his estate in Tedstone Delamere, in trust for his wife Eliza and after that it was to go to their son James, the lawyer. Charles Edward had inherited his property from his uncle, Edward Moore. Because of the

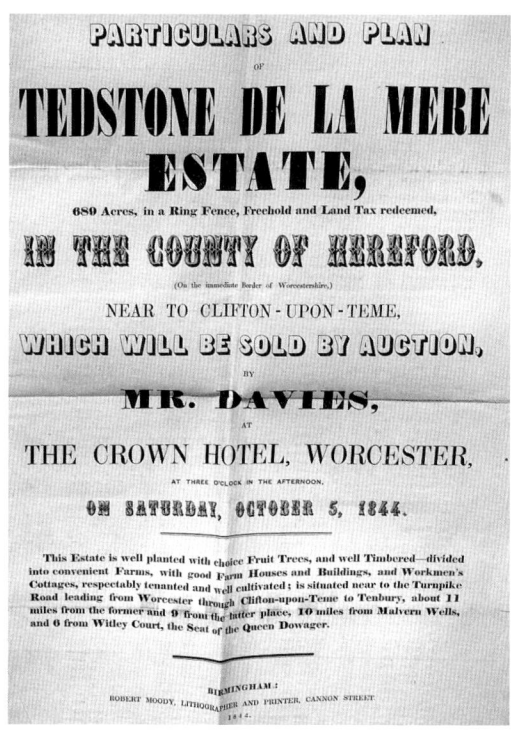

Sale particulars of Charles Edward Moore's estate 1844. It failed to sell.   *Whitbourne Estate*

complications with the inheritance of this property, two affidavits were taken in 1851. The first one was a declaration of George Pritchard of the Shop, Shelsley Beauchamp:

> He said that he had lived in the parish for 50 years and knew Edward Moore of Upper House well, Edward died 5th Dec. 1838. Though a married man he had no children. Pritchard declared that from the respectability of the said Edward and his high standing in the community, it would have been impossible for him to have had children without it being known.

The second affidavit is more useful to us and is the declaration of Ben Grubb, tenant of Woodhall Farm⁎, Tedstone Delamere:

> He is about 70 years old and has lived all his life at Woodend, [today's Woodhall],⁎ having been born there. He has rented the farm from Mr. James Moore since 1847 and previously from 1838 rented the farm from Charles Edward Moore of Upper House, Shelsley Beauchamp. For many years previous to that from about 1811 he rented the farm from Edward Moore, also of the Upper House and uncle of Charles Edward Moore.
>
> He is well acquainted with the Moore Estate in Tedstone Delamere and his father Thomas Grubb rented Woodend Farm under James Moore of Upper House cousin of Edward and further is named in the will of James Moore as one of his tenants. He succeeded to his father's tenancy about 1811.
>
> He has always understood that Woodend Farm and other estates came to James Moore decd. from his brother Robert Moore who purchased the same from various parties at various times. He can remember Robert Moore when he, Ben Grubb, was a boy, and can declare that the various farms and estates at Tedstone Delamere, formerly the property of Robert Moore, then James Moore, then Edward Moore, then Charles Edward Moore then descended to the present owner James Moore, have from time to time and at different times been divided into different farms and under different names, but now are all known and comprised under the names of:
>
> | | |
> |---|---|
> | The Thrift Farm | Ladywood Farm |
> | The Woodend Farm | Holts cottage [now Primrose] and Perkins Cottage and garden |
> | Wooden End Farm | |
> | The New House Farm | |
> | Lee Lay Farm | |
> | The Shop Farm [now Tidbatch] | |
>
> and are now in respective occupations of Thomas Roper, John Davis, myself, Sam Taylor, Richard Powell, Thomas Jones, Thomas Evans, John Davies and William Austin late Thomas Budd, as tenants to the said James Moore.
>
> He declares that the particulars and plan annexed are as they descended from Robert Moore to James Moore except:
> Believes that in 1833 Charles Edward Moore purchased from the Chrees family a cottage and 9 acres of land then called Burbages and now included in New House Farm under the names of the coppice, the close and blackberry orchard, being nos. 95, 98, 99 on plan [see Map 11 page 225]. Shortly before his death in 1847, Charles Edward Moore purchased from the Harris family about 13 acres of woodland called Ladywood and Tidbatch, which though shown on the map are not included in the particulars.
> Signed: Ben Grubb
> Witnessed: George Prothero

⁎ Woodhall was known as 'Woodend' at this time. What is now Woodend Farm used to be called 'Wooden End' Farm. Readers should be aware of this confusion.

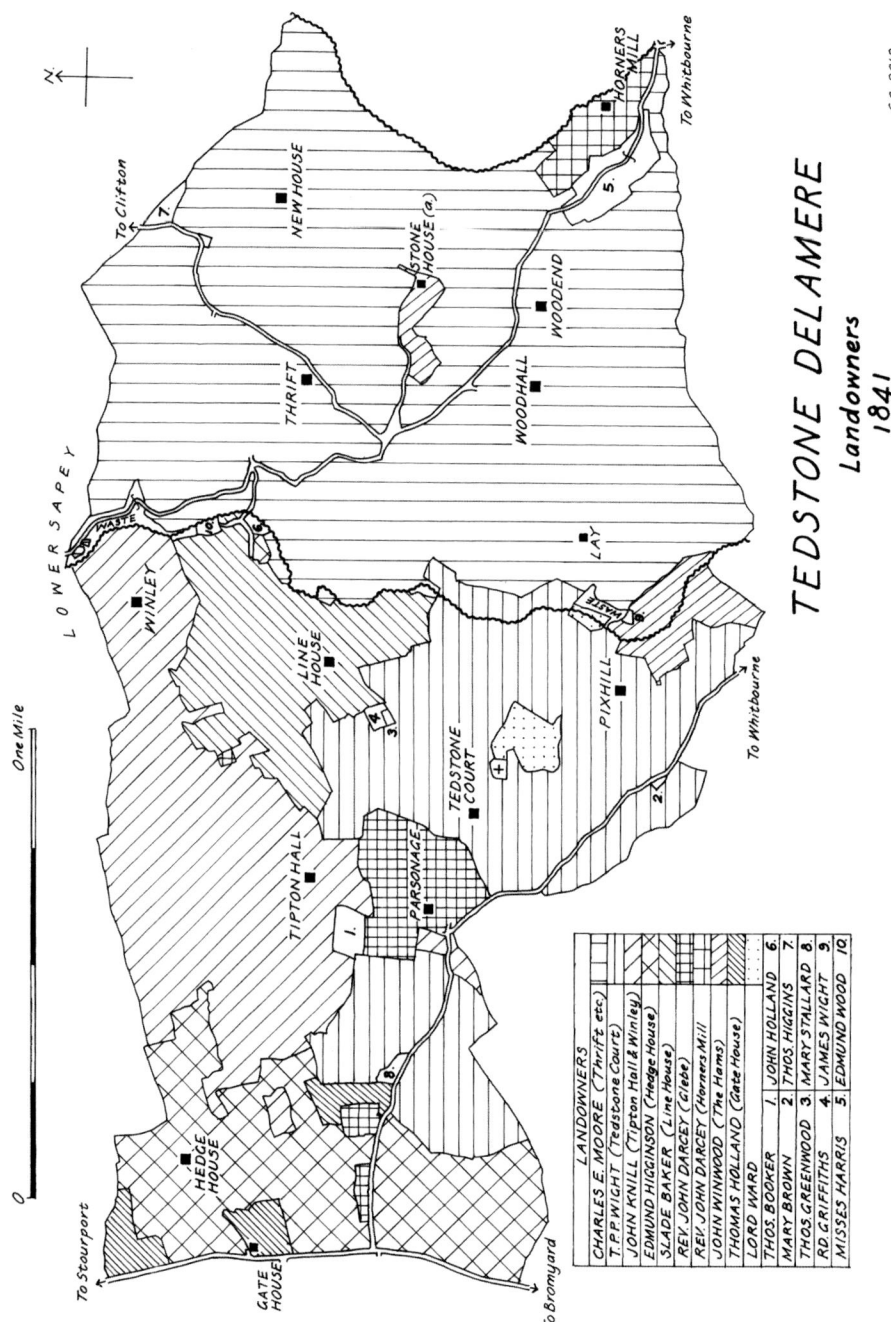

Map 8.

Burbages, mentioned above as being now included amongst New House Farm land, is one of the many cottages and small farms that are mentioned frequently in the records and have now disappeared from the map. It was first mentioned in 1495 when a house called Borbach was the subject of a grant by Humfrey Dor to Thomas and Alice Breton.[3]

When James Moore inherited, he was charged with the payment of £3000 to each of his three brothers, Frederick, who died in 1888; Arthur William, who died at the age of 23 in 1850 but leaving a widow, Eliza; and Henry. Other lands were bequeathed to the younger sons as tenants in common.[4] This may all have been more than the estate could bear; the will of James' father seems to have spelt the end of the Moores' estate in Tedstone Delamere that began in 1726 when Anne Moore's father, George Webb, purchased the manor. Their property became heavily mortgaged as James paid off his brothers and by 1852 the mortgage had increased to £14,000. James Moore died a bachelor in 1871, aged 51, intestate with effects under £800.

2. The Whitbourne Estate

The Moores' estate in Tedstone Delamere was sold in 1860 to a Benjamin Gibbons, but in 1866 it was purchased by Edward Bickerton Evans of Whitbourne Hall. The Evans family came from Wales and were tenants of the Earl of Powys. Edward Evans, Edward Bickerton's father, was a Worcester banker having moved there in 1811, and then, in partnership with a cousin, founded the Hill, Evans Vinegar Works where he made his fortune.

Edward Bickerton Evans was a student of architecture and a keen traveller to Greece, Italy and North Africa; he returned with great plans for a grand house. Apparently he originally looked at the area of the Thrift in Tedstone Delamere for his new house but then found his ideal site at Longlands in Whitbourne. He started to build Whitbourne Hall in 1860, his family moving there in 1862. This very impressive building is said to be influenced by the Erechtheum in Athens; the huge house of attractive grey Bath stone with its Ionic pillars sits dramatically in the Whitbourne landscape. The story goes that Mr. Evans was one day inspecting the work and said to the men laying the foundations: 'It's too small. Double it'!

Edward Bickerton Evans for whom Whitbourne Hall was built.   *Whitbourne Estate*

The Hill Evans Vinegar Works in Worcester. *Whitbourne Estate*

Farming in England had done pretty well since 1750; to feed the rapidly expanding population it had been necessary to grow more corn. The ensuing agricultural prosperity had encouraged industrial tycoons to plough money into the purchase of land and with the need to plough up grassland and orchards for corn had come the amalgamation of smallholdings to create more viable units; this we have already seen in Tedstone Delamere in the second half of the 18th century and the beginning of 19th when the Moore family bought up smallholdings, described in Chapter VI. By 1820 this estate in Eastern Tedstone Delamere was virtually the same as that purchased by E. B. Evans in 1866 except for a smallholding called Burbages that was acquired in 1833 and the smallholding of Stone House A that was purchased by the Evans family. The particular period from 1855 to 1865 was a golden age for farming and Edward Bickerton Evans was entering agriculture at a high point.[5] He quickly bought up the surrounding land as it became available in Whitbourne, Lower Sapey and Tedstone Delamere creating an estate that totalled some 3000 acres. The Tedstone portion was the estate that the Moore family had already created. But this national agricultural prosperity was not to last; in the late 1870s, a period of depression in farming began, which lasted, with a small but short-lived improvement during the 1914–18 War, until the outbreak of the Second World War.

Woodend (formerly Wooden End); cattle shed with swept dormer hay pitch. *B&DLHC*

In 1879, Mr. Evans employed the firm of Murrell, Scobell and Masterman of London to give him a valuation for the purpose of obtaining a mortgage:

> We have viewed the freehold estate belonging to Mr E. B. Evans Esq. ... known as the Tedstone Estate which is 3 miles from Knightwick station.
>
> Schedule: Total acreage: 713a. 3r. 14p.
> Rental value: £947 3s. 4d. as follows:

	acres	roods	perches	£	s	d
Waste Cottage & garden		2	15	06	00	04
Shop Farm [Tidbatch]	17	1	14	32	16	04
Thrift Farm	248	2	20	336	00	00
New House Farm	140	3	30	180	00	00
Woodend [now Woodhall]	104	3	16	128	07	00
Lee Lay Farm	9	3	13	21	00	00
Wooden End [now Woodend]	173	1	19	230	00	00
Ladywood Farm**	18	1	7	13	00	00
Total	713	3	14	947	03	04

** Horner's Mill is not on the list but this may be because it was acquired separately from the main estate

> We find the land in improving condition, Mr. Evans having drained, and is now in the course of draining, considerable portions of the estate. Having regard to the nature of the soil, very beneficial results may be looked to from these operations.
>
> We also noticed that several enclosures have been laid down to permanent pasture, and under the present aspects of agricultural prospects, this must be regarded as decidedly advantageous.
>
> Mr. Evans has also improved the homesteads within the last 10 years, all of which are now in good or substantial condition, well adapted to the farms that they are on.
>
> A good school house has also been erected…, [see Chapter XII].
>
> All existing lettings are yearly, the tenants paying taxes and tithe rent charge. The land tax has been redeemed.
>
> We are of the opinion that the sum of £18,000 may be lent on the property by way of mortgage, with safety to the lender.

It is noted above that Mr. Evans, along with many farmers at that time, was putting land back to permanent grassland, not such an easy thing to do without the improved seed that we have today and probably many rued the day that it had ever been ploughed up. It was not good policy to grow corn when prices were low and grassland farming was less labour intensive.

At almost the same time Mr. Evans listed the tenants on the estate together with the dates their tenancies started. Thomas Evans, James Hodges and Richard Jones had previously been tenants of James Moore:

A recent picture of Woodhall.

Mrs E.B. Evans.

1879 Nov 19th	Woodend Farm	Philip Farmer
1877 Sept 10th	Wooden End Farm	James Poyner
1866 July 21st	Ladywood Farm	Thomas Evans
1866 July 21st	The Shop Farm	James Hodges
1866 July 31st	Lee Lay Farm	Richard Jones
	& also Walls Close	Richard Jones
1879 Feb 12th	Waste Cottage	William Hall

The remainder of farms & lands comprising the estate & consisting of Thrift, New House, parts of Ladywood Farm, in all about 429 acres, are in hand & worked by me until a suitable tenant is accepted.

At this time, the average agricultural weekly wage for labourers in Herefordshire was 13s. 4d.[6] The following extract, taken from Pamela Horn's book: *Labouring Life in the Victorian Countryside,* happens to relate to a Bromyard man and as this is so close to Tedstone Delamere, it is reproduced here. It is the budget of Edward Wood, who was a foreman of farm labourers in Bromyard in 1892:[7]

Budget   Family consists of man, wife, one boy working on farm, and four children aged 9, 7, 5, and 2. One lad at service in gentleman's stable. Two girls in domestic service.

	£	s	d
Wages			
Self		16	00
Boy		6	00
	1	02	00
One Week's Expenditure			
11 loaves of bread at 5d		04	07
1 quarter flour		00	05
7 lb meat at 7d		04	01
3½ lb cheese at 6d		01	09
2 lb butter at 1s. 3d		02	06
½ lb tea		01	00
6 lb sugar at 2d		01	00
4 packets cocoa at 2d		00	08
2 lb rice at 2d		00	04
1 lb candles		00	05
2 quarts lamp oil		00	04½
Club money		00	11½
		18	01
One Year's Clothing Etc.			
7 pairs of boots	2	12	00
Clothing	3	00	00
4 tons coal at 20s.	4	00	00
200 faggots		14	00
	£10	06	00

(averaging 4s. a week).

Rent free.
Gets coat from employer every alternate Christmas.
Gets pair trousers from employer every alternate Christmas.
Gets blanket and flannel every alternate Christmas.
Cast off dress for gowns for children.

The above example relates to a man who, as a foreman, would have had a slightly higher wage than a farm labourer. Clearly any gifts of food or clothing from an employer were a vital part of a budget. It seems likely that Tedstone people would have burnt wood rather than coal.

The Evans family were great benefactors to the parish. In 1901 the Parish Magazine records:

> Mrs. E. B. Evans distributed her presents to the parishioners on Dec 19th and on the following days. We are sure that the recipients of these seasonable and valuable gifts feel most grateful to Mrs. Evans. The choosing of these presents with so much considerate care is no easy task. We are not forgetting too that Mrs. Evans came out herself in such bitter weather to show so much kindness to our parishioners.

Mr. E. B. Evans's elder son, Edward Wallace Evans, died before his parents. After the death of Edward Bickerton Evans's widow in 1910, the Worcestershire part of the estate, some 1200 acres, passed to Mrs. Patrick Evans, the widow of her younger son, and this land became known as the 'Harpley Estate'. Edward Wallace's son, Frank, inherited the Whitbourne and Tedstone Estates, then 1800 acres, on his grandmother's death. He had worked abroad and served in the South African War. He returned to England in 1905 and married Fanny Brierley, the daughter of Whitbourne's much loved and respected rector, settling down to the management of the estate. In 1914, he again volunteered for active service and was wounded on the Somme at the ripe age of 43. After the war, he returned to England and running the estate. He was a typical country squire and loved field sports; Frank's son, Edward

The Grubb family at Woodend. *Evelyn Whistance*

Evans, writing in his book, *Gentleman's Relish,* said his father was the best shot of partridges and pheasants he had ever seen.[8] The shooting and woodland was an important part of the estate, and still is. Frank Evans was a JP, a Herefordshire County Councillor and was chairman of Bromyard RDC for 25 years. He was said to keep a good cellar of port.

He worked the home farm and estate together employing three maintenance men:

> One of the farm men was waggoner and looked after the two shire horses, Dragon and Boxer. Their job was to do all the timber hauling out of the woods, as well as the ploughing and cultivating: there were no tractors then. Timber was sawn on a circular saw driven by a continuous belt powered by an engine fuelled by paraffin. It took about eight people to man the threshing machine. The corn was cut by a reaper and binder – combines had not been invented. When tractors came in, we converted the binder to tractor drawn, and carried on with it for several seasons.
>
> Agricultural wages were about thirty shillings a week, or £1.50 in todays's terms. Farm rents were at a maximum of £2.00 per acre per year.
>
> The estate men's work was practically all maintenance. They fenced round each wood with a solid timber and wire fence. The timber, steeped in creosote by the 'hot and cold' method, was reckoned to last forty years – some of it still good today after sixty. There was digging of drains, laying of concrete round farm yards, endless replacing of roof tiles and battens, endless measures to cure and prevent damp in farmers' living rooms and bedrooms. There were perhaps 40 dwellings on the estate, including 'tied cottages' which paid no rent[**]. Very few tenants would tell you what needed doing; they preferred to wait till my father visited them. He did this steadily year in year out. 'I got round the Captain to build me a pigs cot,' in the words of one tenant, sums up the give and take spirit which I think prevailed.[9]

Edward Evans said that his father's income from rents just exceeded his expenditure on maintenance by about £150 a year. He never took any money out of the estate for his personal use in terms of salary, regularly making a loss which he set against income tax. His income to live on was practically all from shares in Hill, Evans and Co. (the vinegar works). Edward Evans goes on to explain the family feeling that it was important that the estate provided a 'farming ladder' whereby people could climb to better things and some of their workers benefited in this way being offered tenancies as farms became available.

In about 1973, land had gone up in value a great deal and Edward Evans decided to sell some farms thus enabling members of his family to realise their share and also to finance the building of the Dial House in a beautiful setting by the lake, a much more convenient house for modern living than the Hall. Rather than sell the chosen land as a whole to an institution for what would have made a higher price, it was decided to offer it to the tenants. The selected farms were the Thrift, New House, Woodhall and Woodend, all in Tedstone Delamere. The tenant at Woodend did not take up the offer; the other three farms were sold to the tenants but this was a period

---

** The reference here is of course to the Whitbourne Estate as a whole, of which the Tedstone Delamere estate is but a part

of very high interest rates which caused difficulty and one new owner sold his farm at once and it was subsequently broken up, (Woodhall); another gradually sold his off in bits and converted the buildings to housing, (The Thrift); the third soldiered on and his family are still there, (New House). Horner's Mill had previously been sold to its tenant.

Water supply
There are some good springs below New House and a pipeline from these took the water by gravity all the way to Whitbourne Hall; this must have been a huge undertaking! As time went on, the pipes corroded and the estate employed a man almost full time repairing leaks. In the 1950s, a Blake Hydram was installed that pumped water from the springs to a reservoir in Riley Meadow and then it was fed by gravity to Oxhall (in Lower Sapey), Riley and Stone House Cottages, the Thrift, Woodhall, Woodend, Primrose and Lambs Green Cottages and Sunnyside Cottage. The overfill from the ram went to Horner's Mill.[10] Water was never very plentiful, especially further down the line, but the supply never failed until the hot summer in 1976. The water situation had limited the number of cattle that could be kept and made modern dairying difficult at these farms. The mains supply arrived in the 1980s.

The Whitbourne Estate used the Boiling Method.
Journal of Royal Agricultural Society of England, Vol 71, 1910

Electricity
The electricity came through in the 1960s but it was some considerable time before all the properties were connected.

Today the Whitbourne Estate has parted with most of the farmland in Tedstone Delamere, apart from Woodend, but retains the shooting rights. The estate owns about 182 acres of woodland in the parish, of which approximately 85 acres are to the west of the Sapey Brook, being purchased in 1996 at the Bellville sale. Forestry is a major concern today.

CHAPTER X

The Farms and Smallholdings – from 1841

This chapter takes up where Chapters V and VI left off, and makes use of the tithe survey of 1840/41, the censuses 1841–2001, trade directories and other records where available. In 1841, the land on the west side of the brook was owned by several individuals, unlike most of the land to the east which was in virtual single ownership. Glebe Farm is covered in Chapters I and VIII concerning the church. A summary of the tenancy changes can be followed in Tables 6 and 7. Maps 8 and 9 show the landownership and tenure in 1841

FARMS ON THE WEST SIDE WHICH WERE NOT PART OF THE TEDSTONE COURT ESTATE

1. Tipton Hall

Table 8 demonstrates stability in that the acreage remained the same throughout the census years and tenants changed infrequently. In 1840, Tipton (185 acres) was owned by John Knill, the London wharfinger; the tenant was William Blissett whose large household included his wife and three children, his twin brothers, one described as farmer in the census and the other as a cabinetmaker, two female farm servants and three young agricultural workers. At this time, Ireland Cottages were the farm cottages for Tipton housing two more farm workers. Francis Tolley followed as

Charlie Rudd with a Hereford Bull. *Joyce Benbow*

TABLE 6. FARMS & SMALLHOLDINGS IN WESTERN TEDSTONE DELAMERE 1841 - 1901

PROPERTY (acreage 1840)	1841	1851	1861	1871	1881	1891	1901
1. Tipton 185 acres	Willm. Blissett 7f/12h	Francis Tolley - 185a empl. 1 lab - 4f/9h	Jas Ward - 185a empl. 5 labs - 5f	Jas Ward - 185a empl. 6 labs - 5f/7h	Jas Ward 185a - 5f/6h	Mary Ward 3f/7h	Stanley Ward 5f/9h
2. Hedge House 158 acres	Willm Bevan 3f/7h	Willm Bevan - 190a empl.1 lab - 3f/5h	Sarah Hemming - 200a empl. 4 labs - 7f/12h	Jos Chambers - 206a empl. 3 labs - 4f/5h	Dan Nott - 129a 3f/4h	Jos Pantall 7f	Jos Pantall 6f
Tedstone Court 146 acres	Thos Wight 5f/8h	Thos Wight - 217a empl. 5 labs - 3f/6h	[J L Wight] 5f/10h	[J L Wight] 7f/14h	J L Wight - 3f/12h wharfinger	Edgar Wight - retd barrister - 3f/9h	Edgar Wight barrister 4f/10h
3. Line House 108 acres	Thos Wood 3f/5h	Jn Moore - 141a empl. 3 labs - 3f/7h	Jn Moore - 160a empl. 4 labs - 3f/6h	Ann Moore - 140a empl. 8 labs- 2f/4h	Jas Gough - 140a 3f/7h	Jas Gough - 2f/5h	Chas Bowers steward 5f/6h
4. Pixhill 82 acres	John Hill 3f/7h	1. Dan Clews - 250a empl. 8 labs - 2f 2. John Pitt 6f/7h	John Coulson bailiff - 3f	Rich Bullock bailiff - 1f/3f	Thos Herring bailiff - 4f/5h	Chas Sargeant gamekeeper 3f	James Sirrell lab - 3f
5. Upper Grounds 70 acres	-	-	Reynolds*	-	Jos Pantall 7f/8h	Jn Harrington farm manager - 3f/4h	Thos Cooper stockman 3f/4h
6. Winley 50 acres	Ed Jones 5f	Rich Aingell - 45a empl. 1 lab - 5f/6h	Rich Aingell - 39a empl. 2 labs - 2f/5h	Geo Wilson - 48a 3f/4h	Geo Wilson 51a 3f/4h	William Jones 5f	Jn Griffiths stockman - 8f
7. Homs/Hams 31 acres							
8. Gatehouse (alias Yatch) 21a	Willm Tipper shoemaker 6f				Henry Gibbs 75a - 5f/6h	Will Smith lab - 6f	Ernest Boughton 3f/5h

NOTES: names are heads of household. In 1861 & 71, although head of household, J. L. Wight of Tedstone Court lived in London, so name bracketed. Tedstone Crt, Upper Grounds & Pixhill owned by the Wights who purchased Line Hse in 1891. Tipton & Winley owned by the Knills. Hedge Hse was part of the Saltmarshe Estate, as was the Gatehouse sometime after 1840. Hams not in censuses as no farmhouse. a = acres, f = no. in family, h = total no. in household, extras usually living-in servants or ag. labs.

Table 6.

FARMS AND SMALLHOLDINGS FROM 1841

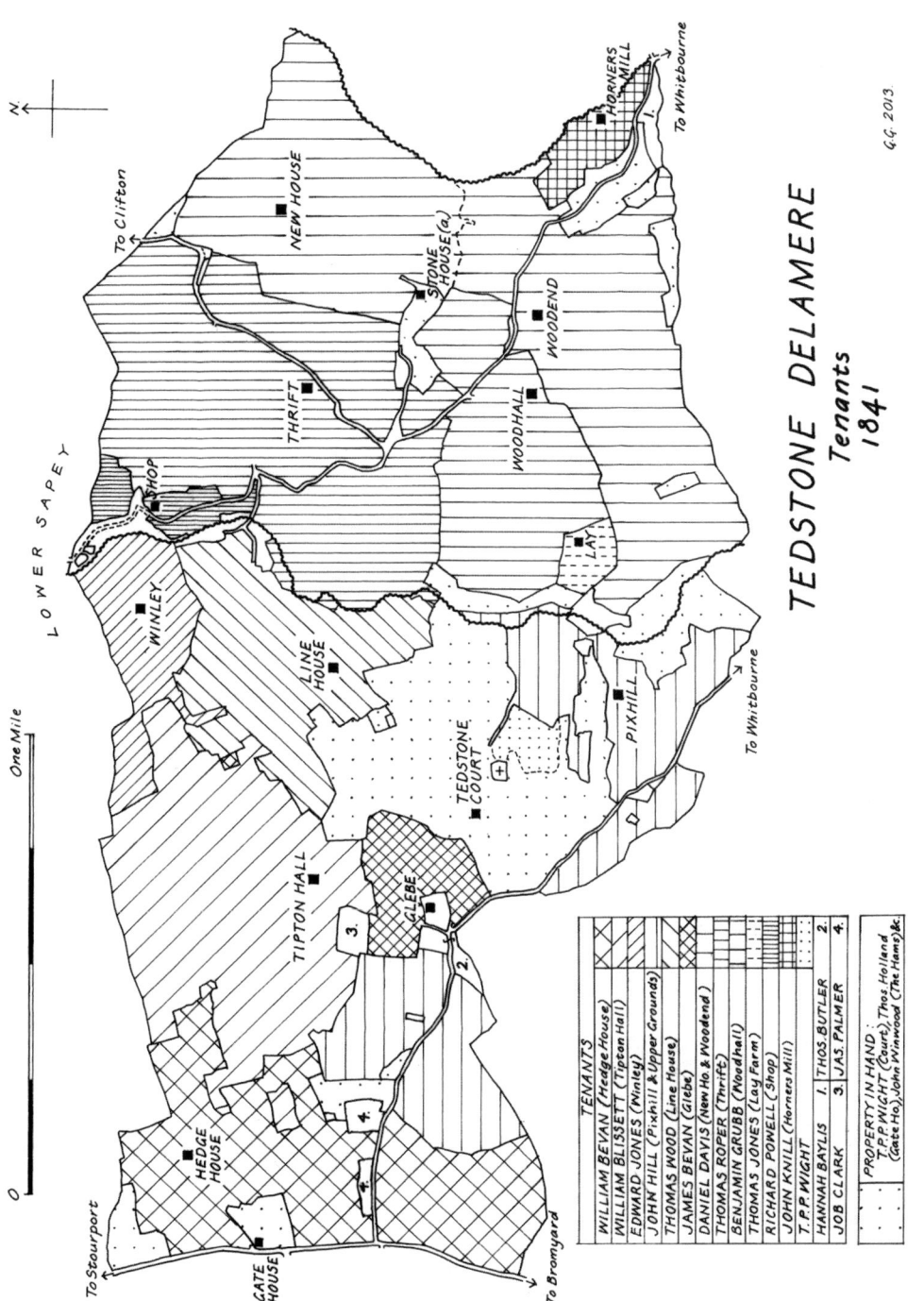

Map 9.

Wedding of Don Rea and Norah Benbow
Joyce Benbow

tenant who, by 1856, had been succeeded by James Ward; the Wards had a large family of seven children. As related on page 153, James Ward took his part in parish duties being the churchwarden for many years, and when the church was closed in the 1860s for the great restoration, services took place in one of the buildings at Tipton. James was eventually succeeded as churchwarden by his son Stanley in 1891. The 1891 census names widowed Mary Ward as the farmer; she had two sons at home: 43-year-old Berrow, who was a commercial traveller; and Stanley, aged 38, with the occupation of 'farmer's son'. By 1901, Stanley had succeeded as farmer and was

Dick Benbow helping.
Joyce Benbow

Dick & Joyce Benbow cutting their cake.
Joyce Benbow

Walter Benbow and Mystery with the cup won in the Clifton Farmers Race at Netherwood 1927.
Joyce Benbow

married with three small children. In 1918, Walter Benbow, having come to Tipton as a tenant, bought the farm from the Knills. Apparently two prize-winning shire horses were sold to enable him to complete his purchase. Walter Benbow was passionate about hunting and horse racing, as was his son Dick who succeeded him. In the 1960s, a serious fire destroyed many buildings at Tipton: the Benbow family had retired to bed but fortunately Rena Easton of Glebe Cottage was returning home late from the pictures and raised the alarm. Today, Walter's grandson, Noel, concentrates on the farming whilst his brother Roger runs a riding school at Cherryfields, the house they have built on Tipton land.

2. Hedge House
In 1841 Hedge House was part of the Saltmarshe Estate owned by Edmund Higginson; the tenants changed frequently and the acreage seemed to vary with each change. At that time, the farm consisted of 167 acres in Tedstone Delamere and 32 in Lower Sapey and was farmed by William Bevan (or Beavan).[1] By the time of the 1851 census, the Tedstone Delamere acreage had increased to 190 acres and it seems likely that it then included Gate House land which had accounted for 21.5 acres in the tithe survey. The Gate House is not included in the 1851 census so the house must have then been empty. As recorded on page 97, in 1855 Maria Beavan, William's widow, was granted her free bench at Hedge House by Bromyard Manorial Court.

A 'free bench' was that part of an estate which a widow had as her dower according to the customs of the manor. Later tenants changed frequently and with each change, the farm acreage was varied. This seems to have been fairly normal for the time as the practice was similar on other estates including those of Whitbourne and Bredenbury.[2] In 1891, the new tenant was Joseph Pantall who had previously been farming at Upper Grounds and he remained for rather longer than most, being still at Hedge House in 1901! He was assisted by his two sons, William and Thomas and his daughter Agnes. At the time of the Saltmarshe sale in 1949, Hedge House, with 163 acres, was for sale with vacant possession, having previously been in the tenancy of Mr. J. F. Dullam at a rental of £164 per annum. The acreage was then 51 acres in Tedstone Wafre, 32 acres in Lower Sapey and 79 acres in Tedstone Delamere; Mr. Burgoyne was the purchaser.[3] In 1966, it was sold to Mr. Coldicott whose son Robert farms it today.

Bob Coldicott with his daughter Susanne before her marriage to Francis Clark, April 1970.

3. The Line House

In 1841, the tithe survey tells us that Slade Baker of Sandbourne, Worcestershire owned the Line House. From 1853 until his resignation in 1875, the Rev. Slade Baker was the incumbent of Clifton-on-Teme. Thomas Wood junior was the tenant farming 108 acres but the 1841 census indicates that 80-year-old Thomas Wood senior still lived and it was he who was named the farmer in the census; it seems that the Baker estate-management policy was rather different from that of the Saltmarshe Estate, for the Wood family had been tenants at the Line House for about 100 years and the Moore family who followed as tenants stayed quite a long time: in 1851, 54-year-old John Moore was farming 141 acres with three labourers (four male servants lived in the house). Ten years later, he was farming 160 acres and employing four men: a carter, James Ward; a carter's boy, 14-year-old Andrew Tyler; and William Green, a cowboy; all lived in the house. In 1871, 70-year-old Ann Moore, widow and her stepdaughter, Sarah, aged 40, were in partnership farming 140 acres at the Line House and employing five men, one boy and two women. In 1881, Sarah Moore had married James Gough who was the new tenant farmer. Her elderly mother, Ann, lived with them still.

Mrs. Wright, daughter of the rector, Prebendary Simcock-Lea, remembers the hop pickers at the Line House:

FARMS AND SMALLHOLDINGS FROM 1841

Market day in Bromyard. Arthur Griffiths, John Roper & John Griffiths.   *Kathleen Harris*

> In addition to the Tedstone pickers, there were the strangers from the Black Country …. They were housed and fed in a big barn at the Line House. To them it was an enjoyable country holiday, for they could not count hop-picking as hard work, compared with that of nail-making. Those Black Country young women had fine voices, and it was wonderful to hear them singing …the strains taken up by the various groups round the hop-cribs floated down the valley ….[4]

In 1891, Edgar Wight of Tedstone Court purchased the Line House and for later history of this farm, the reader should turn to the section: 'Tedstone Court Estate Farms' on page 183.

(Farms: **4. Pixhill** and **5. Upper Grounds** are likewise covered in the section on the Tedstone Court Farms pages 185-188).

6. Winley

At Winley, from left: John Darby; Ernie, Arthur with John & Olive Griffiths; Harold Darby. *Evelyn Whistance*

In 1841, Winley was owned by John Knill, (the London merchant, who also owned Tipton). It was tenanted by Edward Jones who was farming 50 acres. Eleven years later, a new tenant, 62-year-old Richard Aingell, farmed 45 acres and employed one labourer at Winley. He lived here with

The Griffiths family at Winley: Joan, Olive, Agnes, John Griffiths, John Roper, Annie, Arthur & Jessie. There are some fine cabbages. *Kathleen Harris*

his wife, two sons and a daughter. By 1861, Richard Aingell jun. was the head of household and his sister Ann kept house for him. Living-in were carter's boy, Benjamin Jones; farm labourer, Charles Norman; and Mary Ann Griffiths, a servant. In 1871, Richard's sister Ann remained as domestic servant to new tenants who were George and Susannah Wilson. In 1891, the Wilsons had retired and were replaced by young tenants, William and Ann Jones.

The Griffiths family

John and Mary Griffiths were at Winley in 1901; he had the occupation of 'stockman of cattle'. John had been born in Martley and began his married life living at the Hole in Whitbourne parish, a cottage down across the fields south of Hill Cross. They had a large family: Thomas and Sidney, the two elder boys, had been born in Norton; Annie, William and Agnes were born at the Hole, and Ernest, Arthur, Alfred and Gladys were born at Winley. Thomas and Sidney were working on the farm in 1911. Tom later worked for the Bellvilles at the Court. In 1918, John Griffiths purchased Winley through Walter Benbow of Tipton who had requested that the property be conveyed to Griffiths. John

Rescue the Kitten!
John Griffiths followed by Harold Darby at Winley. *Kathleen Harris*

Arthur and Olive buying sheep. The small child in the hat is Evelyn Darby. *Kathleen Harris*

The Clifton Hunt at Winley. William North on foot with camera. Francis Lowden, hunt chairman, about to move off on the right.

Griffiths cut down some woodland and the sale of the timber is said to have paid for the farm. It was then 66 acres and the purchase price was £1200. For some reason, the vendors, who were the mortgagees of Stuart Knill, didn't want to deal with John Griffiths direct. We are again reminded what a bad time it was for farming: the mortgage on the farm had been £3000 so a considerable sum of money had been lost! Stuart Knill was the grandson of John Knill who had owned Tipton and Winley in 1841. John and Mary Griffiths' daughters, Agnes and Annie, both lost their sweethearts in World War 1 and never married. Ernie married Nellie Delahay and farmed at Tidbatch (see page 204). In 1934 their father, John, had a sad end; he was rather stout, overbalanced and fell into the pig swill where he drowned. His son, Arthur, went on to farm both Winley and the Line House (where he lived) as one; Arthur's son John married at the age of 20 and went to live at Winley. Members of the Griffiths family had been at Winley for nearly 100 years and continue to take an important part in parish life to this day. William and Nancy North are today's owners.

7. The Homs / Hams

In 1841, this 23 acre holding, still in the ownership of John Winwood, was in hand. There was no farmhouse but Winwood owned a cottage in the Hams which was let to John Palmer. Today this cottage is the only one still standing at Whitehall (see page 225). A plan of the Tedstone Court Estate in 1908 shows this land and Whitehall Cottage as belonging to Mrs. Evans of Whitbourne Hall.[v]

8. The Gate House

In 1841, the Gate House was a small farm of 21 acres and Thomas Holland was owner-occupier. It was not named in the census, unless it was the house called *Yatch* occupied by William Tipper, a shoemaker. This property was divided and in the other half lived four boys: Richard Perkins, shoemaker's apprentice; Edmund Perry; 15-year-old John Rimmell who was a brickmaker, as was 10-year-old Henry Davis; the old brickworks on the site of the present hunt kennels was not recorded in the tithe survey of 1841 so where the lads worked is unknown. In 1851, the Gate House was unmentioned and was presumably uninhabited. At some unknown date, the property was acquired by the Saltmarshe Estate. In 1861, it was called 'Three Gates' and John Woodhouse, a carrier, lived here with his wife, Elizabeth and son, Edward, 17, who was a farm-worker, and another son, nine-year-old Charles, a scholar. By 1871, an agricultural worker lived at 'Gate House Cottage'.

A farmer in the making. Donald Boughton at the Gate House.

Ten years later, it was a farm; Henry Gibbs was here farming 75 acres. (This land had previously been Hedge House land.) He and his wife Mary and three small children lived at the Gate House and they employed a

Threshing rye at the Gate House in the mid 1940s. Threshing was by H.A. Edwards, Collington; Harold Boughton on the rick, Jack Panthall (Upper Grounds) cutting bands, Ralph Roper on bags, Donald on the ladder, Irene Boughton & Joyce Farr watching.   *Donald Boughton*

living-in farm servant, John Benbow; but by 1891, the Saltmarshe Estate had again demoted it to a farm labourer's cottage. Finally, in 1901, the Gate House was again a farm; Ernest Boughton, his wife Mary and baby son, Harold, lived here; they had a living-in farm servant, Frederick Saunders, who worked as a waggoner; and one lodger, Jenkin Williams, a carpenter. Harold followed his father and in about 1949, he bought the farm; it was then about 50 acres. Today, Harold's son, Donald, lives at the Gate House and farms 118 acres, assisted by his son David. There have now been Boughtons farming the Gate House for over 100 years.

THE TEDSTONE COURT ESTATE FARMS
3. The Line House *cont.*
The Line House farm did not become part of the estate until 1891 when Edgar Wight, James's eldest son who had inherited his father's property, bought it for £2773 5s. 4d. from Col. Robert Broome Baker of Brighton whose family had owned this farm for nearly a century. Edgar Wight purchased the farm with the help of a £1000 mortgage from his parson brother Alfred, who lived in the Isle of Wight, and his sister Emily of Tedstone Court. At that time, James Gough was the tenant. By 1901, the Wight's farm steward, Charles Bowers, lived at the Line House with his wife and three small children. Bowers later emigrated to Canada and did very well out there. In 1948, he wrote to Mr. Griffiths at the Line House asking for news of Tedstone. One of the things he mentioned was that there was a coal mine at Upper Grounds.

Wedding of Arthur Griffiths & Olive Roper. *Kathleen Harris*

Olive & Arthur Griffiths (on the right) at the Line House. *Kathleen Harris*

He had been sworn to secrecy about its whereabouts by Mr. Wight.[6] Just as well perhaps as opencast coal mining across Tedstone is a horrid thought! In 1910, Edgar Wight sold the Line House and various cottages to Henry Archibald Bellville (who by that time had already bought the Court) for £2350, rather less than what he had bought it for some 20 years earlier. By this time, farming was in serious recession. Trade Directories list the following as farming at the Line House: George Bemand 1913 and 1917, Edward Smith 1922 and 1929, and Reginald Mason as being there 1934 and 1941. Arthur Griffiths followed the Masons.

4. Pixhill

Pixhill and the Grey House had been purchased by Robert Moore for the estate in 1790. In 1841, Pixhill was in the tenure of John Hill. There were 82 acres which included land from the former Grey House Farm and a smallholding known as Cullets. Hill employed a couple of living-in male farm workers and a female 'farm servant'. In 1851, the house was divided, in one half lived Daniel Clews who described himself as 'farm bailiff of 250 acres employing eight labourers'. In the other half of the house lived John Pitt, a 'retired farmer', 45 years old, with wife and four small children. In 1861, a new farm bailiff, John Coulson from Northumberland, lived at Pixhill. He didn't last and by 1871, Richard Bullock was the new young 26-year-old bailiff. He had middle-aged Sarah Freeman keeping house for him. There was yet another bailiff in 1881: Thomas Herring with his family. In 1891, Charles Sargeant, gamekeeper, lived here. In 1901, the occupant was James Sirrell, a farm worker. It seems the Wights changed their Pixhill employees quite frequently.

Pixhill was known for its excellent cherries. Fred Mason assisted by Gladys Prosser. *Betty Mason*

Pixhill: From left Fred James, Anne & Betty Mason, Freda Powell, Fred Mason on tractor. *Betty Mason*

Pixhill: Fred Mason checking his cattle. *Betty Mason*

Feeding tiddler lambs at Pixhill. From left: Jen, Anne & Joan Mason. *Betty Mason*

The Mason family.
Fred Mason came as a tenant c1917, moving from Park Cottage opposite the Bringsty Smithy, and his family remained here until 1983. Fred had previously worked as a postman then as a carpenter; Mrs Mason was known for being an expert dresser of poultry. Their son, another Fred, followed his father as tenant and they carried out mixed farming with cattle and sheep. Damsons and blackcurrants were produced and Pixhill was known for its fine cherries.

Mr & Mrs Fred Mason at Pixhill. *Betty Mason*

5. Upper Grounds and Smith's or Forge Cottage

There is no record of when this ground was acquired and it may have been part of the Tedstone Court estate for centuries. Known to be part of the estate in 1824,[7] the land of 70 acres on either side of the road to Whitbourne was 'owned' by T. T. P. (Philip) Wight (as a trustee) in 1841 and along with Pixhill was in the tenancy of John Hill. At this time, there was no house at Upper Grounds. Sometime before 1851, Mr. Wight had built a house; the census tells us that John Gray and family were living in Upper Grounds Cottage and he was farmer of 65 acres employing one labourer. (The cottage may of course have been the future blacksmith's cottage.) Ten years later, there is no doubt for we have both Upper Grounds Farmhouse, and also Upper Grounds Cottage, or Forge Cottage, where Richard Powell, blacksmith, had moved to from Tidbatch. (The Forge is covered in detail in Chapter XI.) The 1871 census has no mention of Upper Grounds Farm so perhaps the house was at that time empty. By 1881, Joseph Pantall was farming at Upper Grounds but by 1891, he had bettered himself by becoming tenant of the larger Hedge House Farm and John Harrington, the Wight's farm manager, was at Upper Grounds. His wife, Mary, managed the dairy and their son, George, was 'working farm bailiff'. In 1901, Thomas Cooper, stockman, his wife, Elizabeth and 16-year-old agricultural worker, Thomas, were at Upper Grounds. The 1908 sale particulars of the Tedstone Court estate tell us that the farm was then let to Thomas Dallow at a rent

Upper Grounds: from sale particulars of the Tedstone Court Estate 1908. *HRO*

of £90 p.a. and the smith's cottage and forge were let to Mr. Powell, blacksmith, at £11 pa. In 1934, Upper Grounds was sold by Mrs. Ethel Bellville and her son Miles to Thomas Pantall and the farm was then 64 acres.[8] It was later farmed by Jack Pantall. In 1950, Upper Grounds was owned by Major Miles Bellville, who must have re-purchased, and Chris Harris went to live there with the post of chief stockman. In 1985, Chris and Kathleen Harris purchased Forge Cottage, where they now live, from Richard Bellville and Upper Grounds was sold to Stewart Clinton-Watkins.

Leslie Griffiths competing at Upper Grounds.
Kathleen Harris

Haymaking at Upper Grounds watched by Archie Bellville & small child 1914-17.   *Bellville Collection*

The Brickworks

As recorded above, the Brickworks does not feature in the tithe survey of 1840/41 but, as noted, two young lads working as brick-makers were then living at the Gate House. The Brickworks became part of the Saltmarshe Estate and featured in the particulars of the estate sale in 1949 as Lot 13: Clifton-on-Teme Hunt Kennels 'situated on an area of land which was formerly a brickworks'.

Clifton-on-Teme Hunt[9]

The hunt was formed in 1920, due to the energy of a small band of sportsman and farmers of the district. The hunt country was loaned from the adjoining hunts: the Worcestershire on the east, the Ludlow on the north and the North Herefordshire on the west; the hounds were to be kennelled at Shelsley Walsh. A hunt handbook of c1939 records:

> The country is hilly, but has always been noted for its stout wild foxes, and for the sport they have shown. The going is mostly on grass, and the enclosures strongly fenced. A horse must be a good performer to get over such a country, and must have plenty of stamina, for a long day on the hills is the test for any hunter, and soon finds out the weed. The horse for this country should be the compact, short coupled sort, with plenty of heart room, and short legged .... There is a fair amount of woodland, about one sixth of the whole area, and the woodlands are dense and call for the perseverance on the part of the hounds and huntsman. But once a fox is forced away he will fly.[10]

The custom then was to send an account of the day's hunting to the local newspapers and cuttings from these papers were pasted into scrap books by the late Mrs. Ethel Bellville; today they make interesting reading.[11] Compared with recent times just before the hunting ban, the most striking differences in the 1920s and 30s were the extraordinarily long runs which the hunt enjoyed when eight or ten mile points were not uncommon. There is probably more than one reason for this: in more recent times, the profitability of shooting to landowners has severely limited the land that could be hunted, and another being the much greater prevalence of wire. Point-to-Points in those early days were held at Netherwood in Thornbury.

In 1936, Audrey Bellville of Tedstone Court became honorary secretary and in the next season, her brother, Miles Bellville, became one of the joint-masters.

Reprinted from the "Bromyard News & Record," October 16th, 1930.

THE LATE CAPT. BELLVILLE.

His Interest in the Clifton Hunt.

A Clifton correspondent writes :—By the death of Capt. Bellville the district has lost a gentleman closely identified with the promotion of all branches of sport in the district generally, and with Clifton fête and races in particular.

The death of his son Dennis, in a motor cycle collision, was a terrible shock to him, and from its effects he never recovered.

He was devoted to horses, and was among the last to drive a carriage and pair abreast, or alternately tandem, in the district, and it was with great reluctance that he allowed a car to displace his horses.

He was a member of a Leicestershire family with a great tradition for hunting, his brother, Captain George Bellville, being at the present time Master of the Woodland Pychley.

He maintained an unswerving interest in the Clifton Hunt from its inception, and very rarely were hounds silent in that excellent fox sanctuary, Tedstone Dingle.

Failing health prevented his following hounds in the saddle of late years, he frequently attended meets on wheels.

A few days before his death, Captain and Mrs. Bellville welcomed the field to breakfast, following an exhilarating morning in the environs of Tedstone Court.

On the day of his death the Cliftons met at Ham Bridge. The Master (Mr. Gerard Joynson) had drawn several coverts in the vale of the Teme, and was proceeding to Whitbourne when he was apprised of the death of Capt. Bellville. Out of respect for one of the Hunt's most ardent supporters, hounds were immediately called off and taken home, and Saturday's meet was cancelled.

Hunt scrap book compiled by Mrs Ethel Bellville is in the care of Francis Lowden

Mr. Miles Bellville, the newly appointed Joint Master of the Clifton Hounds, is well known in hunting circles. He has been a consistent and popular follower for many seasons of the Clifton pack and has frequently figured in the field of neighbouring hunts. Mr. Bellville comes of the stock of a famous Leicestershire hunting family with a great tradition of the chase. Below Tedstone Court, where he resides with Mrs. Bellville, his mother (a staunch preserver of foxes), lies the delectable fox habitation of Tedstone Dingle, which hounds seldom invade without a burst of melody.[12]

Miles Bellville M.F.H.   *Bellville Collection*

The masters hunted hounds themselves and Tom Telfer was first whipper-in and kennel-huntsman. The subscription was voluntary (those were the days!) but a cap would be taken for the 'poultry fund'. This fund was apparently paid out as compensation to anyone in the country who had lost their chickens to a fox!

But war was looming. In September 1939, an emergency meeting of the hunt committee was called. It was resolved to carry on for the moment, but in the event of the master being called up, the policy would be to disband the pack. Most of the dog hounds were to be put down but it was hoped to save a nucleus of the young bitches by placing them out to farmers and other kind friends of the hunt, and to keep the puppies, (three and a half couple) now at walk, till the advent of happier days. Many of the hounds seem to have been kept by Mrs. Bellville at the Court. In 1940, Audrey Bellville resigned as secretary having been called up for hospital duty; Tom Telfer, the kennel-huntsman was given notice.

After peace was declared, the hunt was run by a committee for a number of years with Captain Evans of Whitbourne Hall as chairman. Mr. Springfield, formerly master of the Mendip, came as amateur huntsman. There seemed to be a perennial problem over accommodation for staff, and stabling for the hunt horses. In 1945, the Old Brickyard site was leased from the Saltmarshe Estate and kennels were erected there. In July 1946, the hounds were still being kennelled at Tedstone Court, being moved to the new kennels the following year. In 1949, Mr. Stapleton-Martin was amateur huntsman and acting-master and Bill Millward whipped in and hunted hounds when necessary. At the 1950 AGM, the committee had failed to find a master for the coming season and Bill Millward hunted hounds. The difficulty in attracting suitable masters who would stay seemed to be because of lack of accommodation. At an AGM in 1953, Dick England was appointed master with a guarantee of £1200; it was at this time that a Hunt Supporters' Club was formed to help with the finances and provide good social activities; it was announced that the kennels site had been purchased from the Saltmarshe Estate. Dick England continued as master until 1960 when there seems to have been a difficult season with a distemper epidemic at the kennels which curtailed the number of hunting days resulting in loss of income. The season beginning 1961 saw Ernie Farrelly appointed as huntsman and Major Bellville acting as master for the committee. In 1964, Farrelly, who had been living at Forge Cottage, died in the middle of the season.

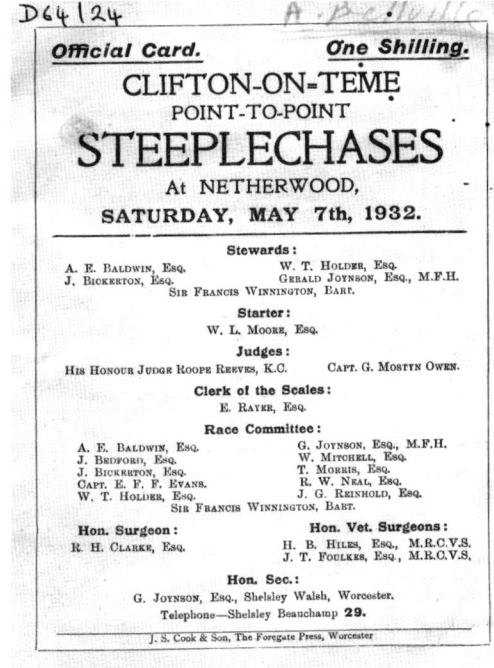

The following is a summary of mastership changes that were to follow:

1966 – 70	John Shearer (it is understood he hunted hounds during his first season)
1971 – 77	John Shearer joint-master with Mrs. Audrey Robinson. Ken Gwyn engaged as huntsman Raymond Rogers started as amateur whip in 1976
1978 – 80	David Palmer master and huntsman
1980 – 82	David Palmer, Ian Haynes and Gwyn Edwards as joint-masters
1982 – 83	Ian Haynes and Gwyn Edwards as joint-masters. Hounds hunted by kennel-huntsman
1983 – 89	David Parker was master & huntsman and stayed for seven years. When he arrived, he and his wife Linda lived in Forge Cottage for a short time whilst the bungalow at the kennels was being built, 1986 / 87. The bungalow was built at a cost of £33,875 accompanied by a massive fund raising exercise. Richard Bellville generously donated six acres of land adjoining the Kennels site.
1990	Roy Tatlow master who stayed for nine seasons
1999	Chris and Jo Burrows-Wood, joint-masters for five seasons
2004	Richard Hill and Clare Hill, joint-masters.

The nature of hunting has changed since the hunting ban but today the hunt thrives, ably supported by a very active Hunt Supporters Club.

FARMS ON THE EAST SIDE

Chapter VI explained how the Moore family of Upper House, Shelsley Beauchamp had come to own virtually all the land on the east side of the Sapey Brook by 1841. James Moore's successor, Edward Bickerton Evans of Whitbourne Hall, who purchased the estate in 1866, let the farms on annual leases; this seemed to be the general practice at the time but it meant that properties changed hands quite often. Towards the end of the century, farming was suffering from depression which may have contributed to the relatively short duration of some of the tenancies. The farms were often in hand, probably because of the difficulty of finding suitable tenants during this difficult farming period. A summary of the tenancy changes can be followed in Table 9.

1. The Thrift

In 1841, Thomas Roper farmed the Thrift, followed by his sons, George and Sandy. They employed four labourers, the youngest being just nine years old. Various changes followed and by 1891, there was a young tenant, John James, who came from Pembrokeshire; his wife, Annie, did the dairy work and it is worth noting that there is a particularly fine dairy at the Thrift. In 1901, John was on his own with five children, the youngest just five years old; James Nottingham, cattle boy and James Perkins, a cattleman, were living in the house. Apparently John James's wife had died in childbirth. John farmed here until at least 1913. Joseph Jackson was at the Thrift c1917 – 29; He was a member of the well known horse racing family of that name. An article in the Bromyard Deanery Magazine in 1920 records that demobilized soldiers were most royally entertained at the Thrift, thanks to the generosity of Mr. Jackson and Mr. Benbow of Tipton. They had an excellent dinner, due chiefly to Mrs. Jackson's arrangements, followed by speeches. After dinner they repaired to the granary when other friends joined them for dancing.

Harold Leighton farmed here between 1934 and 1941.

Bill Richards and his wife Sheila came to the Thrift in 1954. Bill was born on the next door farm at the Hill, Lower Sapey, where his father farmed and Sheila was the daughter of Mr. and Mrs. Harvey Jones of Horner's Mill. They spent 20 happy years at the Thrift bringing up their three children. Their son Harvey recalls salting hams in the large dairy and how the salt caused corrosion to the walls. He remembers how very busy it always seemed with a full household and two farm workers, rather different to a farmer's household today. In the early 1970s, Bill Richards purchased the Thrift

Mrs Jackson of the Thrift, c1920s. *Mrs Ann Jones*

TABLE 7. FARMS AND SMALLHOLDINGS IN EASTERN TEDSTONE DELAMERE 1841 - 1901

PROPERTY (acreage 1840)	1841	1851	1861	1871	1881	1891	1901
1. Thrift 240 acres	Thos Roper 4f/8h	Thos Roper - 240a empl. 3 labs - 4f/9h	George Roper - 244a empl. 3 labs - 2f/6h	Saml Hargrove - 245a empl. 9 labs - 2f/5h	John Taylor ag lab - 3f/4h	John James 5f/9h	John James 6f/8h
2. Woodend 155 acres	Daniel Davies 3f/6h	Saml Taylor - 160a empl. 2 labs - 4f/6h	Thos Pearce - 170a empl. 2 labs - 2f/5h	William Harris - ag lab 3f	Joseph Lewis farm bailiff 6f	James Grubb 8f/9h	James Grubb 6f
3. New House 133 acres	Joseph Passey ag lab - 4f	Rich Cleburey - ag lab 5f	Uninhabited	Geo E Munn - 140a empl. 1 lab - 3f/5h	Henry Andrews farm bailiff - 8f	James Smith ag lab - 5f	Robert Jones 5f/7h
4. Woodhall 103 acres	Ben Grubb 6f/7h	Ben Grubb - 100a 5f/8h	John Farmer - 100a empl. 4 labs - 7f/8h	John Farmer - 105a empl. l lab - 4f/6h	Philip Farmer 2f/3h	Alfred Pitt 8f/10h	Henry T Clarke 5f/7h
5. Horner's Mill 18 acres	Edward Starling miller - 2f	W G Arden - 31a - miller empl. 4 labs - 4f/7h	Thos Moseley - 18a miller - empl. 1 boy - 4f/5h	Thos Moseley - 18a miller - empl. 2 labs - 5f/7h	Alfred Pitt - miller 3f/4h	John Teague miller - 1f/2h	Thos L Jones farmer - 5f
6. Tidbatch (Shop Hse) 17 acres	Richard Powell blacksmith 3f/4h	Richard Powell - 12a blacksmith - 5f/6h	James Hodges blacksmith - 1f/3h	James Hodges - 17a carpenter empl. 1 boy - 1f/5h	James Hodges carpenter - 1f/2h	James Hodges builder - 1f/3h	Sam Young carpenter & joiner - 3f
7. Lee Lay 9 acres	Thos Jones 8f	Thos Jones - 9a 8f	Amelia Jones - 9a - empl. 1 lab* - 2f	Richard Jones - 10a gamekeeper empl. 1 lab - 9f	Richard Jones gamekeeper - 11f	Richard Jones gamekeeper - 6f	Richard Jones 7f
8. Stone House 7 acres	John Smith ag lab - 4f	Thos. Ashcroft - 7a 3f/4h	George Wilson - 7a ag lab - 2f	Thos Wilson - 7a ag lab - 8f	Thos. Wilson - 7a 6f	-	-

NOTES: Censuses 1841-61: the Moores owned all farms except Horners Mill (owned by Rev John Darcy) and Stone House A, together with part of a smallholding called the Hams; (the greater part of the Hams is on the west side of Sapey Brook near Whitehall; the Hams was owned by John Winwood). 1871-1901 E.B.Evans owned whole, except possibly Stone House & the Hams. Every householder was a farmer unless otherwise stated. a = acres, f = no. in family, h = total household, extras in household usually living-in servants or ag. labs...
*1861 Amelia Jones employs 1 lab & '3 more sometimes'.

Table 7.

from Captain Evans. He went on to convert the buildings to housing, creating several attractive dwellings, one of which he lived in himself. The farmhouse was sold and most of the land was sold off separately. Bill's son, Harvey, has built a new modern farmhouse at Lower Thrift and has bought back 100 acres of the land and rents a further 100 acres.

2. Woodend

Woodend is a timber-framed house, built in the latter half of the 17th century and has been described in Chapter VI. A very nice set of traditional farm buildings, nearly all timber-framed, are arranged together with the house as a loose courtyard forming a sheltered cattle yard; all the timber-framed buildings are clad in weatherboarding and have been renewed and refurbished over a period of time. One of the buildings has a swept dormer in the loft over a pitching door, suggesting that the roof may once have been thatched.

Tenants appeared to change fairly frequently until James Grubb became tenant at Woodend c1885 and his descendants farm it to this day:

The Grubb family

James Grubb had previously been a tenant at Crumplebury, one of the Whitbourne Estate farms; it was a smaller farm so he moved to Woodend to better himself. He was not a youngster when he moved; in 1891 he was 53 and he and his wife Elizabeth had a large family: Elvina (or Vinny), Henry, Ada, Ethel, Benjamin, Alice and Bertha with an age range of 15 - 1. James was a public-spirited man and for many years was assistant overseer of the poor. He was also a keen supporter of the church and served as churchwarden for some years; Mrs. Grubb was presented with a silver teapot by Miss Wight of Tedstone Court in recognition of work she did for the church; it is inscribed with her name on it and is now in the possession of Evelyn Whistance, her great-granddaughter. James used to cart the coal to heat Woodend School and his wife helped with concerts at the school in which their daughters used to sing. When Mr. Grubb retired he was succeeded at the farm by his son, Ben. His elder son Henry farmed at Woodhall. Trade directories list Ben Grubb as farming Woodend between 1917 and 1934.

Large barn and foldyard at Woodend.   *B&DLHC*

The Grubb family at Woodend c1906. From left: John, Ethel, Vinnie, Annie, Mr James Henry Grubb, Benjamin, Mrs Elizabeth Jane Grubb, Henry, Alice & Ada. *Evelyn Whistance*

Ernie Jones, who had married Ruth Jones from Horner's Mill, followed at Woodend.[] James Grubb's eldest daughter, Elvina (or Vinny) had married Thomas Lancelot Jones of Horner's Mill and their granddaughter, Beryl, married George Yates, a member of a well known farming family from the Venn at Avenbury. When George Yates had come out of the navy at the end of the 2nd World War, he used to go rabbiting with Bob Jones; Bob was the third generation of the Jones family to be gamekeepers for the Whitbourne Estate and was uncle to Beryl, which of course was how George met his bride. He became bailiff for T. L. Walker & Sons at Ankerdine and this had enabled him and Beryl to get married, later taking on the tenancy of Woodend. At Woodend, the Yates carry out mixed farming with cattle and sheep. Mrs. Yates now lives in retirement, still at Woodend, and her son, Mervyn, is the farmer.

Ruth Jones, daughter of Tom & Vinnie Jones of Horner's Mill, marries Ernie Jones at Whitbourne church. *Evelyn Whistance*

[] Trade directories list *Leslie* Jones at Woodend in 1937 & 1941

John Farmer's sale in 1879. *Julian Westwood*

3. Woodhall

The western timber-framed section of this attractive farmhouse, up to and including the main chimney-stack, is of mid-17th century date and the stone section to the east and the timber-framed section beyond it were added in the early-18th century.[13] This eastern end to the house was formerly a granary and dairy but has been converted by the present owner to domestic use; the fine dairy has become an attractive sitting-room; several very wide doors, probably made on the farm, denote the former agricultural use of this part of the house. The old road to Woodend, marked on both the tithe and the 1848 estate maps, is now not used and has become a watercourse running along the east and south sides of the garden.

Woodhall today.

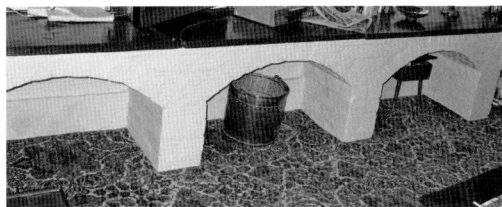

Good use has been made of this former dairy.

In 1851, 70-year-old Ben Grubb and his wife Sarah were assisted on the farm by Ben's brother, William, and a farm-worker, James Lewis. (As far as is known, the Grubbs at Woodhall were not related to the Grubb family who were at Woodend from 1885.) Ben's youngest brother, Samuel, lived with them; Samuel was a miller, probably working at nearby Horner's Mill. Sarah was helped in the house by their niece, 11-year-old Ann Hill. By 1861 they had been succeeded at the farm by their son-in-law, John Farmer, who had married their daughter, Elizabeth. John and Elizabeth had started their married life at Halfway House, a little farm on the road from Bromyard to Pencombe. They had already had eight children when they moved to Woodhall

This wide bedroom door was formerly the door to the granary. It was probably made on the farm.

and a further child, Louisa, was born in Tedstone Delamere; Uncle Sam Grubb, the miller, lived with them still. In 1871, John was being helped on the farm by his son, Charles. John Farmer held a farm sale here on his retirement in 1879. Implements advertised for sale included:

> Set of 1-horse wood harrows, set of iron three-breast harrows with supletrees, heavy iron three-breast harrows with supletrees, set of 2-horse wood harrows, iron chaff furnace, capital iron-wheel plough by *Kell,* iron swing plough - equal to new, light iron hammock plough, iron swede scuffle, excellent 3-furrow wheat drill, two-furrow bean drill, stone hop roll in wood frame, set of 7-tined iron scuffles on wheels, *Avery* patent platform weighing machine, capital winnowing machine, combined swede and manure drill, wood barley roll (barrel cased with iron), capital 2-knife chaff engine by *Richmond & Chandler, Bentall's* patent root pulper, various carts and wagons, a *Whitechapel Cart* with seats & lamps and a gig.

Older farmers today will remember most of the above, but what is an 'iron chaff furnace'? It is clear that hops were grown on the farm, as cribs, hop sacks etc. were included. There were about 70 head of cross-bred sheep, five carthorses, 14 head of Hereford cattle, including a yearling bull descended from J. H. Barneby-Lutley's herd, and three milking cows and some pigs. It is clear that use was made of the dairy for there was a butter churn, cheese press and quite a number of butter and cheese making utensils.

By 1881, their second son, 39-year-old Philip, was the farmer, later moving to the Steps Farm, Clifton. It is worth noting here that this farming family of Grubbs and Farmers had been tenants at Woodhall for nearly 100 years, Philip's great-grandfather Thomas Grubb being mentioned in the land tax assessments for Woodhall in 1790.

By 1891, Alfred and Sarah Pitt were at Woodhall with six small children; lodging with them was Annie James, the village schoolmistress. Between 1900 and 1905, Thomas Clarke farmed here followed by Henry Grubb, eldest son of James Grubb of Woodend. The agricultural depression became worse and he gave up the tenancy in 1934 and was followed by Thomas L. Briscoe, farming in partnership with Percy Orgee who was sadly killed in the war.

Farming became prosperous during and following the war and scrubland was cleared in the 1950s, increasing the land for farming here to 140 acres. In 1964 Roger Powell became tenant; he was the youngest of the Powell children, most of whom were born at Lee Lay but Roger himself was born at Finchers, Whitbourne, after his parents moved there. He remembers salting pigs on the slabs in the dairy at Woodhall and the hams were hung on great hooks in the ceiling; the barrels of cider were stored underneath the granary. Ten years later, Roger purchased the farm from the Evans family early in 1974 but due to financial difficulties caused by the high interest rates at the time, he had to put the farm on the market soon afterwards. At the sale, there was no buyer but later that day, Kenneth Beard, a Leigh Sinton farmer, met Roger Powell in the pub in Clifton and negotiated a purchase. His daughter Sally and son-in-law Julian Westwood purchased the house and about seven acres from him and have created a beautiful home here.[xiv] They are also the owners of Woodend School which they have made into a pleasant house to let. The majority of the land was broken up and the gist of the main transactions is as follows: 30 acres below the lane was sold to Mr. Yeomans of Salford Court; Graham Leake bought about 95 acres and *c*1980 he built a new farmhouse for his Woodhall land, May Farm, and put up a large building there; in 1980, Robin Philips bought 56.5 acres at auction from Mr. Leake and later a further 38 acres and subsequently built the large grain store; in 1985, Allan Wellings bought the house of May Farm which was sold in 1988 to Andrew Hale; in 1994, Geoff, Jennifer and Neil Farmer of Oxhall, Lower Sapey, bought 84 acres at auction.[xv] Geoff is the great-great-grandson of John Farmer who married Elizabeth Grubb and farmed Woodhall in the mid 19th century, the Grubb family having been here since the late-18th century.

4. New House

According to the censuses, from 1841 to 1861, Mr. Moore had the farm in hand and either farm workers lived in the house or it was empty. By 1863, a tenant, George Roper, had been found. In 1866, New House was sold with the rest of the Moore's Tedstone estate to Edward Bickerton Evans. As recorded on page 172, Mr. Evans engaged in waterworks which took water from a spring below New House from where it was fed by gravity all the way to Whitbourne Hall. In the 1950s, a hydraulic ram was installed pumping water from the springs to a reservoir in Riley Meadow, from where it was fed by gravity to farms and cottages. Tenants changed frequently; in 1881 New House was again in hand and a farm bailiff lived here. Robert Jones was farming New House from approximately 1902–1917 inclusive. He was followed by John Jones (no relation) who was here by 1922; his son Bryan succeeded him whose widow and daughter are still farming New House today.

The barn at New House. *B&DLHC*

Harvesting at New House c.1950. Bryan Jones with horse.

New House, granary steps with dog kennel underneath. *B&DLHC*

New House, roof structure in the barn. *B&DLHC*

Bryan Jones with an Oxford ram.
Ann & Sheila Jones

5. Horner's Mill

The Rev. John Darcy, former rector of the parish, had bought Horner's Mill and after his death in 1844, the property passed to his wife and then to his son John. In 1855 John Davies of Lower Sapey purchased Horner's Mill for £1500. The fields were listed and totalled 19 acres. John Davies died and the property was sold in 1864 to Edward Bickerton Evans of Whitbourne Hall.

In 1891, tenant John Teague was farmer and miller, probably the last to use the mill. The W. I. History records that one of the older parishioners could remember fetching flour from Horner's Mill for her mother's baking, so perhaps it was from Mr. Teague.[16] At that time, steam was superseding water power at larger mills and farmers were using horse engines for grinding animal feed and the writing was on the wall for small country mills. In 1895, Joseph Sanders (or Saunders), a carrier, lived here. The following is a story told by the locals:

> For some reason or another Mrs. Saunders used to take the cart quite often to Worcester – one Saturday, having a large bag of gold & not wishing to take it to town with her, she hid it in a haystack – on her return the bag had gone & she presumed it was stolen, however on enquiries from many interested neighbours she was persuaded to search the stack and found eventually that the cows had pulled hay and gold out and most of it was recovered from the mud.[17]

By 1900, Thomas Lancelot Jones was at Horner's Mill. He was a member of that well known Tedstone family of Jones who had been at Lee Lay for several generations and was the youngest son of Richard Jones, Mr. Evans's gamekeeper, himself succeeding as gamekeeper after his father's retirement. Tom Jones married Vinnie Grubb of Woodend. When they were to be married at Tedstone Delamere church,

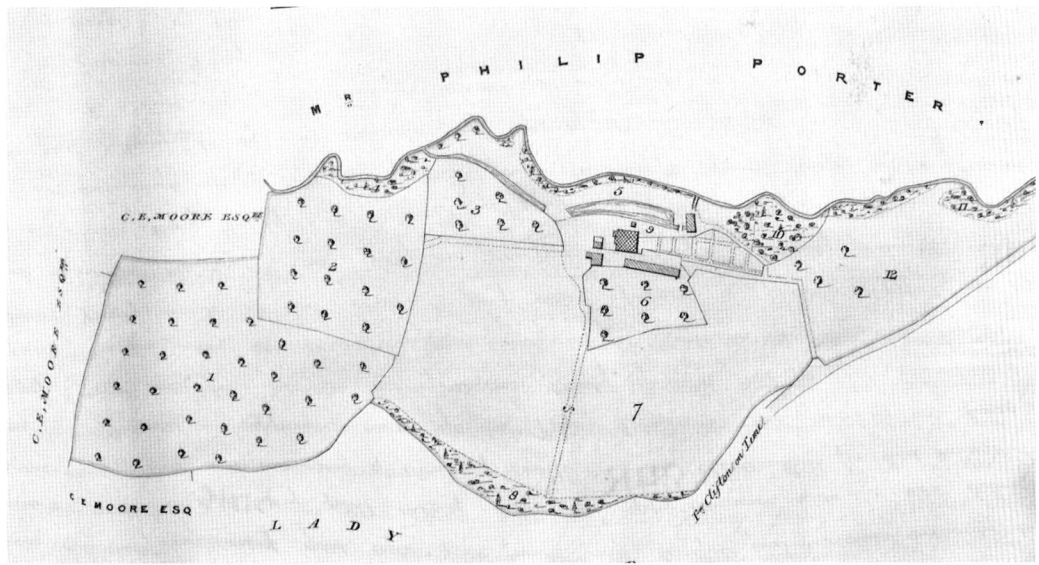

Horner's Mill in 1855. The mill & race are marked. *Whitbourne Estate*

Tom had had rather a good stag night and was still considerably the worse for wear the next day and failed to turn up to church on time. The jilted bride amazingly still married him a week later and indeed she has been described as a lovely lady who kept the family together. Tom was an excellent gamekeeper; his son Harvey, as a small boy, used to go out with the guns and help carry the game. One day there was great excitement because a quail was shot, the first time this had happened; later it was discovered to be missing from the game carrier, being a small bird it had slipped out; Captain Evans told Harvey: 'you retrace your tracks and don't come home until you have found it,' he retraced his tracks and luckily he did find it so all was well.[18] Robin Evans has happy memories of shooting lunches in the 1930s when Tom Jones, by then retired, received them at Horner's Mill; his wife, Vinny, used to produce a superb meal of steak and kidney pie and apple tart.

Buildings at Horner's Mill. *Rosemary Keep*

The Jones family at Horner's Mill. From left: Thomas Lancelot, Vinnie, Harvey, Tom & Vinnie's sister Ethel. Seated: Winnie with Beryl. *Evelyn Whistance*

> Their son, Robert Lancelot or 'Bob' Jones was our gamekeeper then; he lived at Birchy Leasowe and used to educate my brothers and myself in natural history and country lore. When out partridge shooting at the Thrift or New House farms on a hot September day, Bob and the beaters would drop in at a farm for a drink of cider, and when they appeared after what seemed an interminable wait, my father would say: I know where you've been, but for Heaven's sake, don't do it again.[19]

Bob was the third generation of gamekeepers in the family and was said to be quite a character; gamekeeping was in his blood and he was very good at his trade. He lived to be 93. There are more stories about Thomas Lancelot's son, Harvey, who as a lad, used to go to Whitbourne Hall to clean the glass which formed the flat roof over the extremely high hall; apparently someone was needed who was small and light! He was then rewarded by a visit to the kitchen to be fed on cakes. A mill was a good place to play and the boys used to carry a tin bath to the sluice gate which they would open, then be shot off down the race in the bath. In later years, Tom Jones was succeeded at Horner's Mill by Harvey, who together with his wife, had previously moved to Ladywood Cottage nearby so that they could look after his father who was getting frail, moving to the mill on Tom's death in about 1933. The leat was drained as it was considered dangerous for children and later filled in and proved an extremely fertile vegetable plot. They kept cattle and sheep. Mrs. Jones used to go into Worcester each week on the train from Knightwick with baskets full of eggs, rabbits, flowers and other produce to sell. The cherry crop was particularly good at the mill; pickers from Whitbourne were employed and the fruit was sent by rail to Liverpool and Manchester. As recorded on page 195, their daughter, Beryl, married George Yates and later went on to farm at Woodend. She has memories of the hazards associated with the steep hill on the road from Horner's Mill gate: when hauling muck to some ground further up the road, the horses used to slip all over the road; coming back empty was almost as bad and judicious use of the slipper was essential. They would take their horses to Mr. Callow at Whitbourne to be shod. The Jones children used to walk to Whitbourne School, their nearest, now that Woodend School had closed (see page 239). Mr. Jones acquired a car after World War II. He bought Horner's Mill from the Estate in the early 1960s. As recorded, another daughter, Sheila, married Bill Richards who went on to farm the Thrift. Harvey left Horner's Mill to Bill and Sheila's son, another Harvey, who later sold it to Mr. and Mrs. Leek but he retained most of the land. The Leeks carry out a pallet making business here.

6. Tidbatch (alias Shop Farm)

In 1851 the younger Richard Powell had succeeded his father as blacksmith and was living here with his wife Elizabeth and three small daughters. He was assisted in the smithy by 19-year-old Edward Tomkins. Richard must have been a go-ahead man who knew that with the improvements to the roads that took place in the 19th century, his business would do better if it was situated on the western side of the parish on a decent road and by 1861, he had moved. He was succeeded at Tidbatch by another blacksmith, bachelor James Hodges, helped by James Higgins, a journeyman blacksmith. By 1871 James Hodges must have realized that there was not room for two smithies in Tedstone Delamere and was then working as carpenter with two assistants, William Kitchen and James Stephens, and a farm servant, 15-year-old Thomas Mason, all living on the premises. He may well have worked for the Whitbourne Estate, carrying out repairs to cottages, farmhouses and farm-buildings. There must

Cider mill at Tidbatch.

still have been some work for a blacksmith for in 1881, Hodges was employing George Pitt as a smith. By 1901, a new tenant had been found for Tidbatch: Samuel Young was carpenter and joiner, whose son, Richard, carried out the farming. Richard was still here as the tenant in 1929 but by 1934, Ernie Griffiths, a member of the well known Griffiths family from Winley, was farming at Tidbatch. His wife sadly died in childbirth and later his sister Agnes went to live with him. The Whitbourne Estate advertised the property for sale in 1977. It included 35 acres and Mr. Antoni Czerniawski was the purchaser. Tidbatch has been empty for some years and became derelict. After some difficulty over planning permission, the property has recently been demolished and an architect's dream house is planned here.

7. Lee Lay

In 1841, Thomas Jones was farming this nine-acre smallholding with a fantastic view over the valley towards Tedstone Court and the church. He had taken over the tenancy from his father-in-law, Thomas Corbett. (Now, of course, the view has substantially changed, for there are, apparently, far more trees than there used to be.[20]) After her husband's death, his wife Amelia carried on at Lee Lay assisted in 1861 by 'one labourer and three more sometimes'. Her 15-year-old grandson, Ben Grubb, was the 'one labourer'. We know that Amelia had herself taken Ben to be baptised in 1854 and it is clear that she had brought him up. She would have needed extra help at such times as haymaking and fruit picking. By 1867, her 40-year-old son, Richard, and his wife Ann were farming at Lee Lay where they brought up a large family. Richard Jones became gamekeeper to Mr. Evans.

Lee Lay. The cottage from the north-east. *B&DLHC*

The following is a blacksmith's account incurred by Richard Jones: his blacksmith was Richard Powell, who we have just read, had moved his business from Tidbatch to the new forge near Upper Grounds in the west of the parish.

Lee Lay. Possible staddle stones under the granary. *B&DLHC*

Lee Lay. Roof structure at north end of barn.   *B&DLHC*

Mr. Jones,
Lee Lay

		£	s	d
Oct 16th	2 shoes 2 moves landside & fether		04	04
Nov 6	4 shoes		02	04
19	A piece and fether to share		02	00
25	A share point		00	07
28	A flat & plate to a hame peas a arm		01	06
29	1 shoe 3 moves		01	02
Dec 3	Nails ... 3 pieces to strakes rep strakes and putt on one wheel		04	10½
	New strake & nails ... & putt on		12	07½
	2 stop hooks 4 staples		00	07
15	4 shoes		02	04
20	4 shoes		02	04
	Paid	£3	18	06

Compared with the shoeing, the repairs to implements seem very reasonable for they were time consuming.[21] Today, four new shoes would cost £60. Richard was succeeded as gamekeeper by his son, Thomas Lancelot, who went to live at Horner's Mill. After their parents' death, Richard's daughters, Clara and Dora, who didn't marry, continued to live at Lee Lay. Clara worked as cook at Whitbourne Hall. Finally Mr. Evans had other plans for Lee Lay and he found them a home at the Sconce, Badley Wood Common.

For some reason, Lee Lay became known as Primrose Farm for a few years and is listed as such in Kelly's Directories 1926 – 41 when firstly Charles Powell and then Robert James farmed here. Charles Powell had moved from the Gospel Oak, Bringsty c1919.[22] The Powells kept a few cattle and sheep; they milked for the family and for calf rearing. Damson and cherry picking was a very busy time and they used to get pickers from Bromyard. They had a few apples for sale but the apple trees were past their best. The fruit used to be taken to Knightwick Station with horse and four wheeled dray. Apparently the road from Lee Lay to Woodhall used to be absolutely dreadful, a muddy track that was almost impassable in winter. Roly Powell, Charles's son, told of the bad hill by Ladywood and the Horner's Mill gate as being rutted and muddy. Roly earned his first money at Woodhall, cutting string for the threshing and remembered it as a dreadful dirty job that cut his fingers. When he was about 15, he was making the cider and drinking it. They made many gallons of cider. Roly couldn't understand why farmers today no longer make it. There was 'wonderful friendship created by cider'; with no pub and not seeing anybody for days, drinking cider with the Grubbs and other neighbours was their entire social life. He was very friendly with the Masons from Pixhill and he used to ride their pony and go hunting. This was the start of a lifelong interest in fox hunting. The Powell family used to walk down through the muddy valley to church carrying the little ones, not very often but there were the christenings, and as there were eight children at Lee Lay, these happened fairly frequently. Roly didn't know how his parents managed to get them all there through the muddy woods looking clean. In 1930, the Powells moved to Finchers Farm at Whitbourne, a better farm with a much better road. After leaving the army at the end of World War II, Roly worked as woodman on the Whitbourne Estate and came to be regarded as a key person there, for many years as senior to several assistant woodmen. The Powells were succeeded at Lee Lay by the James family.

8. Stone House A
In 1841, Stone House, a smallholding of seven acres, belonged to John Winwood of Whitbourne. George Wilson, followed by Thomas Wilson, are listed in the 1861, 71 and 81 censuses as farming at Stone House but it then became uninhabited. It is marked on the 1904 OS map and local people can remember a building here referring to it by the name of 'Lousehole' but it has now vanished.

Nineteenth - and twentieth - century farming
There have been enormous changes during this period of history, both to farming itself and in the occupations of the inhabitants. Harking back to medieval times, the 13th century saw a large population expansion; it had necessitated ploughing up every available bit of land in order to grow more corn to feed the hungry people (see Chapter II). After the Black Death, the same large quantities of food were no longer required nor were there enough surviving men available to grow it. The land had to be put back to less labour-intensive grassland production, probably with considerable difficulty and much must have just returned to scrub. This same phenomenon of planting more corn in times of need, followed by putting the land back to grass, was to keep repeating itself to a greater or less extent through the ages.[23] The building, in the early-18th century of 12 cottages on the common's wastes at Whitehall and near Tidbatch, demonstrates a growth in the numbers of inhabitants at that time. By the

mid-18th century, the national population was rapidly expanding, and again more corn was needed, contributing to a movement to amalgamate holdings to create larger units and thus greater prosperity for landowners. In the 1820s, there was pressure to repeal the corn laws which had protected farmers from foreign competition. These laws were finally repealed in 1846 but farmers' fears that they would be ruined by low prices did not happen immediately.

In 1841, the tithe apportionment recorded that there were 759 acres of arable land, 653 acres of meadow or pasture land and 146 acres of woodland in the parish. With some minor ups and downs, the period of prosperous farming reached its peak in the 1860s.

In 1870, the crop returns provide the following figures for Tedstone Delamere: 394 acres of corn (wheat, barley, oat, peas and beans) and 867 acres of permanent grassland.[24] There were also 39 acres of temporary leys and 25 acres of vetches and tares, 56 acres of turnips and swedes and six acres of potatoes. The livestock return was made on 25th June when there were 136 head of cattle including 64 in milk, 694 head of sheep, 102 pigs and 67 horses. Fruit was not recorded.

By 1879, recession had struck; there was a huge fall in grain prices and wet harvest followed wet harvest. To start with, people took little action, perhaps hoping that this period would be short-lived. Cheap food including corn was being imported, labourers left the land to find employment elsewhere and again, just as in the 14th century, farmers eventually realised that the only solution was to put land back to grass; this was not such an easy thing without today's improved seed. As expected, the 1910 returns gave a larger permanent grassland acreage of 1074 acres; there were 37 acres of temporary leys. Compared with the 1870 returns, the corn acreage was down to 209 acres. Root crops consisted of 8 acres of potatoes, 29 acres of turnips and swedes, and 11 acres of mangolds. This time, fruit was recorded: somebody was growing 8 acres of currants and gooseberries; the orchards included 92 acres of apples, six acres of pears, 15 acres of cherries and 15 acres of plums; it was also recorded that 130 acres of orchards were also accounted for under permanent grass. We are not told whether the apples were for cider. Many more cattle

> JUARY 18, 1929.
>
> HUNTING.
>
> CLIFTON HOUNDS IN A RUN OF THREE HOURS.
>
> In spite of the wintry conditions the Clifton pack provided an excellent hunt from the Four Chimneys fixture. Captain Bellville had a fox in Tedstone Dingle. Hounds entered that shelter from below Tedstone Court, and their pilot was holloaed away on the opposite bank. He made his way to the school, then took a turn over the grass to Lousehole and run on to Bishops Coppice. Hungry Dean was next invaded, and with a left-hand turn the quarry ran on to the Green Woods. Oxhall Dingle was threaded, and pursuit continued in the direction of Clifton Village. When skirting Mount Pleasant hounds were in close company with their leader, who ran below the village to dip into the Steps Dingle. Curving to the right the fox crossed the Tenbury Road at Salford Drive and continued his ramble to James Wood. He then slipped over the Motor Road at Shelsley Walsh and followed the chain of woodlands to Weymans Wood. Hounds carried the line of their sinking leader over the Stanford Road into the Glebe Spinney beside the Teme, where the pack transferred their attention to a fresh pilot.
> Hounds raced away down the Teme Valley to the Slashes. The trail now intersected the Worcester-Clifton Road, and the chase proceeded over the Green Woods to Hungry Dean. With a right-handed detour the fox rose Tedney Bank, which he left on its far side, and, holding Oxhall Dingle on his right, slipped over the Knightwick Road and plodded on in the direction of the Hope Farm. Hounds were now led by a brace of foxes. Circling round, they ran to the Thrift and regained Bishops Coppice. Oxhall Dingle was revisited, as were the Green Woods, and the Tedney House figured in the picture. Continuing over Mr. Walker's hopyards and holding Tedney Ashbed on his right, their quarry travelled on to the Scar, which held another confederate. Hounds did not waver, but clung to their hunted leader to Rooke Hill, which he left to swim the Teme and continue his tour in Worcestershire territory. The Master (Mr. Gerald Joynson) blew the pack off at this juncture after running continually for over three hours.

Hunt scrap book compiled by Mrs Ethel Bellville is in the care of Francis Lowden

were kept than in 1870: 358 including 100 in milk. Numbers of sheep had also risen to 859 and there were 80 pigs, a fall from 102 in 1870. The number of horses kept for agricultural purposes, breeding and young stock were about the same, as expected. The recession continued with just a short break in World War 1; for the first two years of the war, there was said to be not much change but by 1916, there was again a call for more corn. Six young Tedstone men lost their lives in this sad conflict, a lot for a small parish. People thought that after the war, farming would never be allowed to go back to how it was, but they were wrong; as soon as the war was over, agriculture was in a serious slump and again, land was being put back to grass. The value of land had plummeted, and the recession continued right up to the outbreak of World War 2 when a much more prolonged period of farming prosperity came into being.

Hops

We have said nothing so far about hops in this chapter. Documentary evidence from title deeds and inventories have shown that the growing of hops was widespread in Tedstone Delamere during the 17th and 18th centuries and even included those grown by the rector on his glebe land. In 1840/41, hops were grown at all the farms and smallholdings except the Gate House, then just a few acres; Tidbatch; and Stone House A, although in 1810, hop land was included in an inventory of this last small 5 acre property, (see page 134). The district excise lists show a marked decline in hop growing between 1807 and 1861. Some neighbouring parishes are included in the following list to enable a comparison to be made:

Statute acres of hops grown in each parish[25]

	1807	1811	1821	1831	1841	1851	1861
Tedstone Delamere	161	143	109	72	75	37	39
Thornbury	131	138	132	114	127	52	42
Upper Sapey	90	120	129	138	57	35	66
Whitbourne	400	403	316	253	166		
Bromyard	660	671	632	840	455	189	156

It is likely that the large figures for Bromyard include those of its townships of Norton, Linton and Winslow. The 1851 & 61 figures for Whitbourne are missing

The crop returns used on the previous page provide figures for later years: 44 acres of hops in 1866 in Tedstone Delamere, 54 acres in 1870, 39 acres in 1880, 27 acres in 1890, only 6 acres in 1900 and by 1910, no hops were grown in the parish.

Cider making in the parish has been widespread throughout the documented history and has been part of the local culture. Almost every 17th- and 18th-century inventory included hogsheads and barrels; unused cider mills and presses are still in existence at most properties, often now a feature in the garden.

Tedstone Court hop kilns.

Hop pocketing hole in the cider house at Tipton.
B&DLHC

Roly Powell at the Acreage, Whitbourne.

CHAPTER XI

The Cottages

Of particular interest to Tedstone Delamere people are the remains of a number of ruined cottages, now less apparent than they were fifty or so years ago. A short history written for the Women's Institute in the 1950s records:

> The most obvious [changes] being the desertion of various cottages in the dingles below Tedstone Court which 25 to 30 years ago were lived in. It seems that when horse and cart were the usual means of transport, these rather (now) inaccessible habitations were lived in – usually by keepers and employees at the Court, now they stand empty with roofs blown in and crumbling walls, a mute testimony to those who lived there & enjoyed the wild beauty of woodland and brook and who planted the snowdrops that still bloom in profusion for the delight of any who find their way to these solitary spots.[1]

These cottages in the dingles were not built as keepers' cottages. They were built on the common's wastes at a time when there was less woodland and the land was grazed thus keeping more of the scrub at bay; it would have looked very different then from how it is now. Some of these cottages may have been 'built in a night':

'Built in a night'?
In 1588, for the protection of both the poor and the parish, an act of parliament governed that no cottage was to be built without at least four acres of land which either had to adjoin the cottage or lie in the common open fields of the manor. This act would have been difficult to monitor and was rarely enforced[2] but it is noted that on the rare occasions when cottage deeds date back into the 18th century, they often had a few acres but by the mid 19th century, most of this land had been sold, leaving them with just a small garden. We know that in Tedstone Delamere some cottages were built on the 'commons waste' by squatters. Two field names on the tithe map of 1841 refer to former common land, one being Waste Common and the other was further down the brook, namely Whitehall Common, and there had been others (see Chapter III). It seems probable that this 'commons waste' was at one time more extensive, it mostly being steep land that would only have been used for cultivation when pressure of population warranted it. Many centuries before, in 1496, Humfrey Dore was presented at the manorial court for enclosing common land at the head of 'Vynchurch' (see page 53). It is said to be a fundamental principle of English law that a person who squats on an area of land can eventually achieve a title to that land, the right of an owner to recover possession being limited in time and the possession of that land provides the possessor with title to the same. It may well be that some of these cottages originated from the custom of 'built in a night'. The custom was known in Wales as '*Ty un nos*'; if a family with some helpers could erect a cottage overnight and have a fire lit and smoke issuing from the chimney by sunrise,

then they were entitled to the land on which it stood. They could then at leisure spend time making good the hastily erected building. It is also said that the physical boundaries of the land claimed were based on the distance that the cottager from his doorway could throw an axe in all directions![3] In 1659 there was the following entry in a court roll of Robert Mason:

> We lastly present all those cottagers and others who have made any inclosiers upon the lords waste or commone and paine them three shillings and 4d apiece.[4]

And again in 1713 the lord was still being troubled, as the following were presented at the manorial court:

> Bridgett Collins widow, John Longe, Hannah Longe spinster, William Gabb, Richard Eyton, Thomas Bishopp, Edward Rowley, Francis Howells, Henry Saunders, Susanna Hill widow, George David, Wm. Vaughan …
> For severally and respectively erecting and …[illeg.] cottages and for enclosing commons within the manor. Each laid under pain of 3s. 4d. that they open the enclosed ground within 3 days of notice given.[5]

Note that these 12 people were not asked to take down their cottages but only to open up the ground, which they probably did for a while until people had forgotten about it and then enclosed a garden at a later date. Some of these people appear over twenty years later in another list, dated 1736, of 12 cottagers living upon the waste and it seems almost certain that these would have been the same cottages, see Chapter IV, page 79. Some people appear in both lists, namely John Long, Edward Rowley, Richard Eaton and Susannah Hill; and Henry Saunders (above) must surely be the Henry Sanders in the later list. Nowadays, this waste land along the brook is woodland but at the time the cottages were built, it was grazed at certain times of year by the tenants' livestock. These cottages all seem to have still been occupied in 1841 and this chapter will relate what befell them as the century moved on.

Other cottages had formerly been small farmhouses before the land had been removed by the landowner to enlarge a neighbouring farm. Stone House B is an example of such a property; once a farmhouse, its land was used by Robert Moore, the landowner, to enlarge the Thrift and possibly New House Farm. Such dwellings then became labourers' cottages and, as is the case with Stone House, were sometimes divided for this purpose. Cottagers with a few acres of land and perhaps one or two strips in the open fields and some seasonal work on the farms would have had a living. With this land removed in the landlord's gradual reorganization, the labourers' lot must have been harder, particularly at periods of low wages.

The problem of the poor
The late 18th and early 19th centuries were a time when, nationally, the increasing numbers of the poor were becoming a very serious burden to a parish that, at that time, was responsible for their care. The better off would quite often leave a sum of money or bushels of corn for the poor in their wills, often to be distributed at the funeral or by the priest or churchwarden at church the following Sunday. References

to three charities have been found amongst the Tedstone Delamere records. The first is from the early 17th century and we only have the barest information:

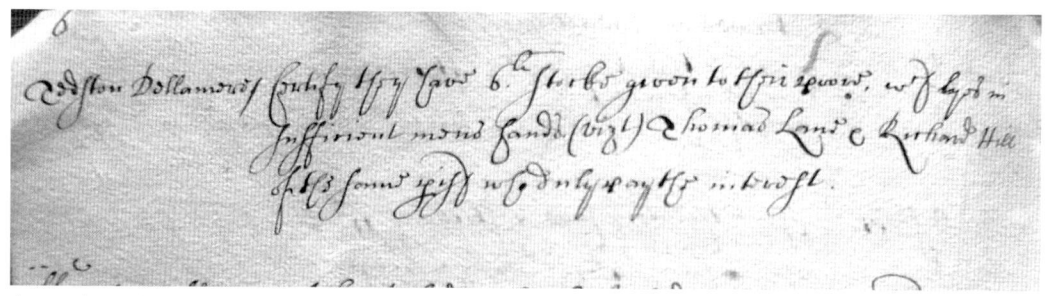

An early 17th century charity. *HRO*

| Tedstone Delamere | Certify they have £6 stock given to the poor which lies in sufficient mens lands (vizt) Thomas Lane & Richard Hill of the same parish … only pay the interest.[6] |

Thomas Lane was from Tipton and Richard Hill was from the Thrift and perhaps the field 'Poor Piece' marked on the tithe map (see Map 4, page 46) is the field that lay in Richard Hill's lands. The second charity was started as the result of a bequest by Robert Mason, late of Tedstone Court, who died in 1736. He left £10 for the benefit of poor widows deposited with John Huck of Lower Poswick, Whitbourne, the then owner of Pixhill; Robert Moore purchased Pixhill in 1791 and notes relating to this charity are to be found with the Pixhill deeds:

Robert Mason's charity for poor widows.[7] *HRO*

The third charity may be the same one as the above but put on a proper footing; at the beginning of the 20th century, trustees appointed by the parish were meeting each year to administer a charity for the benefit of poor widows and submit an account. In 1909, the trustees were: the Rector, Mr. Williams; Stanley Ward of Tipton and John James of the Thrift; they had £27 in the bank.[8]

A Table of DIETARY for the BROMYARD UNION.

Original diet 1837

		Breakfast		Dinner					Supper	
		Bread	Gruel	Bacon	Potatoes and other Vegetables	Soup	Bread	Cheese	Bread	Cheese
		oz.	pints	oz.	lb.	pints	oz.	oz.	oz.	oz.
SUNDAY	Men	8	1½			1½	6		6	1½
	Women	6	1½			1½	5		5	1½
MONDAY	Men	8	1½				7	2	6	1½
	Women	6	1½				6	1½	5	1½
TUESDAY	Men	8	1½	4	1				6	1½
	Women	6	1½	3	1				5	1½
WEDNESDAY	Men	8	1½				7	2	6	1½
	Women	6	1½				6	1½	5	1½
THURSDAY	Men	8	1½			1½	6		6	1½
	Women	6	1½			1½	5		5	1½
FRIDAY	Men	8	1½				7	2	6	1½
	Women	6	1½				6	1½	5	1½
SATURDAY	Men	8	1½	4	1				6	1½
	Women	6	1½	3	1				5	1½

OLD PEOPLE, of 60 Years of age and upwards, may be allowed 1 oz. of Tea, 5 oz. of Butter, and 7 oz. of Sugar per Week, in lieu of Gruel for Breakfast, if deemed expedient to make this change.

CHILDREN, under 9 Years of age, to be dieted at discretion, above 9 to be allowed the same quantities as Women.

SICK, to be dieted as directed by the Medical Officer.

Francis Went, Printer, Leominster and Kin

Workhouse diet 1837.
Saltmarshe Estate papers in the possession of Allan Wyatt

During the 18th and early 19th centuries, the poor rates were becoming a real problem for parishioners; records in Avenbury show that between 1730 and 1806 the disbursements to the poor had increased eightfold and it is likely that what happened in Tedstone Delamere would have been very similar.[9] A Bredenbury rate book dated 1837-41 shows that even lowly cottagers were expected to pay rates to alleviate the parish poor at that time as well as the better off parishioners.[10] The only surviving list of Tedstone Delamere ratepayers, (Appendix E) albeit at the earlier date of 1739, shows that the occupants of smallholdings were rated as well as the farmers.[11] Because of the burden of the poor rates on parishioners, it was necessary for the destitute to prove their 'settlement' in a parish before claiming relief, because quite understandably a parish would not want to take on the responsibility of another parish's poor. Ways of gaining settlement included paying the parish rate, residing in the parish for a year, being bound apprentice to a parishioner or serving as a parish officer. If settlement could not be proven, the parish overseer often spent quite large sums of money travelling to the magistrate and other parishes to try to contest it. Found amongst the Worcestershire Quarter Sessions Rolls are two removal orders, both dated 1829.[12] The first one was to remove George Rowley from Droitwich to Tedstone Delamere and the second was to move James Griffiths and his wife Letitia with four children from Clifton to Tedstone Delamere, the overseers of both Droitwich and Clifton having been determined to hustle these Tedstone people back to whence they came as soon as possible.

The Bromyard Union

Crisis point was finally reached in the early 19th century and culminated in 1836 when the old parochial system was wound up and care of the poor removed from the parish to the hated workhouse. Looking at the Bromyard Union quarterly abstracts which give the number of paupers and expenditure for the years 1837 - 45, the Tedstone Delamere paupers receiving in-door relief (*ie* in the Workhouse) varied between one and eight but averaged 4.3 The numbers receiving out-door relief (*ie* at home) varied between seven and 20 but averaged 13.8. Both these figures included children. The total quarterly expenditure for Tedstone Delamere during these years ranged between £27 and £40 and was charged to the parish to be paid by the ratepayers. This consisted of the out-door relief and a proportion of the in-door maintenance, this being part of the 'establishment charges' which apparently included the cost of the workhouse surgeon. Alterations and repairs to the workhouse building were also charged to the parish to be paid for by the ratepayers. In 1837, the parish was charged 14s. for coffins but thereafter these seem to have been included in the totals and not listed separately. In 1845, the weekly cost per head of indoor relief at the workhouse was given:

Paupers	s.	d.
Food	2	0½
Clothing	0	3½
Total	2	4

A list of pauper children in the Union 'fit for service' included two children from Tedstone Delamere: Mary Green aged 11 and James Passey aged 13. The 1851 census shows the Green and Passey pauper families living in adjoining dwellings at Riley Cottages. It seems therefore possible that Riley Cottages were built as parish houses for the poor. Mary Passey, married and aged 49, was head of household with three children, and clearly had no husband supporting her. Joseph Green, aged 52, an agricultural labourer who had moved from Key Head/Middle Paradise with wife and five children, might perhaps have been unable to work because of sickness or some other reason.[13]

For ease of analysis, the cottages have been divided, as are the farms, into those on either side of the Sapey Brook. There are maps (Maps 10 and 11) and also census tabulations (Tables 8 and 9) to illustrate both the position and also the 19th-century history of each cottage. The cottages are numbered with the prefix CW for the western cottages and EC for those on the east side.

COTTAGES TO THE WEST OF THE SAPEY BROOK[14]

CW1 a & b. Ireland Cottages. In the 16th century a family called 'Irelond' lived in Tedstone Delamere and it is probably their name that has been given to this pair of semi-detached cottages. Some entries appear in the manorial court records about these people, see Chapter III, page 55. Ireland Cottages appear to have been built in the early 19th century and in 1841 these two dwellings were farm cottages for Tipton. Thomas Benbow and his wife, Susan, brought up a family of six children here from 1861 to 1901 inclusive; as far as is known, there was no relationship to the Benbows who were later to buy Tipton. The occupants of the adjoining cottage changed frequently. These cottages are now one attractive house.

CW2. Holland's Cottage. This cottage was under the same ownership as the Gatehouse in 1840/41. It is not mentioned thereafter.

CW3. Forge Cottage. There is confusion as to the dates of building Upper Grounds farmhouse and Upper Grounds Cottage. Upper Grounds Cottage in the 1851 census was lived in by John Gray, farmer, and it may have been either of the above houses. In 1861, Richard Powell, blacksmith, aged 45, lived in Upper Grounds Cottage and as the farm house was also listed at this date, the cottage must be what has now become known as Forge Cottage. Richard Powell, his wife Elizabeth and teenage daughters, Jane and Mary Ann, and nine-year-old son Richard had moved from Tidbatch. Presumably the move was made on business grounds; being close to good roads was of paramount importance. His father, another Richard, had been blacksmith at Tidbatch before him. As with farmers, blacksmiths' businesses tended to pass from father to son, the boys grew up with them, helping in the forges from an early age. Richard Powell was known to be quite a character; he apparently 'wore his hair in the style which is acquired by clipping it round a basin fitted on the head'. He did not 'hold with' doctors, and only rarely patronised one who lived in Tenbury, walking there to consult him.'[15] He was also the census enumerator and was parish clerk for most of his adult life. By 1891, his son, Richard, had succeeded him, both as blacksmith and as parish clerk. One of their account books has survived and tells us much about their business: the accounts date from about 1884 when they had about 21 farming customers.[16] Roughly half the entries in the book were for shoeing and half were for repairs to tools, implements, carts, traps, harness and miscellaneous oddments such as repairs to cooking pots, dairy utensils, lamps and metal tips for clogs. Mr. Lea, the rector, was billed for repairs to a coffee pot and strainer, a watering can and also '4 hooks for tennis'. James Wight of Tedstone Court provided a great deal of work: there was the shoeing of his several horses whose names were Darby, Lively, Boxer, Jack, Lion, Short and Linley; together with repairs to carriages, these feature in his accounts along with such things as repairs to a lawn mower, repairs to a wagon, a pike and 'screwed eyes for the flood gates'. With one exception, all the work was carried out at the forge. The exception was visiting the Rectory to ring the rector's pigs! Prices of course are all relative: four new shoes cost 2s. 4d. or 7d. per shoe, a move or remove cost 3d. per shoe (that's when the shoe is taken off, the foot trimmed and the same shoe put back on). At the time of writing, a set of four new shoes would cost £60 and four removes £40. In 1908, the Bellvilles came to live at the Court and kept many horses which must have been excellent for business. Richard Powell the

Ireland Cottage was formerly two semi-detached cottages. The name is probably derived from a family called Irelond who lived in the parish in the 1500s.

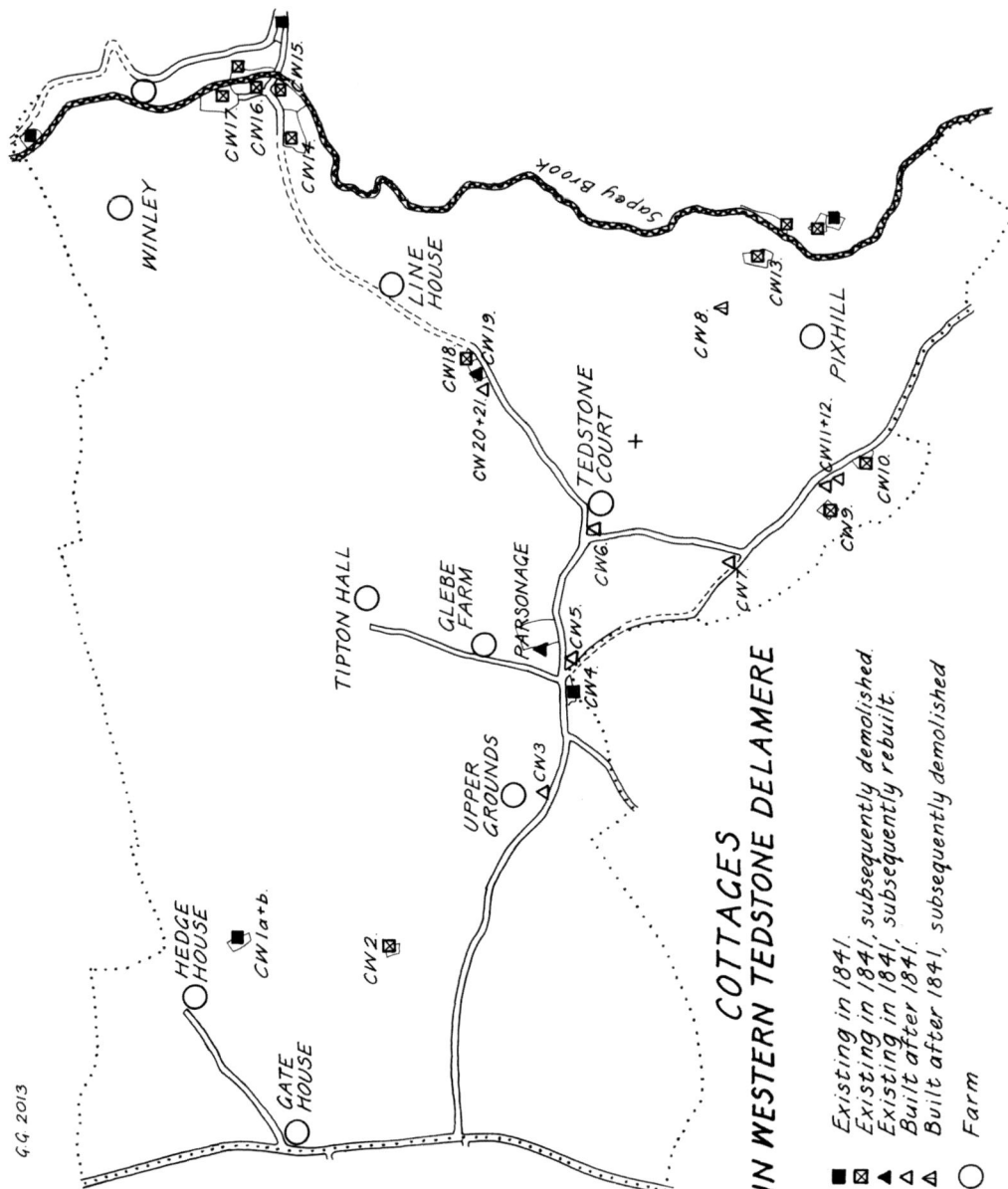

Map 10.

THE COTTAGES

TABLE 8. Occupants of Cottages in Western Tedstone Delamere 1841 - 1901

	Cottage	1841	1851	1861	1871	1881	1891	1901
CW1a	Ireland	Thos Butler 2f	Jn Portman 2f	Thos Benbow 6f	Thos Benbow 7f	Thos Benbow 8f	Thos Benbow 5f	Thos Benbow 5f
CW1b	Ireland	Ed Morris 4f 5h	Willm Green 5f	Thos Phillips 3f	Edwd Jones 7f	Wilm Taylor 8f	John Clark 3f	Thos Foxton 5f
CW2	Holland's Cot	Thos Went 3f 5h						
CW3	Upper Grounds Cot or Forge Cottage			Rrd Powell 5f 7h blacksmith	Rrd Powell 3f blacksmith		Rrd Powell 7f blacksmith	Rrd Powell 9f blacksmith
CW4	Hill Cross	John Knill 5f	T Butler 2f 5h fmr of 13a	Thos Butler 2f fmr 7a / grocer	Sam Bishop 7f	Sam Bishop ? fmr 8a	Sam Bishop 3f fmr	Jas Bishop 2f fmr
CW4a	Hill Cross							Lilian Hunter 1f own means
CW5	Glebe Cottage or New Cottage			Geo Bullock 3f gardener	Geo Bullock 5f gardener	Geo Bullock 5f gardener	Geo Bullock 3f gardener	U
CW6	Back Lodge				Chas Hill 5f gardener	Chas Hill 10f gardener	Chas Hill 7f gardener	Philip Masters gardener 2f 3h
CW7	Lodge			Jas Aldridge 2f gardener	Chas Gouge 3f 6h coachman	Chas Gouge coachman 2f 4h	Chas Gouge coachman 2f 3h	Hen Molyneux coachman 3f 4h
CW8	Wooden House in field				Elizabeth Jay 1f no occ	Elizabeth Jay 1f no occ		
CW9	Upper Cut House	Ed Collins 3f 4h	Ed Collins 5f 8h					
CW10	Lower Cut House	Mary Brown 3f	U					
CW11	New / Brick Cottage			Ed Morris 4f 5h	Jas Merrick 7f 8h gardener	Jas Merrick 6f 7h gardener	Jas Merrick 3f gardener	Jas Merrick 2f gardener
CW12	New / Brick Cottage			Ed Pritchet 4f 5h	Edwd Pritchard 3f	Geo Oliver 6f	Thos Jenkins 3f 5h	Edwd Moss 4f waggoner
CW13	Whitehall or Burberry / Barlary Hill	Geo Smallman 6f 7h	Geo Smallman 3f	Saml Sears 2f		Jos Daniels 5f	Jos. Daniels 2f	U
CW14	Rockmoor Castle 183 tithe	Philip Cooke 4f mole catcher	Phil Cook 4f 7h mole catcher	Willm Budd 6f groom	Willm Smith 8f	Jos Pratt 7f	Jas Symonds 1f	
CW15	1 Keyhead / Lower Paradise	Unoccupied	Thos Phillips 4f 5h	Thos Goodman 2f	Thos Phillips 2f	Ed Symonds 4f mason's lab	B	Francis Wyath 5f
CW16	2 Keyhead / Middle Paradise	Jos Green 5f	Ann Soley 4f	Hen Trehearne 2l	Jas Pitt 5f	Willm Box 8f	Willm. Ray ? 5f	Jas Morris 3f
CW17	3 Keyhead / Paradise	Eliz. Caswell	Eliz Wood 2f	Eliz Wood 2f	Willm Palmer 6f	Edw Jones 4f	Edw Jones 2f	Edw Jones 3f
CW18	Middle Line Hse	Anne Griffiths 2f	Rrd Griffiths 3f gardener	U	Rrd Griffiths 2f 3h	Jane Griffiths dressmaker 1f 2h	James Atkins 7f gamekeeper	Willm Bowers groom 2f 3h
CW19	Upper Line Hse or Brasiers	Thos Greenwood 1f	Edwd Price 1f shoemaker	Eliz Price 2f 4h landed proprietor	Eliz Price 2f 3h school mistress	Rrd Burraston butler 2f	Rrd. Burraston butler 4f	Thos Hollings carter 4f 5h
CW20	Diamond Cot 1							Geo Griffiths waggoner 2f
CW21	Diamond Cot 2							Geo Griffiths 6f head waggoner
	Russels Cot		W Austins 3f 4h					
	No. of inhabited cots	11	11	13	15	15	15	14
	Mean household size	3.7	4	3.8	4.8	5.4	3.8	4
	Mean family size	3.2	3.2	3	4.4	5.1	3.4	3.6

NOTES. All heads of household are agricultural labourers unless otherwise mentioned. 'f' refers to the number of persons in a family, 'h' refers to the total number of persons in a household, extras are usually lodgers. U =uninhabited
1841 Upper Cut Hse & Lower Cut Hse are what were called Cullets Hse & Lower Cutted Hse in title deeds.
1851 It is assumed that the three cottages at Keyhead in 1841 , now not so named, have become 'Paradise'. Russels Cottage is an unknown
1861 It seems that 'Burbery / Barlary Hill' is the 'Whitehall' Cot formerly of John Smallman.
1871 'New Cottages' are near the site of the two 'Cut Houses' which they have replaced, these are the 'Tedstone Village' in 1861. I have assumed that 'Lodge Gate' in 1871 is 'Lodge' in 1861, now inhabited by Charles Gouge, a coachman.
1881 It is assumed that Rectory Cot is the same as New Cot. Now called Glebe Cottage

Younger's son, Arthur, followed on after his father, being the 4th generation of the family to work as a blacksmith in Tedstone Delamere. The brick built forge had a 'pent house and bellows house, two hearths and standing for four horses'. In 1908, it (forge and cottage) was let by Mr. Wight to Mr. Powell at a rent of £11 per annum.'[17] The forge, which was across the road from the cottage, had all its fixtures and fittings removed a few years ago. For many years, the cottage was the used by the Clifton-on-Teme Hunt for housing hunt servants, thanks to the generosity of the Bellville family. In the 1980s, David and Linda Parker, joint masters of the Clifton Hunt, lived at the cottage for a short time whilst the new hunt bungalow was built. Today Chris and Kathleen Harris live at Forge Cottage, having moved from Upper Grounds c1985. Chris was stockman for the Bellvilles and Kathleen is a member of the well known Griffiths family of Winley and the Line House and is current irreplaceable churchwarden.

Mr & Mrs Richard Powell & Arthur. *B&DLHC*

The Powell girls at the Forge. *B&DLHC*

CW4. Hill Cross. This seems to be the property that in 1709 was purchased by Thomas Lane of Tipton from Thomas Farley of Whitbourne, a blacksmith, and described as 'All that Messuage, Smith's shop or tenement ... at or neare a place called the Held Cross. There were three parcels of land totalling 6½ acres. 'Held' or 'Yeld' is probably derived from the Anglo-Saxon word *heild* which means 'a slope'[18] and it is of course on a cross roads. The deeds state the house itself is in Whitbourne which perhaps is an error, as although extremely close to the parish boundary, today's

Blossom time & pretty hats. The Powell girls. B&DLHC

cottage of Hill Cross is just in Tedstone Delamere.[19] In 1713, *Helde Crosse* was listed amongst chief fee farms of the manor for which a rent of 6d. was owed; Richard Jones was the tenant.[20] The present building appears to date from early in the 18th century and is situated on a slope; it is on two and a half levels. The outside door on the south side is wide, possibly for cider or beer barrels and it may be that a beer or cider-seller lived here but there is no evidence for this in the deeds. It is more likely to be an entrance to the former forge or have had some agricultural use. In 1746, Benjamin Lane sold it, together with Tipton, to his brother James. It then passed to James's son-in-law, Richard Jones of the Hope, Edvin Loach. In 1831 it was bought by John Knill for £375. In 1914, Hill Cross with five acres was purchased by Richard Powell of the Forge, from Sir Stuart Knill, Bart. (John Knill's grandson) for £310. In 1979, it was sold by William Charles Powell to Mr. and Mrs. Davis who in turn sold it, in 1990, to Mr. and Mrs. Webb.[21] The cottage has a fantastic view.

CW5. Rectory Cottage or New Cottage, now Glebe Cottage. This was the home of George Bullock and family during the census years 1861 – 91 inclusive. To read about this interesting character, who was the rectory gardener, turn to page 155. The cottage later became the farmhouse for the Glebe Farm where Mr. and Mrs. Easton brought up their family.

CW6 & 7. The Lodges. James Lane Wight built the two lodges between 1851 and 1871. In 1871, Charles Gouge, coachman lived in the larger 'Lodge Gate Cottage' with his wife and daughter, Bertha. It housed two families at this time as Amy Philips, laundress, also lived here with her 18-year-old son, James, who worked as a gardener, and her daughter, Emma, who was at school. The pretty gabled lodge with ogee-headed porch, that guarded the back drive, was lived in by Charles Hill, a gardener for a good number of years. In 1881 he had a large family of eight children.

CW8. Wooden house in field. Someone who seems to have almost become a part of folk lore was 'Betsy Jay'. She lived in a hut the far side of the brook in the late 19th century, later moving to another hut nearer to Grey's Barn (see Map 4, page 46). Mrs. Wright, the daughter of former rector, Rev. F. S. Lea, describes her as:

> That strange half-crazy woman … who used to come to the rectory every week for a bowl of fresh dripping, and other food. She lived in a small hut [writing from the rectory] on the far side of the Sapey Brook, near the footbridge on the way to Woodend School. Children coming back down the steep bank used to throw stones on the roof of the hut, and then Betsy Jay would run out, and storm and shout at them till they would be frightened and run home with alarming tales of the incident. One could tell from her vocabulary that she was not a gipsy or an ignorant peasant. The Miss Wights at the Court were her very good friends. She was quite harmless and in those days must have been young and strong, though she and her raiment always looked old and weather-worn. In the end I heard that the Bromyard Guardians felt that she needed the care and shelter of the workhouse, where presently she died, like a wild bird condemned to captivity.[22]

CW9 – 12. Upper & Lower Cut Houses and the new Brick Cottages. Upper Cut House, formerly a smallholding known as Cullets Hill, was included with Pixhill and Greys in the Wight's marriage settlement of 1809.[23] In 1851, Upper Cut House was the home of Edward Collins, farm-worker and his family of five together with two lodgers, Elizabeth Philips, 36-year-old 'errand girl' and 14-year-old John Mitchell, a farm-worker. 'Lower Cutted House' was the subject of a 1746 lease for a term of 800 years by Frances Smith, widow, of Tedstone Delamere to Samuel and Elizabeth Moore of Docklow. Their granddaughter, Mary Brown, mortgaged it in 1838 to James Wight of Tedstone Court. She lived there in 1841, a farm-worker, with two teenage daughters. The property was valued in 1847:

> … house consists of timber and plaistered walls and thatched roof, the whole slightly built and in bad repair. The timbers are weak and bad and the floors are nearly worn out. There is one chamber and room downstairs with a back room shedded up to the end. The garden is good sound land planted with fruit trees and contains 0a. 1r. 2p. £34 10s.[24]

James Wight purchased the property in 1854; the mortgage and a further mortgage had not been paid off. For it, he paid the princely sum of £3. 3. 0d. Clearly not fit for purpose, both cottages were demolished and a pair of new roomy brick cottages were built for housing the staff at the Court, on the same land (although not on the same footprint). These cottages have a wonderful view.

Brick cottages 1908.

CW13. Whitehall / Burbery / Barlary Hill. It is sometimes difficult to be certain which is which of the cottages at Whitehall but this one seems to be the cottage, garden, orchard and 5a of lands just below Mr. Wight's and near Greys Farm that Robert and Ann Moore demised to John Acton for 99 years by lease in 1768; it was then called 'Brockshall'. Their son, James Moore, was later to purchase the assignment of the lease.[25] In the 19th century, the various tenants recorded in the censuses who lived here were farm-workers, presumably for the Wights at the Court. The cottage was demolished in the latter part of the 20th century by Richard Bellville, all that now remains being a heap of rubble and timber buried in the woodland.

All that remains of cottage CW13; Tom Weale & Sue Haffenden on top of a heap of rubble.

CW14. Rockmore Castle. In 1841 this cottage with the grand name was let by Edmund Higginson of Saltmarshe Castle to Philip Cooke, a mole catcher. In 1851, Cooke and his wife, Mary, both in their fifties, had two small sons aged eight and six. There were also three agricultural labourers lodging with them. In 1861, tenant William Budd, with a wife and four small children, was a groom. It was sold by W. T. Barneby of Saltmarshe Castle to Edgar Wight in 1896 for £100.[26] By 1901, it was uninhabited. Included in the sale of the Line House to H. A. Bellville in 1910 was: 'Piece of land formerly a cottage & garden known as Rockmore Castle with 1a.1r.7p.' and that is the last we hear of it.

CW15. Keyhead / Paradise. The first of the three cottages beside the brook with the curious name of Keyhead or Quayhead was occupied throughout the census years by farm labourers. The name 'Keyhead' is probably what appears in a 1534 court roll as *Causey Hedde,* suggestive of a causeway:

> Richard Dee also ordered to build a common road without overhangings and properly scoured, at Tytbachestone leading from the lower part of Norchards Feld to le Causey Hedde ....[27]

This is yet another cottage that is now just a heap of rubble in the undergrowth; it is the subject of countless legal documents carefully retained for posterity.[28] This was 'the messuage or dwelling house called the Keyhead or Quayhead containing aprox. four acres formerly in the possession or occupation of John Hill and formerly part of a farm called the Freeth (Thrift) that was conveyed to Thomas Colley in 1719 for £26. It was eventually purchased by Slade Baker, the owner of the Line House in 1853 for £160 but then with only an acre of ground and was occupied by Thomas Phillips. It was sold with the Line House to Edgar Wight in 1891.

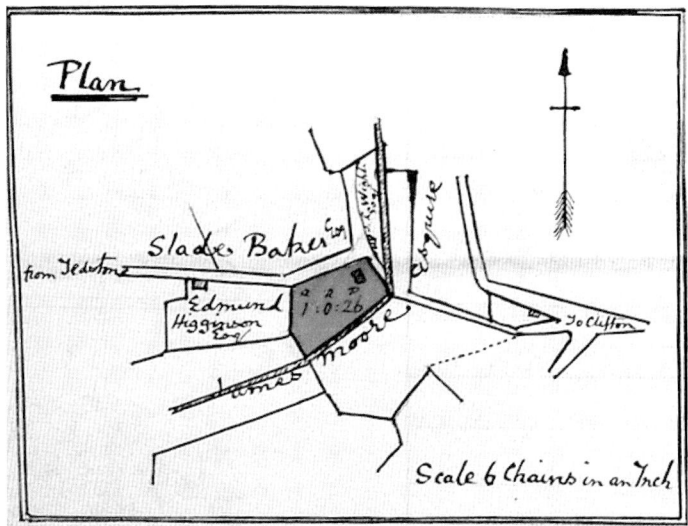

This plan, dated 1853, shows cottages by the bend in the Sapey Brook at Keyhead. On the west side are firstly, CW14, Rockmore Castle owned by Edmund Higginson; then follows , coloured on plan, cottage CW15 owned by Slade Baker with 1a:0r:26p. Just north of this is CW14 owned by J.L. Wight. (Two further cottages to the east of the brook are Lower Tidbatch & Sunnyside)   HRO, AJ49/2

CW16. Keyhead / Middle Paradise belonged to James Wight in 1841 and was let to Joseph Green. It was later included with the Line House in the sale to H. A. Bellville in 1910, then known as 'Box's cottage'. It has now gone.

CW17. Keyhead / Lower Paradise is the cottage belonging to John Holland where Elizabeth Caswell lived in 1841.

CW18. Middle Line House. In 1840/41, Richard Griffiths owned and occupied this cottage with just over an acre of land and lived with his mother, Anne. In later years, he had married Jane, a dressmaker. Richard was described as both agricultural labourer and gardener. In 1874, Richard, then a 'shopkeeper', died bequeathing this property to James Ward of Tipton, in trust, to raise money by mortgage, to discharge his (Griffiths's) debts. After the death of his widow Jane in 1886, the property was auctioned and James Lane Wight bought it for £238.[29] The stone built cottage is now only remembered as a ruin.

CW19. Upper Line House or Brasiers. This property formed part of the estate of Richard Brasier of Tedstone Delamere in 1802. In 1833, it was in the possession of Richard Griffiths who lived in Middle Line House. In 1891, Elizabeth Price who had formerly kept a small 'dame school' was living in what seems to have been a separate part of this cottage, described as 'living on her own means'. Today, 'Stone Cottage', which seems late 19th century, appears to be on the same site.

THE COTTAGES

Jubilee Cottage. Fred Clements (the Bellvilles' chauffeur) with Roy Middemacht (left) & Gustave Middemacht (centre). *B&DLHC*

CW20 & 21. Diamond Cottages 1 & 2. Presumably built at the time of the Diamond Jubilee, these cottages were described in the 1908 Tedstone Court sale particulars as 'recently erected' and each with sitting room, kitchen, pantry, washhouse and three bedrooms. In 1901, they were occupied by George Griffiths, father and son. George senior was 'head waggoner' and his son was 'waggoner'. Now known as Jubilee Cottages, they are two very nice properties with large gardens.

A letter to Stead & Simpson, Bromyard. *B&DLHC*

THE COTTAGES TO THE EAST OF THE SAPEY BROOK

EC1. Waste Cottage. This is now a delightfully situated weekend cottage, built in stone, completely secluded and with no access for cars. Erected on Waste Common, (see map 11) this cottage or one on the same site together with others along the side of the Brook, including the cottages at Whitehall [see below], could originally have been some of those built by the squatters on the commons waste as recorded on pages 210-211 but today Waste Cottage seems to have been rebuilt or much altered. It is one of the few survivors of the many cottages that were built beside the Sapey Brook. In 1841, an agricultural labourer, John Russell lived at Waste Cottage. In 1871 a carpenter lived here who may have worked at neighbouring Tidbatch. In 1914, Frank Evans of Whitbourne Hall put the cottage at Waste Common up for sale. It was then in the occupation of Mr. Craddock at £5 rent per annum.[30]

TABLE 9. Occupants of Cottages in Eastern Tedstone Delamere 1841 - 1901

	Cottage	1841	1851	1861	1871	1881	1891	1901
EC1	Waste	John Russell 1f		Thos Jones 3f	Thos Hanley 4f carpenter	Wm Hall 5f	Jn Gummery 5f	U
EC2	Lower Tidbatch	Ezekiel Portman 2f 3h						
EC3	Pitts, now Sunnyside		Jn Jay 2f	see Summer Bank below	see Summer Bank below			
EC4	Riley (1)	Thos Robinson 5f	Mary.Passey 4f no occ	Thos Passy 5f	Wm Walker 4f	Jn Gummery 3f	U	Ben Barnes 6f waggoner
EC5	Riley (2)		Jos Green 7f	Jas Walton 7f	Wm Walker 5f	Saul Roper 1f	U	Jas Price 2f
EC6	Stone Hse B (1)	Thos Middleton 3f 5h	Edwd Jones 2f	Wm Walker 5f 6h	Caleb Randall 6f 7h dairyman meth. preacher	Jas Collins 5f	Thos Grove 3f 4h	Jas Smith 2f 3h
EC7	Stone Hse B (2)				Jn Phillips 4f 5h	Thos Gwilliam 4f	U	Julia Simmons 3f school mistress
EC8	Burbage (New House f/c?)	Sam Jones 5f 6h	Edwd Jones jun. 5f	Wm Hill 2f				
EC9	Lamb Green	Wm Moss 3f		Jas Green 4f	Wm Gwilliam 6f	Jas Smith 9f	Jas Kennard 3f	
EC10	Dunley alias Woodhall f/c or Woodend f/c		Jn Caswell 4f carpenter			Jas Stephens 4f carpenter	Jas Pitt 2f 3h highway lab	Sarah Pitt 1f 2h charwoman
EC11	Ladywood	Hannah Bayliss	Thomas Evans 2f	Thos Evans 2f	Thos Evans 7f	Thos Evans 5f	Thos Evans 2f	
EC12	Primrose [Holts or Warnells]	Jn Booth 3f 7h ag lab & psh clk.	Jn Davis 3f jockey	Jas Shepherd 2f	Jos Morris 5f	Jas Daniell 4f 5h	Jas Daniels 3f	Hannah Harbour no occ 2f
EC13	Primrose (1)	G.Portman 3f 4h						
EC14	Primrose (2)	Jas Hill 4f						
EC15	Whitehall or Hams	Jn Palmer 4f 5h	Jn Palmer 2f	Jn Palmer 2f	Ben Beeks 5f 6h	Chas Berry 2f	Walter Bridges 7f	U
EC16	Whitehall	Jn Watkins 2f	Wm Hill 2f	Jas Green 3f	Jas Daniels 4f	Wm Yapp 6f	Geo Prichard 6f	U
EC17	Whitehall	Wm Caswell 3f	Edwd Morris 4f	U	U			
	Mortiboys		Jn Walker 3f 5h					
	Dones	John Jay 3f						
	Farmers cottage Dunley ?			Jas Daniel 5f	Jn Grocott 3f			
	Another cottage			Jn Walker 5f				
	Summer Bank or Pitts?			Wm Ward 5f	Jos Coomby 4f	U	U	
	No of Inhabited Cottages	13	11	12	11	10	7	6
	Mean household size	3.9	3.5	4.1	5.2	4.4	4.4	3
	Mean family size	2.9	3.5	4	4.2	4.3	4.1	2.7

Notes:
The first cottages in the list are numbered CE1 - CE17 and these are the ones whose position can be firmly identified and are plotted on the map on p...; the remaining ones cannot be positioned on the map with any certainty; f = number in family; h = total number in household, extras usually lodgers; U = uninhabited. All occupiers are agricultural labourers unless otherwise mentioned.
1861 census: It is likely that Worall & Warnalls are the same property; almost certainly Primrose
Lamp Green is the name of the 20th C cottage that is today in a ruinous state but on the tithe map in 1840, a cottage is marked at the other end of the garden on the tithe map 1840 & was a farm cottage for the Thrift
Wm Tolley, cowman has been placed in Whitehall, W. Tedstone but this could be Whitehall in E. Tedstone

THE COTTAGES

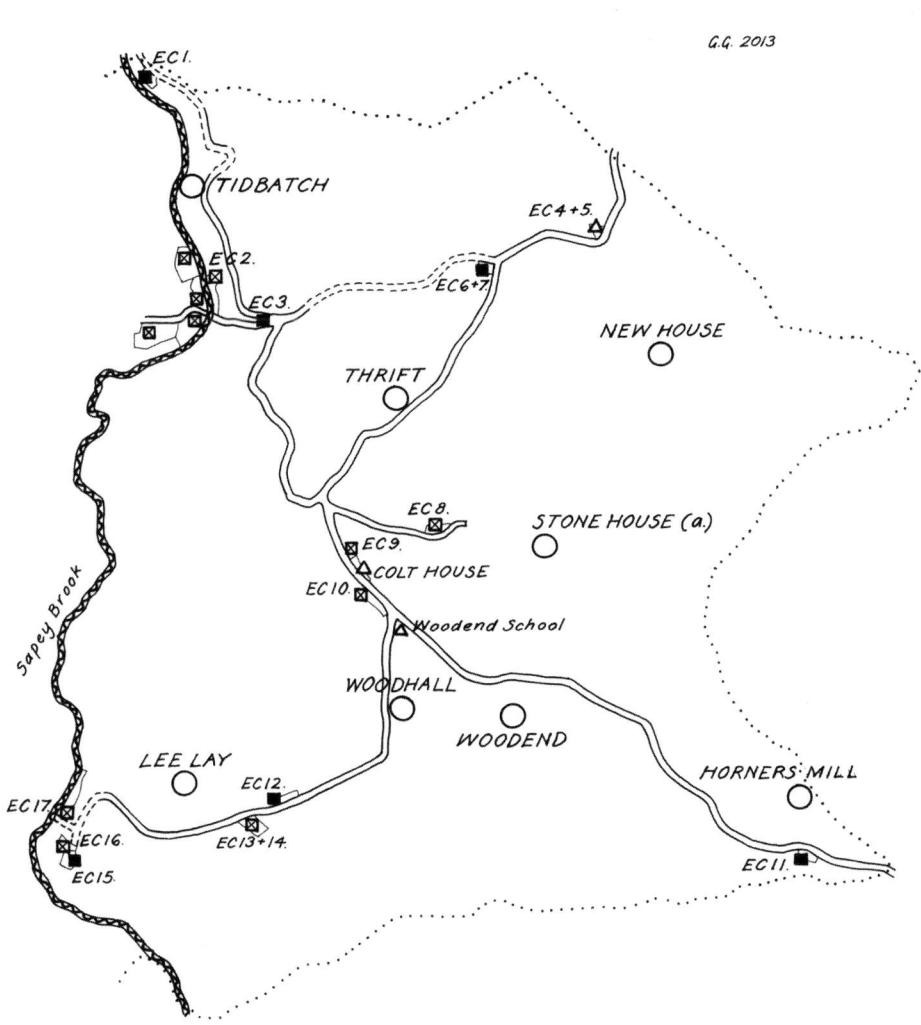

COTTAGES
IN EASTERN TEDSTONE DELAMERE

- ■ Existing in 1841.
- ⊠ Existing in 1841, subsequently demolished.
- ▲ Existing in 1841, subsequently rebuilt.
- △ Built after 1841.
- ○ Farm.

Map 11.

EC2. Lower Tidbatch is marked as being void in the 1840/41 tithe survey but in the 1841 census, Ezekiel Portman, a 60-year-old carpenter, was living here. It was let to Richard Powell, the blacksmith, who at this time was still living at Tidbatch and he may well have been Portman's employer. There is no mention of the cottage after 1841 unless it was the 'Shop Cottage' recorded in the census of 1891. It has now gone almost without trace.

EC3. Sunnyside (formerly called Pitts Cottage). Was this the property called Tennolls that in 1787 was sold by Ben Pitt, a carpenter and joiner, to Robert Moore?[31] In 1840/41 it was part of the Tidbatch (Shop House) estate. Later in the century, it seems to have been called Summer Bank. This late-17th century cottage is situated in a beautiful and isolated spot beside the Sapey Brook.

Sunnyside. The roof on the southern side has been raised in height.

EC4 & 5. Riley. In 1610, William Ingram was presented at the manorial court for enclosing part of the lord's waste at Ryley Green. William claimed he had been given permission to do this by the previous lord, Francis Wysham. Once a medium sized farm, it was assessed at 1s. 4d. poor rate in 1739, see Appendix E.[32] In 1841, it was inhabited by a farm labourer, Thomas Robinson and his family, who at this time were probably living in the old Riley farmhouse, marked on the tithe map but now gone. By 1851, it was entirely rebuilt as two semi-detached cottages. As recorded on page 214, it is possible that these cottages were built by the parish as houses for the poor. The cottages subsequently became farm cottages for New House Farm. They have recently been converted and extended to make one attractive house.

EC6 & 7. Stone House B. This stone-built three-bay small farmhouse, dating seemingly from the late-17th or early-18th century, has a cellar under the west end and a two-storied 19th century extension at the east end. The lean-two extension at the west end is probably of the same date in the 19th century and likely to have been added when the house was divided in the 1860s to provide housing for two farm-workers. This extension contains a bread oven and wash-boiler, perhaps shared between the two families.

When this former small farmhouse was converted to two labourers' cottages in the 19th century, the bread oven and wash-boiler in the small lean-to on the left was probably shared by both families.

In 1841, Stone House B was owned by Charles Edward Moore and was one of the Thrift's farm cottages and inhabited in 1841 by Thomas Middleton, a farm labourer and family. (Stone House A is shown on Map 11 and is dealt with in Chapters VI & X.) By 1871, two families were here: John Phillips, a farm-worker lived in one half with his wife and two small daughters and they also gave board to another farm-worker, William Bloomfield. Caleb Randall who was a dairyman, perhaps selling milk in Clifton or Whitbourne, lived in the other half. Caleb was also a local Methodist preacher; this part of Tedstone Delamere, at such a distance from the parish church, would have been good recruiting ground for the nonconformists. In 1901, Mrs. Julia Simmons, the schoolmistress at Woodend School, lived in part of the Stone House with her teenage daughter and son. The property is now, once again, one house, attractively modernized and enlarged.

EC8. Burbage or New House farm cottage. As early as 1495, Humfrey Dore granted to Thomas and Alice Breton a house with appurtenances called 'Borbach'.[33] In 1735, this nine-acre smallholding was the subject of a marriage settlement between William Chrees & Mary Philips.[34] In 1777, John Chrees of Winley was paying 6s. 8d. land tax for Burbage.[35] Ben Grubb of Woodhall remembered that Charles Edward Moore purchased the holding in 1833.[36] William Hill, a farm worker living here in 1861, appears to be the last person to have inhabited the cottage. It has now been demolished.

EC9. Lamb or Lamp Green. In 1648, James Stallard was ordered 'to put an adequate hedge at his meadow called *Lamps Meadowe* before the Annunciation on pain of 3s 4d'.[37] This unusual name may refer to an endowment to provide a lamp in the parish church.[38] Thomas Roper who farmed the Thrift was the tenant in 1841 and it was then a six acre smallholding which included Badham's Field and Badham's Piece. At this time, it was lived in by William Moss, a farm-worker, who probably worked at the Thrift. In 1877, there were various families who used to hold a 'chapel' service in the cottage.[39] In the 20th century it was a farm cottage for Woodhall before becoming uninhabited. Captain Evans sold it in 1962 to Bill Albright, head of the shooting syndicate that rented the shooting from the Evans's. He replaced the stone cottage with a new Colt House at the other end of the garden and Henry Powell, one of the large family of Powells from Lea Lay, lived in this new house. Henry was the gamekeeper.[40] In 1994, the property was bought by

A rabbit shoot in the 1930s.
From left: Percy Orgee, Jack Jones, Bob Jones, Henry Grubb, Henry Powell (who became gamekeeper).

Neil Farmer of Oxhall.[41] It became derelict and has recently been demolished.

There used to be a village pound for stray animals at Lamb's Green.[42]

EC10. Dunley Cottage. Two fields to the west of this cottage are shown as Upper Dunley and Lower Dunley in the tithe apportionment of 1841; Dunley used to be one of the common fields. John Caswell & family lived at the cottage in 1851, a carpenter who may have worked down the hill at Tidbatch. At other times it has been farm cottage for both Woodend and Woodhall. It has now disappeared.

EC11. Ladywood. In his will of 1573, recorded in Chapter III, page 61, John Callowhill gave to his brothers Richard and Charles: 'three score trees in *Ladie Woode* which trees I had of Mr. Wisham by covenant between him and me which trees shalbe equallie devided between my said brethren'. This seemingly 19th century, brick built cottage with seven acres of land on the edge of an area of woodland, was lived in by Thomas Evans, presumably father and son, through most of the census years. They were described at different dates as either 'farm labourer' or 'farmer of seven acres'. The late Mrs. Jones of Horner's Mill told of a legend that the unusual name was derived from the fact that long ago, a lady sought refuge here from her husband.[43]

EC12. Primrose Cottage. This is a charming late 17th century cottage with fabulous views. It has a raised roof and has been much enlarged in recent years. Primrose belonged to Francis Hill in the 1720s and was let to Ben Baugh at a yearly rent of £31. Primrose, either this property or more likely the buildings that were opposite, was assessed at 1s. 7d. for the poor rate in 1739, putting it on a par with Pixhill and Winley in the pecking order, they both being assessed at 1s. 6d., so it is likely that it was a small farm. In the 1787 sale of Woodham (a lost farm), this property was called Warnalls or Worrells and marked on the plan (see Map 6, page 121). Known as Holts Cottage in 1841, it was let to John Booth, a farm-worker who was also parish clerk at the time. The cottage is situated on the road between Woodhall and Lee Lay. But there could be confusion here because for a short time in the 20th century neighbouring Lee Lay went by the name of Primrose Farm and it is just possible that this had happened in the more distant past as well. The hill at the rear is called Primrose Hill and it may have taken its attractive name from a former inhabitant rather than the flower, although it is said that the nearby fields are a mass of primroses in the spring. However, as recorded in Chapter III, after the Act of Uniformity in 1662, hundreds of ministers either resigned or were ejected from their parishes and amongst these was the Rev. George Primrose M.A. who was removed from his living at

Primrose, a late 17th century cottage with raised roof.

Hereford. He later lived at Tedstone Delamere and was licensed here as a Presbyterian preacher in 1672. He was buried at Tedstone Delamere on September 18th 1695[44] and his will in 1691 denotes a person of some standing. Duncumb, writing in 1812, records the following memorial inscription as being inside the communion rails in the church:

> Mary, wife of George Primrose was also interred here, December 25, 1687[45]

The other names recorded in this position in the church are all of the more important inhabitants such as the rectors and lords of the manor so it is interesting that the wife of a non-conformist preacher and presumably her husband also were granted such a prestigious burial place! It is not known whether the home of George and Mary Primrose was at what is now Primrose Cottage or perhaps on the other side of the road where there was a double dwelling in 1841, also called 'Primrose' and since demolished (see below).

In 1841, John Booth lived in this then small two-bedroomed cottage, with his wife and 10 year-old son and lodging there were Thomas Pitt, a 70-year-old labourer, and Elizabeth Green with a daughter aged 20 and a son of 15. Where on earth did they all sleep?

EC13 & 14. Primrose Cottages was a double dwelling on the other side of the track that was probably the old Primrose farmhouse; in the tithe survey it was two farm cottages for Woodend. In 1841 a young farm labourer and his wife, both aged 20, with their baby son, lived in one section together with a lodger, a seven-year-old 'farm servant'! In the other half lived another farm-worker, James Hill, with his family. The cottages have now gone and are marked only by a slightly raised area of ground.

Whitehall Common. The cottages at Whitehall may have been built by squatters on the Commons Waste. There was once quite a community living at Whitehall. The manorial mill was here, now marked only by two field names *Mill Ground Meadow* and *Mill Rough* on the tithe map of 1841 (map 4). It would once have been a busy place with people bringing their corn to be ground. The WI history, written in the 1950s, tells of an elderly resident who remembered as a child, in about 1880, witnessing a dipping ceremony in the brook below Whitehall 'of presumed Baptists, some 15 to 20 in number, who were totally immersed clad in white robes'. Another WI story relates how an elderly Mrs. Daniel who lived at Whitehall was walking back from the postbox at Badley Wood having previously been poultry plucking at Pixhill, (it was Christmas Eve); it is surmised that her candle lantern went out and that she missed her footing and fell into one of the deeper pools in the Sapey Brook and was drowned.[46] It is stories like this which help one appreciate the difficulties faced by some country dwellers in those days.

A massive pollarded oak at Whitehall. *Rosemary Keep*

James Bayliss and family at Whitehall c1914. James was a gamekeeper. *Jan Davis*

EC15. Whitehall or Hams Cottage is the only cottage now surviving at Whitehall Common and is a timber-framed and stone cottage built close to the brook. This well built cottage appears to date from the late 17th century. Remote and with no road to it, it now makes a delightful holiday cottage. John Winwood owned the property in 1841 when it was occupied by John Palmer, a farm-worker. Winwood, who farmed Rosemore in Whitbourne, also owned the neighbouring smallholding of Homes or Hams which had no house in 1841 so this cottage may have been the farmhouse for the 23 acre holding, see Chapter VI page 135. Winwood also owned Stone House A, another smallholding also described in Chapter VI.

EC16. Whitehall. Now disappeared and marked only by a slight hump in the ground, this seems to have been the cottage that was conveyed by William Saunders to Thomas Knill of Surrey in 1826 for £42; there is also a memorandum that John Knill presented the cottage to his son-in-law, James Lane Wight in 1840.[47] In 1841, John Watkins, a farm-worker and his wife occupied it. It was inhabited until at least 1891.

Views of Whitehall Cottage EC15.

EC17. Whitehall. From its position on the brook, this cottage may have been on the site of the former mill and one would expect it to belong to the lord of the manor. However, if so, the cottage must have been sold for in 1841, it was owned by the Rt. Hon. Lord Ward of Witley Court and occupied by James Caswell, a farm worker. Hedge House and other lands in the parish had for many years belonged to Lord Foley who sold his Witley Court Estate to Lord Ward in 1836. At around the same time, Hedge House was bought for the Saltmarshe Estate. This small cottage seemed somehow to have been missed out of the sale transaction. By 1861, the cottage was uninhabited.

The youngest Bayliss child in a very pretty dress.
Jan Davis

A lost cottage known as **Dones Tenement** near the Thrift was included in the 1841 census. Dones is mentioned in a number of records including a list of ratepayers for a 1739 poor rate (see Appendix E) when it was assessed at 3d.

An analysis of the cottage survey
At the beginning of the 18th century, there were 12 cottages 'recently erected on the lord's waste'. A count of the cottages along the Sapey Brook near Tidbatch and at Whitehall at the later date of 1841 produces a figure of exactly 12. Other cottages had been small farms or smallholdings that had lost their land in the 18th-century reorganization of the estate by lords of the manor. Burbage is an example of a property that had nine acres in 1735; it had deteriorated into being a farm cottage for New House Farm in the 19th century and was last heard of in the 1861 census. Stone House B is another example of a property that was once a small farm, but in the early 19th century its land appears to have been used to enlarge the Thrift and New House farms; between 1861 and 1871, Stone House was divided to make two cottages; it is now once again a single house. The farmhouse at Riley was taken down and a pair of cottages built on an adjoining site. Tables 8 and 9 illustrate how during the course of the 19th century, some of these now landless cottages came to be abandoned when fewer labourers were needed to work the land.

Chief rent of 6d at Whitehall. *HRO*

In 1841, of the 24 cottage heads of household, all of them were farm workers except for one mole-catcher. In 1871, of the 26 cottage heads of household, only 17 were farm labourers but there were now new occupations associated with the rise of the gentrified Tedstone Court as an employer: three gardeners and a coachman. Apart from these occupations, there was also a blacksmith[*], a carpenter and a dairyman / Methodist preacher. By 1901, agriculture was in serious recession and the reduction in householders who were farm labourers had continued, the numbers being down to 12, almost half the 1841 figure, but the total number of cottagers was enlarged by the addition of coachman and gardeners. Cottagers often took lodgers, especially after the children had left home; these were usually other farm workers but in 1871 at Whitehall, Ann Beeks had a different type of lodger; she had three small children

---

[*] R. Powell, the blacksmith, had moved from Tidbatch, a small farm which is covered in Chapters VI and & X

of her own but in addition, had taken in a 'nurse child': Sarah Ann Green, aged eight months. One suspects that most women did piece work or domestic work on the farms but this was often under-recorded in the censuses. In 1841, only four women were recorded as agricultural

Tom Griffiths with Blossom & Blackbird.
Tom worked for the Bellville family. *Bellville collection*

labourers / farm servants, there was one dressmaker, one gloveress and one spinner. In 1871, the numbers were: 13 women recorded as agricultural labourers / farm servants; one dressmaker; Amy Phillips, who lived at one of the lodges, was a laundress, presumably for the Court; Elizabeth Price kept a dame school and Amy Bullock was a laundress at the Rectory. In 1901 there were no women recorded as working on farms; Alice Benbow at Ireland Cottage was a dressmaker, two did domestic work, two were charwomen, there was one laundress, and a school mistress, Julia Simonds, who taught at Woodend School.

One or two cottages to the west of the parish were granted an extended life into the 20th century as they were used to house staff working for the Wights, followed by the Bellvilles, at the Court, and in addition, new cottages were built replacing some of the inaccessible woodland homes: the two lodges, the pair of Brick Cottages which replaced Cutted Cottages or Cullets, and Diamond Cottages in Line House Lane. Forge Cottage and Rectory or Glebe Cottage on the west side were also new. Almost all the cottages on the

Hay making at Tedstone Court. *Bellville collection*

east side of the Sapey Brook were part of Charles Edward Moore's estate in 1841 that was purchased by Edward Bickerton Evans of Whitbourne Hall in 1866. The rebuilding or extension of life for cottages on the west side was not given to the cottages on the east side, being, as they were, much further from the 'big house' at Whitbourne. It seems that no attempt was made to keep the woodland cottages in repair. The reason may have been because they were too inconvenient for people to wish to live in them but another reason could have been that the landlords would have wanted to keep control of the woodlands and didn't particularly want hoards of people there disturbing the pheasants and perhaps poaching. It was only in the latter part of the 20th century that isolated cottages became greatly valuable even though they might be in a ruinous condition, often to the amazement of the locals.

CHAPTER XII

Schooling in the Parish

We have no knowledge of schools in Tedstone Delamere before the 19th century. Perhaps it is significant that none of the 15 people including the two churchwardens who signed the late 16th century glebe terrier were able to write their names, they all signed with a mark. In 1792, eight out of the eleven churchwardens and parishioners who witnessed the signing of the Composition in lieu of Tithes were able to write their names (see page 29). In both cases, the parishioners who signed were the farmers. A better indication of literacy can perhaps be obtained from a study of the marriage registers:[1]

1. During the years 1758 – 67 inclusive, of the 43 Tedstone Delamere people who married in the parish, 30 were unable to write their names and signed the register with a mark.
2. 40 years later, during the years 1808 – 1817 inclusive, of the 18 Tedstone Delamere people who married in the parish, 12 signed with a mark.
3. 40 years later, during the years 1858 – 1867 inclusive, of the 20 Tedstone Delamere people who married in the parish, 9 signed with a mark.

So in the mid 18th and early 19th centuries, approximately 33% could write their names but by the middle of the 19th century, there had been a significant improvement; 65% were sufficiently literate to do so. There may have been some sort of schooling from time to time by the clergy, but it can't have lasted for long. (The figures also suggest a significant drop in the numbers of young adults, if not population, between the mid 18th and the early 19th centuries.) In 1861, 26 children were described as 'scholars' in the Tedstone Delamere census: nine-year-old Charles Woodhouse's father was a carrier who lived at 'Three Gates' (which must be the Gate House) so perhaps he was taken to Bromyard in his father's cart; Thomas, Joseph and James Hemming, aged 12, 10, and 8 from the Hedge House may have attended Bromyard Grammar School; there was also Hannah Benbow, a labourer's daughter from Ireland Cottage. It seems likely that some sort of shared transport to Bromyard was arranged for all these children. The children of Richard Powell, the blacksmith from Upper Grounds: Jane, Mary Ann and Richard, aged 15, 13 and 9, must surely have gone to Bromyard. John Lloyd lived with the rector, the Rev. Gregory Smith, and was likely to have been his pupil, a premium being paid to the rector for his tuition; it was common for sons of gentlemen to be so educated. Alfred and Ada Wight from Tedstone Court were sure to have been educated privately. Berrow, James, Stanley and John Ward from Tipton Hall may have been taken to school in Bromyard. By contrast, hardly any of the children from the east of the parish went to any sort of school at this time. Some of the younger children from the west side would have attended Mrs. Price's dame school at Upper Line House. Mrs. Elizabeth Price had the rather grand description in the census of 'landed proprietor'. Mrs. Wright, the rector's daughter said of her:

The knowledge she imparted to her pupils was doubtless very small, but the help she rendered to busy mothers of large families was a real contribution to the community. I remember her best when she had given up the little school and retired to a smaller cottage near the Linehouse farm. One day I found her with an open Bible before her … she said her eyes were tired so I offered to read aloud to her …. When I laid down the book, she remarked: 'Ain't that nice readin'.[2]

Woodend School

The Education Act of 1870 made provision for all children between the ages of five and 13 to be educated. Following the Act, school boards were set up and members of the gentry played their part in providing suitable buildings. Mr. W. T. Barneby provided the school premises and master's house at Tedstone Wafre known as High Lane School. In Tedstone Delamere, Mr. and Mrs. E. B. Evans of Whitbourne Hall erected a Public Elementary School at Woodend, dated 1871 (see Map 11, page 225); the building remained their property. The school was large enough for 60 children but actual numbers averaged 17 – 25. The 1871 census records 39 children of school age in the parish, 21 living east of the Sapey Brook. This number might have been acceptable if all these children came to school but

Woodend School became a shelter for cattle.

High Lane School in the early 1900s.

B&DLHC

High Lane School c1915. *Jan Davis*

unfortunately school attendance seemed to be a perennial problem. In May 1885, the school was visited by Mr. T. C. Hartley, H.M. Assistant Inspector, who found that owing to the severity of the winter and the past prevalence of colds, the attendance had been very irregular. The Managers hoped that the parents would do their utmost to secure a good attendance during the fine weather of the summer and at this time, a new mistress, Mrs. Whyman, entered her duties.

Attendance was a problem with many schools at this time. Many parents had probably not received education themselves and may have felt that as they had managed without any, so could their children. The older children would have been useful on the land or in the home. In addition there was the difficulty of getting children to school in bad weather; problems with inadequate footwear were likely to have been particularly acute at Woodend School where so many of the children had to walk through muddy woods and across fields. Another difficulty was that schooling was not free; fees of just a few pennies a week were charged but for a family of several children on a labourer's wage, that probably took some finding.

Writing in 1955, the W. I. history relates the following:

> As a small girl an old friend went to school at Woodend and great was the excitement when the Evans carriage drew up from Whitbourne Hall with a pile of sewing and knitting to be done – when this was all finished, again the carriage arrived & every child had a present, books and ornaments & once our story teller remembers having an inkwell in the shape of a rabbit eating cabbage.[3]

One wonders whether the sewing and knitting was for some charity, such as less fortunate children in the London slums.

Every Christmas, year after year, Mrs. Evans sallied forth with a carriage full of presents for the children; in 1898 they were entertained to tea at Whitbourne Hall:

> Toys, books, articles of clothing were given to the children, those who had attended school most regularly during the past year receiving some useful and warm garment. Many of the parents were also recipients of some valuable present from Mrs Evans.[4]

Mrs. Evans was not alone in providing treats. The Lea family at the rectory used to entertain the children. Mrs. Wright, the rector's daughter related:

> My memories of the children centre chiefly round the school-treat on the Rectory lawn in summer, and the carol-singing at Christmas. The numbers at the Treat were never very large and the children were small. I can remember carrying round plates piled high with plum-cake, at sight of which little boys sometimes stuffed an unfinished piece of bread and butter into their pockets for fear of missing a more attractive substitute. After tea we all joined in the popular singing games, new to my sister and me, London bred, but known to even the youngest Tedstone-born child there present.[5]

It would be interesting to know if any local people today can remember playing such games as 'Nuts in May', 'Here come three Spaniards out of Spain' or 'Who goes round my stony wall tonight? Only Johnny Ningo'?

> In preparation for the young carol singers on Christmas Day, my mother would order a goodly supply of buns from the baker at Bromyard who also furnished us with the school-treat cakes. My father would collect a store of pennies and sixpences, to be dealt out with the buns. When the day came, on the table in the hall was a willow pattern dish, holding a mountain of penny buns.

In July 1893, the children of the parish went to tea at the Rectory:

> Those from Woodend School coming with flags, given them by Mrs. Evans, and headed by Miss James, the Mistress of the School. They were given a talk about children in London's East End. Hampers of flowers and occasionally of fruit are sent there from this parish.[6]

Apparently, for some reason, every Monday morning, two children had to walk from Woodend School to Whitbourne Hall across country, a round trip of between two and three miles, to collect a large jar of jam which had then to last the week.[7] The walk must have been considered character building!

H.M.Inspector's report in 1901 relates:

> Woodend C. E. School: Some of the defects in the instruction which were pointed out last year have been partially remedied and the school is now, with a few exceptions, in a fairly efficient condition …. Discipline is quite satisfactory but the children's irregular attendance is a serious obstacle to their becoming proficient, besides entailing financial loss to the School funds.

High Lane School in 1928. B&DLHC

High Lane School in c1948.
From left, back row: Doug Green, Donald Boughton, John Powell, John Griffiths, Doug McNally, Sonny Parsons, Les Griffiths.
Middle row: Joyce Farr, Rene Boughton, Annis Roper, Freda Powell, Lavinia Green, Rose Finch
Front row: Mrs Raneford (head teacher), Ray Phillips, Cicely Richards, Betty Whistance, Vera Powell & Doreen Powell, Patsy Mcnally, Rena Easton, Sandy Raneford.

The 1901 census shows that there had been a fall in the number of school age children in the parish. There were now 23 as opposed to 39 in 1871 but significantly, only 10 of these children were from the eastern side, as opposed to 21 in 1871. This was the writing on the wall for the school; in 1907 after a date for the school's closure had been given, Sir Richard Harington of Whitbourne Court spoke at a County Council meeting, saying that the decision had been taken in opposition to local views:

> Children would [now] have to go a very considerable distance to get to school .... It was obviously not wise to send a child such a long way to school that it would fatigue itself before entering upon the studies of the day (hear, hear). [He thought that] a smaller amount of education at a smaller school under a less competent teacher would not only be sufficient for the lives that most of the children who attended would have to lead, but would be better assimilated than a slightly higher class of instruction at a more distant school when the body was fatigued and the mind consequently less receptive.[8]

It was all in vain. The school closed which was a great loss, not only educationally but also socially, for adult activities took place at the school as well:

> [In 1892] a Magic Lantern Lecture was given by Mr. Ernest Vowles ... and the attendance was encouragingly large. Many of the slides were home-made and showed considerable skill and taste. This was the third of the lectures advertised in October. The money collected at the door on the three occasions amounted to 7s. 5d. which has been expended in the purchase of tin candlesticks for lighting the school.[9]

Unfortunately not all activities were a success:

> [In 1893] Mr Cooper, headmaster of Bromyard Grammar School gave a lecture on Electricity. The evening was very wet which interfered seriously with the experiments and the number of listeners.

The rector used the school for Sunday School and a number of church services were also held here. In 1907, a Harvest Festival Service took place at the school:

> The Schoolroom was very nicely decorated by Mrs Grubb, Mrs Dora Jones etc. The evening proved to be very wet. This however did not prevent a good number attending: all those present were our own parishioners. Another hanging lamp has been placed in the school.

As late as 1916 when the school had closed it was reported in the parish magazine that there was an afternoon service at the school and every seat was taken. Concerts and lectures appeared to continue for a while but it can't have been feasible to keep the building dry and in repair for occasional meetings.

Now the children in the parish had a very long walk to school. The Baylis children from Whitehall whose father worked as a gamekeeper, used to walk all the way to High Lane School at Tedstone Wafre.[10] Other children walked to Whitbourne School and these included the Jones children from Horner's Mill and the Powell children from Lee Lay. Roly Powell remembers how he and his siblings and other children walked to Whitbourne School across the fields from Lee Lay, just under two miles; it wasn't the distance, it was the mud that was the worst part, especially for the little ones. When they emerged onto the road in Whitbourne Village, they left their muddy boots upside down under the hedge and changed into clean boots they had carried!

The Jones children from Horners Mill used to play in Woodend School in the early 1930s, running in and out at will. The building was left unlocked and desks, slates and other furnishings remained as a 'time warp' until finally it deteriorated into a shelter for sheep. It has recently been converted into an attractive house to let by Julian Westwood, the owner of neighbouring Woodhall.

The High Lane School at Tedstone Wafre closed in 1963. It is now converted for domestic use.

Before the village hall was opened, social activities used to take place at High Lane School. A story tells that at a concert held at High Lane School:

> a singer began his song, and, as he completed the first three words, 'Bless this house' there was a loud crackling noise and the floor began to sink, the joists having been unable to sustain the combined weight of the audience. Luckily the floor did not break but merely sank into the foundations which had approximately six feet of water in them at the time.[11]

Saltmarshe Village Hall

Work began on the hall in October 1955. It was built by volunteers following plans made by local architect, John Greenwood. It seemed to take a number of years to reach fruition as it was not opened until 13th June 1963 by Mrs Diana Wells, who was formerly a Barneby. The hall is today used for a great many activities including meetings of the Saltmarshe W.I. and the Saltmarshe Young Farmers Club and harvest suppers.

High Lane Cricket Team 1930.

CHAPTER XIII

The Bellville Family at Tedstone Court 1908 – 1996
by Susan Haffenden (formerly Bellville)

My grandfather, Henry Archibald Bellville, commonly known as Archie or the Captain, bought Tedstone Court as a small sporting estate in 1908. It was actually his formidable mother, Emma, who held most of the purse strings, having been left an extremely rich widow at the age of forty, who completed the purchase for him, through her agent as he was laid up in the Raven Hotel, Droitwich with a bad leg.

Mrs Emma Bellville, a wealthy widow, surrounded by her family; she set up each of her four sons with a sporting estate; Archie, to whom she gave Tedstone Court, is the one on the right. She had made a very good marriage to William John Bellville in 1865; he made a fortune as mustard manufacturer (Keen's Mustard, now a part of Reckitt & Colman). She was widowed at an early age and although exceptionally beautiful, she never remarried.

Bellville Collection

He had recently married for the second time and was determined to set up his own home away from Leicestershire and the rest of the family. He was the epitome of the 'hunting, shooting and fishing' country gentleman and always considered that if the shooting at the Brockhampton estate was good enough for George V, then the Tedstone dingles were good enough for him.

He was passionate about horses and intended to breed race horses and hunters for pleasure as well as to ride to hounds. He also enjoyed having the work horses on the estate; they were used for pulling out the timber from the dingles and also pulled the numerous hay wagons and farm carts. He owned a coach and four, he himself drove a tandem and there were numerous buggies and governess carts and even two donkeys with cane chairs instead of saddles so that the boys could ride at a very tender age. The family photographs always reveal him astride a horse

---

It is also said that Tedstone was bought unseen by Archie's valet on his behalf!

Archie Bellville driving his tandem.

Kennels at the Court.

or with a gun over his arm and always with a pack of dogs at his heels. These varied from setters, spaniels, terriers to his favourite Irish wolfhound, Mick.

Many of the photographs show him out with his three sons: Guy (from his first marriage), Dennis and Miles. They went out shooting rabbits at a very early age; my father owned his first gun before he was eleven.

Archie Bellville with his sons Dennis and Miles. *Bellville Collection*

In the winter Archie would hunt and shoot and in the summer the family would decamp to Carsaig in the Isle of Mull for the fishing. He was a serious fisherman and on his extended honeymoon in 1906/7 he and his wife, Ethel Mary, went on a round the world trip, taking in Canada and New Zealand, mainly for the fishing! Their elder son, Dennis, was born in Wellington, New Zealand in 1907. It seems a fortunate coincidence that Miles, his younger brother, would marry a New Zealander in 1944!

The stable-yard at Tedstone Court. *Bellville Collection*

Archie achieved his ambition of breeding winning race horses from his fine stallion, Dandino, and the fields were full of brood mares and their foals. Archie was often irascible and was quite a demanding boss. My father told me that he used to take the Sunday lunch visitors for a tour of the stables wearing a pair of white gloves. He would summon Stanley the stud groom and proudly stroke

The Bellville Coach; it is election time and the coach is taking the locals to vote. *Bellville Collection*

the horses. When dust appeared on his white gloves, as it always would, the groom would be reprimanded and ordered to be more thorough with his grooming in the future! He was the first person to own a motor car in the parish but the last to give up his beloved coach and four. The old coach was still in the coach house in the 1950s and we used to play in it as children. It was eventually sold to a film company.

My grandmother, Ethel Mary Walton, was the eldest daughter of John Pears Walton J.P. of Acomb High House, Northumberland. Her father and twin brother were also of the shooting and fishing fraternity and they too had horses, so when she married Archie in 1906 she knew what kind of life to expect. She loved the countryside, dogs and gardening and it was she who had the present rose garden at Tedstone created out of an old orchard. Archie and the boys built the crazy-paving path all round the new garden and Ethel planted two straight rows of roses and a wooden summer house was built with shingled roof and diamond-paned windows.

The children learnt to ride at an early age.
Bellville Collection

She also created the tufa stone rockery with a handkerchief tree as a centre piece and added rhododendrons to the shrubbery. Unfortunately the grass tennis court was overshadowed by a bank of dark trees and a monkey puzzle tree obscured light and view from the smoking room. She loved roses and planted all the roses round the moat borders and standard roses along the ha-ha wall.

My grandmother had to organise the indoor staff, appointing a housekeeper, housemaids, nursemaids and later a governess for the three children. She is rarely seen in photographs, mostly I suspect because she was the photographer. She appears in later photographs, always with a hat on and usually with a terrier or pekinese under her arm: 'like a white powder puff' as Bin Richards, a local farmer, told me.

In 1913, the indoor staff consisted of Mrs. Pearce, the cook, with Maggie as

Picnic in the hayfield.   *Bellville Collection*

kitchen maid; Mrs. Brown as head housemaid, with Florence, second housemaid and James as the second footman. The nursemaids came and went and were hired to look after Audrey, the only daughter, born in 1914.

The outside staff consisted of Mr. M. R. Stanley, the stud groom, responsible for the care of 'Dandino', the stallion, and all the brood mares and foals. Mr. Grub and Mr. Green worked in the stable under him. George and Tom Griffiths were employed as first and second carters; in the winter they would use the heavy horses for extracting timber and in the summer these horses pulled the hay wains and harvest wagons. Mr. Humphreys was employed as bailiff, Mr. Vaughan as mason, Brown as estate carpenter, Haywood as woodman, and Wyatt and his son as general estate workers. The head gardener was Mr. Pullen with Mr. Bradford and Mr. Gegg under him; they had the big walled kitchen garden to supervise with two large glass houses full of apricot and peaches and a huge grape vine and all the vegetables and cut flowers to grow for the house. There were also extensive lawns to mow, the shrubbery to attend to with rhododendrons a general favourite and of course the rose garden and herbaceous borders. Mrs. Ethel Bellville was especially fond of her large rockery by the small gate leading to the Church Meadow.

Dennis and Miles with Nanny.

When the 1st World War came, Archie joined up. He served throughout the war in France, taking his favourite horse with him; the 3rd Battalion East Surrey Regiment was a cavalry regiment under Colonel Duborough. There are pictures of him on parade at the camp on this horse but I do not know whether the horse survived. Archie was promoted to Captain and emerged virtually unscathed from the war. However, tragedy struck the family in 1925, when Dennis, his elder son of the second marriage to Ethel, was killed in a motor cycle accident at the age of nineteen. He was a cadet at Sandhurst and was killed returning from Harrow's Founder's Day celebrations.

Stocking the pool with fish.   *Bellville Collection*

The staff at Tedstone Court in 1913.

Archie died at the age of 61 in September 1930. As my father, Miles, was in his last year at Jesus College, Cambridge (where he read economics and agriculture and rowed in the first boat, achieving Head of the River status), Granny Bellville appointed an estate manager. After Archie Bellville's death in 1930, there were large death duties. Miles's birth had not been registered by his eccentric father so legally he did not exist which caused problems as his heir.[1]

Tedstone was then farmed as a mixed farm with more emphasis on the rearing of sheep, cattle and pigs. A small dairy herd was retained for the house and estate needs, and milk, butter and cream were plentiful. The butter was churned by hand in the big dairy wing of the house, an electric separator only being obtained in the 1960s.

The horses were greatly reduced when Grandfather died but hunters were kept for Miles and Audrey who both hunted with the Clifton-on-Teme when at home. Audrey became hunt secretary in 1936 and Miles became joint-master in 1937, hunting hounds himself. When the 2nd World War broke out, Granny agreed to keep several couple of the Clifton hounds at Tedstone 'to save the strain'. My father became MFH again in the early sixties.

During the war, Tedstone was virtually shut down. The lower floor was kept shuttered and Granny made an upstairs sitting room over the porch adjoining her bedroom in the former 'Bachelor's Room'. Audrey and a cousin, Geraldine Milne, both nursing locally, kept her company. A skeleton staff kept the place going.

Miles Bellville had a distinguished youth and war record: he won a gold medal for yachting in the 1936 Olympics; as a marine commando in the 2nd World War he was awarded a Military Cross; he served behind enemy lines in Belgium and was also involved with the taking of Madagascar.[2]

In 1950, my father and mother took over the running of the house and estate after Granny's death. They decided to live there for two years and if they could not make the place pay, they would regretfully sell up. My mother, Nan Bellville, being a practical New Zealander, whom my father had met during the war whilst she was serving as a wren, immediately decided to make two rentable flats of the old dairy/servants' wing and so the Pigeon House and Gracefield took shape. Mother also started a market garden in the walled kitchen garden and we sent many boxes of dahlias and chrysanthemums over the next few years to Birmingham market. Mr. and Mrs. Randall were employed to run this enterprise but we as children and mother especially did a lot of the labour intensive work. My father ran the farm with the invaluable help of Mr. Fred Clements as farm mechanic and chauffeur, Mr. Reg Tarr as estate carpenter, Mr. Joe Whitty as tractor driver and agricultural worker; and Chris Harris in charge of all the animals.

Mr. Jack Mason and Mr. William Nash worked in the garden and their wives were housekeeper and cook respectively. Mrs. Clements was the farm secretary and later

Tedstone Court May 1945. The tenants, staff and other parishioners have been invited to meet Major Miles Bellville's wife, Nancy.
Bellville Collection

Getting in the hay: Fred Clements, Mr Mason, Joe Whitty.

helped mother with the cleaning in the house. The staff, with the exception of Chris Harris, were elderly but all were incredibly loyal to the family and became part of our childhood extended family.

Tedstone was an idyllic place for children to grow up; we had ponies and rode everywhere. We attended Pony Club Camps held at Brockhampton and also at Saltmarshe, pony rallies all over the Clifton Hunt area and of course went hunting alongside my father. Many hours were spent happily in the stable yard, mucking out ponies, cleaning tack and having water fights! Grandfather's gun room was changed into our nursery and later into a schoolroom when Jane and I had a governess for two years from 1956-8, before going to boarding school in North Wales.

Granny's large double drawing room was divided into a study for my father and a beautiful drawing room for Sundays and piano practice on the lovely Bechstein. The hall, smoking room and dining room were used as before but all redecorated by my mother and Mr. Clements, as was the whole house over a period of years. It was a tremendous job as ceilings were high, rooms vast and all previously covered in dark green wallpaper of the pre 1914 period. The former housekeeper's room became the kitchen, with a large Aga replacing the old range and double sinks and fitted cupboards were put in. This room became the centre of the house as mother was an excellent cook and preserver of fruit, maker of marmalade, jam and jellies. We eventually had two big freezers packed full of home-grown vegetables, all picked by mother and anyone else she could rope in to help! The dairy was moved to a new larder in the back passage, with a large meat cage for the game my father shot and the small room next door became the housekeeper's sitting room. Nobody had much time to sit down so eventually it became a boot room where shoes were cleaned, silver polished, and all mother's flower arrangements for the house, local hospital, and her numerous flower demonstrations were prepared. She had trained under Constance

Spry in London before the war and was much in demand for demonstrations, the decoration of Hereford Cathedral at Three Choirs Festival time and many hours of judging at local shows.

The bells in the back passage with the names of all the rooms to which my grandfather and his guests would summon servants were now silent - a symbol of a bygone era. My mother told my father in no uncertain tones not to throw his clothes on the floor as there was only one servant left to pick them up and she wasn't going to do it. My parents chose to sleep in what we called their tower room as it was up another flight of separate stairs – away from noisy children or tiresome guests. The adjoining former dressing room became their bathroom but as it faced north and was vast it was never very inviting. The view from their room was, however, amazing: a panoramic scene taking in the Malvern Hills and even Broadway Tower in the Cotswolds on a clear day and Clifton-on-Teme, the Thrift Farm and Martley and Ankerdine and Bringsty Common in the middle distance and in the foreground, our dingles and the Front Meadow and St James's church. Mother loved this view and created a hospitable house and a beautiful garden so that many others could share it with her. There were numerous visitors at all times of the year: Bellville relations, the Kayes and the Lowlesses; the New Zealand cousins who lived in England such as the Kempston sisters, the Harris and Monro cousins and all visiting New Zealanders were welcome to what my father called 'Little New Zealand House'!

The two main guest rooms were quaintly called the Bachelor's Room and the porch room and three other rooms were occupied by us three children. These rooms were large so all contained at least one if not two spare beds so that our numerous school friends could stay with us. Then there was the linen room with fitted warmly-heated cupboards with all the linen neatly darned and sorted, from damask table napkins to large white damask table cloths and many sheets well over 30 years old and revived by my mother with her endless technique of 'sides to middle' when they looked worn. She was the most amazing practical domestic person and must have saved my father thousands of pounds with her home making skills.

There were three old bathrooms on this middle floor; one for the children, one for the guests with a vast bath and antiquated plug; and the staff bathroom, later used by the girl grooms whom we employed when my father kept the hunt horses at Tedstone in the 60s. The loos were magnificent with chain pulls and mahogany seats which were warm to the touch in an otherwise pretty cold house. We had central heating and splendid fires downstairs but not upstairs and it was very cold as children but we seemed tougher then.

The top floor, where my father and his siblings had had their day and night nurseries, were not used until my mother converted yet another part of the house into a third flat for my brother in the 70s. It was called the Crow's Nest and he had the old billiard room as his sitting room with a lowered roof to keep it warmer, a kitchen and study bedroom and then in the attic his bedroom, spare-room and bathroom. Later, when

Richard moved to Pixhill, this flat was let out to various couples and the rent was always helpful.

The billiard room had been a wonderful playroom for us where we spent many a winter day dressing up and performing plays and devising entertainments for any audience we could persuade to watch. In a pre television and computer childhood we spent hours using our imaginations in such creative play. Later on we had a full-size table-tennis table there which much later was donated to Saltmarshe Village Hall.

Finally there were the Elizabethan cellars which ran below the drawing room, hall and kitchen wing. We used these as discos in the 60s and had many a good party down there with lots of atmosphere and noise which did not penetrate to the rooms above. Together with the granaries, stables, barns and garden with a moat (dry), who could ask for a better place to be brought up. When my father died in 1980, Mother once more showed her talent for adjusting; she made use of the entire house as a Residential Home for the elderly and ran it for nine years very successfully employing 28 people and having 10 or 11 residents at a time. She organised the cooking and staff rotas and had the house altered with new fire doors, wash basins in every room and all the equipment for running such a project. The staff were wonderful and came in on tractors during one very snowy winter. Mother was in her element and when we visited with our children, we slept on the top floor, so all had gone full circle and the fourth generation slept and played in the rooms which had accommodated their grandfather's generation.

Thus the old house welcomed back my sister and her family in the 1990s and was partitioned so that they lived in the west wing with their kitchen made from our old nursery, and mother retained her half until her death in 1996. She died at Tedstone in the smoking room, surrounded by family and loyal local families like the Bethels, Albert Jones, and Chris and Kathleen Harris who had all been so much part of the Tedstone story.

After Major Bellville's retirement in the 1970s, his son Richard took over the running of the farm and estate. Some outlying land was sold, new enterprises were started including a clay pigeon shoot. Richard also became a franchisee of 'The Shooting Box': visiting parties of shooters were supplied with guns, ammunition, and tuition, and were also entertained to refreshments. Deer farming was another profitable new enterprise with meat being sold to local hotels. The area of woodland was increased and a new woodland road built.

Tedstone Court and Estate were sold in 1996 to Stennard Harrison of Worcester who completely renovated the house. He and his wife live there still.

JMW

CHAPTER XIV

The Changing Centuries

This history of Tedstone Delamere demonstrates some great changes that have taken place. Sometimes the pace of change seemed to increase to a gallop, as it must have done after the Black Death when the reduction in manpower that followed the plague sparked changes in the nature of landholding and farming practice. Sometimes the pace of change slowed to a crawl but rarely did it stand still. The manorial records, wills and inventories bring to life the everyday workings of the manor and its inhabitants. The court rolls record 15th-, 16th- and 17th-century holdings that were mostly very small by today's standard.

By the 18th century, the chief-fee tenants of the manor had long been virtually the same as owner-occupiers today; they could sell or bequeath their property to whom they pleased, and only had to pay very small fixed rents to the lord, though the heriots (best beasts) remained a burden. The 18th century brought the rise of the Moore estate as money from industry was invested in land. The lords of the manor and other would-be landowners purchased farms and smallholdings. Enclosure by agreement had been taking place over the centuries but much of the land was still scattered about in small parcels throughout the parish. The new owners reorganised the land into more viable units on which to grow corn to feed an expanding population and in so doing, a number of farms and smallholdings disappeared. Most of these were in the east of the parish. In 1805, James Moore, lord of the manor, bequeathed his Tedstone estate to two cousins: Richard Wight was left Tedstone Court with the now much less important lordship, Edward Moore was left the part of the estate lying to the east of the Sapey Brook. This eastern part was to be purchased by Edward Bickerton Evans of Whitbourne Hall in 1866. The tithe survey of 1841 recorded that, by that time, almost all the holdings were occupied by tenants (apart, of course, from Tedstone Court itself).

The 18th-century manor had become much less important as a unit of local government. Records from other parishes indicate that this function had been largely taken over by the vestry; this is not demonstrated here because of lack of the relevant church records. The last manorial courts took place during the first part of the 18th century, and thereafter the only function of the manor was to attempt to collect the manorial dues, as demonstrated by the plethora of lists of chief rents, heriots and reliefs being owed; there is evidence that these were collected more and more infrequently. It is likely that T. P. P. Wight, in the mid-19th century, was the last to try to collect these manorial dues.

Nineteenth- and twentieth-century population changes

An attempt was made in Chapter III to estimate, only very approximately, the total number of people in the parish by using the 1671 Hearth Tax returns; this produced a figure of 150 persons. Only five years later, another estimate was made based on the Compton Census of 1676; it gave a figure of 132 persons, see pages 56 and 58. The 19th and 20th century census returns give us, for the first time, accurate population figures for the parish that show considerable growth had occurred since the l670s. This growth may be partly accounted for by the occupants of the twelve cottages built on the manor's wastes near Tidbatch and at Whitehall.

TABLE 10
Population in Tedstone Delamere from the Censuses [ ]

	No. of Persons		No. of Persons
1801	245	1901	180
1811	249	1911	189
1821	246	1921	177
1831	230	1931	136
1841	207	1951	102
1851	193	1961	127
1861	205	1971	141
1871	235	1981	136
1881	251	1991	139
1891	203		

There was no census in 1941

The population declined between 1811 and 1851, part of a national trend brought about by changes in estate management which involved merging smallholdings with larger farms (as mentioned above) and the attraction away from the countryside by industrial employment in the cities. In Tedstone Delamere there was a marked population rise during the 30 years that were to follow, owing to the development of the Wights' estate at Tedstone Court with their large indoor and outdoor staff, but before the farming depression had had its effect. The census figures show the population high point as being in 1881. The very serious depression in farming followed, and in Chapter X, the crop returns clearly demonstrate a move to less labour intensive grassland farming. This was combined with a substantial decrease in population as the farm labourers left the land and this trend, which took place from 1881–1951, is clearly shown in Table 10 above. From 1961 the numbers of people started to increase slightly.

One gains the impression that the effect of the Sapey Brook, separating the parish in two, as it does, has become more marked since the advent of the motor car together with better roads. Today, to get to the western side of the parish from the eastern, one has to drive first through Whitbourne or through Clifton-on-Teme. In the old days when one walked or rode, the brook was not important. Most of the

---

[ ] The population summaries are found in the Herefordshire Record Office

people living in the eastern half of the parish now look first to Whitbourne or Clifton, each place having amenities such as a village shop, a school and pubs, all of which Tedstone Delamere lacks. The usual social gatherings take place at the Saltmarshe Village Hall, which is shared by the parishes of Tedstone Delamere, Tedstone Wafre and Edvin Loach. The Clifton-on-Teme Hunt and their Supporters Club provide a number of social activities.

The end of the estates
The later chapters, covering the 19th century, have dealt with changes in landownership in the parish: in 1841, almost all the farms and smallholdings were occupied by tenants; these tenants, with just one or two significant exceptions, changed frequently as did many of the farm workers in the cottages. James Lane Wight made his living as a London merchant and this new money enabled him to invest in his Tedstone Court Estate, building cottages, lodges and Upper Grounds farmhouse in the mid-19th century. The Line House was purchased by his son Edgar in 1891. The farming recession was long lasting. The Tipton/Winley estate of the Knills was sold to the sitting tenants in 1918 making a loss. The Saltmarshe Estate was sold in the mid-20th century and Hedge House and the Gatehouse became owner-occupied. We have read of the difficulties faced by the Moores in trying to keep their eastern estate in the family in the 19th century and the eventual sale to Edward Bickerton Evans at a prosperous time for farming. As recorded, this prosperity was not to last and the depression that followed continued, with just a short break during World War 1, right up to the time of World War 2. Then in the 1970s, after a huge rise in land values, the Whitbourne Estate parted with a large portion of its Tedstone property and two of the three farms sold were subsequently broken up.

Despite the introduction of some Government subsidies, life for farmers today is very different from that led by previous generations; the farm, then, was a bustling place with many people around. Today's farmer must lead a lonely life; with the aid of machinery, and contractors at times such as harvest, he usually works the farm single-handedly and his wife is probably out at work elsewhere. Today, it seems to us extraordinary that in the 16th century a farmer of half a virgate (20 acres) was able to build a fine house like Winley; and in the 17th century, farmers of one virgate (40 acres) were able to build houses such as Woodhall or Pixhill. Today, vastly greater acreages are needed to make an acceptable living and this has led to some farmhouses becoming surplus to requirements.

What has become of the farmhouses in recent years?
The parish today is very different from that of the mid-20th century. There have been great changes in just the last 50 years. Then, all these buildings housed farmers, their families and staff. Today, most of the surviving cottages and some farmhouses in this beautiful countryside have become very desirable country residences for the retired or people with occupations far removed from farming, with perhaps just a few acres retained for hobby farming and horses.

The farmhouses in 2013

House	Working Farm	'Desirable Country Residence'	Other	Notes
1. Tipton Hall	*			
2. Hedge House	*			
3. The Line House		*		
4. Winley		*		
5. The Hams				N/a. No longer a separate farm
6. The Gate House	*			
7. The Thrift		*		Farm buildings converted to housing
8. Woodend	*			
9. Woodhall		*		
10. New House	*			
11. Horner's Mill			*	Pallet making business. Less land
12. Tidbatch		*		Demolished. Modern replacement planned
13. Lee Lay		*		
14. Stone House A			*	Disappeared. Uninhabited after 1881
15. Pixhill		*		
16. Upper Grounds		*		
17. Glebe Farm		*		Land sold c 2000

The 17 working farmhouses are now reduced to five. But there have been two new ones: Lower Thrift is a new farmhouse recently built by Harvey Richards; May Farm was built c 1980 as a farmhouse for some of the Woodhall land but it has now, in its turn, become a 'desirable country residence', its land having been sold.

New 20th-century settlement is restricted to where there are good roads and services: on the west side are the new house at Oldridge on the B4203; the house built by the Boughtons next to the Gate House; the houses down the lane to Hedge House; the six former council houses, 1 – 6 Delamere Road, first occupied in 1952; the 20th century rectory; the bungalow at the kennels; the cottage opposite Hill Cross, Cherry Fields with the riding school; the new house called 'Churchlands' at Glebe Farm and the excellent conversion of buildings at the Court creating two new dwellings. On the east side is the charming new 'hamlet' at the Thrift created by converting the farm buildings, the barn conversion at Stone House, and, as recorded above, the new farmhouses of Lower Thrift and May Farm. The derelict Colt house at Lamp Green has recently been demolished as has Tidbatch.

There is plenty of history still to be discovered: the 20th century has only been partially covered; the National Archives and other repositories contain many documents not yet catalogued; the church is the oldest building in the parish and archaeology at the site near the church may throw more light on that possible Bronze Age enclosure and medieval settlement in that area. Travelling back through time and exploring this most interesting and beautiful parish and attempting to bring to life the people who lived and farmed here centuries ago has been a fascinating project and a great privilege.

APPENDIX A - Lords of the Manor

I am indebted to Bruce Copplestone-Crow for the early part of the descent of the lordship. He tells me that it is difficult to be sure about all of the La Mare family for they were very widespread & it is not always clear which William was intended. Equally, I have found it is difficult to be sure about the numerous Wyshams and sometimes different records give contradictory information. I have used Visitation of Herefordshire 1569; C J Robinson, *Mansions and Manors* ; Herefordshire Record Office, manorial records; & the Bishops Registers

1066	2 manors: a) Church of Hereford (Tedesthorne)	b) Ernwy & Godwin held as two (Chetestor)	
1086	ditto	Gilbert fitzThorold	(Domesday Book ff.181c, 187a)

before 1095   Gilbert fitzThorold had both parts a) & b). At Domesday, he had lands in Herefs, Worcs, Gloucs, Cambs, Essex & Somerset. In Rendcombe & Aylworth in Gloucs, Gilbert had a knight called Walter (de la Mare) as his subtenant, (DB,f.168b)

1095   Bernard de Neufmarche, baron of Brecon, had Tedstone Delamere & part of North Cerney from fitzThorold's barony; these later became part of the earldom of Hereford

1121   Bernard's daughter, Sybil, who was his heir, married Miles of Gloucester

1125   Miles, made earl of Hereford in 1141, died in hunting accident 1143, was succeeded by his son, Earl Roger who d. 1155. Miles had enfeoffed his cousin William de la Mare with several manors, including both parts of Tedstone Delamere

1130   William I de la Mare - held the manor of Tedstone Delamere from Miles together with lands in North Cerney by service of 1 knight & was dead by 1130

1141   William II de la Mare (son of above), lord of Tedstone & Little Hereford

1155   Robert de la Mare (son of above). His younger brother, Oliver, held Little Hereford. In 1166, Robert held lands from earl of Gloucester on which he owed service of 10 knights, (*Red Book of Exchequer*) , 288

1199   William III de la Mare, son of Robert m. Amfelisa, dau. of Gregory de la Mare. By 1199, William de la Mare III was being challenged in his right to one knight's fee at Tedstone and Cerney by Robert and Jordan de la Mare, possibly his brothers. Robert gave up his claim on payment to Jordan of 100s & for ½ mark yearly for life. Soon after this Robert also gave up his claim to another brother, Thomas, the deal was completed by Jordan making over the mill at Tedstone in exchange for 10s. rent in N. Cerney. (Palgrave (ed.), *Rotuli Curiae Regis* , i, 298 & ii,230; *Curia Regis Rolls* ,i,131,197,201,327,462) In 1190 William was amerced 1/2 mark of the forest pleas of Herefs, (*Pipe Roll 2 Henry II),* 47

1200   Thomas de la Mare, son of William III, had 2 knight's fees at Hanley Child & William, Redmarley Adam, Orleton & Doddenham & 1/2 fee in Hardwick from the earldom of Gloucester in 1210-12, *(Red Book of the Exchequer*), 567

1230   William IV de la Mare, son of Thomas m. Parnel (Petronella) de Croun. In 1243 he had 2 hides at Tedstone *la Mare* , held from earl of Hereford by service of 1 knight's fee, (*Book of Fees* , 806) Dead by 1255

APPENDIX

1283	Joan, daughter of William IV & Parnel m. John de Plessey. In 1283 Richard of Wells, killed on campaign in Anglesey, held land at Hampton, Bockleton of the lord of Tedstone, that is Joan, (*Inquisitions Post Mortem*, 1, no. 544)
	Robert de Plessey, died c1301, son of Joan & John de Plessey
1316	Peter de Plessey lord in 1316, (*Feudal Aids*, ii), 384
	Hawise, sister to above m. John of Wysham. There had been a dispute about Hawise's succession to the manor and it was taken into the King's hands. In 1332 there was an order to Robert Chaundos, escheator in Herefordshire, not to inter-meddle further with the manors of Tedstone which were to be restored to Hawise, (*Calendar of Close Rolls*, 1330-3), 516
d. 1356	Sir Richard Wysham, son of John & Hawise, m. dau. of Richard, 2nd lord Talbot
	Richard Wysham of Woodmanton, son of above m. dau of John of Amonsham
held TD 1372	William Wysham m. dau to Corbett of Shropshire
d. by 1418	John Wysham, son of above, m. Elizabeth dau of Edward of Hopton
	Richard Wysham, son of above, m. dau. of Butler of Worcs
1428/9	Richard Wysham, lord of TD, (HRO, manorial records)
1431	John Wysham, (HRO, manorial records 1431, 1493, 1496 - father & son ?)
1500	John Wysham, son of John, was subject of a marriage settlement in 1500: the young couple to have 4 marks annually out of the manor until the death of John sen. when John jun. is to inherit
1552	Thomas Wysham sen; son of above, m. Margaret dau. of Robert Croft of Kyre (HRO, manorial records)
1561	Thomas Wysham (jun.?), (HRO, manorial records)
includes 1561-97	George Wysham m. Anne, dau. of Anthony Dastyn, (HRO, dates taken from manorial & probate records)
1597	Francis Wysham (HRO, manorial & probate records)
1616 - 49	Richard Cresswell & Elizabeth his wife in her right as widow of Francis Wysham (HRO manorial records)
1649 - 84	Robert Mason, m. Hester, d. 1684
1684	Richard Mason, eldest(?) son of above, (unless otherwise mentioned, this information & that below is taken from deeds and marriage settlements in HRO)
1713	Robert Mason, 2nd(?) son of Robert & Hester defaulted on mortgages, manor & estate sold in 1713
1713 - 26	Richard Brompton of Chester Castle, lived at Tedstone Court

1726 - 1757   George Webb the Younger of Shelsley Beauchamp

1757 - 1777   Ann Moore, dau. of above

1777 - 1793   Robert Moore, eldest son of Ann & Robert Moore

1793 - 1805   James Moore, second son of Ann & Robert Moore

1805 - 1821   Richard Wight, cousin of above, m. Maria Shelton of Norton 1809

1821 - 1885   James Lane Wight, son of above m. Sarah Knill

1885 - 1908   Edgar Wight, son of above. Estate sold 1908

1908 - 1930   H. A. Bellville

1930 - 1980   Miles Bellville, son of above

APPENDIX B - Taxes of Henry VIII and the 1542 Herefordshire Muster Book

These assessments reflect the beginnings of the gradual decline of the manor as the primary unit of taxation and its replacement by the parish. In Herefordshire the taxes were levied by county commissioners and the divisions used were those of the ancient hundreds:

a) The Fifteenths and Tenths. The assessments for these taxes hadn't changed since 1332. It was left to the localities to raise their own quota how they could. These particular taxes were known to be an especial burden on the less well off and there was no banding. A collector for each hundred was responsible for raising the money. For example, in 1541, Thomas Wysham (the lord) of Tedstone Delamere was the collector for Broxash Hundred, in 1546 it was Richard Rowden of Thornbury and in 1547 the collector was Roger Hardwick of Winslow.

b) Subsidy and Benevolence Acts during Henry VIII's reign were to raise special 'subsidies' for his various foreign adventures. Taxes were levied on goods, lands or wages, whichever was likely to provide the most money: under the 1523 Subsidy Act, there were, surprisingly, only three people assessed in Tedstone Delamere and these were John Wysham at £4 4s. on land and Thomas and John Callowhill who were both assessed at 40s. on goods. The Callowhills held Woodmanton, Clifton-on-Teme at that time[i] and as mentioned on p..., they held property in Tedstone Delamere that included Winley. The total tax raised for the parish was 6s. Underneath the Tedstone Delamere assessment is written a note that John Wysham died less than a week later.

In Tedstone Delamere, Assessments for the Benevolence of 1545 were made on Thomas Wysham at 20s., John Elte at 8s., Richard Dee at 10s. and Robert Thurston, the rector, at 6s. 8d. (Thomas Wysham had succeeded to the lordship.) We know from the court rolls that John Elte held one of the farms at Woodend and Richard Dee farmed Whitwoods Croft, that lost farm of 1 virgate in the north-east of the parish.

The 1543 Subsidy Act, made in anticipation of a payment in 1545, produced an assessment of 21 taxpayers for Tedstone Delamere:

> John Calowhill and William Lane were each assessed at £9. 18d.
> John Pers and John Stalleward were each assessed at £ £7. 14d.
> Edmund Perkins and Edward Ingram were each assessed at £6. 12d.
> Richard and John Irelond, John Baker and John Thyllam were each assessed at £4. 4d.
> Isatta Calowhill, Richard and John Capper were each assessed at 60s. 3d.
> John Pers junior, William Elte sen, William Elte and Thomas Irelond were each assessed at 40s. 2d.
> John Wall, John Fawkener, Anna Tyle and William Lawton were each assessed at 20s 1d.

It will be noticed that the rate goes up in regular stages suggesting that a banding was in place. A total of 10s. 11d. tax was raised and all 21 were taxed on goods rather than land or wages so it seems fair to presume that they were people in business on their own account *ie* farmers, smallholders or craftsmen etc. 23 people were taxed in Whitbourne, all on goods, raising 20s. 9d. as they were in Tedstone Wafre where 7 were taxed raising 2s. 2d.

We have snatches of information about some of these people from other records: John Pers died in 1558 leaving 4d. to the church of Hereford, 2s. to Tedstone Delamere church, 20s. each to three sons and everything else to his son John; presumably he was the John Pers junior mentioned in the assessment above. Edmund Perkins farmed Winley (he followed the Callowhills), William Lane farmed Tipton which always seems to have been one of the largest farms in the parish. Richard and John Irelond's name is remembered to this day by a property near Hedge House called Ireland Cottage. The Cappers farmed Pixhill and later also farmed the Line House and Winley. William Elte farmed at Woodend. We do not know why Thomas Wysham has been omitted from this last assessment.

The Herefordshire Muster Book of 1542

Because of trouble with Scotland, the king ordered noblemen and leading gentry to muster their own men in their lordships. Negotiations with Scotland failed and the Scots attacked but were thoroughly beaten at Solway Moss on 23rd November where it was likely that the Herefordshire men fought. The 'able' men were:

Tedstarne Delamere & Tedstarn Wafur

B	Thomas Wyseham harness for on man on fote
B	Edmunde Perkyns
B	John Pers
B	John Callowhyll
B	William Loue
A	Richard Dee
A	John Baker
B	John Wall
B	Thomas Elte
b	John Elte junior
A	John Fawkener
B	John Chamberlen
A	Harry Deykyn
A	Richard Loche
A	John Heycokes
A	William Prynse

Abilaments &c
Ha   3pr;   Ho   2

Abbreviations   A = Archer;
B or b = Billman;
Ha = harness;
Ho = horse

Weapons & Armour

bill (usually) a long pole ending in a spike, a concave axe and a spear-point
Thomas Wyseham's harness for a man on foot was his armour
The Abilaments list 3 pairs of armour [or sets?] and 2 horses

The first 11 names are virtually the same as in the Tedstone Delamere 1543 Subsidy Assessment above. The William *Loue* must surely be the William Lane [from Tipton] in the Subsidy Assessment. John Chamb(er)layn and a Richard Deykyns are listed in a Subsidy Assessment for Tedstone Wafre.

APPENDIX C - Probate and Administrative Acts

A recent book by M. A. Faraday, *Calendar of Probate and Administration Acts 1407 – 1581*[i], has provided some very early names of people in the parish. This book lists the names of those featuring in the surviving probate and administration acts recorded in the court books of the diocese for the period 1407 – 1550. This court was mainly an itinerant court, making several circuits of the diocese each year and providing day sessions in each of the thirteen deaneries. Probate cases were usually heard in the deanery where the testator died; presumably it was difficulties of travel which dictated this. The interest of the court was of course in obtaining the fines and fees which resulted from hearing the cases and probate cases were very profitable. The law required that an inventory and valuation should be made on the goods and chattels of the deceased. The fine was based on the value of the deceased's chattels given in the inventories. If the executors failed to come to the court or provide an inventory, there were dire penalties which could be being banned from attending church or even excommunication. The penalties were sometimes commuted to a money fine. The court books are written in abbreviated medieval Latin and entries in the Calendar, a monumental work indeed, are translated and standardised in a concise form so that we can understand them. The first line of the list below, after translation would read something like this: 'On that day and in that place was granted the administration of the goods of John Taylor alias Capryk late rector of the parish of Tedstone Delamere deceased to Alice the mother of the deceased.'

The calendar gives us the following names:

> Sir John Taylor alias Capryk late rector of Tedstone Delamere; E: Alice his mother; [1442 – 3]
> Alice Hunt of Tedstone Delemar; E: John her husband; [1479 – 1480]
> John Elte of Teddiston Dalamare; E: Issabel his R & Thomas his son; [1481 – 2]
> Isobel Hunt of Teddistarn Dalamare; E: John her husband; [1486 – 7]
> William Capper of Teddystarn Delamar; E: Isobel his R; [1490 – 1]
> Alice Calohyll of Teddistarn Delamar; A: …; Bromyard 11th Feb. [1491/2]
> John Hunt senior Alice his wife of Tedston Delamar; A: John Hid of Sucley: 12th Apr. [1490 – 1]
> John Hunt of Tedistarn; E: John Hid of Sucley in Worc. Diocese; [1490 – 1]
> Sir Thomas Walcker of Tedeston Dalamar; A: Thomas Wysham is his ? chief man [1534 – 1536]
> Richard Capper of Teddeston Dalamar; E: John his NS. I: £3 2s. 6½ d. Bromyard 28th April [1546 – 7]
>
> A: administrator
> E: executor
> NS: the natural son of the deceased
> R: the relict of the deceased
> I: inventory of the deceased's goods attached to the will

It is noted that four of the above entries are for the name of Hunt. A John Elte is mentioned in Henry VIII's Taxes, perhaps a grandson of the John Elte listed above and Alice Calohyll must surely be the same family as John and Isatta of that name who were similarly taxed in 1545.

APPENDIX D Patrons & Incumbents

Patron	Incumbent	A.D.
Sir William de Caple	William de la Mare	1275
	Eustace de Chandos	d 1348
Richard de Bagynden	John de la Mare, clerk	1349
Richard de Bagynden	Llewellyn de Blakebache acolyte	1350
?	John de Salghale	resigned 1351
John de Wysham	Thomas de Hylycombe of Odycombe	1351
John de Wysham	William de la More	1354
John de Wysham	Hugh Hawkeleye	1366
Elizabeth Wysham	John Schaull	1424
Elizabeth Wysham	John Smyth, chaplain	1435
Bishop (by lapse)	William Yoppe, chaplain	1441
?	John Taylor alias Caprick#	1442
Richard Wysham	John Chalener, chaplain	1448
Richard Wysham	John Mote, rector of Upper Whitney (exchange)	1462
John Wysham	John Shery	1469
Bishop (hac vice)	John Seabrome*	1476
John Wysham	Thomas Mason	1510
John Wysham	Thomas Walker	1513
Thomas Wysham	Robert Thurstone	1536
Thomas Wysham	Robert Barett	1554
Thomas Wysham	George Longmare	1556
George Wysham	Henry Wellington	1573
?	James Parry, Prebendary	1631
?	John Baker M.A.	1671

\# M.A.Faraday, *Calendar of Probate and Administration Acts 1407 – 1550 in the Consistory Court of the Bishops of Hereford* (2009)

* John Seabrome was Vicar of St Peter's, Hereford. He had dispensation to hold more than one benefice

Patron	Incumbent	A.D.
Robert Mason	Thomas Doleman M.A.	1671
Robert Mason	George Hay M.A.	1691
Elizabeth Hay, widow	John Hay M.A	1729
Ann Hay, spinster, with consent of guardian, Charles Holland	Richard Wilding M.A.	1739
Ditto	John Holland M.A.	1744
Ann Hay	John Landon B.A.	1749
Wakeman Long	Thomas Cox	1782
Thomas Cox, clerk & Barbara his wife	P.G Tomkins, LL.D.	1790
Richard Blakemere	Luke Booker LL.D.	1805
Brasenose College, Oxford	John Darcy	1812
Ditto	Edward Hartopp Grove M.A.	1843
Ditto	Isaac Gregory Smith M.A.	1854
Ditto	Fredk. Simcock Lea M.A.	1873
Ditto	George Wm. Sandford M.A.	1894
Ditto	Charles Williams	1897
	(Evan James appointed priest-in-charge of merged parishes of Tedstone Delamere & Edvin Loach with Tedstone Wafre)	1939
Ditto	Donald Edward Jones, rector of b(above	1947
Tom Barneby	Frederick Massey - ditto	1955
	Leigh Simpson - ditto	1960
	Frank Cherrington - ditto and priest-in-charge of Upper Sapey & Wolferlow	1968
	Robert Colby, rector of Tedstone I Delamere with Tedstone Wafre, Upper Sapey, Whitbourne & Wolferlow	1980
	David Paul Howell - ditto	1997

Sources: The Bishops' Registers
    J. Duncumb, Collections, Vol II, 200
      A. T. Bannister, *Diocese of Hereford Institutions (AD 1539-1900)*

APPENDIX E

A Lewne made by the overseers of the Poore of the parish of Tedstone Delamere for collecting Money for the poore at 2d in the pound to be collected monthly as oft as needful in the year 1739 Comensing the 29th Oct[i]

	£	s	d		£	s	d
The Rectory	0	04	00	Widow Philpots	0	00	02
The Lindhouse [Line House]	0	02	02	Held Cross	0	00	01½
The Court	0	04	02	Richard Brasier	0	00	02
The Mill land	0	00	06	Norgroves	0	00	03
Mr Roberts [Tipton?]	0	04	00	The Frith [Thrift]	0	00	10
The Hedge House	0	03	08	Peter Branch	0	00	03
Farn [illeg.] Meadow	0	00	06	Tidbatch	0	00	07
Pixall	0	01	06				
Winley	0	01	06	Totall	2	03	07½
The Homs	0	01	06				
Thos Brasier	0	01	06				
Greys Farm	0	01	02				
Ryley	0	01	04	I alow of this to be just			
Aron Cook [Woodhall]	0	01	11	Arundel Roberts - Churchwarden			
Woodend	0	03	00	Peter Broome - Overseer			
Mr Cooks land	0	02	00				
Mr Wheelers [Woodham]	0	01	09				
Impey	0	00	10				
Primrose	0	01	07				
Wm Caswall [Horners Mill]	0	00	10				
Thos Norman [Gate House]	0	00	10				
Mazer	0	00	05				
John Price	0	00	05				
Mr Crees [Burbage]	0	00	04				
Doon	0	00	03				
Wm Acton	0	00	02				

Wee do alow this to be just
Richard Brasier
John Huck
E Price
Wm Chrees

---

[i] Birmingham Archives, poor rate, 1739

NOTES AND REFERENCES

Abbreviations

B&DLHC	Bromyard and District Local History Centre
HRO	Herefordshire Record Office
TNA	National Archives
RCHME	Royal Commission on Historical Monuments, England, Herefordshire East, Vol. 2, (1932), now English Heritage NMR
TWNFC	Transactions of the Woolhope Naturalists' Field Club
VCH	Victoria County History, Worcestershire

Notes and References

Introduction. Early Beginnings

1. I am indebted to Rosemary Keep who has generously allowed me to make full use of her unpublished undergraduate project, 'Parish Survey, Tedstone Delamere and Tedstone Wafer'
2. Phyllis Williams, *Whitbourne A Bishop's Manor* (1979), 14
3. Phyllis Williams, *Avenbury and the Ruined Church of St Mary* (2000), 11
4. Jean Hopkinson, *Little Cowarne, A Herefordshire Village* (1983), 14
5. P. D. Williams, 'Manor and Manor Foreign' in J. Hillaby & E Pearson (eds.) *Bromyard a Local History* (1970), 29. One of the Bromyard common fields was called Pleggenyat in 1575, The corruption of the name to Flaggoners Green is confirmed by title deeds: B&DLHC, abstracted deeds of Northfields, Avenbury, provenance unknown
6. Bruce Coplestone-Crow, *Herefordshire Place-Names* (1989)
7. Ed. Frank and Caroline Thorn (eds), *Domesday Book, Herefordshire* (1983), 2, 3; 25, 8; 10, 68. I am grateful to Bruce Coplestone-Crow for his unpublished research: The latest edition of DB for Herefordshire Thorn (ed) (1983), 25.8 note) seems to doubt whether Gilbert fitz Thorold's *Chetestor* was at Tedstone. However, the fact that it is annotated *Ketestorna* in HDB (p67: this form accords very well with the form *Kedestorhne* recorded in the Curia Regis Rolls for 1199: RCR iii, 174) and that in 1243 there were 2 hides (the DB assessment) at a *Thoddesthorne la Mare* (Fees, 806), makes the identification with Tedstone – and Tedstone Delamere in particular – virtually certain. Fairly certainly, also, the bishop's estate of *Tedesthorne* was at Tedstone Delamere. It is said in DB that the bishop's manor here and at three other places 'paid tax with Bishop Walter before 1066' (i.e. 1061 – 66). No other details are given for them and the implication is that though they belonged to the bishop they had been in the hands of other men since the Conquest. This supposition is borne out by a list of hides in Herefordshire drawn up at a date subsequent to DB and included with the material bound up with Balliol MS 350 (HDB 77). The list says that four men have the four estates *de qua geldabat cum episcopo* listed in f181b. Three of these tally with the place-names and hideages given in DB but the fourth does not. This says that Gilbert fitz Thorold now has 2½ hides at *Salberga* (Sawbury near Bromyard) that paid tax with the bishop, rather than 2½ hides at Tedestherne as DB says. However, since the three other place-names and hideages tally – and the hideage at least tallies in this case – it seems likely that the writer has simply got the place-name wrong. I therefore think that the bishop's manor lay adjacent to Gilbert fitz Thorold's in Tedstone Delamere and had come into his hands since the Conquest.
8. Information from Bruce Coplestone-Crow
9. S. C. Stanford, *The Archaeology of the Welsh Marches* (1980)
10. D. Sylvester, *The Rural Landscape of the Welsh Borderland*, 1969 quoted by R. Keep, *Loc. Cit.*
11. HRO, A100, manorial records
12. R. Keep, *Loc. Cit.*
13. Eve McLaughlin, *Manorial Records* (1996), 30

Chapter 1

1. Edna D. Pearson, 'The Parish Church', in J. Hillaby & E. Pearson (eds) *Bromyard: a Local History* (1970), 5
2. Allan Wyatt's manuscript for his forthcoming history of Edvin Loach
3. Information from Tim Bridges
4. Tim Bridges, *Churches of Worcestershire* (2005), 113
5. St Bede's *Ecclesiastical History of the English people* (Book 1)
6. H. M & J. Taylor, *Anglo-Saxon Architecture* II (1965), 607- 608
7. H. M. Taylor, *Anglo-Saxon Architecture*, Vol III (1978)
8. A. Brooks & N. Pevsner (eds), *The Buildings of England. Herefordshire* (2nd ed, 2012), 621-2
9. Information from Tim Bridges

10 H. M. Taylor, 839, 863
11 Archaeology by Archaeological Investigations Ltd of Hereford. Report by A J Walker, RCD Radio Carbon Dating, The Old Stables, East Locking, Wantage
12 Sarah Robinson, 'Rediscovering the Past in the Present' in *The Churches Conservation Trust, Review and Report* (1997-1998)
13 *V.C.H.* v4, Wiliam Page, J. W. Willis-Bund (eds) (1924), 328-331
14 J. Hillaby, 'The Early Church in Herefordshire: Columban and Roman' in Malpas & others (eds) *The Early Church in Herefordshire* Leominster History Society Study Group (2001), 64
15 *Ibid.*
16 *RCHME*
17 *Ibid.*
18 J. Duncumb, *Collections towards the history and antiquities of the county of Hereford* (1812), II, 92
19 William J. Dohar, *The Black Death and Pastoral Leadership* (1995), 46
20 *Register of Bishop Trillek,* 375
21 *Register of Bishop Trillek,* 383
22 *Register of Bishop Trillek,* 385
23 *Register of Bishop Orleton*, II, 390
24 *Register of Bishop Thomas Charltone*, 72,
25 Wyatt, as in note 2
26 HRO, A100/279, agreement concerning small tithes
27 J. H. Bettey, *Church and Parish, A guide for Local Historians* (1987), 114
28 W. E. Tate, *The Parish Chest* (1983), 126
29 HRO, Tedstone Delamere glebe terrier
30 HRO, HD4/1/158, Tedstone Delamere Acts of Office, 1600-1610. I am grateful to Sue Hubbard for sending me a translation of this document
31 HRO, will of George Wysham, 1597
32 W. E. Tate, 67 - 69
33 Hereford Cathedral Archives, 6 A VI, *A Puritan's Survey of the Ministry in the County of Hereford* (1642)
34 HRO, A100/277-297, papers relating to glebe exchange
35 HRO, A100/277, lease of rectory and tithes
36 HRO, A100/278-291, papers concerning agreements over tithes due to the Rev P G Tomkins, 1792

Chapter II
1 F. & C. Thorn (eds), *Domesday Book, Herefordshire* (1983), 2, 3; 10, 68; quoted by Bruce Coplestone-Crow
2 Coplestone-Crow, *Place-Names of Herefordshire* (1989), 188
3 I am indebted to Bruce Coplestone-Crow for information on the early history of the manor and a number of the following references marked (BC-C) are his
4 Text on a board in Clifton church
5 *RCHME,* surveyor's notes
6 *Inquisitions Post Mortem*, Henry VII, ii, no 373 (BC-C)
7 Pleas, ii, no 3032 (BC-C)
8 *Register of Bishop Swinfield*, 308
9 Taxatio. 173 (BC-C)
10 John Duncumb, *Collections towards the History and Antiquities of the County of Herefordshire,* Vol II (1812), 200
11 HRO, A100/172, abstract of Mr. George Webb's title to the manor of Tedstone Delamere
12 *Feudal Aids*, ii, 384 (BC-C)
13 Tim Bridges, 71
14 Jabez Allies, *The British, Roman, and Saxon antiquities and folklore of Worcestershire* (1852), 215-253
15 Calendar of Charter Rolls, vol. IV, 1327-41
16 J. Severn Walker, *Architectural Sketches, Ecclesiastical, Secular and Domestic – Worcestershire and its Borders, with historical and descriptive notes* (1862-63), 11 & 14
17 HRO, 'Swithun Butterfield's Survey', quoted in Phyllis Williams, *Whitbourne, A Bishop's Manor* (1979), 37
18 Jennifer Weale, *A History of Bredenbury and its Landed Estate* (1997), 33
19 HRO, A100/81, court roll, 1545. I am grateful to Sue Hubbard for an explanation of the meaning of 'bounds and meres'
20 M. A. Faraday, *Herefordshire Militia Assessments of 1663* (1972)
21 HRO, will of George Wysham, 1597
22 TNA, C142/300/175, *Inquisition Post Mortem*, 1616/17, Chancery Records
23 HRO, HD4/1/158, Tedstone Delamere Acts of Office, 1600-1601

NOTES AND REFERENCES

24   TNA, PCC will of Elizabeth Cresswell, 1645
25   HRO, A100/162-172, manor of Tedstone Delamere, title deeds
26   State Papers (Domestic) Chas. I., Addenda. p751
27   HRO, will of Mary Marston, 1673
28   Duncumb, 201
29   *Ibid.*

Chapter III

1   M. A. Faraday, *Herefordshire Taxes in the Reign of Henry VIII* (2005)
2   M. A. Faraday, *The Herefordshire Musters of 1539 and 1542* (2012), 157
3   M. A. Faraday, *Calendar of Probate and Administration Acts 1407 – 158* (2008)
4   HRO, A100, Tedstone Delamere court rolls; I am greatly indebted to Sue Hubbard, former manager of Herefordshire Record Office, who has most generously and painstakingly translated nearly all the surviving Latin court rolls for Tedstone Delamere
Books that I have used: Eve McLaughlin, *Manorial Records;* N. W. Alcock, *Old Title Deeds ;* Dennis Stuart, *Manorial Records (1992)*
5   HRO, will of Edward Ingram, 1556
6   HRO, A100/74
7   HRO, A100/76
8   HRO, A100/88
9   HRO, A100/116a
10   HRO, A100/105
11   *Ibid.*
12   HRO, A100/115
13   Whitbourne Estate records kept at the Dial House, Whitbourne, deeds of the Thrift Farm
14   HRO, A100/85
15   *Ibid.*
16   HRO, A100/74
17   HRO, A100/113
18   HRO, A100/78
19   Victoria County History, Lower Sapey, P.C.C., 28 Home
20   *Inquisition Post Mortem*, Henry VII, II, 232-3 quoted in Phyllis Williams, *Bromyard, Minster, Manor & Town* (1987), 95
21   As in note 18
22   HRO, A100/98
23   HRO, A100/97
24   HRO, A100/81
25   There is a field called Hoarstone, shared between Bishopstone and Bridge Sollars, which had mere stones, presumably as boundary markers, information from Sue Hubbard; see John Field, *A History of English Field-Names* (1993), 146
26   HRO, A100/122
27   As in note 6
28   HRO, A100/112
29   HRO, A100/114
30   John Duncumb, *Collections towards the History and Antiquities of the County of Hereford*, Part 1 of Vol. II (1812), 195
31   A history collated by members of the Saltmarshe & District Women's Institute, 1953 - 77
32   As in note 8
33   HRO, A100/79
34   HRO, A100/126
35   M. A. Faraday, *Herefordshire Militia Assessments of 1663* (1972)
36   *V.C.H. Worcs.* Nash, *Hist. of Worcs.* I (DATE?), 247
37   HRO, Hearth Tax records; copies are in B&DLHC
38   M. A. Faraday, 'The Hearth Tax in Herefordshire', *TWNFC* (1973), 82
39   Ann Whiteman, *The Compton Census of 1676* (1986), 261
40   Information supplied by Allan Wyatt
41   HRO, Tedstone Delamere wills and inventories; a small number of PCC wills have been found in the National Archives on line; I am most grateful to Polly Rubery who has transcribed some of the more difficult wills
42   TNA, PCC will of John Callowhill of Worcester, 1573

43 HRO, Q/SO/3, Quarter Sessions papers, quoted in Phyllis Williams, *Avenbury and the ruined church of St Mary* (2000), 194

Chapter IV
1   It seems that Duncumb was in error in writing that Robert Mason was succeeded by his son William in 1684, who in turn was succeeded by his son Richard in 1693, see Appendix A
2   HRO, A100/162-172, manor of Tedstone Delamere, title deeds
3   1840 - 41, Tithe Survey
4   John Field, *A History of English Field-Names* (1993), 136
5   HRO, A100/131
6   HRO, A100/136
7   HRO, A100/140
8   HRO, wills and inventories
9   HRO, Q/Rel, land tax
10 John West, *Village Records* (1962), 199
11 HRO, A100/299
12 James M. Gaynor, Nancy L. Hagedorn, *Tools: working wood in eighteenth-century America* (1997), 4
13 Birmingham City Archives, directory information
14 Deeds of the properties in the east of the parish were found amongst the Whitbourne Estate records kept at the Dial House, Whitbourne, by kind permission of Mr. and Mrs. Chris Evans; the deeds of Pixhill, Grays Farm and Cullets House are stored at Herefordshire Record Office
15 HRO, A100/300
16 TNA, PCC will of James Moore of Shelsley Beauchamp
17 *Ibid*

Chapter V
1   Eilert Ekwall, *The Oxford Dictionary of English Place-Names* (1960), 404
2   John Duncumb, *Collections towards the History and Antiquities of the County of Hereford,* Vol. II (1812), 196, 197
3   Jennifer Westwood, *Albion. A guide to legendary Britain* (1986), 262
4   SMR, Herefordshire Through Time
5   TNA, *Thwypelton* 1292 Assize Roll, JUST1/302 m.8d [Wm de - , pledge of Thos. Heymok, re Bromyard] information supplied by John Freeman
6   HRO, A100/172, abstract of title to the manor of Tedstone Delamere,
7   HRO, A100/76, court roll, 1440
8   HRO, A100/98, court roll, 1588
9   J.W.Tonkin, 'Tipton Hall, Tedstone Delamere' in *Journal 10, of the Bromyard & District Local History Society*; also published in *Bromyard Round and About,* Ed. D. Waller, (1991), 59 - 61
10 B&DLHC, A25, Tipton deeds
11 John Field, *A History of English Field-Names* (1993), 176; Janet Cooper, Sylvia Pinches & Joan Grundy, 'Deadwoman and Deadman',in *Friends of Hereford Record Office Newsletter*, No. 91, January 2012
12 HRO, inventory & will of Elizabeth Lane, 1714
13 HRO, inventory of Thomas Lane, 1731
14 J. W. Tonkin, as in note 9
15 HRO, Q/Rel, land tax records
16 HRO, A100/172, abstract of Mr. George Webb's title to the manor of Tedstone Delamere
17 S. C. Stanford, *The Archaeology of the Welsh Marches* (1980)
18 Clarissa Dixon Wright & Johnny Scott, *The Game Cook Book* (2012), 98
19 Field, 141 - 2
20 Feet of F. Worcs. Mich. 21 Chas. II quoted in VCH, Worcs, Lower Sapey
21 Recov. R. Hil.29 & 30 Chas. II, m. 167, conveyance of the advowson of Shelsley Beauchamp quoted in VCH, Worcs, Lower Sapey,
22 HRO, A100/278-291, papers concerning agreements over tithes due to the Rev. P. G. Tomkins, 1792; HRO, as in note 15
23 *Burkes Peerage*. Bill Pardoe, *Witley Court: Witley Court and Church: Life and Luxury in a great country house* (Peter Huxtable Designs Ltd 1986), 6
24 HRO, A100/131, a list of the inhabitants of Tedstone Delamere
25 HRO, as in note 15
26 *Thomas Foley, 4th Baron Foley – Wikipedia the free encyclopedia,* related web pages

NOTES AND REFERENCES

27 HRO, Saltmarshe Estate papers awaiting cataloguing; B&DLHC, Tedstone Delamere tithe map. A small part of Tedstone Delamere did belong to Lord Ward in 1840 (see page 112)
28 HRO, CB 26/1, sale particulars
29 HRO, B54/1, plans of Saltmarshe Estate, 1841-2
30 Field, 146
31 A. H. Smith, *Place Names of Gloucestershire,* Part 3, Lower Severn Valley & Forest of Dean, 231, 227
32 Field, 246
33 Old Series Map, 149, Cassini (Hereford & Leominster) 1:50,000
34 B&DLHC, A25/5, deeds of Held Cross (Hill Cross)
35 HRO, as in note 15
36 HRO, A63/1, manorial records of Bromyard and Bromyard Foreign
37 TNA, Assize Rolls m.52, information from John Freeman
38 I am grateful to John Freeman for giving this information on the early meaning of 'Line House'. He also says that there seems to be an exact parallel in Surrey: Lynehouse Farm (Lingfield par.) was *le Lynde* in 1418 and was probably the home of *John de la Linde* in 1270
39 *Inquisitions Post Mortem,* 13 Hen.VII, 232/3
40 TNA, Chancery Proceedings, 8th February 1622/23
41 M. A. Faraday, *Herefordshire Militia Assessments* (1972), 43
42 B&DLHC, hearth tax records
43 HRO, AJ 49/26 - 28, deeds of the Line House
44 HRO, A100/167, deeds of Tedstone Court & Manor
45 I*bid.*
46 HRO, A100/172, abstract of title to the manor of Tedstone Delamere. I am grateful to John Freeman for information on the meaning of the place-name 'Pixhill'
47 HRO, A100/80, court roll, 1550
48 HRO, A100/98, 97, court rolls, 1588 & 89
49 *RCHME,* surveyor's record sheet
50 HRO, A100/174 – 185, Pixhill deeds
51 Eve McLaughlin, *Manorial Records* (1996), 4
52 HRO, A100/75, manorial records
53 The name, *Team Side,* also occurs in Whitbourne where the property is beside R. Teme but there is no reason to think that this was the Whitbourne property
54 TNA, Assize Roll m.52., 1292. The reference is supplied by John Freeman
55 I am grateful to John Freeman for information regarding this place-name
56 HRO, A100/74, court roll, 1428
57 HRO, A100/77, court roll, 1451
58 HRO, A100/79, court roll, 1551
59 *RCHME,* surveyor's record sheet
60 B&DLHC, Tedstone Delamere parish registers
61 HRO, A100/166-167, deeds of Tedstone Court & Manor
62 TNA, PCC will of John Chrees of Winley, proved 19th May 1815
63 I*bid.*
64 HRO, A100/145-159, papers concerning chief rents & heriots
65 A Plan of the Tedstone Court Estate, 1824. The plan is in the possession of Gail Belville of Pixhill
66 Pleas, ii, no 3032, quoted by Bruce Copplestone-Crow, who also suggests that Gatley was probably held by *Eliam filius Willelmi* who appeared in 1200 as Thomas de Mara's essoiner in the case with Jordan de Mara. He is probably the *Elye* in whose demesne lands Great Malvern Priory had 2/3 tithes (see Chapter I, p...).
67 VCH, Worcs, Lower Sapey, PCC, 28 Home
68 HRO, A100/79, court roll, 1551. The name 'Gatteley' is likely to be the 'Catley' mentioned in an Assize Roll, 1292, see note 54
69 Information supplied by Donald Boughton
70 HRO, K68/43, deeds of property near the Hedge House

Chapter VI
1 TNA, PCC will of James Moore of Shelsley Beauchamp, 1805
2 TNA, PCC will of Edward Moore of Shelsley Beauchamp, 1838
3 In 1297, the king required the Sheriff of Herefs. to let Robert de Plessy have seizing of a messuage & 5 acres of land in Tedstone Delamere held by Adam de *Fevre,* who was outlawed for felony [Close Rolls 1296 – 1302, 19; Ipm (1st Series, no 71).] Could 'Freeth' be a corruption of 'Fevre'?
4 Whitbourne Estate records kept at the Dial House; I am indebted to Ann and Chris Evans who generously allowed me access, & also to Phyllis Williams who has made abstracts of most of the deeds & these are now stored at the B&DLHC

5   HRO, A100/76, court roll, 1443
6   HRO, A100/83, court roll, 1534
7   B&DLHC, Hearth Tax, 1664
8   Birmingham City Archives, Barnard 43, list of Tedstone Delamere ratepayers for relief of the poor, 1739
9   See note 4
10 HRO, land tax Q/Rel
11 B&DLHC, tithe survey and 1841 census
12 HRO, A100/166-167, lease & release of Tedstone Court including lordship of the manor, 1713
13 I*bid.*
14 Jennifer Weale, *A History of Bredenbury and its Landed Estate* (1997), 2
15 HRO, A100/88, court roll, 1559
16 HRO, A100/101, court roll, 1621
17 HRO, A100/125, court roll, 1656
18 HRO, A100/124, court roll, 1656
19 Worcester Record Office, Quarter Sessions Rolls, 1/1/66/6
20 HRO, A100/166-167, Tedstone Court deeds
21 As in note 11
22 As in note 20
23 John Duncumb, *Collections towards the History and Antiquities of the County of Hereford* II (1812), 202
24 B&DLHC, 'Recollections of Tedstone Delamere 1873 – 1894' by Mrs. Elizabeth Mary Wright, daughter of the Rev. Frederick Simcock Lea 'who died 1893 beloved by all'
25 As in note 8
26 HRO, A100 Manorial records
27 M. A. Faraday, *Herefordshire Militia Assessments of 1663* (1972), 43; also B&DLHC, Hearth Tax 1664
28 John Field, *A History of English Field-Names* (1993), 67
29 B&DLHC, tithe survey and 1841 census
30 *RCHME*, surveyor's record cards for Tedstone Delamere
31 As in note 10
32 B&DLHC, tithe survey and 1841 census
33 HRO, A100/85, court roll, 1532
34 HRO, A100/88, court roll, 1558
35 HRO, A100/166-167, deeds of Tedstone Court & Manor
36 I am grateful to John Freeman for information on this place-name
37 HRO, A100/166-167, Tedstone Court deeds
38 As in note 8
39 HRO, will of Thomas Brazier, 1742
40 Whitbourne Estate records, as in note 4
41 HRO, A100/85, court roll, 1532
42 Field, 96
43 Whitbourne Estate records, as in note 4
44 I am grateful to Dr. Katherine Lack for information about the Winwoods
45 HRO, A100/120, court roll
46 HRO, A100/166-167, deeds
47 Rosemary Keep, 'Parish survey, Tedstone Delamere and Tedstone Wafre', project undertaken when an archaeology undergraduate

Chapter VII
1   B&DLHC, Tedstone Delamere parish registers
2   TNA, PCC will of James Moore of Shelsley Beauchamp, 1805
3   HRO, A100/302, marriage settlement
4   Information supplied by Nuala Cockburn whose husband is the great-great-grandson of Eliza Lane, the fifth child of Richard and Maria Wight
5   HRO, as in note 3
6   B&DLHC, H73, deeds of dental surgery, 32 High Street
7   Duncan James, *Bromyard, Herefordshire. An analysis of the historic fabric of fifty buildings in the central area of the town* (2009), 81
8   Jennifer Weale, *A History of Bredenbury and its Landed Estate* (1997), 78
9   HRO, MS/30B/6, Tedstone Court sale particulars, 1908
10 HRO, A100/303, marriage settlement
11 B&DLHC, censuses

NOTES AND REFERENCES

12 HRO, A100/144, file of papers concerning chief rents
13 *Ibid*
14 HRO, A100/145-159 papers concerning enquiries relating to chief rents & heriots arising from Winley
15 *Ibid*
16 R. B. Pugh, *How to Write a Parish History* (1954), 61, 68
17 A larger ram, now in the Hereford Waterworks Museum, was installed in 1929. This ram was a Blake with an 8 inch drive pipe laid half a mile from the stream to achieve the right fall. The spring water fell 90ft. to the ram & was then pumped to the reservoir 400ft. higher. In 1930, there was a storm which washed away the dam. The ram was not used again
18 HRO, Tedstone Court sale particulars, 1908; Hereford Waterworks Museum, paper entitled 'Tedstone Court Estate Water Supply' by Richard Bellville
19 B&DLHC, D9/203, Mrs. Elizabeth Mary Wright, 'Recollections of Tedstone Delamere, 1873 to 1894', 12
20 Edna Pearson, *Two Churches: Two Communities* (1993), 47

Chapter VIII
1 John Duncumb, *Collections towards the History and Antiquities of the County of Hereford,* Vol. II (1812), 198
2 www. Blackcountrygenealogyandfamilyhistory.co.uk
3 *Burke's Peerage & Baronetage*, 106th edition, 691
4 B&DLHC, note in Tedstone Delamere parish register
5 HRO, diocesan records, Annual Box, 1845
6 *Ibid*
7 Roy Strong, *A Little History of the English Country Church* (2007), 208
8 *Ibid*
9 Hereford City Library, Pilley Collection, album of watercolours by C. F. Walker
10 John Leonard (ed) *Sir Stephen Glynne's Church Notes for Herefordshire,* with water-colours by Charles F. Walker, (2006), xi
11 HRO, BO41/9, Tedstone Delamere churchwardens' accounts, 1842 - 95
12 Frederick Sharpe F. S. A., *The Church Bells of Herefordshire* (1972), Vol. IV, 497
13 B&DLHC, D9/203, a typed manuscript entitled 'Recollections of Tedstone Delamere - 1873 to 1894' by Mrs. Elizabeth Wright, daughter of the Rev. Frederick Simcock-Lea who died 1893 'beloved by all'
14 Berkeley Scudamore Stanhope, *The Church Plate of the County of Hereford* (1903), 166 - 68
15 As in note 11
16 The late Barry Phillips pointed out to us the holes which he had spotted, now filled with neat dowels, in some of the pews towards the west end of the church
17 As in note 11
18 Herefordshire Through Time, SMR Number 30812, Monument Detail,
19 Herefordshire Federation of Women's Institutes, *The Herefordshire Village Book*
20 D. M. Annett, *The Churches of the Bromyard Deanery, An Informal Guide* (revised edition 2003), 43
21 A. Brooks & N. Pevsner (eds) *The Buildings of England. Herefordshire* (2nd ed, 2012), 622
22 HRO, CL19/3, Terrier & Inventory 1897
23 Story told me by Sue Haffenden, née Bellville
24 I am grateful to Allan Wyatt for this information
25 An open letter to parishioners, neighbours and friends with an appeal for the restoration. Further information is supplied by Churchwarden Mrs Kathleen Harris

Chapter IX
1 To avoid repetition, unless otherwise mentioned, all information regarding land ownership in this chapter is taken from the Whitbourne Estate records generously made available for my inspection at the Dial House, Whitbourne by Anne and Chris Evans. I have been much helped by detailed abstracts of these made by Phyllis Williams and deposited in the Bromyard and District Local History Centre
2 B&DLHC, tithe survey 1840/41
3 Hereford City Library, LC Deed 3859, Borbach
4 TNA, PCC will of Charles Edward Moore, 1847
5 Books used: Joan Thirsk, *Alternative Agriculture, A History from the Black Death to the Present Day* (1997); Pamela Horn, *Labouring Life in the Victorian Countryside* (1987)
6 *Ibid* Horn, 259
7 *Royal Commission on Labour: The Agricultural Labourer*, Parliamentary Papers 1893 – 94, XXXV
8 Edward Evans, *Gentleman's Relish* (1963), 3 - 6
9 *Ibid*
10 I am grateful to Ann and Sheila Jones of New House Farm for this information about the water supply

Chapter X

1. HRO, Saltmarshe Estate Survey, 1841/2
2. Whitbourne Estate records at the Dial House, Whitbourne, valuation of E. B. Evans's Tedstone Delamere Estate, 1879; Jennifer Weale, *A History of Bredenbury and its Landed Estate* (1997), chapter VII
3. B&DLHC, F13/22, sale of outlying portions of the Saltmarshe and Clater Estates, 1949. There are errors in the acreages given in this document
4. B&DLHC, D9/203, a typed manuscript entitled 'Recollections of Tedstone Delamere - 1873 to 1894' by Mrs. Elizabeth Wright, daughter of the Rev. Frederick Simcock-Lea who died 1893 'beloved by all'
5. HRO, AJ 49/86
6. Letters in the possession of Kathleen Harris
7. Plan of the Tedstone Court Estate, 1824, in the possession of Gail Bellville
8. Deed in the possession of Gail Bellville
9. Minutes books of the Clifton-on-Teme Hunt, 1920 - 1989
10. 'Sonech', *The North Ledbury, Croome and Clifton-on-Teme Hunts, Official Handbook,* (undated but *c* 1939), 35
11. Clifton-on-Teme Hunt scrap books are in the custody of Francis Lowden, Lower House Farm, Stanford Bishop
12. *Ibid.*
13. *Ibid.*
14. Information from Julian Westwood of Woodhall
15. I am grateful to Jennifer Farmer of Oxhall, Lower Sapey for providing details of land transactions and extracts from the Farmer family history
16. B&DLHC, W.I. History, M33/2, a history compiled by Saltmarshe & District Women's Institute, 1953 – 1977
17. *Ibid.*
18. I thank Harvey Richards of Lower Thrift for these stories
19. Recollections of Robin Evans of Longlands Barn, Whitbourne
20. Information from Roly Powell of Whitbourne
21. B&DLHC, C52, account book of Richard Powell, blacksmith, of Tedstone Delamere (1870s). Mike Roberts of Bringsty, blacksmith, has kindly commented on the account book
22. I am indebted to Roly Powell for his recollections of Lee Lay
23. Joan Thirsk, *Alternative Agriculture, A History* (1997)
24. B&DLHC, A54/43, photocopies of crop returns
25. B&DLHC, D9/318, excise lists of parishes growing hops, copied from the Parliamentary Sessional papers housed in the State paper room at the British Museum by the late Inett Homes

Chapter XI

1. B&DLHC, M32/2, W. I. History
2. Phyllis Williams, *Bromyard: Minster, Manor and Town* (1987), 180
3. *Ibid.*
4. HRO, A100/119, court baron of Robert Mason, 1659
5. HRO, A100/127, ditto, 1713
6. HRO, F44/1, a charity
7. HRO, A100/205 – 246, bundle of papers relating to Pixhill and Greyhouse properties
8. HRO, AP55/23, Poor Widows' Charity
9. HRO, AR90/11 – 12, Avenbury overseers' accounts
10. Jennifer Weale, *The History of Bredenbury and its Landed Estate* (1997), 72
11. Birmingham City Archives, Barnard 43, list of Tedstone Delamere ratepayers for relief of the poor, 1739
12. Worcester Record Office, 1/1/684,685, Worcestershire Quarter Sessions Rolls
13. Saltmarshe Estate records now deposited in the Herefordshire Record Office and awaiting cataloguing; Bromyard Union, extracts from the quarterly abstracts showing the numbers of paupers relieved and the amount of money expended and the balances due to and from the several parishes. Photocopies are to be deposited in the Bromyard Local History Centre
14. B&DLHC, unless particularly mentioned, information is taken from the tithe survey of 1840/41 and the censuses
15. B&DLHC, D9/203, Mrs. E. M. Wright, 'Recollections of Tedstone Delamere, 1873 – 1894'
16. B&DLHC, C52, blacksmith's account book
17. HRO, MS/30B/6, Tedstone Court sale particulars, 1908
18. John Field, *A History of English Field-Names* (1993), 44
19. B&DLHC, A25, deeds of Tipton (including Hill Cross)
20. HRO, A100/166-167, deeds of Tedstone Court & Manor

NOTES AND REFERENCES

21 Copy of Hill Cross deeds in the possession of Mr. & Mrs. Stuart Beare
22 Mrs. E.M. Wright, as in note 15
23 HRO, A100/303, settlement on the marriage of Maria Shelton & Richard Wight, 1809
24 HRO, AJ49/1 – 5, deeds of Lower Cutted House, 1746 - 1854
25 HRO, A100/266 – 276, deeds of cottage called Whitehall
26 HRO, AJ 49/66 – 70, deeds of cottage called Rockmore Castle
27 HRO, A100/83, manorial court roll, 1534
28 HRO, AJ 49/14 – 25, deeds of cottage at Keyhead
29 HRO, AJ 49/58 – 64, deeds of a cottage called Middle Line House
30 B&DLHC, A56/3, *Sale Particulars*, Bentley, Hobbs & Mytton, June 18th 1914
31 Whitbourne Estate records kept at The Dial House, Whitbourne, deeds of Tennolls
32 Birmingham City Archives, as in note 11
33 HRO, LC Deed 3859, Borbach
34 Whitbourne Estate records, deeds of Burbage
35 HRO, Q/Rel., land tax assessments
36 Whitbourne Estate records, declaration of Ben Grubb 1851
37 HRO, A100/118, manorial ourt roll
38 Field, 202
39 B&DLHC, M33/2, a history compiled by Saltmarshe & District Women's Institute, 1953 – 1977
40 Information from Julian Westwood of Woodhall
41 Information from Mrs. Elizabeth Farmer of Oxhall for information regarding property transactions
42 Information supplied by Mrs. Beryl Yates of Woodend
43 B&DLHC, Mrs. E. M. Wright, as in note 15
44 Deborah Waller, 'Various Places of Worship' in Hillaby & Pearson (eds) *Bromyard: A Local History* (1970), 88
45 Duncumb, *Collections towards the History and Antiquities of the County of Hereford*, II (1812), 201
46 W. I. history, as in note 1
47 HRO, AJ 49/13, deeds of a cottage at Whitehall, feoffment, 1826

Chapter XII
1 The parish registers are on microfilm in the Bromyard and District Local History Centre
2 B&DLHC, D9/203, 'Recollections of Tedstone Delamere 1873 – 1894' by Mrs. Elizabeth Mary Wright, daughter of the Preb. Frederick Simcock Lea who died 1893 'beloved by all'
3 B&DLHC, M33/2, a history compiled by Saltmarshe & District Women's Institute, 1953 – 1977
4 B&DLHC, Deanery Magazine
5 B&DLHC, Mrs. E. M. Wright, as in note 2
6 As in note 4
7 Information from Mrs. Evelyn Whistance
8 B&DLHC, *Bromyard News and Record*
9 This and the following two quotations are all from the Deanery Magazine
10 Information supplied by Jan Davis whose grandfather was a gamekeeper living at Whitehall and whose mother attended High Lane School, Tedstone Wafre
11 B&DLHC, W. I. history, as in note 3, the story was apparently told by the pianist at the concert and confirmed by the School Log Book.

Chapter XIII
1 Information from Jane Hawksley, formerly Bellville
2 *Ibid*

Index

Abevan, Richard 40
Acton, Elizabeth 131; John 49, 56, 111; William 56, 79, 94, 131
Adams, William 54
advowson 17, 77, 146
affidavits 163
agricultural wages 171
Aiden, Ann 62; Zacy 62
Aingell, Ann 180; Richard 179; Richard jun. 180
Albright, Bill 227
Alledge 94
Annett, David 157
apples 144
Arden, Robert 49
Arnold's Mill, see under Horner's Mill
Austin, William 163, 169
axe-head, stone 1, 2

Bagyndon, Richard de 17
bailiff 139
Baker, Col. Robert Broome; 183Isobel 99; Richard 51; Rev Slade 80, 99, 178, 221; Thomas 20; William 20, 50
Ballescote 98
baptists 229
Barber, Rev F.H. curate 147
Barcroft, see under Bearcroft
Barnbrook/Barnbrooke, John 101; Joseph 28, 84, 212
Barneby, W.T. 235
Barnes, Anne 99; Christiana/Cristiana 62; 25, 106; Elizabeth 99; Francis 99; John 56, 62, 64-65; 73-74, 79, 98, 106, 108; Mary 99; Richard 57, 58, 98; Rowland 65; Thomas 99, 108; William 65, 99, 108
Bateman/Batman, Frances 124; James 56, 79, 123, 124; John 56; Mr 81
Baugh, Benjamin 80, 81, 228
Baylis children 238
Baylis/Bayliss, James 230; Mr 128; Sarah 124
Bearcroft/Barcroft 51, 132, 133
Beard, Kenneth 198; William 28
Beddinton/Bedington/Bedintun, James 118; John 28, 84, 118; Mr 26
Beeks, Ann 232
bell turret 152
bells 152
Bellville family **241-251**
Bellville, Audrey 189, 245, 248; Emma 241; Ethel 189, 244, 248; Dennis 243, 245; Henry Archibald (Archie) 188, 241, 242, 243, 245, 247; Miles 158, 189, 190, 191, 243, 247, 248; Nan 158, 247, 248; Richard 251; William John 241;
Bemand, George 184
Benbow, Dick 173, 177; John 183; Joyce 176; Mr 192 Mrs 248, 248; Noel 177; Norah 176; Roger 177, 159; Susan 214; Thomas 214; Walter 177, Walter 248
benefice, value of 147
Bennett, George 55
Berrow, Giles 28
Berry, John 84
Best, John 78; 130
Bethels 251
Bevan/Beavan, James 30, 159; Maria 94; William 94, 153
Bine Field 100
Birch, Benjamin 28, 84, 109, 130; Elizabeth 109, 130

Bishop/Bishopp, Sarah 159; Thomas 211
Black Death 16, 38, 39, 44
blackcurrants 187
blacksmith 131, 156, 203, 204, 215, 218; blacksmith's account book 215; forge 218
Blakebache, Llewellen de 17
Blissett, James 94; William 173
Bloomfield, William 227
Booker, Anne 146; Edward 146; Elizabeth 146; memorial 146; Phyllis Ann 146; Rev. Dr Luke 113, **145-146**; Thomas, 113, 146;
Booth, John 228
Boss Croft 98
Boswoode, Anne 64
Boteler, John 89, 90
Bough, Benjamin 24
Boughton, David 183; Donald 182, 183, 238; Ernest 183; Harold 183; Irene 183; Rene 238
boundaries, parish 4, 14
Bowers, Charles 183; Mr 157
Bowling Green 94
Bradford, 245; Joan 49; John 49
Branch, Peter 82
Brasenose College 17, 146
Brasier/Brazier, Ann 132; Martha 28, 84; Richard 79, 80, 117, 131, 222; Sarah 82; Thomas 79-82, 131; Thomas's inventory 132
Brick Cottages 22, 142
brickworks 188
bridges 51
Brierley, Fanny 170
Brierley/Bryells/Bryalls 48, 49, 50, 51, 61, 81, 118
Briscoe, Thomas L. 198;
Broad, John 24
Brompton, Richard 77
Bromyard Union 213, 214
Broome, Peter 80; Rev 84, 85; Rev John 99
Brown, Brown, estate carpenter 245; Mary 220, 148; Mrs, head housemaid 245; William 53
Brucking, Ann 62
Bruton, Isobel 54
Budd, Thomas 163; William - groom 221
budget of Edward Wood, foreman of farm labourers 169
Bufton, William 80
Bullock, George 153, 155, 159; Richard 185
Burbage/Burbages 49, 50, 55, 61, 108, 163, 164, 227
Burgoyne, Mr 178
burials in woollen 22
Burraston, Ann 128; William 128
Burrow Meadow 55
Burrows-Wood, Chris MFH 191; Jo MFH 191
Burton Court 52, 57, 94
Bury, John 28
butler 142
Butler, Robert 99
butter 155
buttresses 149
Byrche, John 52

cab 155
Callowhill/Calluhulle/Caluhill, Alice 60, 105; Anthony 60;

The appendices on pages 256-264 and the census tables 6, 7, 8, and 9 on pages 174, 193, 217 & 224 are not indexed.

INDEX

Charles 60; family 36, 50; Francis 60; John 45, 55, 60, 105; Richard 36, 60; William 45, 52, 54, 10
Caple, William de 17
Capper, Ann/Anne 49, 62, 100; Edmond 57; family 50; John 20, 48-53, 62, 98, 100, 101; Margaret 98; Richard 62; Thomas 52; William 20, 21, 62, 100
carpenter 203
carrier 201
Caswal/Caswell, Edmund 112; Elizabeth 79, 222; James 231; John 84, 128, 228; Joseph 28; Mary 109, 140; Thomas 130; William 129
Catley, see under Gatehouse
Catteley, John 45
Chaleston, Thomas 45
chalice 152
Chandos, Eustace de 17
charities 212
Charletts 77
cherries 185
Cherrington, Rev Frank 160, 161
Cherryfields 177
chief fee farms 77, 81
chief rent at Winley 108
chief rents 80
Childs, Anne 142
Chrees/Chreese Benjamin 108; Elizabeth 108; family **108-109**; John, 26, 28, 29, 84, 85, 108, 141; Mary 227; Mr 140; Mrs 140; Thomas 80; William 79, 81, 82, 108, 141
church **9-30, 145 – 160**; bells 152; bell turret 152; choir 157; font 15; furnace 157; gallery 152; hour-glass stand 152; offerings 19; offertory 154; organ 152; organist 157; plate 152; pulpit 15, 152; repairs 1842 149; screen 15, 16; sketch before restoration 149
Churchlands 159
Churchwarden/s 24, 176, 194; accounts 149, 153, 154; William Bevans's account 149
cider 206, 208; cider mill 203
Civil War 75
Clark, Francis 1
Clarke, Thomas 198
Clements, Fred 247, 248, 249; Mrs 247, 248
Clews, Daniel 139, 185
Clifton-on-Teme Hunt 94, 181, **189-191**, 218
Clinton-Watkins, Stuart 188
coach 243
coachman 142
coal mine 183
coffin lids, 34
Coldicott, Bob 178, Robert 178, Susanne 178
Colley, Roger 111; Thomas 57, 221
Collins, Bridgett 211; Daniel 64, 123; Edward 220; Richard 99; Simon 56; William 64
Colt house 227
common fields, 38, 79
commons' wastes 53
Compton Census 58
concerts at school 194
Coney/Cony, Catherine 68, 73, 74; Richard 80
Coninge/Conynge, Ann 62; Anthony 61, 62; Katherine 56; Margaret 49, 51; Mary 61, 62; Miles 61, 62; Richard 62; Roger 20, 73; Thomas 55, 61, 62, 73
Cook/Cooke, Aaron 25, 80; Elizabeth 125; John 56, John the elder 73, 74, John the tanner 70, 73, 75, 125; Richard 79-82, 125; Richard's inventory 125

Cooke, Mary 221; Philip – mole catcher 221
Coombey, George 129
Cooper, Elizabeth 187; Thomas 187
Corbet/Corbett, Amelia 133; Ann 133; Judith 111; Richard 57; Thomas 28, 84, 133, 153
cordswainer 132
Coterel, Isaac 139
cottage survey analysis 232, 233
cottagers living upon waste 81
cottages **210-233**; 'built in a night' 210, 211
Coulson, John 185
court baron 44, 77
court rolls 44
Cowgley, Baldwin 49, 50
Cox, Mr 28
Craddock, John 84, 123
Craddock, Mr 223
creosoting 172
Cresswell, Elizabeth 40 71, 73; Richard 40
cricket 240
crop returns 207
Cullets 102
Czerniawski, Antoni 204

dairy at Thrift 192
dairyman 227
Dallabere, Walter 54
Dallow, Thomas 187
dame school 134, 222
damsons 187
Daniel, Mrs 229
Darby, Evelyn 181; Harold 179; John 179
Darcy, Rev 85, 130, 146, 201
David, George 211
Davies/Davis, Daniel 124, 128, 163; Henry 182; John 28, 201; Mr & Mrs 219
Deakin, Thomas 94
Dedman's Furlonge 91
Dee, John 51; Richard 38, 49, 51, 53
deer park 5, 94, 110
Delahay, Nellie 182
Delamere House 158
demesne 77
Deykins, John 52
Dial House 171
Diamond Cottages – see under Jubilee Cottages
ditches 51
Dodson, Ann 64
Dodying, John 53
dog wheel 102
Dolman, George 71, Thomas 22, 23, 73
domesday survey 31
Dones Tenement 231
Dore, Humfrey/Humphrey 35, 52, 53, 98, 110
dovecote 54, 79
Dowding, Margaret 137
Dr Booker's Land 113, 146
Dudley, Rev Jos 137
Dullam, J.F. 178
Dunley Cottage 228
Dyll, Edward 45

Easton family 219; John 248; Mr & Mrs 159; Rena 238
Eaton, Francis 28, John 108, 109; Mary 108, 109, Richard 79

The appendices on pages 256-264 and the census tables 6, 7, 8, and 9 on pages 174, 193, 217 & 224 are not indexed.

Eckley, Thomas 49, 129
edge toolmaker 85, 86
Education Act 1870 235
Edwards, Gwyn MFH 191; H.A. 183; Harriet 142
eggs 155
electoral roll 146
electricity 172
Eliam/Elye 35
Elt/Elte, Edward 20, 48; John 51; Margaret 120; Richard 48, 49, 120; Thomas 52; William 120
enclosure, pre-historic 1, 10
encroachments 53
England, Dick MFH 191
Ernwy, 31
Evans family as benefactors 170
Evans, Edward 171; Edward Bickerton 199, 201, **165, 169**; Edward Wallace 170; Fanny 158; Frank 158, 170, 171, 190, 223; Mrs E.B. 168, 235; Mrs Patrick 170; Robin 202; Thomas 163, 168, 228
Eyton, Richard 211

Farley, Thomas 218
farm bailiff 185, 187; farm rents 171; farm sale – see under sale particulars
Farmer, Elizabeth 197; Geoff; 199; Jennifer 199; John 195, 197; Louisa 197; Neil 199, 228; Philip 198, 169
farmhouses in 2013 - 255
farming depression 166, 207, 208; farming in 19th & 20th century 206-209;
Farr, Joyce 183, 238
Farrelly, Ernie 191
Fawkener, Thomas 55
Ffisor, Richard 117
Fidoe, Thomas 49
Finch, Rose 238; William 57
fire at Gatehouse 111; fire at Tipton 177
fish 55, 245
fish ponds 120
flagon 152
flax 131
Florence, 2nd housemaid 245
Floyd, John 57
Foley, Lord 26, 84, 85, 94
footman 142
Ford, Mary 80; Richard 82
forestry 172
Forge Cottage 187, 215, 218
Foulk, Frances 99
free warren 54
free-bench 94
Freeman, Sarah 185; Thomas 142
Fudger, Richard 55
furniture van (horse drawn) 155

Gabb/Gabbe, William 64, 211
Gabbes 77
gallery (in church) 152
gamekeeper 185, 201, 202, 204, 227, 230
gardens at Court 143
gas supply at Court 143, 144
Gate House /Catley/Gatley 35, 45, 50-52, 57, 74, 82, 94, **110-112, 182-183**
Gate House Cottage 182
Gatley, see under Gatehouse

Gegg 245
ghost 160
Gibbons, Benjamin 165
Gibbs, Henry 182; Mary 182
Gilbert, son of Thorold, 31, 33
Gillam, Dr 137, 144
Gittins, James 28
glebe & tithes, mortgage of 148
Glebe Cottage 157, 159, 219
glebe exchange 25; farm 26, 30; 159, 160; land 19, 147, 159; terrier 19
Godwin, 31
Gouge, Bertha 219; Charles 142, 219
Gough, Anne 64, 73; James 142, 178, 183
Gracefield 247
Gray, John 187
Gray's Barn/Farm 49-51, 81, 88, 102, **103-104**
Green, Elizabeth 229; Doug 238; Joseph 214, 222; Lavinia 238; Mary 150, 214; Mr 245; Sarah Ann 233; William 150, 178
Greenwiche, William clerk 55
Greenwood, John 240
Gregory-Smith, Rev Isaac 148, 152
Grey House, see under Gray's
Grey, Richard 54
Griffiths, Agnes 180, 182, 204; Alfred 180; Ann/Anne 133, 222; Annie 180, 182; Arthur 178, 180, 181, 184, 248; Ernie 179, 182, 204; Fra 80; George 223, 245; Gladys 180; James 213; Jessie 180; Joan 180; John 178, 180, 182, 238; Leslie 188, 238; Letitia 213; Mary 180; Mary Ann 180; Mrs T. 248; Olive 179, 180, 181, 184, 248; Philip 84, 133; Richard 222; Sidney 180; Thomas 180, 245, 248; William 28, 180
Grubb, Ada 194, 195; Alice 194, 195; Benjamin 127, 194, 195, 197, 204; Bertha 194; Elizabeth 194, 195; Elvina/Vinny 194, 195, 201; Ethel 194, 195; family 170; Hariet 127; Henry 194, 195, 198, 227; James 194, 195; Mr 248; Mrs. 238; Samuel 197, 198; Sarah 127, 197; Thomas 28, 84, 127; 198; William 127, 197
Grye, John de 88, 103
Gunny, William 57
Gwyn, Ken 191

Hacklett/Hackluitt, Richard 56, 73-75
Haines, Thomas 13
Hall, Elizabeth 49; Francis 49, Thomas; William 169
Hamans/Hamons, John 55; Philip 57
hams 155
Hams/Homs/Homes 50, 57, 85, **135, 182**
Hancocks 80
Harpley Church 149
Harpley Estate 170
Harrington, George 187; John 187; Mary 187
Harris, Chris 188, 218, 247; Elizabeth 101; John 133; Kathleen 188, 218, 251
Harrison, Stennard 251
Hartopp-Cradock, Edward – see under Hartopp-Grove
Hartopp-Grove, Rev. Edward 146
Haukeleye, Hugh 17
Hawker, Edward 81, 127
Hay, Ann 23; Elizabeth 99, 116; Rev. George 17, 77, 79, 82, 99; John 23
haymaking 188
Haynes, Edward 28, Ian MFH 191; Thomas 80, 84, 85
Haywood, woodman 245
Hearth Tax 57

The appendices on pages 256-264 and the census tables 6, 7, 8, and 9 on pages 174, 193, 217 & 224 are not indexed.

Hedge House 33, 57, **94-97,** 112, **177–178**
hedges 51
Helme, John 103; Joan 103
Hereford, Earl of 33
heriot 45, 47, 81, 141
Herring, Thomas, 185
hide 31
Higgins, James 118, 203; Mr 80
Higginson, Edmund 221
High Lane cricket team 240
High Lane School 235, 236, 238; social activities 240
Hill Cross/Held Cross 81, 94, 218, 219
Hill Evans Vinegar Works 165, 166, 171
Hill, Ada 197; Charles 143, 219; Clare, MFH 191; Eliza 117; Elizabeth 116, 117; Francis 117, 228; John 58, 110, 116, 117, 123, 185, 187, 221; Mary 116, 117; Richard 56, 57, 66, 67, 73, 74, 82, 116, 117, 212; Richard MFH 191; Robert 117; Sarah 91; Susannah 79, 211; William 57, 117, 227
Hodgekins, Frank 40
Hodges, James 129, 168, 169, 203; Jane 129; Unett 79, 129, 130
Holder/Howlder, Edward 65; Elizabeth 56
Holder's cottage 103
Holland, John 222; Thomas 112, 182
Holland's Cottage 215
homage 44
Homes – see under Hams
hops 144, 208; hop kiln at Winley 107; hop kilns at Tedstone Court 209; hop pickers 178; hop pocketing hole at Tipton 209; hop-yard 144
Hopton, John 49, 88; Richard 88
Horner/Hornar, Augustine 20, 49, 72, 73, 129; Edward 48, 129; Eleanor 49; Elizabeth 49, 129; Joan/Joanne 129; John 129
Horner's Mill/Peck/Perke Mill/House 33, 49, 51, **128-130,** 167, 172, 195, **201-203**
horses 241; horses for heriots 141
Hostler, William 55
hour-glass stand 15
house platforms 7
Howan 116
Howell/Howells, Francis 211; William 20, 21, 48, 49
Howey, Dr E.V. 137
Huck, Elizabeth 81, 101, 102; John 101, 104
Humphries, Mr. bailiff 245
Hunt Supporters' Club 191
Hunt, Hunte, Roger, 20, 21, 49, 50, 120
hunting 206
hydraulic ram 199
Hylycombe, Thomas de 17

Impey/Impy 49, 118
Ingland, Thomas 56
Ingram, Edward 45, 73; William 226
Ireland Cottage/ Cottages 1, 2, 173, 214
Ireland/Irelond, Richard 51, 55

Jackson, Joseph 192; Mrs 192
James, 2nd footman 245; Annie 192, 198; Fred 185; John 192; Rev Evan 160; Robert 205
Jarvis, Arthur 88
Jay, Betsy 220
Jones, Albert 251; Ann 180, 204; Amelia 204; Benjamin 180; Bert 248; Beryl 195; Bob 201, 227; Bryan 199, 200; Clara 205; Dora 205, 238; Edward 109, 179; George 111; Harvey 202, 203; Jack 227; James 85; John 199; Margaret 111; Mr 26;

Rev Donald Edward 160; Richard 84, 94, 163, 168, 169; 199, 204, 205, 218; Robert 199; Ruth 195; Sheila 203; Thomas 28, 133, 204; Thomas Lancelot 195, 201; William 180
Jubilee/Diamond Cottages 143, 223

kennels 190, kennels at the Court 242
Kerry, Elizabeth 82, William 82
Keyhead /Paradise 221
Kitchen, William 203
Knill, John 94, 141,17 9, 219, 231; Mr 80; Sarah 141; Sarah 137; Stuart 141, 182, 219; Thomas 28, 84, 94, 109
Kynnett, John 49

La Mare family 35; Joan de 36; William de 34
lady's maid 142
Ladywood/Ladiewood 61, 105, 163, 167, 169, 203, 228
Lamb/Lamp Green 227; chapel service at Lamb Green 227
lambs 186
land tax 84
Landers, John 123;
Landon, John 23, 99
Lane, Benjamin 79, 94, 218; Bridgett 111; Elizabeth 82; George 56, 73, 74, 88, 89; 91, 94 111, 112; James 84, 94, 218; Jane 94; Joan 56, 88; John 88; Margaret 21; marriage settlement 91; Mary 137; Mr 26, 81; William 88; Richard 94; Thomas 82, 91, 94, 212, 218; Thomas's inventory 92, 93
Langeford 40; Ann 49
Lawrence, John 28, 84, 85, 94; William 94
Lea, Anthony 56; Elizabeth 154, 157; Margaret 157; memorial 157; Mrs 157; Thomas 157; Rev Frederick Simcox 143, 152, 154, 157
Leake, Graham 199, 203
Lee Lay 82; **131-133,** 163, 167, 169, **204-206;** barn roof 205
Leighton, Harold 192
Lewis, Ann 56, James 197; Thomas 57
Ley, George 57
license for non-residence 147
lime kiln 135
Line House 23, 50-52, 62, 64, 66, 74, 81, 85, **98-99,** 139, **178-179, 183-184**
literacy 71
Little Riley 118
Lloyd, John
lodges 142, 219
Lokyer, William 28
Long/Longe, Hannah 211; John 79, 211
Love, Nicholas 45
Lowden, Francis 181
Lower Cut House 220
Lower Sapey church 13
Lower Thrift 194
Lower Tidbatch 222, 223

Maggie, the kitchen maid 244
Malvern Priory 35
Mann, Mary 128; William 128
manor 31; lordship of **31 – 42**; manor house 39, 40; manor in 18th century **77- 86**
manorial mill 229
Mare, More, John de la 17
markets 33
Marston, Mary 40, 73; Richard 40, 44, 73-75
Mason bequest for poor widows 212
Mason, Anne 185, 186; Betty 185; family 41; Fred 185, 186, 187;

The appendices on pages 256-264 and the census tables 6, 7, 8, and 9 on pages 174, 193, 217 & 224 are not indexed.

248; Hester 40; Jack 247, 248; Jen 186; Joan 186; Mr 245, 248; Mrs 187; Reginald 184; Richard 40, 44; Robert 56, 57, 82; Robert I 41; Robert II 41; Robert III 77; Thomas 203; William 41
Massey/Massy, John 88; Rev Frederick 160
Mathewes, John 56
May Farm 199
Mayo, William 57
Mazer 118, 123
McNally, Doug 238; Mrs 248; Patsy 238
memorial slabs 152
Merrick, James 142
methodist preacher 227
Middle Line House 222
Middleton, Thomas 227
Midlefield 49
Miles of Gloucester 34
militia assessments 56
milk 155
mill 33, 38, 77, 78; mill race 203
Millward, Bill 190; John 20
minster, Bromyard 9, 10; Clifton 10
Mitchell, John 220
Moore Estate 116, **162-165**; sale particulars 162
Moore, Ann 114, 115, 178; Anthony 79; Arthur 115; Arthur William 162, 165; Charles Edward 162; Edward 85, 114, 115, 162; Eliza 115, 162; Elizabeth 220; family 85, **114-116**; family tomb 115; Frederick 115, 162, 165; Henry 115, 162, 165; James 84, 114, 115, 140, 162, 165; John 178; Mary 115; Mr 199; Robert 25-26, 28, 29-30, 51, 79, 102, 104, 118, 114, 124, 126; Samuel 220; Sarah 178
Moorehouse Meadow 105
mortgages
Mortiboys, John 28; Mary 84
Mortimer 4, 5; family 94, 110; Roger 33
Moss, William 227
Moxam, Edward 146; Phyllis Ann 146
Mylwood John 105; Matilda 105

Nash, Jim 248; Mrs J 248; William 247
Neufmarche, Bernard de 33; Sybil 34
New House **127-128**, 163, 164, 167, 169, 171, 172; **199-200**, 226; barn 199, barn roof 200; harvesting 200; kennel 200; RCHME survey 127
Nicholls, Geoffrey 50
noke/nooke 38
nonconformists 58
Norgrave/Norgrove, Henry 56, 73, 74
Norman, Anthony 80, 84, 85, 112; Charles 180; Kitty 112; Thomas 79, 81, 112; William 84, 85
North, Nancy 182; William 181, 182
Nottingham, James 192

Orgee, Percy 198
Orgee, Percy 227
overseer 213
Owen, Richard 54

Pagan of Tipton
Palmer, David MFH 191; John 135, 182, 231
Pantall, Agnes 178; Jack 183, 188; Joseph 187, 178; Mr & Mrs 248; Thomas 178, 188; William 178
papists 58
Paradise - see under Keyhead

Pardoe, Eliza 142
parish mergers 160
parish registers 22
Parker, David MFH 191
Parkes, Adam 125; Ann 125; Joseph 125; Samuel 125; Thomas 125
Parkhorn Farm 94
Parry, James 56, 68, 69, 73, 74; Mr 22, 23
parsonage - see under rectory
Parsons, Francis 79; Sonny 238
Passey, James 214; Joseph 128; Mary 214
pauper children 214
Pearce, Mrs 244
Pechar, John 103
Peck Mill - see under Horner's Mill
Perkins/Perkyn, Anne 62; Catherine 82; Edward/Edmund 52, 62, 105, 106; Elizabeth 62; family 50; James 192; John 106; Katherine 62; Lettie 248; Moses 82; Richard 49, 59, 73, 106, 182; Richus 20; Roger 62; Susane 62
Perre/Peyrs John 20, 73
Perry, Edmund 182
Philips/Phillips, Amy 219; Elizabeth 220; Emma 219; James 219; John 79, 82, 227; Mary 227; Ray 238; Robin 199; Thomas 221
Philpotts, Widow 80, 81
Pigeon House 247
pigs 54, 155
Pitt/Pytt/Pytte, Alfred 198; Anne 56; George 204; Henry 21, 49,50, 54; John 185; Sarah 198; Thomas 229
Pitts Land 50
Pixhill 45, 49-51, 62, 81, **100-103,** 139, 141, **185-187**; RCHME survey 100
Plegelgate Hundred 3
Plessey, Edward de 36; Hawise de 36; Hugh de 36; John de 36, 37; Peter de 36; Robert de 36
ploughs 31
point-to-point 191
pools at Tipton 88
poor 55, 211; bequests to 82; lewne for 83
Poor Piece 212
poor rates 213
population from the censuses 253
Porter, Agnes 45
Portman,
Portman, Ezekiel 226; John 28; Richard 84
Postans, Humphrey 82, 112; Jeremiah 82
poultry 187
Powell, Agnes 142; Arthur 218; Charles 205, 219; Doreen 238; Elizabeth 131, Elizabeth 215; family 144, 203; Frank 248; Freda 185, 238; girls 219; Henry 227; Jane 215; John 238; Margaret 40; Mary Ann 215; Richard 131, 156, 163, 203, 204, 215, 218, 226; Roger 198; Roly 206, 209, 238; Vera 238
Poyner, James 169
Prattenton, John 73
presbyterian preacher 229
Price, Ann 123, 134; Edward 28, 82, 84, 128, 134; Elizabeth 222, 234; Hugh 54; John 28, 79, 123, 134; Joseph 134; Mary 128
Primrose Cottage/Warnalls/Worrells/Holts Cottage 124, 125, 228
Primrose, George 59, 73, 228; Mary 59, 228
Pritchard, George 163
Prosser, Gladys 185
Pullen, Mr. head gardener 245
puritan's survey 22
Pykeshale, see under Pixhill

The appendices on pages 256-264 and the census tables 6, 7, 8, and 9 on pages 174, 193, 217 & 224 are not indexed.

INDEX

rabbit shoot 227
rabbits 54
Randall, Caleb 227; Mr & Mrs 247
Raneford, Mrs 238; Sandy 238
Raymond, Rev W.S. 148, 152
Rea, John 176
rectory, 23, 77; coach house 152; dilapidations 148; garden 155; gardener 153; location of 25; pew 157; survey 147; life at 154, 158; saddle room 152; Victorian rebuilding **146 – 148**
Reform Act (1832) 146
relief 45, 80
reservoir 144
Richards, Cicely 238; Frederick 133; Harvey 192, 194; Bill 192; Richard Brazier 133; Sarah 133; Sheila 192
riding school 177
Riley - see under Ryley
road hazards 203, 204
roads 51
Robinson, Audrey 191; Thomas 226
Rockmore Castle 221, 222
Rogers, Raymond 191
Roper, Ann 118, Annis; 192, 199; John 118, 178; Ralph 183; Sandy 118, 192; Thomas 118, 163, 192, 227
Rowley, Edward 211; George 213; Richard 79
Rudd, Charlie 173
Rufforde, Francis 64; Roger 64
Rumney, Elizabeth 91
Russell, John 223
Ryley 49-51, 57, 78, 118, 226; Ryley Cottages 214

Salloway/Sallway/Salway, Frances 123; Humphrey 123; John 78; Mr 56
salting pigs 198
Saltmarshe village hall 240, 251
Sanders/Saunders, Frederick 183; Henry 211; Joseph 201; the Goodwife 64, Thomas 79; William 231
Sapey Brook 55, 87, 88
Sargeant, Charles 185
Saunders - see under Sanders
Saxon church 10, 11; doorway 12; quoins, 12, 13
school house 167; mistress 198, mistress at Woodend School 227
school tea at Whitbourne Hall 237; tea at rectory 237
schooling 234 – 240
Scott, George Gilbert 150
scrapers, flint 1, 2
seal depicting William & Mary 132
Serre, John
settlement 6, 7, 88
Sewalles/Shewelles 45, 47, 49, 50, 116
Shangold, Mrs 28
Sheare, John 100
Shearer, John MFH 191
Shelton, Brown 137, 138; Brown the younger 138; Maria 137; Mary 137, 138; John Brown 138, 144
Sherree, John 20
shoemaker 182
shooting rights 172
Shop House - see under Tidbatch
Showley Heath see under Shewelles
Simmons/Simons Julia 227, Richard 55
Simpson, Rev Leigh 160
Sirrell, James 185
skeleton 13

Smith, Edward 184; Frances 220; Francis 79; John 26, 134; William 26, 79, 84
smoke hood 106, 107
soldiers at rectory 158
Somers – see under Summers
South Lodge 143
Southhall, William 57
Springfield, Mr 190
squatters on commons' wastes 210
St Agnes 158; St Agnes's well 157
staddle-stones 204
staff at the Court 246
staircase at 32 High Street, Bromyard, 138
Stallard/Stallward/Stalleward, Anne 73; Edward 49, 61; Ellinor/Ellenor 22, 61; James 61, 73; John 20; 49, 73, 88, 112; Richard 56, 57
Stanley M.R., stud groom 245
Stapleton-Martin, Mr 190
Starling, Edward 130; John 130
Stephens/Stevens, James 203; Susannah 133
Stone Cottage 222
Stone House A **133-135, 206**
Stone House B 226, 227
Summers, Ann 79; Joseph 80; Richard 70, 73, 74
Sunnyside/Pitts Cottage/Summer Bank 222, 226

tandem 242
tannery 125
Tarr, Reg 247
Tatlow, Roy MFH 191
Taylor, Sam 163
Teague, John 201
Team Side 103
Tedstone Court 39, 44, **241-251**; cider press 144; estate **137-144**; gardens 143, 244; gas &water supplies 143; hayfield 244; house 137-138; kennels 242; stable yard 243
Tedstone Wafre 4
Telfer, Tom 190
Tennall 82
tennis parties 156
Tennolls 226
Thomas, Blanche 21
threshing 183
Thrift 66, **116-119**, 163, 165, 167, 169, 171, 172, **192-194**; farmhouse 119
Tidbatch, Lower 131
Tidbatch/Shop House/Upper Tidbatch 77, **130-131**, 163, 167, 169, **203-204**
timber frame 103
Timmings, Edward 101
Tipper, William 182
Tipton 49-51, 82, 85, **88-94;** 150, 155, **173 - 177**; architectural description 90;
Titbach, Hugh 130; John 130; William 130
tithe/tithes 18; agreement 26, 27; commutation act 30; tithe-dinner 156
Tolley, Francis 153, 173
Tombs, Mrs 141
Tomkins, Edward 203
Tomkyns, Rev George Packington 25, 28, 29, 84
trespass 52
Turford, William 21, 73
Turner, John 57

The appendices on pages 256-264 and the census tables 6, 7, 8, and 9 on pages 174, 193, 217 & 224 are not indexed.

Turton, W 248
Tyler, Andrew 178
Tymmings, John 62

Unett, George 129
Upfill, Maria 142
Upper Cut House/Cullets Hill 220
Upper Grounds **110**, 139, 141, 178, **187-188**
Upper House/the Manor, Shelsley Beauchamp 115
Upper Line House/Braziers 222, 234

Vaughan, Mr 245; William 211
Victorian restoration of church, **148 - 152**; architect 150; consecration 151; foundation stone 152; sketch after restoration 151;   21st century restoration 161;
village pound 228
Viltes 54
virgate 37
visitation, archdeacon's 24; episcopal 21, 24

Walker, Anne 40; Elienor 40, Frank 40
Walshe/Welshe, Ann 49
Walter, Bishop of Hereford 32, 33
War 190; memorial 157
Ward, Berrow 176; James 153, 176, 178; Lord 112; Mary 176; Stanley 153, 176
Ward, Lord 231
warren, free 37
Waste Common 210
Waste Cottage 167, 169
Waste Cottage 223
water supply at Tedstone Court 143; Whitbourne Estate supply 172
waterworks 199
Weaver 70
Webb, Anne 115; George 78, 79, 81 115, 117; Mary 115
Webb, Mr & Mrs 219
Wellings, Allan 199
Wells, Diana 240
Welonde, William 45
West, William 55
Westwood, Julian 198; Sally 198
wharfinger 94, 141
Wheeler, Mr 124
Whettall, Richard 130; Thomas 130
Whistance, Betty 238; Evelyn 194
Whitbourne Estate **165-172**; Hall 203
Whitbourne School 239
Whitehall Common 210, 229
Whitehall Cottage 112, 135, 182
Whitehall/Burbery/Barlary Hill/Brockshall Cottage 221
Whitehall/Hams Cottage 231
Whiteing/Whitinge/Whyting, George 54; Thomas 54, 56
Whitewoods/Whitwoods Croft 49, 50, 51, 61
Whitledge/Whitlegg, John 20, 49, 50, 73

Whitty, Joe 247; 249
Whitwoods Croft 116
Whyman, Mrs 236
Wight family **137-144**; grave 141
Wight, Ada 137, 142, 144; Alfred 137, 142, 144; Clara 137, 152; Edgar 137, 141, 144, 159, 183, 221; Edith 137; Ellen Phillipa 137; Eliza Lane 137; Elizabeth137; Emily 137, 142, 144; Florence 137, 142, 144; James Lane 137, 141, 143, 144, 231; Laura 137, 143; Margery 139; Maria 137, 138, 139, 140; Marianne 137, 138; Mary 137, 142, 143, 144, 154; memorial of Richard & Maria Wight 139; Miss 143; Richard 28, 84, 85, 137, 138, 141; Richard Thomas 137; Sarah 137, 142; Thomas 139; T.P.P./Philip 109, 110, 137, 139, 140, 141; T.P.P. the Younger 137, 139
Williams (see also Wylyams) Ann 79; Rev Charles 157-159
Williams, Jenkin 183
Williams, Mrs 223
wills 59, 82
Wilson, George 180; Susannah 180
Winley 48-51, 64, 82, 85, **104-109, 179-182**; Duncan James's findings 106-108; Perry report 106; RCHME survey 106;
Winwood, John 85, 134, 135, 182, 231; Thomas 134; Thomas's inventory 134
Wisham - see under Wysham
Witley Court 94
Wood/Woode, Mr 139; Thomas 84, 99; Thomas junior 140, 178; Thomas senior 178
Woodam/Woodhall/ Woodend/ Wooden End confusion 119
Woodend School 194, 198, 235, 236, 237; adult activities 239
Woodend/Wooden End 49-51, 54, 77, 82, **120-124**, 163, 167, 169, 170, 171, 172, **194-195**; barn 194; farmhouse 194; RCHME survey 124;
Woodhall 57, 70, 82, **125-127, 196-199**; dairy 197; farmhouse 197; granary door 197; sale particulars 195, 198
Woodham/Woodham Hall 81, **124-125**; plan 121
Woodhouse, Charles 182; Edward 182; Elizabeth 182; John 182
woodland 54
Woodmanton 36, 37
Workhouse diet 213, 214
World War 2 247
World War 1 245
Wright, Mrs E.M. 143, 155
Wyatt 245
Wylyams (see also under Williams) John 52; Roger 52
Wynleslond 45
Wynne, William 56, 135
Wyse, John 45
Wysham, Francis 21, 40, 49; George 21, 40, 73; John 36; Ralph, 37; Thomas 38, 52

Yapp, James 81; John 130, Mr 80
Yates, Beryl 195; George 195; Mervyn 195
Yelds Cross – see under Hill Cross
Yeomans 135; Mr 199
Young, Richard 204; Samuel 204

The appendices on pages 256-264 and the census tables 6, 7, 8, and 9 on pages 174, 193, 217 & 224 are not indexed.